böhlau

KÄTE HAMBURGER KOLLEG MÜNSTER
EINHEIT & VIELFALT IM RECHT
LEGAL UNITY & PLURALISM

Edited by Ulrike Ludwig and Peter Oestmann

Volume 4

Die Reihe versteht Rechtsvielfalt als ein überzeitliches und überregionales Strukturmerkmal von Recht schlechthin. Es kann demnach von einem relationalen und historisch wandelbaren Zusammenhang von Einheit und Vielfalt im Recht gesprochen werden. Die Schriftenreihe möchte diesen Zusammenhang in seiner kulturellen Vielgestaltigkeit umfassend beleuchten: interdisziplinär, räumlich übergreifend und interepochal. Die Bände erscheinen in deutscher und englischer Sprache und sind überwiegend im Open Access zugänglich.

The book series conceptualises legal pluralism as a structural characteristic of law itself. We can therefore speak of a relational and historically changeable association between unity and pluralism in law. The book series intends to comprehensively illuminate these connections in their cultural polymorphy interdisciplinarily, transspatially and interepochally. The volumes are published in German and English and will be predominantly open access.

Die Herausgeber/the editors

Hans Beck / Kaja Harter-Uibopuu (eds.)

Ancient Greek Law

Vectors of Unity and Local Idiosyncrasy

BÖHLAU

This publication was made possible by the Käte Hamburger Kolleg "Legal Unity and Pluralism" at the University of Münster, funded by the Federal Ministry of Research, Technology and Space (BMFTR).

Bibliographic information published by the Deutsche Nationalbibliothek:
The Deutsche Nationalbibliothek lists this publication in the Deutsche Nationalbibliografie; detailed bibliographic data available online: https://dnb.de.

Cover image: Lex Sacra: Festivals of Demeter, Dyme (3rd cent. BCE). © A. Rizakis, 2007

Cover design: Michael Haderer, Wien
Proofreading: Bird und Hübner GbR, Berlin
Typesetting: SchwabScantechnik, Göttingen
Printed and bound: CPI print, Ulm
Printed in the EU

Vandenhoeck & Ruprecht Verlage | www.vandenhoeck-ruprecht-verlage.com
E-Mail: info@v-r.de

ISBN 978-3-412-53311-3 (print)
ISBN 978-3-412-53312-0 (digital)

Content

Abbreviations

AE	L'Année épigraphique, Paris 1888 –.
AGER, Arbitrations	AGER, Sheila L., Interstate Arbitrations in the Greek World, 337–90 B. C., Berkeley 1996.
BGU	Berliner Griechische Urkunden, Berlin 2014–.
BE	Bulletin épigraphique in Revue des études grecques, Paris 1888–.
BNJ	WORTHINGTON, Ian (ed.), Brill's New Jacoby, Leiden/Boston 2006–.
Choix Delphes	JACQUEMIN, Anne/MULLIEZ, Dominique/ROUGEMONT, Georges (eds.), Choix d'inscriptions de Delphes, traduites et commentées, Paris 2012.
CID	Corpus des inscriptions de Delphes, Paris 1977–.
CIG	Corpus inscriptionum Graecarum, Berlin 1828–1877.
CRAWFORD, Roman Statutes	CRAWFORD, Michael Hewson (ed.), Roman Statutes [vol. 1–2], London 1996.
CRNG	CARBON, Jan-Mathieu/PEELS-MATTHEY, Saskia/PIRENNE-DELFORGE, Vinciane, Collection of Greek Ritual Norms (CGRN), 2017–.
F.Delphes III	Fouilles de Delphes III. Épigraphie, Paris 1909–1985.
FrGHist	JACOBY, Felix (ed.), Fragmente Griechischer Historiker, Berlin 1923–.
GAGARIN/PERLMAN, Laws of Crete	GAGARIN, Michael/PERLMAN, Paula, The Laws of Ancient Crete c.650–400 BCE, Oxford 2016.
GEI	Greek Economic Inscriptions, 10.25429/sns.it/lettere/gei000
I.Aphrodisias Performers	ROUECHÉ, Charlotte Mary, Performers and Partisans at Aphrodisias in the Roman and late Roman Periods. A Study based on Inscriptions from the Current Excavations at Aphrodisias in Caria, London 1993.
I.Amphipolis actes	HATZOPOULOS, Miltiades, Actes de vente d'Amphipolis, Athens 1991 (Μελετήματα 14).
I.Beroia	GOUNAROPOULOU, Loukretia/HATZOPOULOS, Miltiades, Epigraphes Katō Makedonias (metaxy tou Vermiou orous kai tou Axiou potamou). Teuchos A'. Epigraphes Veroias, Athens 1998.
I.Chalcidique actes	HATZOPOULOS, Miltiades, Actes de vente de la Chalcidique centrale, Athens 1988 (Μελετήματα 6).
I.Cret.	GUARDUCCI, Margherita, Inscriptiones Creticae [vol. 1–4], Rome 1935–1950.

I.Délos	Dürrbach, Felix (ed.), Inscriptions de Délos, Paris 1926–1937.
I.dial. Sicile II	Dubois, Laurent, Inscriptions grecques dialectales de Sicile [vol. 2], Geneva 2008.
I.Didyma	Rehm, Albert/Harder, Richard (eds.), Didyma II. Die Inschriften, Berlin 1958.
I.Ephesos	Wankel, Hermann/Merkelbach, Reinhold/Knibbe, Dieter/Meriç, Recep/Nollé, Johannes/Wankel, Hermann/Börker, Christoph (eds.), Die Inschriften von Ephesos, [vol. 1–7], Bonn 1979–1984 (IGSK 11–17).
I.Epidauros Askleipieion	Peek, Werner, Inschriften aus dem Asklepieion von Epidauros, Berlin 1969.
I.Erythrai Klazomenai	Engelmann, Helmut/Merkelbach, Reinhold (eds.), Die Inschriften von Erythrai und Klazomenai, [vol. 1–2], Bonn 1972–1973 (IGSK 1–2).
IG	Inscriptiones Graecae, Berlin 1873–.
IG Napoli	Miranda, Elena, Iscrizoni greche d'Italia. Napoli, [vol. 1–2], Rome 1990–1995.
I.Iasos	Blümel, Wolfgang, Die Inschriften von Iasos Bonn 1985 (IGSK 28/1–2).
I.Kalchedon	Merkelbach, Reinhold/Dörner, Friederich Karl/Sencer, Şahin (eds.), Die Inschriften von Kalchedon, Bonn 1980 (IGSK 20).
I.Kios	Corsten, Thomas, Die Inschriften von Kios, Bonn 1985 (IGSK 29).
I.Magnesia	Kern, Otto, Die Inschriften von Magnesia am Maeander, Berlin 1900.
I.Milet	Milet VI. Inschriften von Milet, [vol. 1–3], Berlin 1997–2006.
IMT Kaikos	Barth, Matthias/Stauber, Josef (eds.), Inschriften Mysia & Troas, München 1996.
I.Olympia	Dittenberger, Wilhelm/Purgold, Karl (eds.), Die Inschriften von Olympia, Berlin 1896.
I.Olympia Suppl.	Siewert, Peter/Taeuber, Hans (eds.), Neue Inschriften von Olympia. Die ab 1896 veröffentlichten Texte, Wien 2013 (Tyche Sonderband 7).
IOSPE I²	Latyschev, Basilius (ed.), Inscriptiones Tyrae, Olbiae, Chersonesi Tauricae, aliorum locorum a Danubio usque ad regnum Bosporanum iterum, St. Petersburg 1916.
I.Lindos	Blinkenberg, Christian, Lindos. Fouilles et recherches, II. Fouilles de l'acropole. Inscriptions, Berlin 1941.
IPArk	Thür, Gerhard/Taeuber, Hans, Prozessrechtliche Inschriften der griechischen Poleis. Arkadien (IPArk), Wien 1994 (Österreichische Akademie der Wissenschaft Philosophisch-historische Klasse. Sitzungsberichte 607)

I.Pergamon	Fraenkel, Max, Altertümer von Pergamon. VIII. Die Inschriften von Pergamon, [vol. 1–2], Berlin 1890–1895.
I.Priene	Hiller von Gaertringen, Friederich, Inschriften von Priene, Berlin 1906.
I.Priene B-M	Blümel, Wolfgang/Merkelbach, Reinhard, Die Inschriften von Priene, [vol. 1–2], Bonn 2014 (IGSK 69).
I.Sestos	Krauss, Johannes, Die Inschriften von Sestos und der thrakischen Chersones, Bonn 1980 (Inschriften Griechischer Städte aus Kleinasien 19).
I.Smyrna	Petzl, Georg, Die Inschriften von Smyrna, I–II/1–2, Bonn 1982–1990 (Inschriften Griechischer Städte aus Kleinasien 23–24/1–2).
I.Tomis	Stoian, Iorgu, Inscriptiones Scythiae minoris Graecae et Latinae II. Tomis et territorium, Bucharest 1987.
LegDrSol	Schmitz, Winfried, Leges Draconis et Solonis. Eine neue Edition der Gesetze Drakons und Solons mit Übersetzung und historischer Einordnung, Stuttgart 2023 (Historia Einzelschriften 270).
Minon, I.dial. éléennes	Minon, Sophie, Les inscriptions éléennes dialectales (VIe–IIe siècle avant J.-C.), Geneva 2007.
Meiggs/Lewis, GHI	Meiggs, Russell/Lewis, David (eds.), A Selection of Greek Historical Inscriptions to the End of the Fifth Century B. C., Oxford 1969.
Migeotte, Emprunt	Migeotte, Leopold, L'emprunt public dans les cités grecques, Québec 1984.
Migeotte, Souscriptions	Migeotte, Leopold, Les souscriptions publiques dans les cités grecques, Geneva 1992.
OGIS	Dittenberger, Wilhelm, Orientis graeci inscriptiones selectae, Leipzig 1903–1905)
Osborne/Rhodes, GHI	Osborne, Russell/Rhodes, Peter John (eds.), Greek Historical Inscriptions, 478–404 B. C., Oxford 2017.
P.Eleph 1	Rubensohn, Otto, Elephantine Papyri. Ägyptische Urkunden aus den königlichen Museen zu Berlin. Griechische Urkunden. Sonderheft, Berlin 1907.
Pernin, Baux ruraux	Pernin, Isabelle, Les baux ruraux en Grèce ancienne, Lyon 2014.
Rigsby, Asylia	Rigsby, Kent, Asylia. Territorial Inviolability in the Hellenistic World, Berkeley 1996.
Rizakis, Achaïe III	Rizakis, Athanasio, Achaïe III. Les cités achéennes: épigraphie et histoire, Athènes 2008

RPC I	Burnett, Andrew/Amandry, Michel/Ripollès, Pere Pau (eds.), Roman Provincial Coinage. [Vol 1], From the Death of Caesar to the Death of Vitellius, London/Paris 1992.
SEG	Supplementum Epigraphicum Graecum, Leiden 1923–.
Sherk, RDGE	Sherk, Robert K., Roman Documents from the Greek East. Senatus Consulta and Epistulae to the Age of Augustus, Baltimore 1969.
$Syll^3$	Dittenberger, Wilhelm, Sylloge inscriptionum graecarum, Leipzig 1915–1924.
TAM	Tituli Asiae Minoris, Vienna 1901–.
Van Effenterre/ Ruzé, Nomima	van Effenterre, Henri/Ruzé, Françoise (eds.), Nomima. Recueil d'inscriptions politiques et juridiques de l'archaisme grec [vol. 1–2], Rome 1994–1995.

Preface

The conference from which these proceedings are presented here was held in Münster on February 23 and 24, 2023, under the auspices of the Käte Hamburger Kolleg 'Legal Unity and Pluralism'. Organized by the editors, it brought together 14 speakers from Europe and North America, all of them experts in the fields of Ancient Greek History and the History of Law in Antiquity. The aim was to explore new concepts and perspectives on the dynamics between local law and legal coherence from Archaic to Hellenistic times. The idea for the workshop grew out of two separate but also converging research trajectories: the notion of the unity of Greek Law on the one hand and new, rising interest in localism and local legal idiosyncrasies on the other hand.

Scholarly debates on early Greek law have diversified significantly over the past two decades. For the longest time, divisions between the fields of the History of Law and Ancient Greek History, the former concentrating on the concepts of legal theory and the latter on the 'realities' of adjudication and administration, had left their marks on scholarship. This segregation has been largely superseded today by cross-fertilization and indeed cooperation. As conversations unfold, the field also benefits from the discovery of new sources hailing from various corners of the Greek world that complement, and sometimes challenge, the prominence previous scholarship has assigned to Athens and Crete as unique loci of study. This expanded corpus, especially at the intersection of history and archaeology, has significantly enriched our understanding.

Law in the Greek polis was – as in all other premodern communities – always closely connected to questions of the solution of pending problems, thus closer to modern case law systems than to the civil law concept based on Roman legal tradition. It is therefore not surprising that the first regulations to be found in our written sources seem to be more oriented towards problem-solving rather than broad conceptions and grand legal ideas. There is no doubt that already in the early city-states certain legal principles existed and were well conceptualized, but it remains formidably more difficult to uncover these than in other ancient legal systems. Where almost one thousand more or less independent communities established rules for specific problems, each one arising under unique conditions, the solutions will not always have looked the same. Each polis created its own tools for legal transactions and dispute resolution, and each polis implemented them accordingly. At the same time, there were many undeniable, profound similarities in the structure and application of these legal instruments. The question remains whether these shared principles were either generated by the close interconnectedness of *poleis* and the tight network of their mutual exchanges or, rather, point to a communal archetypal law, as has often been argued. In other words: were they the basis of a connected Greek world or the outcome of this interplay? The Homeric epics have been taken as a starting point for a unified Greek Law, which then diversified over time. Still, recent studies have shown that the practical view of the Iliad and the Odyssey as sources for a common Greek culture, while convenient at the outset, falls well short of critical historical questioning. Thus, rather than reconstructing a primordial stage of law that was the very same in all peasant communities, *poleis,* and ethne in Asia Minor, the mainland, the islands, and Magna Graecia, the local perspective appears more promising.

Did the members of different cities simply adapt and copy from their peers where they thought these had found an apt solution to challenges within? If so, where did the related processes of communication and adaptation take place? Was there even an – inherent or explicit – necessity to adopt certain approaches, and if so, by whom? Did shared experience in politics lead also to the standardization of regulatory legal practices? And, did standardization provide certain advantages in a polis-world that was moving gradually closer together? The latter question, at least, should be answered in affirmative fashion – as such, it hints at a progression from diversity to unity. Through the ever-closer contacts between individual city-states and through supraregional structures, common legal traditions emerged that fostered and indeed facilitated coexistence. The Hellenistic koine found expression, in rudimentary form, also in law, as is posited in the later contributions to this volume. Yet this conformity ought not be interpreted, and certainly not inevitably so, as a return to Homeric unity; the very idea of this unity is problematized in the opening chapter.

Variety and difference in legal structures were deliberate, as cities asserted their place in a world subject to the tensions of independence and union with others. However, this tension also created room and opportunity for common, or rather comparable institutions in law, not because of a common legal heritage or let alone similar dogmatic views, but because everyday life was easier to handle when there was agreement on certain legal processes and procedures, e.g., common principles in the question of the accessibility of local courts for non-citizens, in cross-polis marriages, or in trans-polis trade, among others.

We believe it is desirable for historians and law scholars to embrace these issues together. A glance not only at the older scholarly literature shows that time and again – and quite rightly so – criticism has been articulated at both ends of the table. Trained jurists have grasped notions of contractual framework, but they might have paid little attention to its historical setting: the political situation, the position of the individuals involved within their community, economic conditions, or, most eminently, religious implications. Historians, on the other hand, cast a keen eye on all these issues, but at times are not so well equipped to unlock some of the quintessential legal details. Both scholars might defend their position by arguing that their perspective would be the one at hand and hence of importance (that is, to themselves). Our workshop – and this is the case for the Käte Hamburger Kolleg in Münster overall – was therefore intended to bring together representatives from these different disciplines and foster the exchange between them.

The papers assembled for publication represent the workshop's main vectors of inquiry: public law and sanctions, Greek ritual norms, economy and trade, and private law. They have been regrouped here for the purpose of narrative coherence. In the opening chapter, Hans Beck examines the evolution of law in Thebes, focusing on inheritance law and the legal reforms of the lawgiver Philolaos. His enactments were examples of local legislation, yet they display striking resemblances with legal frameworks in other *poleis.* Recent epigraphic findings betray the integration of diverse local legal systems into more coherent structures of emerging federal states. Athina Dimopoulou follows up on diversity and unity of legal spheres on the island of Lesbos. Drawing on epigraphic evidence from Mytilene, Methymna, and Eresos, she points to both shared legislative and political structures as well as local variations in administrative details, for instance, in the designation and duties of officials. Donatella Erdas' contribution is written in this vein of inquiry. She discusses the processes of buying, owning, selling, and at times partially alienating land and houses, showing that Greek city-states typically stepped up to secure individual property rights, through magistrates and/or land registrations in archives. The practice was widespread, the legal mechanisms to safeguard private property widely acknowledged. Its implication, as Erdas demonstrates, was however subject to highly localized practices.

The volume then moves on to the realm of the economy. In the chapter that was delivered as a public keynote, Alain Bresson introduces regulations on the use of coinage in the Greek world, focusing on its economic role in the eastern Mediterranean; doing so, he provides the example of an arena in which common interests across the borders of single city-states were of outstanding importance. Bresson explores how various *poleis* regulated the production and circulation of currency, presenting a wide range of epigraphic examples. Economic issues were of pivotal importance to both public and private law. Dorothea Rohde examines infrequent instances of debt cancellations in ancient Greek history. She attributes the rarity of such measures to the broadly acknowledged economic difficulties they might entail; in cases where debts were canceled, this was typically influenced by local legal customs and usually prompted by contextual crises, including civil unrest or military conflict. The absence of certain legal actions, following Rohde, can be seen as a common Greek legal conception. Quite the opposite holds true for the subsequent chapter by Ruben Post. An inscription from Dyme in northwestern Achaia regulated a loan from citizens to magistrates for federal projects of the Achaian League. Close analysis of the document reflects early challenges for federalism in the local adaptation of supra-polis regulations.

The cultural norms and rules of behavior for festivals and athletic competitions bear witness to local idiosyncrasies and generally accepted legal concepts alike. Turning to regulations governing attire in religious settings, Laura Gawlinski exposes the coexistence of widespread cultural practices and regional variation. Her study highlights how local traditions shaped clothing norms across individual cities, particularly in Asia Minor, while certain sanctuaries advocated for more localized practices. Zinon Papakonstantinou explores regulations for athletic competitions, focusing on the Sebasta in Naples and thus extending the scope of the investigation into Roman imperial times. He highlights local differences in event organization but notes also that basic rules for sports remained largely consistent across regions, showcasing the balance between local diversity and overarching uniformity. Rome's rise to power in Greece from the 2nd century BCE did in any case not, as is sometimes stated, mark the end of Greek law. In her contribution on Roman legal enactments in mainland Greece, Lina Girdvainyte shows how Greek local judicial institutions implemented Roman laws and blended them with existing Greek legal practices. Again, the broad variety of local adaptations and applications is remarkable and also fascinating. Patrick Sänger's re-examination of the well-known marriage contract P.Eleph. 1 shows both the influence of local Egyptian legal traditions on a Greek marriage contract as well as the embedding of the document in the broader juristic culture of a growing Hellenistic legal koine; his article reflects broader trends in cross-cultural legal pluralism. In the concluding chapter, Philipp Scheibelreiter looks beyond the borders of the Greek world to Rome in his comparison of the notion of homology in Athenian and early Roman law. He demonstrates that – despite the obvious differences of both culture spheres –the concepts and contents of the legal instruments at hand were indeed quite comparable.

This takes us back to the starting point of our considerations. Despite the local differences in the legal systems of ancient Greek city-states that figure so prominently in the assembled chapters, it is obvious, we believe, that analogous processes and developments are traceable in many places, at roughly the same time; that parallels are visible that arose on the same cultural and economic bases; and that direct influences can be detected in the typical contact zones between *poleis*, in trade, supraregional festivals, and in supranational federal alliances.

We would like to thank all the speakers at the meeting for their contributions and the guests for stimulating discussions. We would also like to express our gratitude to the Käte Hamburger Kolleg, its directors Ulrike Ludwig and Peter Oestmann, as well as Claudia Lieb, Andre Dechert, Lennart Pieper, and Nadine Zielinski for their assistance with the event. The conference and subsequent publication of this volume were supported with funds from the Federal Ministry of Education and Research. In the Department of Ancient History at the University of Münster, David Westerkamp, Natalie Wieser, and Emilia Bachmann lent a helping hand with the preparation of the print version of manuscripts, for which we are particularly grateful.

Hans Beck, Münster
Kaja Harter-Uibopuu, Hamburg

Hans Beck (University of Münster)

Land and law in Archaic Thebes*

Vectors of Greek law: pluralization and fragmentation

Ancient Greek law is a posterchild for the study of legal unity and diversity. Among the classic cases that speak to the issue is the legislation on landed property. The standard succession in the ownership of a *kleros* was that the estate, at the death of the proprietor, was shared among his legitimate sons. If there were no sons but a daughter, the heiress *(epikleros)* was obliged to marry the closest relative of the deceased who then took possession of the family property. In Athens, where the corresponding legislation was applied with particular rigor, the *epikleros* could not refuse to marry the man who claimed that he was entitled to the union; the existence of property forced her into marriage. The so-called Great Code from Gortyn (I.Cret. 4.72) stipulated, on the other hand, that daughters might inherit half of the holdings transferred to a son (4.31–43). If there were no legitimate male descendants at all, they might refuse to marry (7.52 to 8.8), although under noticeable loss of her property. Furthermore, in Gortyn, although limited to a defined ceiling, the dowry *(proix)* was handed over as liquid assets to the female (4.48–51), while in Athens, it typically comprised a small piece of property presented to the head of the household into which she married.

The point is reasonably clear. Leaving aside the fact that women were disempowered by the Athenian model – the Cretan legislation put them in a stronger position – Athens and Gortyn established different inheritance regimes with, effectively, significant societal consequences. At the same time, these differences might be seen as varied responses to similar challenges. In the rising urban communities across Archaic Greece, political participation and social status were intertwined with the possession of property, no matter how defined. The core unit where property was accumulated, aggrandized, and passed on from one generation to the next was the family. Early Greek legislation was therefore driven by the desire to

* Acknowledgements: This paper was written during my 2022–23 fellowship at the Käte Hamburger Kolleg *Einheit und Vielfalt im Recht* in Münster. I would like to thank the Kolleg, its directors Ulrike Ludwig and Peter Oestmann plus the vibrant cohort of fellows from around the globe for the insight and inspiration they provided. Among the various research activities in the Kolleg, conversations revolving around the *Münster Glossary on Legal Unity and Pluralism* have left deep impressions on my understanding of Greek law. Beyond the Kolleg, Lene Rubinstein (London) and Kaja Harter-Uibopuu (Hamburg) offered generous advice and critical feedback. Lukas Duisen and Emilia Bachmann have helped with some of the documentation. I am very grateful to all. Translations of the Greek are mine unless indicated otherwise.

govern this unit by law, that is, to solidify the ties between its members, structure and prioritize different levels of belonging, and protect the associated family possessions as they ventured through the critical moments in the cycle of life: birth, marriage, and death.

Scholarly debates about early Greek law have happily diversified over the past two decades. To begin with, the specialized discussion complements the 'big picture' in the study of Greek history; the days of Athenocentric renderings have passed, also in the field of Greek law. Cretan legislation – due to the exceptional state of preservation of legislative acts a crown witness to the issue at hand – too, forfeits its role as a sole beacon in the study of ancient Greek law: not so because evidence from the island is not instructive but because it is now supplemented by new, recently discovered material from elsewhere. At the fruitful intersection of history and archaeology, the last two decades have witnessed a rapid growth of the available corpus of legal texts; exciting discoveries from different corners of the Greek Mediterranean fuse the study of Greek law with new material and insight. In the sphere of sacred laws or *leges sacrae*, now more commonly labeled ritual norms, the field has witnessed a particularly rich expansion of the available bodies of evidence.[1] As a consequence, the emerging picture is not only more diverse and nuanced but also more complicated.

Conceptual advances add to the new picture. Already in 2004, Lene Rubinstein and Edward Harris established that "the concept of 'Greek Law' has been out of fashion in mainstream scholarship for several decades."[2] The punchline was that the debate on the universality of law, shaped by Ludwig Mitteis' idea of common juristic conceptions among the Greeks for so long, had long fallen out of sync with some of the new intellectual mantras of Classical Studies, the notion of diverse local encodings of Greek culture in particular. Moses Finley's interventions against Mitteis from the 1960s, while remarkable at the time,[3] set very demanding criteria for the identification of any type of common legal conception. Combined with a notoriously Athenocentric point of view, Finley's objections in the long run offer no helpful compass to navigate through the variegated nature of the new evidence. Revivals of the debate in the early 2000s by Michael Gagarin and Gerhard Thür reopened the trenches between Anglo-American scholarship and continental traditions, yet they also fostered a new operational consensus that appeared agreeable to unitarians and pluralists alike.[4] The consensus by and large informs current conceptions of Greek law to date: on the one hand, the legal spaces of Greek city-

1 See the online Collection of Greek Ritual Norms, http://cgrn.ulg.ac.be/.

2 Rubenstein/Harris 2004, p. 3.

3 See Finley 1951 and then especially Finley 1966/1975.

4 Gagarin 2005a; Thür 2006. See also the complementary debate on the codification of Greek law and the nature of a Greek law code, Hölkeskamp 2005; Gagarin 2005b.

states were clearly not subject to coherent formulations of substantive law. Positive legislation differed widely throughout Greece. On the other hand, there was an undeniable level of structural consistency that united these spaces both in their conception of law and in legal practice: for instance, a high degree of orality and a corresponding low degree of formalism, as well as a common understanding of the guiding procedures in the application of laws.[5]

Disagreement persists, however, on the historical development of the threads of unity and diversity. According to Gagarin, procedural unity was grounded in the legal practices of the Archaic and Classical periods; hence, whatever conformity there was emerged from the lateral exchanges and shared experiences between entities whose legal conceptions cross-fertilized one another and, over time, became increasingly similar.[6] Contrarily, Thür has argued that the visible moments of coherence were the remnants of a common Homeric heritage: "Das homerische Modell war ... der gemeinsame Ausgangspunkt der unterschiedlichen Ausformungen des Prozesses in den späteren griechischen Poleis."[7] Once the map of Hellas was shaped by highly politicized city-states, these units, accentuating their role viz other communities, moved away from common conceptions of law to assert legal authority through idiosyncrasy. The former position describes unity through pluralization of legal phenomena, the latter builds on the idea of fragmentation. Or, in other words: one position charts a road to unity, the other that to diversity. The purpose of this chapter is not to reconcile these vectors. Rather, the following discussion shifts the focus from diverse substantive law and unifying procedures toward the historical process of their formation. In doing so, this contribution seeks to unravel the historical threads that weave legal unity and diversity together.

Hesiod's family estate: litigation and legal transformation

One of the curious blind spots in the debate is the legislation of Archaic Thebes. Outside the community of scholars in Boiotian Studies, Thebes has received only little attention in discussions of early Greek law, which might be explained with the limited body of evidence available; we will turn to this shortly. On the other hand, both the Bronze Age pedigree and the Iron Age impulse are exceptionally strong in Thebes, so much so that the Kadmeia is an obvious, if not compelling object of inquiry. Whether Thebes was the most eminent Bronze Age palace in mainland Greece or not – the debate continues – the recovery rate after the fall of the palaces was demonstrably higher and faster in Boiotia than anywhere else in Greece. In

5 Cf. Foxhall/Lewis 1996.
6 Gagarin 2005a, p. 40.
7 Thür 2006, p. 44.

Homer and Hesiod respectively, Thebes' Bronze Age legacy and Iron Age present resonate louder than that of most places in the Greek world.[8]

Homer's poetry speaks of Thebes and its inhabitants in ambiguous terms. In the *Odyssey,* the place is called Thebes, but its people, consistently so, Kadmeians.[9] The *Iliad* draws the same distinction (5.804; cf. 23.676–680; and elsewhere). In the *Catalog of Ships,* Thebes is listed simply as "Hypothebai, the well-built citadel" (2.505). The depiction of its people is flavored with dismissive undertones. Sent on an embassy to demand the reinstatement of Polyneikes, Tydeus, father of Diomedes, finds the Kadmeians feasting in the house of Eteokles. He challenges them to feats of courage and defeats each of his opponents. His request however falls flat. En route back to his camp Tydeus is ambushed by 50 Theban youths whom he slaughters one by one, with the exception of Maion, son of Haimon (Iliad 4.364–400). The unraveling image of Kadmeians is one of deceit and weakness, disregard for binding cultural conventions of old: Tydeus comes in peace and defeats his opponents in tests of courage, yet he is assaulted. As the ambush turns into fair combat, he prevails over his enemies who are far superior in number.[10]

The locus of Hesiod's poetry was c. 25 kilometers west of Thebes in Askra, a local dependency of Thespiai.[11] While Thespiai is conspicuously absent from the Hesiodic corpus, Thebes is present by the inclusion of the legends of Kadmos and Oedipus and by a reference to the seven gates (Works and Days 161–165). It has been argued that Hesiod might offer a "Thebanocentric riposte,"[12] a narrative crafted in response to the image of Thebes in Homer. Note, for instance, how Hesiod pays particular attention to Kadmos as well as Herakles' ties to Thebes.[13] Also, the *Catalog of Ships,* the main section in the Homeric poems to pay reverence to the prestige of cities, downplays Thebes: it is accounted for only toward the end of the list of the Boiotian communities and is addressed, as we have noted, simply as Hypothebai (2.505). Thespiai, on the other hand, appears early (2.498, sixth place).[14] It is difficult to fully substantiate the idea of a pro-Theban thrust in his poetry, but it is clear that Hesiod and his hometown Askra were not only drawn into the boundaries of Thespiai but also oriented toward Thebes as the most prominent regional hub in

8 Cf. Beck 2025 for an extensive overview; recovery rate: Schachter 2016, pp. 6–7.

9 E.g., 11.263, 265 (Thebes), 11.276 (Kadmeioi); cf. also Hesiod, Theogony 978 and Works and Days 162 (Thebes), Theogony 326, 940.

10 Cf. also Iliad 23.676–680, where at the funeral games of Oedipus, Mekisteus, son of Talaos, defeats "all sons of Kadmos." For a narratological approach to Homer's Thebes, see Barker/Christensen 2019.

11 Freitag 1999, pp. 160–163; Edwards 2004, pp. 30–79.

12 Larson 2018, p. 32.

13 Theogony 314–319, 937–955, 982–983.

14 Cf. Eder 2003, pp. 301–304.

commerce and culture. Circumstances in Thebes were more important to the political, legal, and economic conditions discussed by Hesiod than is typically assumed.

When speaking of political communities in an abstract manner, Hesiod uses the term polis (Works and Days 222, 227); Askra is labeled a *kome* (639–40). Hesiod's polis, as is well known, was composed of gatherings and assemblies *(agorai)*, people (*laoi)* as well as kings (*basileis)* who govern their communities through councils of elders or leaders of clans. They are in a position to settle disputes and pronounce judgments. Sometimes they do so all too eagerly. The critical stance adopted by Hesiod toward the leaders is unmistakable: they are described as "eaters of gifts" (βασιλῆας δωροφάγους, Works and Days 38–9, 220–2, 263–5), self-inflated swaggerers, with "sweet dew upon (their) tongue, and from (their) lips flow honeyed words" (γλυκερή οἱ ἀπὸ στόματος ῥέει αὐδή, Theogony 97, cf. 80–93).

How much was this moralistic undertone informed by Hesiod's notorious dispute with his brother Perses over the land inherited from their father? The passage that rolls out the quarrel in *Works and Days* (27–39) has attracted much scholarly attention. The passage is important enough to be spelled out in full:

ὦ Πέρση, σὺ δὲ ταῦτα τεῷ ἐνικάτθεο θυμῷ,
μηδέ σ᾽Ἔρις κακόχαρτος ἀπ᾽ ἔργου θυμὸν ἐρύκοι
νείκε᾽ ὀπιπεύοντ᾽ ἀγορῆς ἐπακουὸν ἐόντα.
ὥρη γάρ τ᾽ ὀλίγη πέλεται νεικέων τ᾽ ἀγορέων τε,
ᾧτινι μὴ βίος ἔνδον ἐπηετανὸς κατάκειται
ὡραῖος, τὸν γαῖα φέρει, Δημήτερος ἀκτήν.
τοῦ κε κορεσσάμενος νείκεα καὶ δῆριν ὀφέλλοις
κτήμασ᾽ ἐπ᾽ ἀλλοτρίοις: σοὶ δ᾽ οὐκέτι δεύτερον ἔσται
ὧδ᾽ ἔρδειν: ἀλλ᾽ αὖθι διακρινώμεθα νεῖκος
ἰθείῃσι δίκῃς, αἵ τ᾽ ἐκ Διός εἰσιν ἄρισται.
ἤδη μὲν γὰρ κλῆρον ἐδασσάμεθ᾽, ἀλλὰ τὰ πολλὰ
ἁρπάζων ἐφόρεις μέγα κυδαίνων βασιλῆας
δωροφάγους, οἳ τήνδε δίκην ἐθέλουσι δίκασσαι.

"Perses, do store this up in your spirit, lest gloating Strife keep your spirit away from work, gazing at legal strife and hanging out in the agora. For he has little care for quarrels and assemblies, whoever does not have plentiful means of life stored up indoors in good season, what the earth bears, Demeter's grain. When you can take your fill of that, then you might foster quarrels and conflict over other men's possessions. But you will not have a second chance to act this way – no, let us decide our quarrel right here with straight judgments, which come from Zeus, the best ones. For already we had divided up our allotment, but you snatched much more besides and went carrying it off, greatly honoring the kings, those gift-eaters, who want to pass this judgment" (trans. Most, with modifications indicated above).

We do not know for sure whether the dispute was factual or rather a narrative trope that allowed Hesiod to unpack his moralistic agenda – maybe it was a creative write-up of the former to magnify the effects of the latter. No matter if authentic or not, the passage makes it clear that inheritance issues, questions pertaining to the passing on of land from one generation to the next were a matter of concern. As the incident involved agents and bodies of authority vested with the power to settle the dispute between two individuals, it follows that the household was intertwined with and subject to communal processes. The possession of land was a condition amendable to legal regulations at a level higher than private arrangements.

We ought to note that it is not certain if, as is commonly assumed, litigation had been filed by Perses at the moment of Hesiod's poetic rebuttal. The future tense in line 34, followed by the call to "decide our quarrel right here with straight judgments" (αὖθι διακρινώμεθα νεῖκος ἰθείῃσι δίκῃς, 35–36) signals that the case was pending. Anthony Edwards has argued that the initial division of their father's *kleros* (37) was most likely handled between the two brothers within prevailing legal practices of the community; hence, no court was required. Maybe Perses became dismayed with the arrangement (whether the division provided both sons with equal shares we do not know) and had sought legal action against his brother; this would explain Hesiod's comment that Perses will not be given a "second chance" (δεύτερον, 34) to sue him.[15] Perses in any case seems to have relied on support from his brother to stay afloat economically (37), an arrangement Hesiod soon grew unwilling to perpetuate. When Hesiod cut him off, Perses, in indignant fashion, turned to Thespiai for support from another authority (the gift-eating kings there, βασιλῆας δωροφάγους, 38–39), possibly seeking review of the original division of the farm.[16] Hesiod warned Perses about taking that route. Line 33–34 reads: "When you can take your fill of that, then you might foster quarrels and conflict over other men's possessions" (τοῦ κε κορεσσάμενος νείκεα καὶ δῆριν ὀφέλλοις κτήμασ' ἐπ' ἀλλοτρίοις), which either hinted at the costs of litigation or, more moralistically, reminded Perses of his wrong priorities in life. Either way, "gazing at legal strife and hanging out in the agora" (νείκε' ὀπιπεύοντ' ἀγορῆς ἐπακουὸν ἐόντα, 29) inevitably had sent Perses on a trajectory to ruin, no matter what justice might ultimately be rendered by the *basileis*.

Hesiod's quarrel was subject to ongoing legal transformation. Little was set – literally – in stone. The initial division of the *kleros* was made between brothers

15 Cf. Edwards 2004, pp. 38–44.

16 Gagarin 1974 dismissed the moral undertone of Hesiod's verdict on the *basileis*, arguing that "gift-eating" merely alluded to the fact that litigant parties had to pay court fees to the judges (in analogy to Homer, Iliad 18.508, the meaning of which is however notoriously puzzling).

and within the family, but the subsequent dispute elicited public scrutiny; action on behalf of the community adhered to traditional norms and the judgment of new legal authorities; and it was indicative of the volatile stance of these authorities, their status as an elite class on the one hand and the need to vindicate their elevated position in the civic arena on the other. Amidst those tensions, the inheritance and division of an estate could be a potentially precarious affair. If a dispute arose, conflicts between various agents, conceptions of law, and bodies vested with legal authority made both the course of the case and its outcome rather unpredictable. While the Homeric tradition looks at civic processes in Thebes from a heroic perspective, with *basileis* firmly positioned to lead the community and, by implication, render judgment, the legal horizon in Hesiod is more convoluted. It betrays a proto-politicization of communal affairs, both in terms of civic administration and justice, as much as a growing political sensibility among the people. Scholars are notoriously divided on when the related processes, conveniently labeled 'the rise of the polis,' actually began: it appears wise to look for different timelines in different places of Aegean Greece. It is clear, however, that from the mid-8th century, several communities in Boiotia experienced a sweeping wave of political and cultural innovation that placed them in the center of precisely these developments. The arrival of a regional variant of the Greek alphabetic script, itself associated with the local development in Thebes (below), also suggests that various cultural threads ran together in Boiotia. In turn, the application of an all-new media – writing – to the field of law triggered dynamic processes of establishing and advancing the political body of the community and its legal practices. We shall return to this aspect below.

Philolaos, paidopoiia, and 'set laws'

For the period immediately after Homer and Hesiod a diverse body of legal evidence becomes available. According to the strand of a tradition preserved by Aristotle, Philolaos, a member of the Bacchiad family of Corinth, migrated to Thebes to act as lawgiver. Aristotle says (Politics 2.1274b.2–6):

> νομοθέτης δ᾽αὐτοῖς ἐγένετο Φιλόλαος περί τ᾽ἄλλων τινῶν καὶ περὶ τῆς παιδοποιίας, οὓς καλοῦσιν ἐκεῖνοι νόμους θετικούς· καὶ τοῦτ᾽ ἐστὶν ἰδίως ὑπ᾽ ἐκείνου νενομοθετημένον, ὅπως ὁ ἀριθμὸς σῴζηται τῶν κλήρων.

> Philolaos became the Thebans' lawgiver in regard to various matters, among others the size of families – the laws called by the Thebans the laws of adoption (νόμους θετικούς); about this Philolaos enacted special legislation, in order that the number of the estates in land might be preserved. (trans. Rackham)

The nature and date of Philolaos' legislation have been subject to debate. A few lines earlier (1274a.31-b2), Aristotle says that Philolaos was the lover of a certain Diokles who appears in the list of Olympic victors under the year 728.[17] Both men were said to have left Corinth because of Diokles' difficult relationship to his mother Alkyone; they lived in Thebes until their death. In Aristotle's days, the tombs were still visible, one oriented toward Corinth, the other, that of Diokles, facing away from his hometown in ostentatious fashion. Aristotle's early chronology, derived from the Olympic lists, has been questioned both on the grounds of source criticism and of more general observations on early Greek legal practice. The second half of the 8th century, more than 50 years prior to the earliest epigraphic attestation of legal texts from Dreros and Lokroi Epizephyrioi, appears too soon for the passing of νόμοι θετικοί (below). The story about the tombs of Philolaos and Diokles was in any case most likely an etiological tradition that explained the diametrical orientation of the graves.[18] It is preferable to see Philolaos as one of the exiles who were forced to leave Corinth in the events that led to the downfall of the Bacchiads around 660 (Herodotus 5.92, below); hence, the return to his hometown was out of the picture. If correct, his legislation reverberated with circumstances around the mid-7th century BCE.

A more general approach to Aristotle's passage suggests that the distribution of land lots was an issue of concern at the time. Preservation of "the number of the estates" indicates that the grand total of *kleroi* was somehow in jeopardy. In other words: the measure concerned not the size of plots as such but their actual number, although the two issues were inherently related. In the case of a growing concentration of land lots in the hands of fewer people, brought about for instance by sales or inheritance, some estates grew larger, while their overall number dropped. The former fostered economic hierarchies, but the true point of concern was the latter, because ownership of a *kleros* was the critical requirement for enjoying entitlement and political participation rights in the developing community of Thebes.[19] Philolaos' legislation thus intersected with the core issue of the political and social order

---

17 Moretti 1957, no. 13.

18 Cf. Hölkeskamp 1999, p. 247; Christesen 2007, pp. 157–160. The trope of difficult ties between mother and son, Alkyone and Diokles, smacks of a rationalizing attempt too. A historical figure in Aristotle, Alkyone was considered by Hesiod (fragment 118.2, 157 Most) the daughter of Atlas or Aiolos. The first Alkyone was raped by Poseidon (cf. Pausanias 3.18.10, Throne of Amyklai) while the latter was notorious for exuberant sex with her husband Keyx. In both variants, she is subsequently turned into a kingfisher by Zeus. Aristotle's text is unclear in that it not does state whether Diokles loathed for the love of his mother for other men or for himself: ὡς ἐκεῖνος [Diokles] τὴν πόλιν ἔλιπε διαμισήσας τὸν ἔρωτα τὸν τῆς μητρὸς Ἀλκυόνης: 1274a.34–35). That is, did Diokles disapprove of his mother's sexual exaltation or her love for him? If the latter, the story resembled that of Oedipus and Iokaste, and it followed the same itinerary between Corinth and Thebes.

19 Cf. only Buck 1979, p. 92.

of Thebes; the interrelation between both topics is a key theme in book 2 of the *Politics,* which provides the overall context for Aristotle's discussion of his measures.

So the legislative measure to preserve the number of estates in the Theban countryside was designed to avoid broadscale downward social mobility. But how was the freeze brought about, i. e., by what legal stipulation? In Rackham's translation, Philolaos turned to the legal tool of laws of adoption; the purpose of the legislation could have been establishing guidelines for the (obligatory?) adoption of an heir by childless landowners, or to govern the legal succession of heirs so that properties were not folded into someone else's possession. We ought to note however that νόμοι θετικοί does not translate as "laws of adoption" but simply "set laws," in the sense of fixed or statute laws. The formulation pertains to the status of νόμοι, not to their contents. The meaning of adoption laws transpires only in connection with the previous παιδοποιία, freely translated by Rackham as "the size of families" but, more literally, "the making of children," that is, their status definition through law (below). The grammatical connection οὓς (plural) makes it clear that the measure concerning παιδοποιία was but one item among the νόμοι Philolaos had stipulated περί τ' ἄλλων τινῶν. This reading is endorsed also by the subsequent τοῦτ' ἐστὶν ... νενομοθετημένον, which envisions an overall package of laws rather than one legal matter alone. A more accurate translation of the section reads, therefore, "Philolaos became the Thebans' lawgiver in regard to various matters, including the legal status of children, which they call statute laws; and this (i. e., the overall package) was specifically enacted by him so that the number of the *kleroi* might be preserved."

It is quite possible, although impossible to prove, that Philolaos' legislation marked the beginnings of stipulating, that is, decreeing, writing down, and recording laws in Thebes. Referencing this body of legal texts as νόμοι θετικοί, a label that signals the departure from previous legal practice, points in this direction. Measures regarding the land were a common legal subject matter in the surviving corpus of early Greek legislation, they are widely attested elsewhere.[20] Depending on how serious the situation in Thebes was, Philolaos might have initiated a thoroughgoing redistribution of land lots.[21] Another possibility is that landowners were assured of their right of ownership, no matter how large (or small) the estate was.[22] The latter would imply the existence of some kind of cadaster or land registry in which the community kept basic information about *kleroi,* including their size and maybe their value, even though the collection and organization of this type of information in the early polis might raise suspicion among scholars; we shall return to this below.

---

20 See below.

21 Gehrke 1985, p. 373.

22 Cloché 1952, p. 26.

Paidopoiia was in any case but one measure that was implemented to preserve the number of *kleroi*. A few sections earlier in the *Politics* (1265b.12–16), still under the same thematic rubric in book 2, Aristotle reports a curious piece of legislation at Corinth that adds context and nuance to Philolaos' enactment in Thebes. Pheidon the Corinthian, who is qualified as one of the earliest legislators, put forth measures for birth control, designed to limit the number of potential heirs and, effectively, to safeguard the size of landed property. His legislation stipulated that the number of houses had to equal the number of citizens; it appears to have served to protect the owners of plots of land and to maintain the balance of land ownership ratios. If it was an authentic measure from the late 7th century BCE, if not slightly earlier, Pheidon's law was in use at the time of the Bacchiad regime, although it did not deliver the sociopolitical redemption its originator had hoped for. By the mid-7th century, Corinth was thrown into civic strife that brought about the end of the Bacchiad dynasty. Maybe Pheidon's law – controversies over its passing or its subsequent implementation, or both – contributed to the quarrels rather than easing social tensions.[23]

The thematic nexus with Philolaos' legislation, in addition to the joint Corinthian backdrop, has led scholars to view both acts as quintessentially similar, if not identical. Both regulations targeted the connection between land ownership and political status; and both emphasized the role of children in the process of reconciliation between the subjects at hand. But there were also marked differences. Aristotle introduces Pheidon's legislation with an expression of surprise over the fact that, although many attempts have been made to freeze the number of properties, few have bothered to "regulate the number of citizens; the issue of τεκνοποιία is left undealt with by many. ... It might instead be thought that it is the τεκνοποιία rather than the properties that should be restricted, so as not to allow the birth of a certain number of children ... Leaving this question unanswered, as happens in most states, will inevitably lead to poverty among the citizens, and poverty produces revolt and crime" (1265a.41-b14). Now comes Pheidon's part (1265b.14–16):

> Φείδων μὲν οὖν ὁ Κορίνθιος, ὢν νομοθέτης τῶν ἀρχαιοτάτων, τοὺς οἴκους ἴσους ᾠήθη δεῖν διαμένειν καὶ τὸ πλῆθος τῶν πολιτῶν, καὶ εἰ τὸ πρῶτον τοὺς κλήρους ἀνίσους εἶχον πάντες κατὰ μέγεθος.
>
> The Corinthian Pheidon in fact, one of the most ancient lawgivers, thought that the households and the citizen population ought to remain at the same numbers, even though at the outset the estates of all were unequal in size. (trans. Rackham).

23 Hölkeskamp 1999, pp. 150–157.

So Pheidon believed that through τεκνοποιία the number of citizens might be kept in sync with the number of *kleroi*. The English translation of τεκνοποιία in Rackham's edition is "control of birth-rate," which is somewhat abstract for the more literal meaning "procreation of children." We just noted that in Philolaos' case Aristotle speaks of παιδοποιία, which sounds very similar – the making of παῖδες and τέκνα respectively. While τεκνοποιία is used frequently in Aristotle's corpus (19 occurrences), παιδοποιία appears only once, in the Philolaos passage in *Politics* 1274b. Plato, on the other hand, speaks variously and in different contexts of παιδοποιία, with a meaning that resembles Aristotle's usage of τεκνοποιία. By the 4th century BCE, both words seem to have been used by and large synonymously.[24]

The single reference to παιδοποιία foregrounds the context to which it is applied by Aristotle. It has been argued that παῖς and τέκνον, in early Greek legal conceptions, pointed to two different principles of establishing status. While the former, the making of legal παῖδες, whether through procreation or adoption, built on the notion of patrilineal descent, the original meaning of τεκνοποιία pointed to matrilineal customs, especially female rights to the tenure of property and land. In Corinth, matrilineal rights were in place until the mid-7th century BCE: the tradition of the uprising against the ruling clan of Bacchiads builds off the idea that Kypselos, the main protagonist, staked his matrilineal claim to power.[25] Drawing on information from the collection of constitutions of Greek cities that served as the database of the *Politics*, Aristotle might thus indeed have encountered in his sources that the Corinthian Philolaos, a man from a matrilineal community, enacted a piece of legislation in Thebes that resonated with patrilineal traditions there – hence, παιδοποιία.[26] If the different choice of words was indeed indicative of gender-distinct conditions in the legal framework in Corinth and Thebes, Philolaos' and Pheidon's substantive legislation was nonetheless different. Pheidon sought to maintain a given ratio of estates and the number of citizens through a law that governed the number of children with legal capacity; Aristotle cited this for the novelty of the approach. While Philolaos, in order to preserve the stock of *kleroi*, issued a series of statute laws that pertained to the land, either through redistribution or principal endorsement of the quality of *kleroi* to generate political status, no matter how small the land lot might have been. In other words, the one approach targeted people, the other the land.

In another passage in the *Politics* (1321a.26–29), Aristotle declares that "when the people get a share in governing it should happen either in the previously stated way and recipients should be those who have the property qualification or, as it

24 Cf. Fossey 1993/2019. *Paidopoiia* in Plato: Symposion 192b.1; Theages 121c.4; Timaios 18c.6; 91c2; Laws 783e.5; 784b.1; Politeia 424a.1; 449d.2; 459a.4; 459d.5; 460d.6.

25 Herodotus 5.92; Nikolaos BNJ 90 fr. 57.

26 This argument has been put forth by Fossey 1993/2019, esp. pp. 79–81.

is the practice in Thebes, participation should go to people who, for some while, have abstained from manual labor." The observation is made with reference to the oligarchic backbone of the Theban *politeia* in the Classical period, the well-attested distribution of all active citizens among local councils *(boulai)* as well as the federal bodies of the Boiotian *koinon.*[27] Political participation, in this arrangement, was disconnected from property qualification, i. e., citizens were not required to possess a piece of land of a certain size. Rather, the defining element of status had shifted toward profession and income, the latter secured through a variety of conceivable practices (e. g., trade, money lending, leases), whereas others were deemed unsuitable to generate the right to participate in politics ("manual labor"). Status was of course not dissociated from landowning altogether, because property holding will have been among the most common sources of revenue. The Theban measure to link political participation with a defined amount of income can however easily be understood as a long-term legacy of Philolaos' legislation and its strike against large-scale *kleroi* as the sole basis of political status.

In sum, then, the challenges Philolaos had encountered in Thebes were similar to those elsewhere in mainland Greece and the Peloponnese. In the developing political and legal culture of the city-state, emphasis on individual participation and collective privilege of the citizen body almost naturally produced tensions about how civic status was defined, secured, and passed on from one generation to the next. The responses to these challenges were deeply local – Philolaos' and Pheidon's legislative acts make this obvious – formulated in recognition of local circumstances, and accounting for pre-existing ways and traditions, following local idiosyncrasies. In Thebes, this gave rise to the first-time constitution of a body of statute laws; the issue was of metajurisdictional quality (below). All the while, local response to challenges encountered by others, in neighboring communities as much as beyond the regional horizon, added to the formation of a body of legal practices and procedures that were, in principle, similar and structurally comparable, and that contributed to the growth of a common legal culture. We will return to the fine-tuned mechanics of this local-translocal interplay again soon.

---

27 According to another law referenced by Aristotle "no one who had not kept out of trade for the last ten years might be admitted to office [in Thebes]" (Politics 1278a.25–6). Oligarchic councils: Hellenika Oxyrhynchia 19 Chambers; Thucydides 5.38.2; Cartledge 2000; Beck/Ganter 2015; Beck 2025.

Propraxia and its proxies

There was for the longest time no epigraphic evidence to support our reading of the situation in Thebes at the time of Philolaos' legal enactments and in the decades thereafter. Unlike the rich material for instance from Crete, excavations in Thebes had not released any inscribed laws or legal charters. This situation changed when archaeological work at the Sanctuary of Herakles in the southeastern corner of the Kadmeia and in the modern suburb of Pyri in the early 2000s brought to light a wealth of new evidence. Among the inscribed findings were five bronze tablets from the late Archaic or early Classical periods. Only one of them has been published to date by means of an editio princeps. It is a bronze pinax from the Herakleion with holes in the upper and lower right corners and one hole on the left, which appears to have been the middle of the original bronze: the left half is broken off. The surviving part is c. 11 cm high and 16 cm wide. The text is written stoichedon with visible horizontal guidelines except for the final line, the last letters of which continue upwards along the right edge of the tablet. It is on display in the Museum in Thebes (TM 41063 = SEG 60.509). The first edition of the text by Vasilis Aravantinos (2014) reads:

[- - - - - -]τ̣õε Ἀριστ-
[- - - - - -]τ̣õε Ἀθανα-
[- - - - - - κ]αὶ παίδε-
[σσι- - - -]Ṭ̣ΕΓΟΑΝ⁝α
[- - - - - - -]π̣ρ̣οπραχ-
[σίαν - - -] ἔ̈δον α-
[- - -] Θ[ε]βαε̃ος v
[- - -]αδ̣α̣ο̣βοιοταρχίοντος

Historically, the bronze is certainly a spectacular find, while its contribution to the understanding of early alphabetic writing, especially the rise and dissemination of epichoric scriptures in Boiotia make it a "small gem."[28] We ought to begin our discussion of the text however with the observation that its basic nature is unclear. What can be drawn from the remaining section is that one, two, or more individuals (ll. 1–3), together with their children (ll. 3–4), were reassured of certain privileges or were first-time recipients of these privileges, including the right of προπραξία (l. 5). The names of the individuals are battered, further rights in addition to *propraxia* irrecoverable.[29] Assurance of existing rights or the award of new ones points to an honorific decree, which raises the question of the issuing authority. The text is

28 Papazarkadas 2021, p. 274.
29 Aravantinos 2014, pp. 199–202.

relatively short, even if the preserved section is only half of the original document. Several individuals plus reference to children makes for a crowded space. Toward the end, one of these individuals is identified as a Theban (l. 7). He is syntactically and thematically separated from the recipients of rights through their children. The local qualification of the person in line 7 makes it unlikely that the decree was issued by the city of Thebes: in a public document from Thebes such an identification was hardly necessary. Vice versa, it is likely that the individuals at the beginning were not from Thebes; again, an all-Theban background of the parties involved would have made their local identification redundant. Reference to a boiotarch in line 8 settles the issue in favor of a translocal issuing authority. As has been noted by scholars, this is the first epigraphic attestation of the office of boiotarchs, which disperses all doubts in Herodotus' mention of boiotarchs in the Battle of Plataia. Against all concerns raised by scholars earlier, the beginnings of the office date to the (late?) 6th century BCE.[30] The Theban official in line 7, together with at least one more colleague in line 8, through their office represented the Boiotian League as issuing authority. Incidentally, dialectal distinction also seems to point to the regional horizon of Boiotia, suggesting influences on the scripture from Tanagra.[31]

As a federal rather than a polis decree, the bronze had a wide catchment area. Its authority to govern legal matters revolving around *propraxia* applied to a larger legal framework. Similar honorific documents of the *koinon* from later periods typically awarded recipients with various rights and privileges, including *ateleia, asylia, proxenia, enktesis,* and *epigameia.* These honors were effective tools to establish ties with cities outside the *koinon* and streamline foreign relations near and far; in reverse direction, many Boiotians are known to have been the recipients of corresponding honors elsewhere.[32] By means of comparison, *propraxia* prima facie looks like a minor, technical privilege, a granulated regulation. Its only other attestation in the epigraphy from pre-Hellenistic times is in a decree from the city of Stratos (IG IX 1^2 2.390) from c. 400 BCE which grants several rights to three foreigners as well as their descendants: προξενίαν δόμεν καὶ προνομίαν καὶ προπραξίαν αὐτοῖς καὶ γενεᾶι (ll. 4–7).

What is *propraxia?* The editio princeps of the boiotarch-inscription suggests to see it as priority in negotiations or in having one's financial demands fulfilled.[33] In similar fashion, Alain Bresson has commented that *propraxia* in the city-decree

30 Cf. Herodotus 9.15.1; Beck 2025. The bronze most likely dates from exactly that time, the late 6th cent., and no later than 475 BCE: Papazarkadas 2021, p. 273.

31 Ma 2016 considers Tanagra as the inscription's point of origin, from where it had come to Thebes under unknown circumstances. Note that the linguistic case rests on the spelling of one single diphthong in line 7 (Θ[ε]βαεος for Θ[ε]βαιος in line 7), which appears characteristic of Tanagra, cf. Aravantinos 2014, p. 201.

32 Fossey 2014, pp. 83–104.

33 Aravantinos 2014, p. 201; in similar fashion: Ma 2016: "priority in recovering debt."

of Stratos presumably implied "the privilege of benefiting from an immediate judicial enforcement ... or perhaps a privilege of guarantee for a seizure of property at the expense of a citizen of Stratos."[34] Such an interpretation is echoed by the literary tradition, although the term occurs only once in the corpus of texts from the Archaic and Classical periods. In Aischylos' *Libation Bearers,* the chorus, in an otherwise murky intervention, urges Orestes to put his plan to kill Klytemnestra into action and "exact satisfaction" (πρόπρασσε χάριν: 834–5) to avenge his father's death.[35]

The line-up of *proxenia, pronomia* – most likely access to the council and/or assembly of the polis – and *propraxia* in the Stratos decree makes the latter again look like a specialized award: prioritizing claims when recovering debts. The issue was evidently important enough to be spelled out and, prospectively, secured for the children of the creditor. We can only surmise the obvious, that is, that the securing of creditor rights, for instance by the guarantee for the seizure of property, was a key aspect in the legal governance of households. Property claims feature prominently among early Greek inscriptions, which hints at a certain degree of insecurity, both within the communities and also in families (we already encountered Hesiod's quarrels above). Second, assurances of priority entitlement must have been a prime enticement. In the famous *thetmion* from the early 5th century BCE for settlers sent out from East Lokris to Naupaktos to establish a new settlement there, various legal assurances are listed, evidently to dispel concerns about potential legal disadvantages of the settlers once they had left their hometown. Among these was the right to obtain priority access to the lawcourts, which suggests that the issue was a matter of concern to the people who at that time of future litigation had forfeited their citizenship privileges.[36] For foreigners, *propraxia* was a robust asset when conducting business in town. As a universal award, similar to, for instance, *ateleia, propraxia* secured their investment against claims raised by a member of the citizen community. Maybe this implied also that no citizen-agent

34 Bresson 2018, p. 289, note 11. Cf. also the *proproxia* awards in I.Iasos 23.

35 Marshall 2017, p. 112–113.

36 Meiggs/Lewis, GHI 20 = van Effenterre/Ruzé, Nomima I, no. 43, ll. 32–35 (after Beck 1999):
τοὺς ἐπιϝοίϘους ⁝ ἐν Ναύπακτον ⁝ τὰν δίκαν πρόδιϘον ⁝ *h*αρέσται πὸ τοὺς δ-
ικαστε̃ρας, ⁝ *h*αρέσται ⁝ καὶ δόμεν ⁝ ἐν Ὀπόεντι κατὰ ϝέος αὐταμαρόν. ⁝ ΛοϘ-
ρο̃ν το̃ν *h*υποκναμιδίον ⁝ προστάταν καταστᾶσαι ⁝ το̃ν ΛοϘρο̃ν τὀπιϝ-
οίϘοι ⁝ καὶ το̃ν ἐπιϝοίϘον το̃ι ΛοϘρο̃ι, ⁝ *h*οίτινές κα ‹πιατὲς ἔντιμοι ες ⁝
"The settlers in Naupaktos shall be given priority in access to the law, and it shall be given before the lawcourts, and in Opus it shall be given against him on the same day. For the Hypoknemidian Lokrian a legal guardian shall be instated from the local Lokrians and a settler for the Lokrians who hold citizen rights."

was required to enforce the priority of claims of the *xenos*, which further provided substance and legal security to the precarious status of foreigners.[37]

In material terms, *propraxia* shifted the focus from granted rights to procedural law. Such a nature of *propraxia* hints at another possible background to the boiotarch-inscription. If *propraxia* was issued with regard to a specific title and/or a concrete land lot rather than a universal grant, the decree might have had the character of a *horos* inscription. Placed on the wall of a property or a wooden plank, *horoi* were used to identify sacred lands or, less frequently, to mark out public property, for instance if it was leased out for profit-making purposes.[38] In cases of private property, *horos* inscriptions proclaimed that ownership of the *kleros* was formally transferred to a creditor. Potential buyers were reminded that a property was either sold as a security or, if the property was mortgaged and the current occupant unable to pay in due time, that someone was entitled to have their financial demands fulfilled first.[39] Maybe the inscription from the Herakleion was a copy of an *horos* on site, deposited in the sanctuary to place the agreement under the tutelage of the deity. Alternatively, it was used to demarcate a property and transferred to the sanctuary once the financial demands were fulfilled. A third possibility, although rich in presumptions, is that it belonged to an archive in the Herakleion that kept track of debts levied on specific properties, including their location, size, and value, as well as the names of creditors. Set up in one of the city's most prestigious sanctuaries, such an archive highlighted the communal authority over the record and any legal pronouncement arising from it in the future. In other words, the polis as a whole, in sacred covenant with the gods, vouched for the creditor's access to their legal title, reminding the citizenry of the supreme authority behind the agreement.[40]

It is difficult to decide with certainty whether *propraxia* in the text from the Herakleion applied to one property or was awarded as a universal privilege and to determine, effectively, whether the inscription was a *horos* marker or an honorific decree. Similarity in syntax, structure, and style to the Stratos decree might suggest the latter. Either way, *propraxia* was linked to other procedural practices. It empow-

37 Note how the regulations in Lokris required the appointment of a local citizen agent to defend the claims in court. The precise meaning of the passage (previous note) is however muddled, cf. Koerner 1993, pp. 196–197 ("der Inhalt ... ist nicht wirklich zu klären").

38 Cf. Maffi 2005, p. 262; Horster 2010, pp. 404–442.

39 Horster 2010, p. 442 (examples); see also the contribution in this volume by Donatella Erdas on the procedures of selling land and houses.

40 See IPArk 1 from Tegea (c. 450 BCE) for a similar case.

ered certain individuals from outside of Thebes to have their economic status solidified: whether the recipients were from another Boiotian city or somewhere else we do not know, nor is it certain where the right of *propraxia* was to be utilized, in Thebes, another city, or universally throughout Boiotia. All of these possibilities were united by the fact that *propraxia* required a legal framework beyond a single city in Boiotia. Note, however, that the right of preferential treatment implied the existence of additional prescriptions and institutions to handle the prioritization of financial demands. To begin with, schemes for the repayment of debts had to be laid down by law. If someone submitted their claim for *propraxia,* the marking out of the property, its size and binding value had to be legally ascertainable. Furthermore, the role of legal children needed to be defined in the process, and, if there were no *paides,* measures had to be in place to identify and authenticate hereditary collateral relatives; with property disputes within families being commonplace, the legal context of ownership and its defense against rival claims had to be defined. And for foreigners, there must have been a legal protocol for how appeals were handled and before what court, and if the litigation made communal exaction of the property necessary, how this was carried out.

So we have a wide panorama of legislation before us that accompanied *propraxia* and was necessary to make the proper execution of priority rights possible. Maybe the juristic complexity, the intertwinement with other legal prescriptions, had something to do with the rarity with which the award was granted: it was relatively easy for the polis to put grants of universal tax exemption into action or the right to marry and own property, but it was more complicated to issue a legal title that interfered with the fine-tuned mechanics of procedural law. Late Archaic and Classical legislation offers of course a full array of highly specialized, locally idiosyncratic regulations to address the relevant areas of material law. In Thebes, the corresponding body of laws most likely contributed to and evolved in conversation with Philolaos' earliest *nomoi thetikoi.* Land and property inheritance issues were part and parcel of this type of legislation, and of the conception of law overall. Judging from the quantitative record alone, more than one third of all attested Archaic legal inscriptions were dedicated to regulating property, which highlights the precarious nature of land ownership.[41]

Indeed, land legislation was critical to the early Greek polis in more ways than one. Emily Mackil has reminded us that the communal settlement of disputes about ownership and/or inheritance of landed property, while inspiring and advancing a new legal chapter of the polis, also contributed significantly to the rise of auton-

41 Calculations after Mackil 2017, p. 69, based on her quantification of the evidence assembled in van Effenterre/Ruzé, Nomima 1994–1995.

omous state authority. Archaic legislation, adjudication, and, if necessary, enforcement of laws pertaining to the land is typically referenced for its quality as substantive law, that is, its content-related dimension. Yet in settling conflicts relating to the land, the corresponding statutes created a new form of "territorial jurisdiction," a gradual recognition that the land as such was brought under the control and made subject to the laws and institutions of the community; and in turn, that the laws were considered binding within the boundaries of the polis. Such a juristic seizure of the land added, secondly, to the gradual enhancement of a "metajurisdictional authority," that is, the polis' exclusive authority to issue and alter its own jurisdiction in and over a territory that was considered an integral, constituent part of the community. Litigation about landed property was therefore always a conversation or, rather, an ongoing negotiation about the conception of legal practice and its governing juristic institutions.[42] *Propraxia* appears as a prime example of the advancing of territorial jurisdiction through material law. Judging from its rare application, however, it turned out to be an awkward legal measure because it seems to have been at odds with metajurisdictional claims of the community, since priority in litigation potentially conflicted with legal procedures considered under the unrivaled prerogative of the polis.

New material from Thebes: adumbrating a thicket of laws and legal administration

We noted in passing that the inscription from the Herakleion was issued before the regional backdrop of the Boiotian League. Its claim for recognition extended beyond the local horizon of the single city. Regional perspectivation relates back to our opening conversation about unity and plurality of Greek law, and multiple scales of legal encoding in between. The discovery of four new bronze tablets in Thebes makes a substantive contribution to this debate. As we shall see in this section, some of the texts relate, in unique fashion, to a regional regime of property regulations that evidence the establishment of an all-new jurisdictional authority in Boiotia. The main impediment to the study of the documents is that they have not yet been fully published. They are showcased in the Museum in Thebes where they eagerly await publication.

Angelos Matthaiou offered a prepublication of the material in 2014. All four bronze tablets were retrieved 2001–2002 by the local Ephorate of Antiquities from a tomb-like cist found at the Madhis plot in Pyri, c. 800 m northwest of the Kadmeia, with finds including palmette antefixes, fragments of Archaic sculpture and

42 Mackil 2017 (quotes 79).

of a perirrhanterion, a bone stylus, a few bronze phialai, and an inscribed late-Archaic column fragment. The disparate deposit was deliberately covered with earth and other debris in the early decades of the 4th century BCE.[43] Judging from the form of the letters, the tentative date provided for the epigraphic batch is the late 6th to early 5th century BCE. Given the demanding state of preservation of the plaques (oxidation of the metal makes the texts in various sections difficult to read), the absence of full-fledged editiones principes makes the in-depth study of the documents impossible to date. The prepublication provides, however, valuable data on the nature and contents of the tablets. The following conspectus is based on the information given by Matthaiou.

Table 1: Conspectus of recent discoveries of Archaic inscriptions from Thebes

Reference	Format	Contents
SEG 60.505 TM 35908 Matthaiou 2014, 212, no. 1	intact bronze tablet (4.5 by 18 cm) with ring attached to the left; writing on 1 side	account statement
SEG 60.506 TM 35913 Matthaiou 2014, 213–215, no. 2	largely intact bronze tablet (originally measuring 10.1 by 19 cm), writing on 1 side	record of arbitration over disputed land
SEG 60.507 TM 35909 Matthaiou 2014, 215–220, no. 3	intact bronze tablet, writing on both sides (no dimensions given)	record of leased or sold landed properties
SEG 60.508 TM 35914 Matthaiou 2014, 221, no. 4	intact bronze tablet, writing on both sides (no dimensions given)	regulations concerning a sacred feast

SEG 60.505 documents the deposit of a large cash sum under the tutelage of a public treasury or a sanctuary. It is the earliest evidence for the practice of placing monetary funds in a communal treasury in Thebes. By implication, the bronze is also the earliest example for the archival practice of keeping financial records and placing these under the authority of the deity and/or polis. The plaque appears intact but its lower part, roughly half of it, is kept empty. If this was intentional, there might

43 Matthaiou 2014, p. 211; cf. Aravantinos 2006 on an inscribed late-Archaic column drum from the same find spot. Ma 2016 thinks that such dumping points to an upheaval in Theban history, maybe at the time of the Spartan coup 382 BCE.

have been room for new information pertaining to future deposits, for instance, if legal circumstances changed or the entitlement was transferred to another person. The stated figure of 5,635 drachms and 2 1/2 obols was calculated after a tithe was subtracted from the initial amount, exacted from the creditor. Maybe this tithe was a tax/fee for deposits in the treasury, or an offering to a deity. The language makes it clear that it was levied upon the fund in authoritative fashion. Evidently the polis reserved the right to exact the fee, asserting its role as legal guarantor of the transaction.

SEG 60.506 is largely intact. The lower right corner of the tablet is broken off, it can however be restored from three small adjoining pieces that complete the damaged section. Writing is evenly distributed and the text preserved in its entirety. Corrosion poses a substantial challenge to legibility. Most likely the bronze pertains to an arbitration over a certain piece of land. The listed parties to the dispute are Megara (l. 4) and Thebes with Eleutherai (ll. 5 and 6). The dispute arose when the Megarians used or took possession of lands that belonged to a community referenced as Ϝασ[.]οι or Ϝασ[.]ιεῖς (l. 4). Lines 7 to 10 list the names of two judges and three witnesses.[44] No ethnikon is given, hence, they belonged to the (unknown) city that issued the arbitration. The document from the cist is thus most likely a copy of the final verdict delivered to Thebes.

Thebes is listed in the inscription as a polis of its own, in close union with Eleutherai: hα πόλις hα Θεβαί|ον κἐλευθεραίο[ν]. No mention to a federal backdrop is made in the legible sections of the text; presumably plans about the *koinon* were just about to appear on the horizon. Union with Eleutherai suggests that the dispute arose before the last decade of the 6th century and maybe before c. 519 BCE (a date inferred from Thucydides 3.68), when the Thebans sought to make Plataia, the main stakeholder across the Asopos and in the direction of Eleutherai, "to partake in the Boiotian League" (Herodotus 6.108.5). The Plataians refused and placed themselves under the protection of the Athenians. Before battle between Thebans and Athenians was joined, the Corinthians arbitrated between the two sides and set a boundary, with the condition that the Thebans would not "force such of the Boiotians to be Thebans as did not want to be such." Despite the arbitration, the Thebans attacked the Athenians as they made ready to leave and were defeated, whereupon a new boundary was created: "they set the river Asopos as a boundary for Hysiai and Plataia against the Thebans" (6.108.6).

Plataian allegiance with Athens further complicated the situation in the muddled borderlands. As late as 506 BCE, volatile conditions in the area saw the The-

44 Matthaiou 2014, p. 214.

bans lead a military campaign as far as Eleusis toward the Saronic coast.[45] Finds from the Antiopi cave (Pausanias 1.38.9) in the vicinity of the later city-walls of Eleutherai indicate that Theban engagement in the area did not end with the establishment of the Asopos borderline, on the contrary. The earliest ceramics from Eleutherai so far date from the early 5th century, which is also the time when the first fortress was built there. Sylvian Fachard has pointed to the high density of massive border fortifications in the area, which underpins the character of the region as a genuinely contested space.[46] It is well conceivable, then, that the dispute with Megara, in addition to quarrels with Athens over Plataia and zones of influence in the Mazi plain, was causally related with the Thebans' decision to strengthen their foothold in the area by aiding Eleutherai's cause: through support for the expensive construction of its monumental fortifications and through assistance with its claims for disputed pastures.

The contested land itself must have been somewhere in the region south of Eleutherai – Megarian engagement north of Eleutherai is very unlikely – presumably in the rugged terrain of the western sectors of Mt. Pateras toward Aigosthenai. The Wasioi (?) cannot be associated with any of the attested settlements in the region or in southern Boiotia, for that matter. Most likely they were a kome, a village and satellite of Thebes: by the mid-6th century, the Thebans had several such villages in their possession, in various directions: towards Haliartos, Tanagra, and into the Parasopia. The land in dispute thus cannot have been a large-scale area but rather a pocket of land, not more than a few square kilometers. What follows from these observations is that Thebes, in union with Eleutherai, had not only a clear understanding of the microtopography of the area some 30 km south of the city, but the drive to bring patches of land there under its administrative grip. In other words, the Thebans not only staked claims to territorial jurisdiction in the region but also to act as legal guardians of the land, vested with the authority to execute whatever verdict emanated from the arbitration. Such a juristic seizure of territory, far remote from the polis and its genuine *chora,* added to the city's meta-jurisdictional authority. It fueled the understanding of the Thebans that they were empowered to issue legal decisions over land that was considered an integral, constituent part of their community.

45 Herodotus' account of these events is complemented by the new *kioniskos* from Thebes (Aravantinos 2006 = SEG 56.521) that sheds a curiously different light on the incident. Cf. now the most comprehensive account on Theban-Athenian relations in the area by van Wijk 2024, pp. 179–206.

46 Fachard 2013; Fachard et al. 2020; cf. van Wijk 2024, pp. 175–178. The large fortress whose monumental remains occupy the hilltop at the Kaza defile, 500 m west of the Eleutherai settlement, is of a younger date (mid-4th cent. BCE; van Wijk 2024, pp. 201–202).

SEG 60.508 is complete and opisthographic. Due to bad erosion only the back side can be deciphered, and only with utmost effort. The text seems to spell out regulations for a meal at a common banquet, most likely held in a sanctuary. It then lists a board of 22 partakers in the feast, who are subsumed under the heading of "feast givers" (θοίνατροι). Nothing else can be said about the contents at this time. The more general observation to be drawn from the battered text is that the community kept records of certain rights and privileges granted to individual citizens, in this case participation in an event rich in communal purpose and prestige.

The most instructive document for our purposes is SEG 60.507, listed as a record of landed properties. The tablet is opisthographic, inscribed by the same hand on both sides. No dimensions are given. Judging from display in the Museum of Thebes, it is about 10 cm high and 34.5 cm wide. On both sides, landed properties are listed to be leased or sold. Each entry details the following information: the current owner, location, and size.[47] Since the notice is dated after and the transaction overseen by Theban officials, the public character of the document is evident. Some of the attested local institutions were previously unknown. The first is a board of so-called πρόραρχοι. Only those of the *prorarchoi* are mentioned who were present at the deed of sale. They are headed by a person named Oligos – a rare name in Boiotia and throughout Greece, most likely identifiable with the same man who had dedicated an inscribed bronze vessel at Olympia in the concluding decades of the 6th century.[48] Furthermore, a council (βολά) was involved in the process, which was in office at "the time of Agelas," presumably an eponymous archon; another entry attests to "the time of Ptoiodoros." Finally, a board of πρατίδιοι ("sellers" or "makers") is involved in the process. The name could derive from a place or a tribal group. Their role in the text suggests however, more plausibly, that they represented a board involved with the sale of properties, hence, they might have been the facilitators of the deed of sale, through representation of the registry that kept the information pertaining to each property. Such a reading is corroborated by the verb used to describe the nature of the transaction, ἀνέλασαν, aorist of an otherwise unattested verb ἀνελαύνω. According to Matthaiou, this is best understood as "to sell, most likely after confiscation. The verb, that is, denotes the act of public auction."[49] Maybe the *pratidioi* were the ones

47 Cf. Matthaiou 2014, p. 218 on referenced sizes. Of these, only two are attested to date: the *blethron/plethron,* a square with 100 ft on each side, i. e., c. 27 to 35 m ≈ 900 m² (Montanari s.v.); and the *sphura,* lit. "hammer," maybe to demarcate a "balk between the furrows of ploughed land" (LSJ s.v.); cf. IG VII 2415, line 22 on Theban private grounds in the *chora* of Plataia (2nd cent. CE) and IG IX 1.61, line 39 f. (Daulis). One property is labeled an *aula,* "farm" or "farmstead."

48 SEG 42.382.

49 Matthaiou 2014, p. 216.

who had administered the confiscation and now carried it through with the action. After the change in ownership, their agency would be responsible for compiling the new record for each *kleros.*

A total of at least 22 properties were sold or leased, for which seven proprietors are listed, including six of an individual named Aristogeiton, five of Iaron and another 5 of Phithe, two or three of Kleudoros and two more to a person whose name is not preserved, one to Hippokleiadas. There is also the curious case of an inheritance of Daikleidas, which had come up for auction as well. Maybe there were no legal heirs or the property was levied with a mortgage. Between the information on ownership and size, each entry details the location of properties. Several of these were located near and across the Asopos River (ἐπ' Ἀσοπõι, δι' Ἀσοπõ), two of them north of Thebes in the region of Mt. Hypatos (ποτ' Ὑπάτοι). One property was "near the Trophonion" (ποτ' Τροπονίοι). If this was the well-known sanctuary of Trophonios near Lebadeia, the land in question was c. 45 km west of Thebes, far beyond the Theban countryside. Matthaiou conjectures that a property as remote as this was owned most likely by a Theban under the legal framework of the Boiotian League;[50] we have already encountered the *koinon*'s legal authority in law cases revolving around landed properties earlier. The same might hold true as well for some of the other properties in the Asopos Valley and near Mt. Hypatos; the boundaries of the Theban *chora* were malleable and in any case unclear at the time.

There is a captivating dynamic of spatial and legal paradigms at play in the document. For it seems that legislative action pertaining to the listed properties, expressed by a broad variety of administrative and juristic practices, itself added to and endorsed the territorial jurisdiction of Thebes. In this sense, legislative action was not subject to set areas of validity, but rather it demarcated the *chora* of the polis in the first place, shaping boundaries for the application of laws and adherence to them within that space – in contrast to the legal space in locations without. Note that of the localizable properties, at this point in the decipherment of the tablet, none was situated in the city of Thebes or its immediate surroundings. The deed of sale of properties further away put a whole phalanx of legal issues on the agenda, precisely because the territorial and metajurisdictional implications were so precarious. Similar to the disputed lands from the Megarian arbitration, some of the patches of territory were brought under the legal prerogative of Thebes (if that was the outcome of the arbitration). In other, more remote regions like that of Mt. Hypatos and in the vicinity of Lebadeia, this authority ought to have been more indirect, transmitted through moments of mediation and exchange. For example, Theban institutions might have claimed the authority to oversee the deed of sale,

50 Matthaiou 2014, p. 220.

but most likely this was done in conversation with other legal entities in the region that supported and in any case respected the binding force of the sale. Before the backdrop of the corresponding communications between Thebes, Lebadeia, and other stakeholders, the rise of federalism in Boiotia was thus informed by and fostered through the rise of the new territorial and soon enough metajurisdictional authority of a political entity that governed exchanges and provided legal security at a level beyond that of a single city.

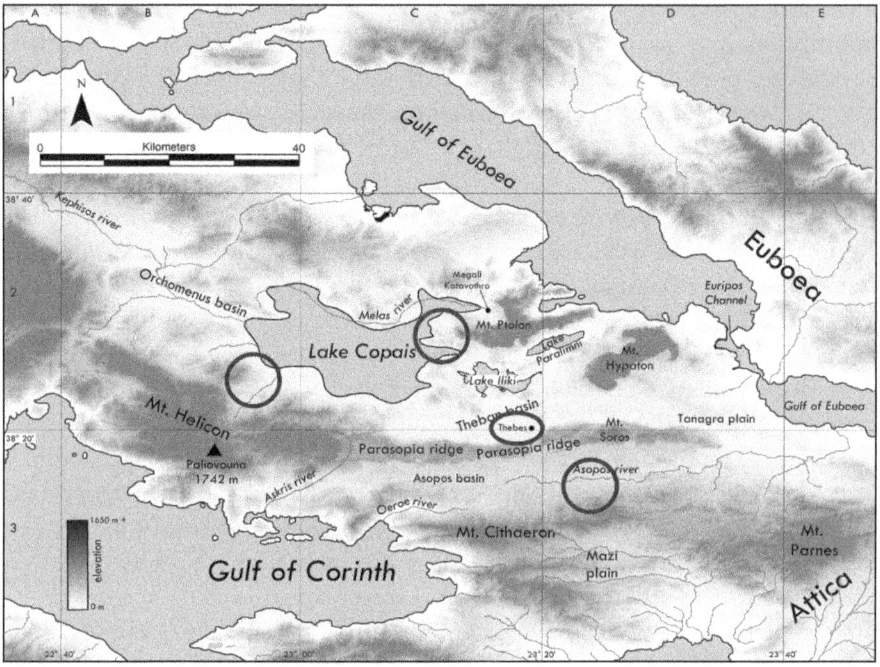

Fig. 1: Thebes and approximate distribution of properties in TM 35909 = SEG 60.507 across Boiotia. Note that the location of at least two other properties is unknown. Map adapted from H. Beck, Thebes, in: The Oxford History of the Archaic Greek World (Oxford 2025). © P. Christesen.

What unites these variegated texts is their desire to regulate and administer communal concerns, not by means of doctrinal statements, but through a growing authority of the community to take up and address these concerns, and to apply its legislative action to its members in binding fashion. On the one hand, this was done through material governance: ownership issues and social privileges were formulated, participation rights stipulated, etc. On the other hand, the process was complemented by a new archival practice, that is, the practice of recording in writing rights, privileges, and laws and storing the resulting tablets in one or several archives. The practice had a deep history in Thebes: it extended back to the Bronze Age palace whose administrative apparatus, as indicated by the particularly rich record of Linear B tablets, was very extensive.[51] It has been argued that, from the 7th century on, encounters with Kadmeian legacies from the Bronze Age were particularly prominent in Thebes, as documented, for instance, in the orientation and monumental design of the Temple of Apollo on the Ismenian hill.[52] If this was indeed the case, scattered encounters with clay tablets of old also inspired conversations and in turn triggered questions about the legal practices pertaining to these tablets. The dialogue coincided with the rediscovery of writing, a development associated in ancient traditions far and wide with the city of Thebes itself and that lent an all-new quality to legends about its heroic past as well. The new alphabet preserved communal discourses in records and narratives, including the preservation of thoughts, ideas, and guiding concepts of hitherto oral expressions. In the field of law, the arrival of the script elicited both an administrative and conceptual quantum leap.[53] The same was valid for the materiality of the tablets onto which the new administrative acts were written. Handy, durable, and valuable, they vouched for what was stipulated, making contents both communicable and tangible. If monumental legal texts like the Great Code of Gortyn have been seen as representing "in symbolic form ... for which the community as a whole stood,"[54] the skillfully crafted bronze tablets were miniature counterparts to the imposing display of communal authority in stone. All the while, the rich tapestry of their contents suggests that the new epigraphic material merely represents an offshoot of random examples, dumped into a pit on the edge of town, that stood at the tip of the iceberg of similar documents. The new finds do give us a hunch, then, how legislative action permeated the political and social organization of Thebes in the late-Archaic period.

Summary conclusion

This article set out to make the laws and legislation of Archaic Thebes a fruitful object of inquiry in the study of early Greek law. The notoriousness of Hesiod's battle over his inheritance, along with Philolaos' laws on the legal status of children make it obvious that ownership and inheritance issues were as critical to the developing communities of Thebes and in Boiotia as elsewhere in Archaic Greece. Philolaos' legislation is typically approached with regard to the particular area of material law it covered, that of *paidopoiia*. In addition to its contents, there was

51 To date Thebes ranks third in the overall number of Linear B tablets recovered (after Knossos and Pylos) and first in terms of inscribed clay sealings and stirrup jars.

52 Larson 2018, pp. 34–36; Beck 2025.

53 Cf. only Thomas 2005; Whitley 2017; Knodell 2021, pp. 215–222 ("a media revolution").

54 Whitley 1997, p. 660.

however a discursive dimension to Philolaos' *nomoi*. Bringing in a *nomothetes* from somewhere else who was vested with the authority to give new laws to the Thebans initiated a wide range of questions about practices and procedures that required firm answers. Given their gravity, each one of them ought to have put in motion complicated negotiations – effectively, the outcome of these negotiations was mostly fixed in writing by means of what later authorities considered the growing body of 'set laws'. How was legal ownership of landed property secured and transferred from one generation to the next? How was the status of legally entitled children defined? How did properties in question relate to the expanding *chora* of Thebes? Who was the governing authority to employ Philolaos, and finally, how was the body of entitled *politai* organized, in operational terms, so as to implement and oversee adherence to the new legislation? The boiotarch-inscription from the Herakleion, along with new finds from Pyri corroborate and lend depth to isolated references to Philolaos in the literary sources. They offer a glimpse at the consistent development of the genre and cause of *nomoi thetikoi*. Scanty as the evidence is, it documents again that issues of land ownership were among the key areas of legal action in Archaic Thebes. As the public administration of the city took shape in the 7th and 6th centuries, one of the primary concerns was the regulation and, presumably, ongoing re-negotiation of legal prescriptions that were key to its socio-economic and political management.

All the while, the regional horizon of Theban polis legislation, its implication with other local legal spheres and progressive amalgamation into a federal frame of reference, relates back to questions about unity and plurality of Greek law, and multiple scales of legal encoding in between. If we return to the initial agenda of shifting the focus from material law and procedures to the historical processes of their formation, it becomes obvious that the rise of the polis was among those very processes that wove vectors of legal unity and diversity together. On the one hand, the rise of the city-state unleashed all sorts of dynamic forces and potentially contentious negotiations that directed communal conversations toward the local horizon of the city. On the other hand, those conversations were led in close interaction with translocal developments: the shaping of ethnic and regional identity formation and, from the mid-6th century, the rise of federalism. If we remind ourselves that the latter processes took place everywhere across Greece, not only in Boiotia, although not necessarily simultaneously and with varying degrees of intensity, it becomes obvious that federalism provided both the infrastructure and framework for local legal entities to branch out and extend spheres of legal validity, applicability, and reliability.[55] Ancient Greek law, from the moment of its inception, then, was destined

55 For further discussion, cf. the chapter by Ruben Post on the Hellenistic Achaian League.

to grow together in rhizomatic fashion: to accentuate nodes of impact that were locally distinct and increasingly similar at the same time, and to connect, merge, and blend these nodes into the shared frame of reference of ancient Greek law.

Bibliography

Aravantinos, Vassilis (2006) A New Inscribed Kioniskos from Thebes, in: Annual of the British School at Athens 101, 369–377.

Aravantinos, Vassilis (2014) The Inscriptions from the Sanctuary of Herakles at Thebes: An Overview, in: Zinon Papazarkadas (ed.), 149–210.

Barker, Elton T. E./Joel P. Christensen (2019) Homer's Thebes. Epic Rivalries and the Appropriation of Mythical Pasts, Washington/DC.

Beck, Hans (1999) Ostlokris und die Tausend Opuntier. Neue Überlegungen zum Siedlergesetz für Naupaktos, in: Zeitschrift für Papyrologie und Epigraphik 124, 53–62.

Beck, Hans (2025) Thebes, in: Paul Cartlegde/Paul Christesen (eds.), The Oxford History of the Archaic Greek World (in press).

Bresson, Alain (2018) The Making of the Ancient Greek Economy: Institutions, Markets, and Growth in the City-States, Princeton.

Buck, Robert J. (1979) A History of Boeotia, Edmonton.

Christesen, Paul (2007) Olympic Victor Lists and Ancient Greek History, Cambridge.

Cloché, Paul (1952) Thèbes de Béotie, des origines à la conquête romaine, Namur.

Eder, Birgitta (2003) Noch einmal: Der homerische Schiffskatalog, in: Christoph Ulf (ed.), Der neue Streit um Troia. Eine Bilanz, Munich, 287–308.

Edwards, Anthony T. (2004) Hesiod's Ascra, Berkeley.

Fachard, Sylvian (2013) Eleutherai as the Gates to Boeotia, in: Revue des études militaires anciennes 6, 81–106.

Fachard, Sylvian et al. (2020) The Fortress of Eleutherai. New Insights from Survey, Architecture, and Epigraphy, in: Hesperia 89, 476–549.

Finley, Moses I. (1951) Some Problems of Greek Law (review of F. Pringsheim: The Greek Law of Sale, 1950), in: Seminar 9, 72–91.

Finley, Moses I. (1966/1975) The Problem of the Unity of Greek Law, in: La storia del diritto nel quadro delle scienze storiche, Florence, 129–142 (reprinted in The Use and Abuse of History, London, 134–152 and notes 236–237).

Fossey, John M. (1993/2019) Paidopoiia in Archaic Thebai, in: John M. Fossey (ed.), Boiotia in Ancient Times. Some Studies of its Topography, History, Cults and Myths, Leiden, 77–87.

Fossey, John M. (2014) Epigraphica Boeotica II. Further Studies on Boiotian Inscriptions, Leiden.

Foxhall, Lin/Lewis, A. D. E. (eds.) (1996) Greek Law in its Political Setting. Justification, not Justice, Oxford.

Freitag, Klaus (1999) Der Golf von Korinth. Historisch-topographische Untersuchungen von der Archaik bis in das 1. Jh. v. Chr., Munich.

Gagarin, Michael (1974) Hesiod's Dispute with Perses, in: Transactions of the American Philological Association 104, 103–111.

Gagarin, Michael (2005a) The Unity of Greek Law, in: Michael Gagarin/David Cohen (eds.), The Cambridge Companion to Ancient Greek Law, Cambridge, 29–40.

Gagarin, Michael (2005b) Early Greek Law, in: Michael Gagarin/David Cohen (eds.), The Cambridge Companion to Ancient Greek Law, Cambridge, 82–94.

Gagarin, Michael/Cohen, David (eds.) (2005) The Cambridge Companion to Ancient Greek Law, Cambridge.

Gehrke, Hans-Joachim (1985) Stasis: Untersuchungen zu den inneren Kriegen in den griechischen Staaten des 5. und 4. Jahrhunderts v. Chr., Munich.

Hölkeskamp, Karl-Joachim (1999) Schiedsrichter, Gesetzgeber und Gesetzgebung im archaischen Griechenland, Stuttgart.

Hölkeskamp, Karl-Joachim (2005) What's in a Code?, in: Hermes 133, 280–293.

Horster, Marietta (2010) Religious Landscape and Sacred Ground: Relationships between Space and Cult in the Greek World, in: Revue de l'histoire des religions 227, 435–458.

Knodell, Alex R. (2021) Societies in Transition in Early Greece. An Archaeological History, Oakland.

Koerner, Reinhard (1993) Inschriftliche Gesetzestexte der frühen griechischen Polis, Cologne.

Larson, Stephanie (2018) Seventh-Century Material Culture in Boiotia, in: Alexander Loney/Stephen Scully (eds.), The Oxford Handbook of Hesiod, New York, 31–42.

Ma, John (2016) Review of Papazarkadas 2014, in: Bryn Mawr Classical Review 2016.07.11.

Mackil, Emily (2017) Property Claims and State Formation in the Archaic Greek World, in: Clifford Ando/Seth F. C. Richardson (eds.), Ancient States and Infrastructural Power: Europe, Asia, and America, Philadelphia, 63–90.

Maffi, Alberto (2005) Family and Property Law, in: Michael Gagarin/David Cohen (eds.), The Cambridge Companion to Ancient Greek Law, Cambridge, 254–266.

Matthaiou, Angelos (2014) Four Inscribed Bronze Tablets from Thebes: Preliminary Notes, in: Zinon Papazarkadas (ed.), 211–222.

Marshall, C. W. (2017) Aeschylus: Libation Bearers, London.

Moretti, Luigi (1957) Olympionikai, i vincitori negli antichi agoni olimpici, in: Memorie della Accademia Nazionale dei Lincei, Classe di Scienze Morali, Storiche e Filologiche 8, 53–198.

Papazarkadas, Nikolaos (2014) Two New Epigrams from Thebes, in: Nikolaos Papazarkadas (ed.), 223–251.

Papazarkadas, Nikolaos (ed.) (2014) The Epigraphy and History of Boeotia. New Finds, New Prospects, Leiden.

Papazarkadas, Nikolaos (2021) Boiotian Inscriptions in Epichoric Script: a Conspectus of Recent Discoveries, in: R. Parker/P. M. Steele (eds.) The Early Greek Alphabets. Origin, Diffusion, Uses, Oxford, 267–292.

Rubinstein, Lene/Harris, Edward (eds.) (2004) The Law and the Courts in Ancient Greece, London.

Schachter, Albert (2016) Boiotian Beginnings. The Creation of an Ethnos, in: Albert Schachter (2016) Boiotia in Antiquity. Selected Papers, Cambridge, 3–22.

Thomas, Rosalind (2005) Writing, Law, and Written Law, in: Michael Gagarin/David Cohen (eds.), The Cambridge Companion to Ancient Greek Law, Cambridge, 41–60.

Thür, Gerhard (2006) Die Einheit des Griechischen Rechts. Gedanken zum Prozessrecht in den griechischen Poleis, in: Dike 9, 23–62.

Van Wijk, Roy (2024) Athens and Boiotia. Interstate Relations in the Archaic and Classical Periods, Cambridge.

Whitley, James (1997) Cretan Laws and Cretan Literacy, in: American Journal of Archaeology 101, 635–661.

Whitley, James (2017) The Material Entanglements of Writing Things Down, in: L. Nevett (ed.) Theoretical Approaches to the Archaeology of Ancient Greece. Manipulating Material Culture, Ann Arbor, 71–103.

Athina A. Dimopoulou (National and Kapodistrian University of Athens)

Diversity and unity of public institutions and sanctions

The case of the cities of Lesbos (Archaic to Hellenistic Times)

On most Greek islands, their relatively small size and lack of sufficient means did not favor the coexistence and growth of many autonomous cities. The large and prosperous island of Lesbos, in contrast, nurtured more independent *poleis* than any other Greek island:[1] Mytilene, Methymna, Antissa and Eresos divided the 1,636 km² of the island among themselves.[2] Mytilene and Methymna[3] also controlled lands on their *peraia*, on the shore of Asia Minor. Olive oil and wine production sustained a wealthy landed aristocracy. The island was known for its strong naval tradition, thanks to ample access to timber and its unique strategic location, allowing the control of naval routes linking the Aegean with the Hellespont and the Black Sea. The large size and high mountains of Lesbos rendered land communication between the cities difficult and slow, up until the 19th century. To cover the approximatively 65 km from Mytilene to Methymna on foot required at least two days of travel, while Eresos lay even further on the western coast, a fact that did not facilitate cooperation among them. The *poleis* of Lesbos, therefore, developed as autonomous and often competing entities. This, despite the island's inhabitants sharing a common heritage as carriers of the Aeolic civilization flourishing in the northeastern Aegean, speaking the same dialect of Aeolic Greek and sharing a panhellenic reputation of excellence in the culture of poetry and music.[4]

The cities of Lesbos were typical examples of medium- and small-sized Greek cities. Each had its own army, fleet, and fortifications and minted its own coins. Throughout their history, they faced similar challenges. In their evolution, they

---

1 Spencer 1980, pp. 68–81.

2 Very little is known about the institutions of the city of Arisbe, which was early on absorbed by Methymna. The city of Pyrra will be destroyed by an earthquake in the 3rd cent. Antissa will be destroyed by the Romans and its territory will be absorbed by Methymna. For the borders of the territories belonging to Mytilene and to Methymna and the enmity between the two cities, see Mason 1993, pp. 225–250 and Kontis 1978, pp. 127–129.

3 Mytilene's *peraia* was called *Mytilineon aigialos*. For the possible existence of the *peraia* of Methymna, see Robert 1951, pp. 95–97.

4 Lesbos was the native island, among other famous poets and musicians, of Sapho, Alkaios, Terpander, Arion. The Lesvians were considered the most expert in music among the Greeks. They also developed distinct artistic and architectural features, such as the Lesvian masonry and the Aeolic capitals.

closely followed the great trends of both mainland Greece and Asia Minor, home to several cities with which they were in constant exchange. The 6th century BCE is a period of violent *stasis.* Successive attempts to seize power and the establishment of tyrannies opposed the island's aristocratic families, events on which the unique contemporary source of Alkaios' poems provide details. Peace was restored in Mytilene when the lawgiver Pittacos was elected *aisymnetes,* establishing the rule of written law by his legislative reforms.[5] In the 5th cent., following the submission of the revolt by Mytilene against the first Athenian Confederacy, Athenian cleruchies were established on the island.[6] In the 4th cent., a new wave of tyrants ruled in all the cities on Lesbos, with the support of the Persians. Democracy was finally restored by Alexander, who ordered the return of the exiles, the restitution of their properties and for the cities' tyrants to be put to trial.[7]

Aristotle, who spent two years in Lesbos studying the flora of the island, must have included in the Greek cities' *Constitutions* written in his Peripatetic school some dedicated to the cities of Lesbos, none of which survives though. In the extant writings of his favorite pupil and successor at the *Lycaeum,* Theophrastus, a native of Eresos, few references are included to the legislation of the cities of Lesbos. Our main source of information on the laws and institutions of the cities of Lesbos are the surviving inscriptions, coming mainly from Mytilene (over 700, public and private), but also from Methymna and Eresos, dating from the 6th cent. BCE to the Roman times. The inscriptions include decrees issued on the occasion of extraordinary events, such as the decree on Concord from Mytilene following the restoration of democracy under Alexander (SEG 36.750), and the decree on the restitution of properties of the returning exiles (IG XII 2.6);[8] international treaties, such as the between Mytilene and Phocea for minting coins of the same value in order to limit currency exchange expenses (SEG 34.849); *asylia* decrees with the Aitolians (IG XII 2.15.16); grants of *isopoliteia,* such as between Mytilene and Larissa (SEG 55.605); sacred laws; construction projects; land registers. Several honorific decrees award *proxenia,* and privileges such as *isolopoliteia, ateleia, asylia, proedria, prodikia.* Regarding the administration of justice, the stele of the trials of the tyrants and their descendants from Eresos (IG XII 2.526) is a precious source on an extraordinary series of trials, while information can be also drawn from several honorific decrees for foreign judges and inscriptions regarding international arbitrations. The information collected from these inscriptions allow us to draw a comparative tableau of the function of different public organs throughout Les-

5 Dimopoulou 2017.
6 Dimopoulou-Piliouni 2015, pp. 163–183.
7 Dimopoulou-Piliouni 2015, pp. 199–272.
8 Dimopoulou 2018.

bos, several of which are close to the Athenian point of reference, attesting that the islands' sister cities developed quite similar civic and legal institutions, with minor local differentiations.

Citizen divisions

The inhabitants of the cities of Lesbos comprised citizens, permanent residents called κάτοικοι, and foreigners.[9] The number of Mytilene's citizens in the 5th cent. BCE is calculated at approximatively 56,000. In all cities they were organized in tribes (φυλαί), some decrees of which survive from Methymna,[10] attesting to their own internal organization under the *phylarchos*. Seven honorific decrees from Methymna attest to a particular form of citizen organization,[11] the χέλληστυς,[12] by one thousand persons, with its own internal rules of organization, hierarchy, and elected administrative bodies, an institution known also from several Ionian cities.

Ecclesia

The first reference to citizens (πολίταν) participating in the *boule* (βόλλα) and the assembly (ἀγόρα) in Mytilene is found in the verses of Alkaios,[13] who during his exile regrets the loss of the privilege of participation in these organs that his father and grandfather also enjoyed before him, therefore probably a hereditary right connected at the time to the ownership of land. Despite the strong oligarchic tradition prevailing in the cities of Lesbos, in the Hellenistic Period, possibly all adult male citizens were entitled to participate in the assembly of the *demos* in all the cities of the island. No *misthophoria* is mentioned for citizen participation, nor for any public function. Local and foreign ambassadors could address the assembly and, after reading out the decrees and letters they had conveyed to the city,[14] they would elaborate on the matter at hand.[15]

---

9 Dimopoulou-Piliouni 2015, pp. 381–408.

10 IG XII 2.505.

11 Similar organizations, for which however we have no evidence from Methymna, are the ἑκατοστύες (subdivisions of one hundred) and the πεντακοστύες (of five hundred).

12 Debord 1984, pp. 201–211; Buchholz 1975, pp. 158–160. For this institution see Jones 1940, p. 189.

13 Alkaios, fragment 130, l.18.20.

14 IG XII 2.15, ll. 13–15: περὶ ὧν οἱ στρόταγοι προτίθεισι προσταξαίσας τ[ᾶς βόλ/λ]ας καὶ οἱ πρέσβεις οἱ ἀποστάλεντες εἰς Αἰτω[λίαν/ἀ]παγγέλλοισι καὶ δόγμα ἤνικαν πάρ τῶ κοίνω Αἰτ[ώλων].

15 As the ambassadors of Magnesia did (IG XII Suppl. 138, l. 19–21): διελέχθησαν δὲ καὶ οἱ πρέσβευται ἀκο/λ[ού]θως τοῖς ἐν τῶι ψαφίσματι γεγραμμένο[ισι]/τᾶς [φι]λοτιμίας οὖδεν ἐλλείποντες.

In Mytilene, the assembly was convened for a specific number of meetings each year.[16] By law, certain sessions were reserved for specific issues. The first *ecclesia* possibly had a legislative mandate.[17] The assembly voted for the laws and decrees issued by the city. No law survives intact from Lesbos, only references to laws in decrees. The decree on Concord from Mytilene (SEG 36.750) mentions laws determining the penalties to be imposed by the courts for various crimes,[18] and the tyrant's stele from Eresos (IG XII 2.526) refers to the law on tyranny. Other references include laws regulating the amount of public expenditure on sacrifices, on honors[19] such as the value of the honorary crowns,[20] hospitality expenses, such as the banquets that the city offered at the Prytaneum, and on the classification and priority of public expenses (κατάταξις), among others for the publication of decrees.[21]

The legal procedure for public voting on the decrees is depicted in their structure, which often preserve the relevant four main stages: a motion by a citizen before the *boule,* its discussion by the *boule,* the introduction of the *probouleuma* to the assembly, and the assembly reaching a decision. However, the structure of the decrees of the Lesvian cities is not always consistent, nor the decision-making procedure uniform.[22] The citizens who wished to propose draft decrees would do so before the *boule,* not before the assembly. The *boule* could authorize the presentation of a decree to the assembly of the *demos* by the citizen who had made the proposal, as indicated by the mention in a decree of Mytilene Ἀρ̣ιφρ[ά]δ̣ης ...

---

16 In Athens, the assembly of the *demos* convened to four ordinary meetings for each one of the ten *prytanies* of the year, of which one was called ἐκκλησία κυρία (main assembly), [Aristoteles], Constitution of the Athenians 43.3–6. Rhodes/Lewis 1997, pp. 13–14.

17 As it is derived from a related reference in an honorary decree of Mytilene about the Erythrean judges (IG XII Suppl. 137 = I.Erythrai Klazomenai 122, l. 37), in which the *strategoi* are commanded to introduce for discussion the award of *proxenia* and civic rights at the time fixed by the law (ἐν τοῖς χρόνοις τοῖς ἐκ τῶ νόμω).

18 In the Decree on Concord the law fixing the penalties of death and exile is mentioned, SEG 36.750, l. 14–15: αἰ μὲγ κὲ τις δίκας γενομένας κατ τὸν νόμον φύγηι ἐκ τᾶς πόλιος ἤ ἀπυθάνη, [χ]ρῆσθαι τῶι νόμωι.

19 In the decree for the Magnesians (IG XII Suppl. 138) there is reference to a law that provided for the hospitality expenses for the *theoroi* who announce the Pythia, in this case applied analogously, and to the expenses of the ambassadors, which amount to 200 coins "according to the law" (ἐν νόμωι διακό[σια]).

20 SEG 26.909, IG XII Suppl. 2.3, IG XII 2.18 (all from Mytilene). In the honorary decrees of the χελληστύς of Methymna and in the decree honoring the Milesian judges (IG XII 2.505, IG XII Suppl. 139.B.18), it is stated that the honoree is awarded the "golden crown prescribed by law" (στεφάνῳ χρυσῷ τῷ [ἐ]κ τοῦ νόμου).

21 As in the decree of Methymna in honor of the *agoranomoi,* IG XII Suppl. 114: καταγράφη εἰς τὰν κατάτ̣α̣ξιν ἐν [τῶ] μῆνν[ι τῶ Δίω], ὅπως κε δόθη τὸ γενό[με]ν[ον ἀνάλ]ωμα εἰ[ς τὰν σ]τάλλαν καὶ τὰν ἀναγράφα[ν τῶ] ψαφίσματος ὑπὸ τῶν δειχθησομένων ἐπὶ τ[ᾶς] [ἀγ]όρας.

22 In Mytilene's decree honoring the Erythrean judges, IG XII Suppl. 137, the decision of the *demos* is mentioned first then that the *boule* had issued a *probouleuma* (ἔγνω δᾶμος· περὶ ὤν ἀ βόλλα προεβόλλευσε).

εἶπε.[23] Voting usually took place by raising hands (χειροτονία).[24] Secret ballots were reserved for reaching important decisions, such as the decree on Concord from Mytilene, where it is specifically stated (SEG 36.750.13–14) ἐψάφισθαι τᾶι βόλλα καὶ τῶι δάμωι.[25] We do not know whether a minimum number of citizens was required in order to form a quorum for certain matters.

The preamble of the decrees contained the essential introductory elements: the bodies of the city that reached the decision, the name of the citizen who proposed the decree (εἶπε), the confirmatory verb (ἔγνω), and the dating by citing the *eponymous archon* (ἐπὶ προτάνιος) of the city. Sometimes the standard invocation of Ἀγαθή Τύχη (Good Fortune) was added.[26] The introductory phrase of some decrees from the cities of Lesbos, ἔγνω βόλλα/δᾶμος, differs considerably from the respective Athenian (ἔδοξε τῷ δήμῳ, or ἔδοξε τῇ βουλῇ καὶ τῷ δήμῳ), while in the Aeolian dialect the use of the infinitive γιγνώσκειν refers to reaching a decision by decree.[27] This however does not mean that in the cities of Lesbos the procedure of introducing, discussing, and voting on decrees differed significantly from the respective Athenian procedure.

Entrenchment clauses were sometimes included,[28] as in the honorary decree of Eresos in favor of Agemortus Bacchius, prohibiting any future amendments of the decision and the introduction of any related motion to the *boule* or the *demos:* μηδ'εἴπην ἐν βόλλα μήδε ἐν δάμω μήδενα ὡς δεῖ περιβάλεσθαι τὰν θυσίαν, μηδὲ τὸ ἀργύριον εἰς ἄλλο κατάταξαι μῆδεν.[29] The opposite could also be resolved, as in Mytilene's honorary decree for Athanas,[30] where it is provided that no one should obstruct the *demos* from reaching decisions (μηδεὶς κωλύσει χρη[ματίζην τὸν δᾶμο]ν).[31] After a decree was voted on it was made public by engraving the decrees in stone and posting them in front of the *boule,* but also in sanctuaries: in Mytilene those of Asclepius and Athena, in Eresos in the city's *agora* and the sanctuary of Athena.[32]

---

23 IG XII 2.5.

24 IG XII Suppl. 137, l. 49: χηροτόνησαι δὲ καὶ πρεσβεύταν ἐκ πάντων τῶμ πολίταν; IG XII Suppl. 138, l. 37–38: χειροτονήτω ὁ δᾶμος … θεώροις.

25 SEG 36.750.

26 For Ἀγαθή Τύχη in the decrees of the cities, see Dimopoulou-Piliouni 2012, pp. 167–180.

27 Rhodes/Lewis 1997, p. 258, 557.

28 For these entrenchment clauses of the decrees, see Rhodes/Lewis 1997, pp. 524–525.

29 IG XII 2.529.

30 Pistorius 1913, pp. 147–148.

31 IG XII 2.4.

32 IG XII Suppl. 121.

Boule

The members of the archaic *boule* of Mytilene mentioned by Alkaios[33] were probably wealthy landowners. As in all the Greek cities that embraced democratic institutions, it would evolve into the sovereign body of the city, along with the assembly of the *demos.* In all the cities of Lesbos the *boule* prepared the draft of the decree to be voted on after deliberation at the assembly, called προβούλευσις or πρόθεσις.[34] The proposal was made, in writing or verbally, by a member of the *boule* or an ordinary citizen (which was the sign of a democratic regime), whose name is in a few cases mentioned in the decree, such as that of Bacchius, son of Kaikos, who in Mytilene introduced a proposal to invite the Thessalians.[35] The text of the προβούλευμα has been preserved[36] in its entirety in Mytilene's honorary decree for the Athenian Cleosthenes, son of Cleophon,[37] and in Eresos' honorary decree for Damon, son of Polyarchos.[38] The procedure of the προβούλευσις is recorded in the introductory phrase of a decree from Eresos: περὶ ὤν ἀ βόλλα προεβόλλ[ευσε] καὶ ο[ἰ] ἄρχοντες προτίθισι.[39] The *boule,* assisted by the γραμματεὺς (secretary) also drew up the agenda for the assembly, and proposed the conclusion of bilateral treaties to the assembly.[40] In some cases, the *boule* reached a decision directly, for example to award honors to certain persons.[41] The *boule* also admitted ambassadors from other cities to its sessions.

Prytanis

The cities of Lesbos had several archons, with common titles and responsibilities. The πρύτανης was the *eponymous archon* of all the cities of Lesbos. The function of the *eponymous prytanis* is known for only ten other Greek cities, Chios being the only other insular one.[42] He probably served for a term of one year and could

33 Alkaios, fragment 130 (b).

34 For the content and the operation of Athenian προβουλεύματα, see Rhodes/Lewis 1997, pp. 484–490. However, the term used by modern scholars, προβούλευσις, does not appear as such in the ancient sources.

35 IG XII Suppl. 3.

36 Many inscriptions survive only partially, and so we do not know in how many cases the text of the preliminary decree of the *boule* preceded, on the same stele, the text of the decree of the assembly of the *demos.*

37 IG XII 2.18.

38 IG XII 2.527.

39 IG XII Suppl. 121.

40 For the institution of embassies, see Dimakis 1997, pp. 87–91.

41 IG XII 2.96.97.

42 The others are the Corinthian colonies of Kerkyra, Apollonia and Epidanos, Kassope in Epirus, Kymi of Aiolis in Asia Minor, Komana in Cappadocia, Colophon and Ephesus in Ionia, and the *koinon* of the Valaeitians. See Sherk 1990 I; ibid. 1990 II (for Lesbos pp. 273–275); ibid. 1991, pp. 225–260. See also Labarre 1996, pp. 162–163.

serve more than once. The *prytanis* exercised important duties. In Theophrastus' work Περὶ νόμων,[43] assigning the sale and purchase of landed property to the prytanis, along with the βασιλεῖς, is attributed to Pittacus. In Mytilene the *prytanis* was responsible for introducing the *probouleumata* to the assembly for discussion and voting, sometimes in collaboration with the στρατηγοὶ. Along with the βασιλεῖς, he was responsible for announcing, during the celebration of the *Dionysia*, the golden crowns for the city's benefactors.[44] Among his religious duties was to lead the sacred procession that led to the sacrificial altar.[45] In Eresos, for which the philosopher Phaenias had dedicated a work entitled Περὶ πρυτάνεων Ἐρεσίων,[46] the *prytanis* had similar responsibilities and was also the *eponymous archon* of the city.[47]

At the heart of every city in Lesbos stood the Πρυτανεῖον, the symbolic center of the city. Sacred processions started there during religious celebrations, as stated in a religious calendar.[48] The brother of Sappho served as wine attendant in the archaic Prytaneum of Mytilene,[49] a way for young aristocrats to acquaint themselves with politics. The honorary distinction of ξενία is attested in several inscriptions, an invitation to a banquet at the κοινὴ ἑστία, the common dining hall of the Prytaneum, for persons whom the city wished to honor, such as the Erythrean judges.[50]

Basileis

In Mytilene, the βασιλεῖς were among the earliest officials, dating from the Archaic Period and retained down to the Classical and Hellenistic years.[51] As in many ancient cities with similar traditions, the βασιλεῖς are a development of the authority exercised by the house of the deposed kings, the Penthilids, in the Archaic Period.[52] They were already archons of the city at the time of Pittacus, who assigned jointly to the βασιλεῖς and the *prytanis* the supervision of sales and purchases of

---

43 Stobaios 44.22.1: Οἱ μὲν οὖν ὑπὸ κήρυκος κελεύουσι πωλεῖν καὶ προκηρύττειν ἐκ πλειόνων ἡμερῶν, οἱ δὲ παρ'ἀρχῇ τινι, καθάπερ καὶ Πιττακὸς παρὰ βασιλεῦσι καὶ πρυτάνει.

44 IG VII 2.19, XII Suppl. 137.

45 IG XII 2.7.

46 Athenaios 8.333a

47 IG XII 2.562, IG XII Suppl. 124. Sherk 1990 II, pp. 273–274.

48 IG XII Suppl. 29: μηνὸς Δείου δ' ἡ ἀνάβασις τῆς θεοῦ τῇ ζ'/ἡ ὑδροποσία μηνὸς Ἰουλαίου νουμηνίᾳ/ἡ πομπὴ ἐκ πρυτανείου ι'/τὰ νεώματα μηνὸς Ἀπολλωνίου ιε'/ἡ δύσις τῆς θεοῦ μηνὸς Ἡφαιστίου δ'/ἡ κατάκλησις μηνὸς Ποσιδείου ιε'/κατὰ κέλευσιν τῆς θεοῦ Ἀρίστιππος Ἀριστίππου/ἐπέγραψα.

49 Athenaios 10.425a.

50 Schmitt-Pantel 1992, pp. 163–168.

51 Carlier 1984, pp. 457–458.

52 For the origin and the role of the βασιλεῖς in Epizephyrian Locroi, see Costabile 1992, pp. 139–149.

landed property.[53] This reference indicates that they evolved into a *collegium* of archons, whose authority was gradually limited by the joint power of the *prytanis.*[54] Reference to βασιλεῖς acting jointly with the *prytanis* is encountered again in the Hellenistic Period in texts from Mytilene (and in one from Eresos), and therefore the office was still in existence at the time as one of the highest-ranking in these cities. We do not know how they were elected, though they were probably not φυλοβασιλεῖς (elected by each tribe).

The office of the βασιλεῖς is mentioned four times in Mytilene's decree about the return of the exiles (IG XII 2.6),[55] in plural (οἱ βασίληες), while king Alexander is referred to in the singular, as ὁ βασίληας. They are tasked with determining the penalties to be imposed upon citizens who refuse to comply with the terms of the arbitration that would decide about the return of the exiles' properties. In Mytilene, the βασιλεῖς undertook important public religious functions, as is also known for Athens, where the ἄρχων βασιλεῦς supervised the organization of the city's religious ceremonies. In the decree on Concord (SEG 36.750) they are appointed to supervise the performance of annual sacrifices to the gods. In three decrees, dating from the 3rd through the 2nd centuries BCE, the βασιλεῖς, during the celebration of the *Dionysia,* undertake to announce, according to the law, the golden crowns awarded to the Athenians Cleosthenes,[56] Atrometus,[57] and to the Erythrean judges who adjudicated disputes in Mytilene.[58] In Methymna, honorary inscriptions for the ἀγορανόμοι and the Milesian judges[59] also confirm the existence of a βασιλεῦς. If the office is mentioned in the singular, this does not necessarily mean that only one person held it, since (one) βασιλεῦς could be the named head of the body of archons bearing that title.[60] The *basileus* worked together with the *prytanis* in Methymna too, and so we can infer that the βασιλεῖς had a similar origin and possibly some similar duties to the respective office in Mytilene. In Methymna however, contrary to the case in Mytilene, the βασιλεῖς did not announce the award of golden crowns to the persons who the city was honoring, this duty being reserved for the *strategoi.* In Eresos, the existence of archons bearing the title βασιλεῖς is

53 Stobaios 44.22.1.

54 Sherk 1990 II, p. 274, Labarre 1996, p. 166.

55 IG XII 2.6 = SEG 36.752, ll. 1, 9, 13, 45–46.

56 IG XII 2.18, ll. 11–14.

57 IG XII Suppl. 2.

58 IG XII Suppl. 137. An honorary decree for a judge from Megara [IG VII 2.19], in which the name of the city that awarded it has not been preserved, is attributed to Mytilene, because the βασιλεῖς have been restored in its text in conjunction with the *prytaneis,* on the model of the honorary decree for the Erythrean judges.

59 IG XII Suppl. 139.

60 This hypothesis is also based on the fact that the office was a collective one in both Mytilene and Eresos.

also attested in several decrees, including a decree of the Hellenistic years in honor of Agemortus and the honorary decree for the Milesian judges.[61] The βασιλεῖς, together with the *prytanis,* invite the foreign judges and their escorts to a banquet at the *Prytaneum.*[62] The institution of the βασιλεῖς proved long-lived in Eresos, where it is attested down to Roman times.

Strategoi

In Mytilene the *strategoi* were among the senior archons of the city. They certainly had military responsibilities, as is known for other Greek cities, though we have no related evidence for Mytilene specifically. They were probably elected by the assembly of the *demos,* their term of office was for one year, and the extent of their duties allows us to infer that, unless they were remunerated, they must have been wealthy citizens, able to dedicate considerable time to public affairs. In the *probouleuma* for the honorary decree in favor of Cleosthenes, the *strategoi* are possibly instructed by the *boule* to introduce the motion for a vote by the assembly,[63] and the *boule* also instructs them to perform the same function for the decree in honor of the Aitolians.[64] In the first lines of Mytilene's honorary decree for the Erythrean judges, it is stated that the decree was introduced to the assembly by Polydeuces, son of Megon, who bears the title ὁ τεταγμένος στράταγος ἐπὶ πάντων,[65] the *strategos* of general assignment. He was therefore the senior *strategos,* who enjoyed enhanced powers as head of the body of *strategoi* and of the army.

In Mytilene's decree for the return of the exiles (IG XII 2.6), the *strategoi* are ordered to enforce the arbitration decisions about the related disputes upon any citizen who refuses to comply therewith, and in particular to attribute immediately possession of the disputed land to the opposite party.[66] In the inscription of the treaty forming the *koinon* of the Lesvians (IG XII Supp. 136), it is stated that the *strategoi* are responsible for conducting a census of the citizens of the member-cities of the *koinon.* The office of *strategos* existed therefore in all Lesvian cit-

---

61 IG XII 2.529.

62 IG XII Suppl. 139, ll. 100–101: ὁ δὲ πρύτανις καὶ ὁ βασίλευς καλεσσάτωσαν τοῖς τε δικάσταις καὶ τὸν ἀγώγεαν εἰς τὸ πρυτανηίον ἐπὶ τὰν κο<ί>ναν ἐστίαν τᾶς πόλιος. Sherk 1990 II, p. 274, considers that the singular number for the two offices is surprising, and may be an error by the engraver of the inscription.

63 IG XII 2.18, ll. 18–20: ὡς δὲ καὶ τ/[ιμάσε]ται Κλεοσθένης κατ' ἀξίαν τοὶ στρότα/[γοι εἰσάγοντον κα]ὶ τῶ/δάμω.

64 IG XII 2.15, ll. 13–15: περὶ ὦν οἱ στρόταγοι προτίθεισι προσταξαίσας τ[ᾶς βόλ/λ]ας καὶ οἱ πρέσβεις οἱ ἀποστάλεντες εἰς Αἰτω[λίαν/ἀ]παγγέλλοισι.

65 IG XII Suppl. 137. The introduction of the decree was made jointly with the ἀντιγραφέας Aeschyles.

66 SEG 36.750, l. 13.

ies, including Eresos and Antissa for which no related evidence has survived. In Methymna, the *strategoi* were responsible for drawing up the agenda of the assembly of the *demos.*[67] Along with the ἐξετασταὶ and the ἀντιγραφεὶς, they also welcomed foreign judges and attended to their stay in the city, and were assigned to make the public announcement of certain honorary crowns.[68]

Archons with judicial responsibilities

In Mytilene, according to the decree on Concord (SEG 36.750), judicial duties were assigned to the δικασκόποι and the περίδρομοι. It has been suggested that the δικασκόποι supervised the correct implementation of court decisions, and the περίδρομοι were what we might call circuit judges who circulated within the *chora*, the countryside surrounding the city of Mytilene. They were perhaps responsible for resolving minor disputes and supervising the enforcement of court decisions.[69] According to Mytilene's decree for the return of the exiles (IG XII 2.6), they introduce the case to be heard at the court and forbid the hearing of cases in violation of the provisions of the decree: μηδ' αἴ κέ τις δίκαν γράφηται περὶ τ[ο]ύτων, μὴ εἰσά[γοντον οἱ περί]δρομοι καὶ οἱ δικάσκοποι.[70] They were also responsible, along with the other archons, for the condemnation of those who violated the ordinances contained in this decree.

In Eresos, for the trial of the tyrants, a decree of the demos (IG XII 2.526) set up a special court consisting of 891 judges according to the laws of the city, after Alexander's decision to send back the tyrants to be judged in the city: [ὁδὲ δᾶμος ἀκο]ύ[σ]αις τὰ[ν] διαγράφαν δικαστήριο[ν καλέ]<σ>σα[ι]ς κ[ατὰ] τοὶς νόμοις. The city is represented in this trial by 10 συνήγοροι, acting as the equivalent of modern-day district attorneys. Applicable law consists in the laws of the city, including the law against tyranny, Alexander's *diagraphai,* and the general concept of δίκαια (conception of justice). Two votes took place among the juries, first by secret ballot on the guilt of the accused, then by raising hands (χειροτονία) on the sentence to be imposed. A unique epigraphic reference to the right of ἀντιτίμησις of the tyrant Eurysilaos shows that this was an ἀγὼν τιμητὸς, where the accused could propose a sentence as in the Athenian procedure. In one of the texts of the stele the oath of the judges is preserved. They swear to judge the trial "as provided in law and in accordance with the law, and otherwise I will make every effort to judge as well and justly as possible, and if I condemn, I will impose sentence correctly and fairly." The same stele

67 IG XII Suppl. 114.
68 Honorary decree for Damon, son of Orios, IG XII Suppl. 115, ll. 14–15: τᾶς δὲ ἀναγο[ρεύ]σιος τ[ῶ στεφάνω ἐπίμελες ποίησ]/θαι τοὶς στ[ροτά]γοις ἄι τοὶ[ς/ἐνέοντας.
69 Carlier 1984, p. 458.
70 IG XII 2.6, l. 11.

preserves a very rare epigraphic recording of the verdict by which one of the tyrants was condemned with a very large majority, as well as of the sentence, which included the death penalty, confiscation of property, and exile of the tyrant's descendants.[71]

Several honorific inscriptions for foreign judges from Lesbos also attest that the three main cities of Lesbos actively participated in the exchange of judges among Greek cities, both as senders thereof and as recipients, with the usual process of invitation, the escort of the judges by a *dikastagogos,* intensive sessions of arbitration or judging in the hosting city and finally the honors attributed to the judges by the city.[72] In Mytilene and Eresos, as in many other Greek cities, the δικασταγωγοί[73] were assigned to escort judges from third cities who were invited to resolve local disputes to and from their country.

Mytilene is also attested as being involved in international arbitrations, either as arbiter, in the case of the synoecism between Teos and Levedos and the land dispute between Messene and Megalopolis, or as party, as in the long inscription recording the arbitration of Pergamon between Mytilene and Pitane regarding lands disputed on the *peraia.*[74]

Other officials

To represent the city before other cities or kings, the *demos* of Mytilene elected πρέσβεις (ambassadors) or ἀγγέλους (emissaries),[75] who conveyed honorary and other decrees and messages.[76] Θεωροί were sent by Mytilene to announce religious celebrations to third cities.[77] In Methymna, the κήρυκες (heralds) made the official and public announcements on behalf of the city or subsidiary groups of its citizens, such as the φυλαὶ[78]and the χελληστύες.[79]

In Mytilene, the ἀντιγραφεὺς,[80] in the honorary decree for the Erythrean judges, assists the *strategos* in presenting the *probouleuma* to the assembly of the *demos,* perhaps by reading it aloud. In Methymna, he was assigned duties related

71 In Mytilene a unique inscription has been found, still unpublished, recording a court's decision imposing the death sentence and exile followed by a long list of names of citizens and foreigners "from Alexandria," see Archontidou/Acheilara 2000.

72 Dimopoulou-Piliouni 2015, pp. 414–433.

73 IG XII Suppl. 137 (Mytilene); IG XII Suppl. 139.C.58 (Eresos).

74 Dimopoulou-Piliouni 2015, pp. 434–454.

75 For the dispatch of ἄγγελοι to Alexander, see IG XII 2.6 = SEG 36.752.

76 IG XII Suppl. 137.

77 For this function of the *theoroi,* see the monograph Boesch 1908.

78 IG XII 2.505, ll. 12, 20.

79 IG XII Suppl. 114, l. 7.

80 For the ἀντιγραφείς, whose duties at this time mainly comprised the drafting of copies, see Dmitriev 2005, pp. 241–242.

to the reception of judges.[81] The φοινικογράφος, mentioned in an inscription from Mytilene, engraved the decrees in scarlet-colored letters.[82] In Methymna, in the honorary decree for the Milesian judges,[83] after the reference to the *boule* and the *strategoi,* it is stated that τῶν τιμώχων καὶ πρεσβυτέρων οἱ παρέοντες ἔπηλθον. The τιμούχοι and the πρεσβύτεροι, terms that do not appear in any other of the city's inscriptions, in this case present the decree to the assembly of the *demos,* a responsibility that in Mytilene, by contrast, was assigned to the *strategoi.*[84] The τιμούχοι are known from Teos and other cities, and were responsible for making public announcements.[85] The πρεσβύτεροι, comprising mature citizens, also known from other cities,[86] did not hold a public office, but were an association of citizens undertaking duties related to the organization of celebrations or games in the city.[87] In the Methymna decree it is stated that only the παρέοντες, i.e., only a part of the body, presented the draft plan for the proposed decree to the assembly of the *demos.* In another decree of the same city in honor of two ἀγορανόμοι, after the reference to the *boule* and the *strategoi,* there follows a list with ten names,[88] who may have been the τιμούχοι and πρεσβύτεροι.[89]

In the cities of Lesbos the ἐξετασταὶ had duties related to public finances. They were the only officials who could issue an order approving expenditure from the public treasury, for example for the purchase of sacrificial animals, as in the following inscription from Mytilene. The ἐξετασταὶ were commanded to inscribe the decrees on a stone stele and erect the steles at places that are sometimes specified in the city's decree,[90] probably in the sense of obtaining approval for the disbursement of the required expenses from the public treasury, in which the revenues of the city were collected. Such revenue was mainly derived from the exploitation of public land, the *liturgies* of wealthy citizens who undertook to cover public expenses, taxes, and other resources, which were allocated each year in a type of budget drawn up by the public administration: [τὸ δὲ ἀνάλωμα δότω ὁ] ταμίας ἐκ

81 IG XII Suppl. 137 (Mytilene); 139.A.1 (Methymna).
82 IG XII 2.96. See Chantraine 1972, pp. 7–15.
83 IG XII Suppl. 139.A.1, B.18. For the πρεσβύτεροι, who are mentioned in an inscription of Roman times in Lesbos, see Euangelides 1920–1921, pp. 107–108.
84 Buchholz 1975, p. 157.
85 Meiggs/Lewis, GHI 30; Gottlieb 1967.
86 I.Iasos 84, where the body of the πρεσβύτεροι is assigned the task of collecting funds.
87 For the function of the institution in general, see Giannakopoulos 2008.
88 IG XII Suppl. 114.
89 Labarre 1996, p. 175.
90 IG XII 2.5 a, ll. 13–16: οἱ ἐξέ[ταστοι δὲ ἐπιμελήθεντον ὄπ]ως ἀναγ[ρ]αφήσεται τὸ ψάφισμα τοῦτο] εἰς στάλαν λι[θίναν καὶ τεθήσεται εἰς] τὸ ἶρον τᾶς Ἀθά[νας. See also the decree of the Aitolians, IG XII 2.15. For these responsibilities see Frölich 2004, pp. 137, 143 n. 94, 166.

τῶν κα[τ' ἔτος χερριζομένων ε]ἰς διοίκ̣ησιν.[91] The ταμίαι (treasurers) executed payment orders which had been issued by the ἐξετασταὶ[92] in implementing decrees of the *demos.* In the immunity decree of the *koinon* of the Aitolians, the treasurer of Mytilene called the one "ἐπί τᾶς διοκέσιος,"[93] is commanded to disburse the ransom money to be paid for liberating the captive Mytilenians and the expenses for the sacrifices. In other decrees the treasurers are ordered to disburse the expenses required for inscribing the decrees on stone or to give to third parties, such as the *proxenos* Atrometus, the gifts "that are usually given in similar cases."[94] The existence of the above officials, their special powers and duties, and the arrangement of categories of expenditure, indicate that Mytilene enjoyed a well-organized fiscal administration, exercising control over the state budget through dedicated officials. The ἐξετασταὶ and the ἀντιγραφεὺς also appear in Methymna.[95] In the honorary decree for the Milesian judges, they are ordered, along with the *strategoi,* to attend to the stay (ἐνδαμία) of the judges.[96] There too, the ταμίαι have the same responsibilities similar to these of their colleagues in Mytilene. They are ordered to pay the money required for the annual sacrifices,[97] for the invitation of the two ἀγορανόμοι to a banquet at the *Prytaneum,*[98] for the travel expenses of the Milesian judges.[99] In Eresos, in the honorary decree in favor of the judges who had been sent to Parium, the ἐξετασταὶ were also responsible for inscribing the decree on a stele, in the sense of obtaining approval for the related public expense.[100] In the decree in honor of the Milesian judges, their duty includes inscribing the judge's names, including his patronymic and city, on a stele.[101]

The ταμίας (treasurer), an office mentioned in two inscriptions from Eresos in the singular in the honorary decree for the Milesian judges, is ordered to disburse various sums to cover specific expenses, which are specified either (l. 106) "[κατὰ τὰν κατάταξιν, κ]ατότι ὁ δᾶμος ἐχειροτόνησε," i.e., according to a special table of expenses approved by open ballot, or are provided for (ll. 103–104) in "τὰ ἐν νόμωι διακείμενα," i.e., in a law of the city.[102] The expenses that are subject to this κατάταξη

---

91 IG XII 2.5. See also IG XII Suppl. 114. According to Schuler 2005, pp. 385–403, the διοίκησις was a treasury administered by the *demos.* According to Robert 1963, p. 56, it was the entire budget; this meaning is more probable in the case of Mytilene.
92 Frölich 2004, pp. 134–135, 261.
93 Migeotte 2006, pp. 77–97.
94 IG XII Suppl. 2.
95 Frölich 2004, pp. 155, 166.
96 IG XII Suppl. 139.
97 IG XII Suppl. 115.
98 IG XII Suppl. 114.
99 IG XII Suppl. 139.
100 IG XII Suppl. 121.
101 IG XII Suppl. 139, Frölich 2004, p. 146.
102 IG XII 2.508.

concern the meals of the judges at the *Prytaneum* iand the expenses for their escort, and those that are provided for in the law concern the travel and hospitality expenses for the judges by the Eresian *proxenoi* of the Milesians. In the honorary decree for Damon, son of Polyarchus, the ταμίας and the ἐξετασταὶ are ordered to give to the honoree certain sums of money from the city's revenues for performing sacrifices and other expenses.[103] He must also disburse the expenses for engraving the inscription on a stone stele "ἐκ [τῶν] χει[ρ]ι[ζ]ομέν[ων] κατ›ενί[αυτον εἰς διοίκησιν χρημάτων]." Possibly, the text (restored at this point, l. 55–56) of the honorary decree for Damon, son of Polyarchus, states that both the εξετασταί and the ταμίαι are subject to an audit (εὐθύναις)[104] of their management of public funds after their term of office has expired. This procedure of giving account and attributing responsibility at the end of the terms of office of archons who manage public funds, also known from Athens and other cities,[105] was an element typical of a democratic government. It was probably also practiced in Eresos and perhaps in the other Lesvian cities too.

Agoranomoi

The ἀγορανόμοι are only attested in Methymna and Eresos, but they certainly existed in Mytilene too. An honorary decree for the ἀγορανόμοι in Methymna, bearing two engraved crowns, is dated to the second half of the 3rd century BCE. The *agoranomoi,* who appear in many Greek cities,[106] were responsible for supervising the smooth operation of the markets. They inspected the commodities and their prices, and in general took care to ensure that the consumers, as we would say today, of market produce, were not defrauded. In Methymna the *agoranomoi* had another responsibility, which in Athens was assigned to the σιτοφύλακες, the supervision of the grain trade, which was very important for the city, lying as it did across the maritime and commercial routes linking the Aegean with the grain-producing areas of the Black Sea. Sufficiency in grain supply was an important factor for sustainability and social peace for all Greek cities, which explains the particular significance of this office. The *agoranomoi* of Methymna are honored because they exercised their duties justly and in the public interest, i. e., they resolved disputes between merchants and citizens, buyers and sellers fairly. They were probably awarded these honors after their term of office had expired and the procedure of auditing their performance of their duties had been completed.[107]

---

103 IG XII 2.527.

104 For the εὔθυνα in Athens, see [Aristoteles], Athenian Constitution 54.2, 48.4–5.

105 Rhodes/Lewis 1997, pp. 528–29.

106 For their duties, see Jones 1940, pp. 215–216; Stanley 1979, pp. 72–79; Jakab 1997, pp. 70–80, 82–85; Migeotte 2001, pp. 287–301; Harris 2005, pp. 159–176.

107 Frölich 2004, pp. 390, 397.

In Eresos, the *agoranomi* were also responsible for the supervision of markets, commodities, and transactions. The honorary decree for Hyperochidas, son of Saylus, describes how the *agoranomos* benefited the city during his tenure of office. This *agoranomos* not only exercised his duties as market inspector diligently and fairly but also protected citizens' interests by ensuring that the price of grains and olive oil remained affordable. Keeping the prices of these two staples at consistently low levels would be sufficient to earn the gratitude of the citizens, but this *agoranomos* also instituted the privilege of ἀτέλησαν, i. e., exemption from paying τέλη (tax duties) for the products of cookshops and bakeries that the city normally levied. Since the same decree also states that Hyperochides acted as sponsor, this out of his own funds, perhaps his sponsorship consisted of undertaking, at his own expense, to cover the public expense corresponding to these tax duties.[108] In any case, all of these beneficent actions earned him, beyond the gratitude of his fellow citizens, a golden crown and the extraordinary honor of having a bronze statue of his likeness erected in the city. Similarly, in the 2nd century BCE, the πρύτανις and ἀγορανόμος Euchelaus, son of Koisios,[109] was honored in Eresos. He assumed public expenses, performed sacrifices, and sponsored public banquets but also offered services such as embassies and missions connected to Lampsacus, and provided hospitality to persons from Chios and to a Roman official named Cneus Junius.

Priests, priestesses, *gynaikonomoi*

In Mytilene, the ἱερεὶς and the ἱέρειαι (priests and priestesses) performed a public function. They were elected by lot and were associated with the divinity and the sanctuary they undertook to serve. In the decree of Concord (SEG 36.750), the δημόσιοι public priests of Mytilene, are ordered to open the temples for the *demos* to pray there.[110] The priests' term of office was for one year, and at its expiration they were also under the obligation to account for their actions, since the temples, beyond their other functions, undertook, as treasuries, banking activities too. In the inscription about attributing honors to the *koinon* of the Thessalians, there is a reference to an ἱεροκήρυκας (sacred herald), who was associated with the cult of Asclepius and is commanded to pray for the prosperity of the Thessalians.[111] In Methymna, duties of a religious nature were exercised by the ἐπιμήνιοι, who in the decree of the Aeolian tribe for the *phylarch*, Aristophanes son of Aristophon,[112] supervised the disposition of sacrificial animals (female lambs) that the honoree

108 Labarre 1996, p. 183.
109 IG XII 2.528 [1].
110 SEG 36.750, ll. 42–44.
111 IG XII Suppl. 3.
112 IG XII 2.505, l. 4.

sacrifices to Athena. The title of the archons indicates that they performed their duties on specific days or in specific months of the year and were linked to a specific tribe. The μισθούμενα ἱερεία referred to in the inscription were animals intended to be sacrificed at public sacrifices,[113] procured with funds from the tribe's treasury.[114] The ἱεροπεὶς (if this title has been correctly restored in an inscription of the early 2nd century BCE related to the association of the Samothracians) also had religion-related duties and are associated with the cult and the mysteries of the *Cabeiri* in Methymna.[115] They appear in many other Greek cities, and were the administrators of the sanctuaries' property; their duties included the safeguarding of offerings and granting loans from the sanctuary's treasury. In a Hellenistic inscription from Methymna preserving the text of a sacred law, there is a reference to the γυναικόνομος (superintendent of women), attested for in other ancient Greek cities as well,[116] who was responsible for supervising the women during religious ceremonies in honor of Dionysus. The γυναικονόμος, who had to have reached the (mature) age of forty years so he could resist temptation, was responsible for keeping men away from the part of the celebration reserved for women.

Gymnasiarchs, agonothetai

As of the 3rd century BCE, in Mytilene the institution of the Γυμνάσιονis recorded where the ἔφηβοι of the city exercised in athletics and trained in the military arts, preparing for their duties as adult citizens, under the supervision of the γυμνασίαρχος.[117] This office was a *liturgy* and was usually exercised by wealthy citizens, due to the considerable expense it entailed. The term of the *gymnasiarch* in Mytilene was possibly for two years. The operation of a gymnasium in Methymna arises from the reference to gymnasiarchs in an inscription of the 2nd century BCE. In Eresos it is attested in the honorary decree for the judges sent by the city to

---

113 Cf. [Xenophon], Constitution of the Athenians 2.9: ...θύουσιν οὖν μὲν δημοσίᾳ ἡ πόλις ἱερεία πολλά.

114 Robert 1928, pp. 16–164.

115 IG XII 2.506. Labarre 1996, pp. 176–177.

116 Γυναικονόμοι are possibly attested for in Ephesos (I.Ephesos 230), Andaneia in Messenia (IG V 1.1390), Magnesia on the Maeander (I.Magnesia 2), Kaikos in Mysia (IMT Kaikos 922), Didyma (I.Didyma 163.462), Sparta (IG V (1).170.209), see Parker 2004, p. 61. For the institution of the γυναικονόμοι in Athens and other Greek cities, see Wehrli 1962, pp. 33–38; Banfi 2007, pp. 17–29.

117 The attendance and access to the *gymnasium* of different age classes of young people (ἔφηβοι, νέοι, ἀλειφόμενοι), and the duties of the γυμνασίαρχος for their protection from undesirable influence were sometimes regulated by detailed laws, such as the law of the 2nd century BCE found in Veroia, see Gauthier/Hatzopoulos 1993. No such law has been found in Lesbos.

Parium.[118] Further information about the institution is given in the honorary decree of Eresos for Aglanor son of Periander, dated to 209–204 BCE,[119] who directed the gymnasium, which at this time was called the *Ptolemaion.* Eresos, following a motion by four citizens, honors the γυμνασίαρχος for his contribution to training the youth. Previously, the νέοι had awarded him a golden crown, but also the extraordinary honor of a statue (εἰκόνος). The νέοι who honor Aglanor are probably graduates of the age-group of ἐφηβεία, who continue to frequent the Γυμνάσιον and attend a program of military training for a specific period. In addition to them, the ἀλειφόμενοι, who were probably slightly older than the νέοι, could also participate in the military training, though not mandatorily. The honoree had attended to the conduct of sacrifices, offered a public banquet,[120] sponsored contests in athletics, by, *inter alia,* providing the weapons that were given as prizes to the winners and for the journey of the νέοι to the limits of the *chora* of Eresos, i. e., close to its borders, in an armed procession (ἐν ὅπλοις) that was part of their military training. The honors were awarded after the celebration of the *Hermaea,* during which (as also with the *Heracleia*) the school year usually ended with games and sacrifices in the Hellenistic *gymnasia.*[121]

In Mytilene, the ἀγωνοθέται direct the games that the city organizes and award prizes to the winners, call upon the benefactors to take the presidential seats in the theater, and conduct the theatrical contests that are held during the *Dionysia.*[122] The ἐπιμελητὴς τοῦ θεάτρου (superintendent of the theater) mainly attends to the theater, though it is not known whether he was also responsible for the theater grounds or the conduct of the theatrical performances. We are also informed about the existence of χορηγοί (sponsors), evidently connected to the performance of the related official functions.[123] In Eresos, the χοροστάτης was responsible for announcing honors bestowed upon citizens during the theatrical contests that were part of the celebrations of the *Dionysia.*[124]

---

118 IG XII Suppl. 121. For the functions of the Hellenistic Γυμνάσιον and the inscription of Eresos, see Schuler 2004, pp. 163–191; Kah/Scholz 2004.

119 For a commentary on the decree, see Chankowski 2010, pp. 264–265, 323–325.

120 For public banquets in the ancient city, see Schmitt-Pantel 1992.

121 The related reference from Eresos is the earliest known for a model of celebrations that would be very broadly disseminated in the Hellenistic world. See Chankowski 2010, p. 294.

122 IG XII 2.5.

123 IG XII 2.447, Charitonidis 1968, no. 16.

124 IG XII Suppl. 121.

Koinon of the Lesvians

In the Hellenistic period, following the general trend of the time, the cities of Lesbos will establish their own confederation, the *koinon* of the Lesvians,[125] seated at the Temple of Messon, which, as its name suggests, was a shared place of worship at the very center of the island. The international treaty (συνθήκα)[126] founding the *koinon*, agreed upon among the cities of Mytilene, Methymna, Antissa, and Eresos[127] (IG XI 4.1064),[128] dating between 197/6 and 167 BCE,[129] was found separately in three fragments in Delos,[130] which were later identified as parts of a single text.[131] The treaty was concluded at the very sanctuary of Messon (referred to in l. 5), certainly following long negotiations among representatives of the four cities and the ratification of the relevant decision within each city of Lesbos. The administrative bodies of the *koinon* referred to in this fragmentary inscription included a common mercenary army (to which Eresos contributed 600 soldiers, Methymna 400, for Mytilene the number is lost), the assembly (ἐκλησία) of the *koinon*, and elected representatives (οἱ ὑπὸ τῷ κοί[ν]ω δεδείγμενοι ἐπ'ἀρχ[...]). Monetary contributions from the revenue from sales of produce grown on public lands financed the common fund of the *koinon*. *Isopoliteia* was granted between the citizen, allowing all citizens to be inscribed before the *strategoi* to the tribe of their choice in another Lesvian city. The *koinon* would adopt a body of common laws in the first assembly, each city proposing a certain number, probably proportionally to their population: Mytilene 11 laws, Methymna 6, the number for Eresos is lost. A dispute-resolution process was instituted, which would take place in the sanctuary of Messon. After agreeing on the constitution of the court ([---ὀμογν]

125 Labarre 1994, Dimopoulou-Piliouni 2015, pp. 307–333.

126 Text B, l. 36.51.

127 The archaeological findings include different indications as to when the temple was founded, and so it is possible that its construction took time to complete.

128 Robert 1960, p. 308, has suggested that the existence of the *koinon* and its connection to the sanctuary of Messon are quite earlier than the inscription of Delos. This view is not based on written evidence but on the founding of the temple, as a place of common worship with pan-Lesvian prestige, at a point located at the limits of the most important Lesvian cities. It is suggested that the founding of a splendid temple in the late 4th century BCE on the location of an earlier temple, at a conspicuous, central, but uninhabited place near the bay of Pyrra, is linked to the existence at the same time of a broader cooperation between the Lesvian cities and that the establishment of the *koinon* dates from the same time.

129 See references to Mytilene (text A, l. 1, text B, ll. 15, 30); Methymna (text A, ll. 2, 8, text B, ll. 5, 30); Eresos (text A, l. 3 restoration, text B, l. 5 restoration); and Antissa (text A, l. 3, text B, l. 30). The reference to Eresos is the product of restoration, but it is certain that the city participated in the *koinon* since in another line of the inscription there is mention of four cities (l. 42).

130 IG XII Suppl. 136 (=IG XI 4.1064). Cassayre 2010, pp. 83–85.

131 Wilhelm 1909, pp. 315–316.

ωμονέωσι περὶ τῷ κριτηρίῳ), third cities (λαχοίσαν πολίων) would be drawn by lot (ἀποκλήρωσις) from a list to act as judges. An illustration of this dispute-resolution process among the cities of Lesbos is preserved in an inscription from Miletus (IG XII Suppl. 139) containing two decrees by Methymna and one by Eresos, honoring Milesian judges who resolved disputes between the citizens of the two Lesvian cities at the sanctuary of Messon.

Conclusion

To what extent does the extant information on the laws and public institutions of the cities of Lesbos allow us to reach conclusions about the existence of a common legal background, a certain unity of their law,[132] and, on a second level, on a perception of common identity among the Lesvians?[133] Throughout their history the cities were linked both by a belief in common ancestry and by their belonging to the same large Aegean island. They faced the same problems and similar political upheavals: *stasis,* the eternal strife between democrats and oligarchists, succeeded by periods of tyrannies, perennial threats from the East, the issue of the exiles and the challenges connected to their return and reintegration into the citizen body. The information drawn from the epigraphical and literary evidence examined, despite the randomness of the material that has survived and its unequal distribution, geographically and in time, outlines certain common parameters. The existence of several Lesvian cities that constituted autonomous civic entities and independent states, each pursuing its own public and international policy, having its own archons, set of laws, coins, fortifications, and armies, did not prevent them from sharing many common perceptions about the law and from operating quite similar civic institutions. All the cities of Lesbos demonstrate many common features in the structure of their political and legal systems and within their civic bodies. Their political life was organized (except for periods of tyranny), around the assembly of the *demos* and the *boule,* the issue of laws and decrees regulating every aspect of public life, the dispensation of justice, their state-operated religious worship. The titles and responsibilities of the various archons feature common elements in all Lesvian cities and attest to their similar civic organization, with slight variations.[134]

---

132 For the issue of the unity (or not) of law in ancient Greek cities, see GAGARIN 2005, pp. 29–40, who considers that there was unity in procedural matters but not in substantive law. THÜR 2007, pp. 25–54, suggests that the background of differing legal institutions in the Greek city-states conceals common perceptions about law.

133 CHANKOWSKI 1999, pp. 1211–1214.

134 An element of civic differentiation is the χέλληστυς of the people of Methymna, though the information that has survived does not allow us to be certain that similar (or differently named) citizen associations did not exist in the other cities of Lesbos.

All the cities of Lesbos also participated actively in exchanging judges with other cities of the Hellenistic world. The citizens' contribution to public affairs was considered of primary importance and benefactors were honored in the same manner, applying a similar legal framework. Their citizens were actively involved in public functions, in the running of the gymnasiums, in citizen associations, while participating in the cultural and artistic life for which Lesbos was famous.

It is not paradoxical that the parallel legal and institutional systems of the Lesvian cities co-existed with their – sometimes acute their – competition, especially the tendency of the biggest city, Mytilene, to aspire to primacy over its sisters on the island. The internal strife and rivalries that often divided the citizens of the Lesvian cities – also an expression of the agonistic Greek spirit – were not an exception, but the rule amongst Greeks everywhere. Being though conscious of the need for collaboration in view of external threats, the *koinon* of the Lesvians was a deliberate effort to forge a lasting coalition between them, in a deliberate attempt to bring about the "[αὔ]ξησιν καὶ ὀμόνοιαν τῶν Λεσβίων," the Lesvians' prosperity and concord,[135] though its activity never overshadowed the independence of each city participating in it. This concord remained an elusive concept, both within the cities, as indicated by the decree on Concord of Mytilene (SEG 36.750), as among the Lesvians and the Greeks in general. Later, the cities of Lesbos were unable to form a common front against the Romans: each shaped its own policy towards them, and each suffered its own fate, although the island will finally be fully integrated to Roman rule, its cities will be awarded privileges and enjoy a new period of prosperity under the *Pax Romana.*[136]

Even so, throughout their ancient history, the surviving sources make evident that the Lesvians, other than a common heritage and a belief in ancestral kinship, shared many common legal institutions. Onomastics in inscriptions attest that the Lesvians conceived their ethnic identity as composed of concentric circles: their city of birth being at the center, surrounded by the island of Lesbos, then by the wider Greek world. Among the common elements shared in this multifaceted identity, lies a certain coherence of the cities of Lesbos' legal systems and the adoption of mostly similar public institutions among them.

135 IG XII Supp. 136.b.1, l. 33.
136 Dimopoulou 2020.

Bibliography

Archontidou, Aglaia (2000) Λ. Αχειλαρά, Μυτιλήνη, Οδός Ερμού 273–291, in: Αρχαιολογικόν Δελτίον 55 Β'2, 922–923.

Banfi, Antonio (2007) Gynaikonomein. Intorno ad una magistratura ateniese del IV secolo ed alla sua presenza nelle fonti teatrali greche e romane, in: Eva Cantarella/Lorenzo Gagliardi (eds.), Diritto e Teatro in Grecia e a Roma, Milan, 17–29.

Boesch, Paul (1908) Theoros, Untersuchung zur Epangelie griechischer Feste, Berlin.

Buchholz, Hans-Günther (1975) Methymna, Mainz.

Carlier, Pierre (1984) La Royauté en Grèce avant Alexandre, Strasbourg.

Cassayre, Aude (2010) La Justice dans les cités grecques. De la formation des royaumes hellénistiques au legs d'Attale, Rennes.

Chankowski, Andrzej S. (2010) L'Éphébie hellénistique. Étude d'une institution civique dans les cités grecques des îles de la Mer Égée et de l'Asie Mineure, Paris.

Chankowski, Véronique (1999) Compte-rendu de G. Labarre. Les cités de Lesvos aux époques Hellénistique et Impériale, Lyon (1996), in: Annales 54, 1211–1214.

Chantraine, Pierre (1972) A propos du nom des Phéniciens et des noms de la pourpre, in: Studii Clasice 14, 7–15.

Charitonodis, Serafim (1968) Αἱ ἐπιγραφαί τῆς Λέσβου. Συμπλήρωμα, Athens.

Charitonides, Seraphim (1968) Ai epigraphai tēs Lesbu: symplērōma, Athens.

Costabile, Felice (1992) La contribuzione al re: Ruolo finanziario e cronologia dei magistrati Locresi, in: Felice Costabile (ed.), Polis ed Olympieion a Locri Epizeifiri. Constituzione, economia e finanze di una città della Magna Grecia, Catanzaro, 139–149.

Debord, Pierre (1984) 'Chiliastys', in: Revue des Études Anciennes 86, 201–211.

Dimakis, Panayotis (1997) Les ambassadeurs dans la Grèce Antique, in: Bullettino dell'Istituto di Diritto romano 39, 87–91.

Dimopoulou-Piliouni, Athina (2012) La Bonne Fortune et son rôle civique dans les cités grecques et romaines, in: Bernard Legras (ed.), Transferts culturels et droits dans le monde grec et hellénistique, Paris, 167–180.

Dimopoulou-Piliouni, Athina (2015) Λεσβίων Πολιτεἰαι. Πολίτευμα και δίκαιο των πόλεων της Λέσβου (αρχαϊκοί, κλασικοί, ελληνιστικοί, ρωμαϊκοι χρόνοι), Athens.

Dimopoulou, Athina (2017) The Lion and the Sage: writing the Law in Archaic Lesbos, in: RDE VII, ΝΟΜΟΣ ΒΑΣΙΛΕΥΣ, La regalità del diritto in Grecia antica, 19–36.

Dimopoulou, Athina (2018) The decree of Mytilene for the return of the exiles, in: Barbara Biscotti (ed.), Kallistos Nomos. Scritti in onore di Alberto Maffi, Torino, 71–82.

Dimopoulou, Athina (2020) Lesbos in the Roman Empire. Treaties, Legal Institutions, and Local Sentiment towards Roman Rule, in: Kimberly Czajikowski/Benedikt Eckhardt/Meret Strothmann (eds.), Law in the Roman Provinces, Oxford Studies in Roman Society and Law, Oxford, 267–283.

Dmitriev, Sviatoslav (2005) City Government in Hellenistic and Roman Asia Minor, Oxford.

Euangelides, Demetrios (1920–1921) Λέσβου ἐπιγραφαί, in: ΑΔ 6, 107–108.

Frölich, Pierre (2004) Les cités grecques et le contrôle des magistrats (IVe-Ier siècle avant J.-C.), Geneva.

Gagarin, Michael (2005) The Unity of Greek Law, in: Michael Gagarin/David Cohen (eds.): The Cambridge Companion to Ancient Greek Law, Cambridge, 29–40.

Gauthier, Philippe/Hatzopoulos, Militiades (1993) La loi gymnasiarchique de Beroia, Athens.

Giannakopoulos, Nikos (2008) Ο Θεσμός της Γερουσίας των ελληνικών πόλεων κατά τους Ρωμαϊκούς Χρόνους. Οργάνωση και Λειτουργίες, Thessaloniki.

Gottlieb, Gunther (1967) Timuchen: Ein Beitrag zum Griechischen Staatsrecht, Heidelberg.

Harris, Edward (2005) Who Enforced the Law in Classical Athens?, in: Symposion, 159–176.

Jakab, Éva (1997) Praedicere und cavere beim Marktkauf. Sachmängel im griechischen und römischen Recht, Munich.

Jones, Arnold Hugh Martin (1940) The Greek City from Alexander to Justinian, Oxford.

Jones, Nicholas F. (1987) Public Organization in Ancient Greece. A Documentary Study, Philadelphia.

Kah, Daniel/Scholz, Peter (2004) Das Hellenistische Gymnasion, Berlin.

Kontis, Ioannis D. (1978) Η Λέσβος και η μικρασιατική της περιοχή, Athens.

Labarre, Guy (1996) Les cités de Lesvos aux époques Hellénistique et Impériale, Paris.

Labarre, Guy (1994) ΚΟΙΝΟΝ ΛΕΣΒΙΩΝ, in: Revue des Études Anciennes 96, 415–446.

Mason, Hugh J. (1993) Mytilene and Methymna. Quarrels, Borders and Topography, in: Echos du Monde Classique/Classical Views 37(12), 225–250.

Meiggs, Russell/Lewis, David (eds.) (1971) A Selection of Greek Historical Inscriptions to the End of the Fifth Century B. C., Oxford.

Migeotte, Léopold (2001) Les pouvoirs des agoranomes dans les cités grecques, in: Symposion, 287–301.

Migeotte, Léopold (2006) La planification des dépenses publiques dans les cités hellénistiques, in: Studi Ellenistici 19, 77–97.

Parker, Robert (2004) What are Sacred Laws?, in: Edward Monroe Harris/Lene Rubinstein (eds.) The Law and the Courts in Ancient Greece, London, 57–70.

Pistorius, Hans (1913) Beiträge zur Geschichte von Lesbos im vierten Jahrhundert v. Ch., Bonn.

Rhodes, Peter John/Lewis, David M. (1997) The Decrees of the Greek States, Oxford.

Robert, Louis (1928) Notes d'Épigraphie Hellénistique, in: Bulletin de Correspondance Hellénique 52, 16–164.

Robert, Louis (1951) Études de numismatique grecque, Paris.

Robert, Louis (1960) Recheches Épigraphiques, IV. Une pierre errante en Écosse. Inscription du Dumbartonshire, in: Revue des Études Anciennes 62, 276–285.

Robert, Louis (1963) Samothrace 2, 1: Fraser, The Inscriptions on Stone, in: Gnomon 35, 56.

Schmitt-Pantel, Pauline (1992) La cité au banquet: histoire des repas publics dans les cités grecques, Rome.

Schuler, Christof (2005) Die διοίκησις τῆς πόλεως im öffentlichen Finanzwesen der hellenistischen Poleis, in: Chiron 35, 385–403.

Schuler, Christof (2004) Die Gymnasiarchie in hellenistische Zeit, in: Daniel Kah/Peter Scholz (eds.), Das hellenistische Gymnasion, Berlin, 163–191.

Sherk, Robert K. (1990) The Eponymous Officials of Greek Cities I, in: Zeitschrift für Papyrologie und Epigraphik 83, 249–288.

Sherk, Robert K. (1990) The Eponymous Officials of Greek Cities II. Mainland, Greece and the Adjacent Islandes, in: Zeitschrift für Papyrologie und Epigraphik 84, 273–274.

Sherk, Robert K. (1991) The Eponymous Officials of Greek Cities III. The Register, Thrace, Black Sea, Asia Minor, in: Zeitschrift für Papyrologie und Epigraphik 88, 225–260.

Spencer, Nigel (2003) Exchange and Stasis in Archaic Mytilene, in: Roger Brock/Stephen Hodkison (eds.), Alternatives to Athens. Varieties of Political Organization and Community in Ancient Greece, Oxford, 68–81.

Stanley, Phillip V. (1979) Agoranomoi and Metronomoi. Athenian Market Regulations and Officials, in: Ancient World 1, 72–79.

Thür, Gerhard (2007) Die Einheit des Griechischen Rechts. Gedanken zum Prozessrecht in den griechischen Poleis, in: Etica & Politica IX(1), 25–54.

Wilhelm, Adolf (1909) Beiträge zur griechischen Inschriftenkunde, Vienna.

Wehrli, Christoph (1962) Les Gynéconomes, in: Museum Helveticum 19, 33–38.

Donatella Erdas (University of Milan)

Selling land and houses in the ancient Greek poleis

Some notes on procedures, liabilities, and parties involved

The basis for the knowledge of the laws governing sales in the Greek *poleis* is a long fragment of Theophrastus' *Nomoi* quoted by Stobaios (fragment 97 Szegedy-Maszak = 650 Fortenbaugh, *apud* Stobaios 4.2.20 Hense). The most valuable section is dedicated to contracts (Περὶ συμβολαίων). In paragraphs 1–3 Theophrastus reviews several forms of publicity for real estate transactions in use in some Greek *poleis*. The plurality of legal contexts described by Theophrastus makes one obvious fact clear, namely that each polis, in protecting sales between private individuals of real estate, applied procedures that best suited its needs. In this respect local institutions took the socioeconomic context into account when producing ad hoc legislation.

This said, how sales actually worked can be deduced mainly from the deeds of sale, particularly in those cases where – and they are not few – we possess what could be called a dossier of documents. Here the resulting data go far beyond their original legal function. And yet the comparison between different socioeconomic contexts can nevertheless provide elements of interest for some thought on the unitary aspects of Greek law.[1] This can be said taking into account what the same Theophrastus wrote in conclusion of the section mentioned above as a general rule: the sale is legally accomplished for the purpose of possession when the price has been paid and when the obligations prescribed by law regarding publicity have been fulfilled (κυρία ἡ ὠνὴ καὶ ἡ πρᾶσις εἰς μὲν κτῆσιν, ὅταν ἡ τιμὴ δοθῇ καὶ τὰ ἐκ τῶν νόμων ποιήσωσιν).[2]

A passage from the *Dikaiomata* of Alexandria (par. XI, ll. 252-256) shows a similar prescription. The sale is considered complete when the seller has received the price and the *amphourion* has been paid. The *amphourion* literally means 'ascer-

1 Without discussing the long standing debate concerning the unity or diversity of ancient Greek law, I refer here to the summaries of GAGARIN 2005 (on the substantive diversity of law within common legal procedures), THÜR 2007 (on the unity of law on the basis of common juristic conceptions), and HARRIS 2024 (on the prevailing unity of law in substantive and constitutional matters, and with regard to legal terminology), esp. pp. 139–141 for the similarities in property law. On the development of the concept of the unity of Greek Law in modern scholarship see now TODD 2023 with ARNAOUTOGLOU 2023.

2 Theophrastus, fragment 97 Szegedy-Maszak = 650 Fortenbaugh, 35–36. On the payment of the price as a condition for the transfer of ownership, which in fact excludes the existence of forms of obligations on sale in Greek law, see PRINGSHEIM 1950, pp. 90–92 with critical remarks by GERNET 1951, and now FARAGUNA 2021, pp. 311, 327 and FARAGUNA 2023, pp. 241–242.

tainment of the boundaries', thus it is probably a registration fee on the property. This kind of fee can also be found in an inscription of a Rhodian *koinon* from the end of the 2nd century BCE concerning the sale of some properties. A similar tax is also present at Paros (SEG 54.798, end of the 3rd cent. BCE), where it is significantly called περιήγητα. The main argumentation is that this fee probably implies the transcription and registration of the deeds.[3]

In light of these preliminary remarks, we could therefore state that a common basis for the sale of real estate in the Greek *poleis* was the payment of the sale price and the fulfillment of the obligations associated with the transaction: that is, publicity of the acts and/or deed registration fees. Publicity of the acts and deed registration fees serve the same purpose of avoiding claims around the property and the regularity of the transaction.

Several documents recording the sale of land and houses between private individuals have been found in the Greek world from between the 4th and 1st cent. BCE. In most cases, these are synthetic documents that present more or less succinctly the basic data on the sale: the date, the name of the buyer, the name of the seller, the description of the property being sold from a physical and topographical point of view, the sale price, the guarantors, and the witnesses involved.

The function of these deeds is not the same for all types of documents: sometimes they provide publicity for the transaction between the parties and the inscription is placed near the property, in other cases the texts appear to be a copy of a public record, produced by the official in charge for the use of one of the parties. Evidence shows that Greek *poleis* formalized real estate sales in different ways, but some of the abovementioned data were always present in sale deeds: the name of the buyer, the name of the seller, the description of the property being sold from a topographical point of view, the sale price.

However, there are texts which, also because of their conciseness, cannot be easily ascribed to a single model. Alongside deeds recording the definitive and irrevocable sale of a property, there are also deeds in which the asset is transferred on a temporary basis: here, consequently, the sale is only the first part of the transaction, while the second consists in the release of the property previously sold (πρᾶσις ἐπὶ λύσει). Formally, there is no difference in the vocabulary used and the structure between deeds of definitive sale and *praseis epi lysei*.[4] In documents recording the latter procedure, however, the deed of sale is followed by the conditions of release,[5] in which the possibility of redeeming the property by the seller is indicated and,

---

3 This issue is dealt with in detail by Faraguna 2021, pp. 309–317.

4 Since Harris 1988.

5 In sales records organized by date the two deeds may not be contiguous, as for example in the Tenos register, on which see below. On the presence (or not) of *praseis epi lysei* in deeds of sale from the Macedonian area see Youni 1986; Hennig 1987; Thür 2008; Harris 2008.

sometimes, the time within which release is required. While formally there is no difference between deeds of sale and *praseis epi lysei,* there are, however, indicators that make it possible to better specify the nature of the deeds. One of these is the presence of one or more guarantors. The latter are usually (though not always) present and have the function of providing security for the integrity of the property being sold, and sometimes for the solvency of the seller, whereas they are never present in deeds of sale on condition of release.[6]

That being said, it is legitimate to ask how widespread and widely practiced the alienation of real estate in the Greek *poleis* was. The starting point is that sales of land and houses between private individuals constituted a phenomenon that affected much of the Greek world, and which we know about not only through epigraphic documentation attesting to deeds of sale from different parts of the Greek world but also, as far as Athens is concerned, through the disputes over ownership witnessed in orations. The documentation hardly goes back any further than the 4th century BCE, while most evidence dates from this century and the next, and in a few cases even beyond.[7]

Buying, owning, selling, or partially alienating land and houses is thus a recognized right in the Greek world, and the Greek city-states secure individual property rights through magistrates and/or land registration in archives.[8] Knowledge of the extent to which this right was exercised, however, depends entirely on the documentation available to us: this inevitably conditions any discussion of the spread of the phenomenon of private land sales. This said, however, the existence of sales records and private documents testifying to their existence clearly demonstrate that land (and house) transactions were a common practice throughout the Greek world.[9]

In some specific cases, however, one can identify specific causes in the large-scale alienation of land and houses other than the individual initiative of private individuals, such as phases of economic crisis, or widespread phenomena at the city level of money circulation. This is undoubtedly what happened on the island of Tenos in the 4th century BCE. The deeds recorded in a large stone stele and other smaller fragments in Tenos are a peculiar case of real estate sales. Firstly, because for the most part they are sales on condition of release and not definitive sales; secondly, because it is now proven that the list of sales registers records a large credit transaction involving entire families, in which definitive sales or *praseis epi lysei* served

---

6 Erdas 2012, pp. 350–352. For the guarantors in sale deeds see below.

7 The later acts come from Sicily, and in particular from Morgantina, where they date back to the 2nd and 1st centuries BCE (see Game 2008, p. 147).

8 Thus Aristotle, Rhetoric 1361a15–25. See recently Bresson 2016, p. 225 (security on property as a condition of economic growth), Harris 2016 (the protection provided by the registration of sales deeds secures assets and contributes to economic growth), and Mackil 2018, pp. 318–319 (property security does not contribute significantly to economic growth).

9 Faraguna 2021, pp. 365–367. The existence of laws prohibiting the alienation of property under certain circumstances also shows that the phenomenon was widespread.

as investment of private money.[10] These operations were very common, both on a large scale, as in this case, and even more so in the smaller family sphere. By way of example one may recall the case described by Iseus of the trierarch Euctemon, who wishing to transform his property from real estate to cash carried out a series of sales, investing the money in various forms of credit, including the mortgage of a house, which he renounced once the credit was recovered (6.33, 394/3 BCE).[11]

A similar situation occurred in the territory of Mylasa in Caria between the end of the 2nd and the beginning of the 1st century BCE. Here, however, it must be pointed out that the complex system consisting of the acquisition of private lands for the benefit of the sanctuary and their subsequent exploitation through *misthosis* to the former owners of the land itself, was managed entirely by the state through appointed magistrates.[12]

Who is entitled to sell?

It is a widespread and widely shared idea that only those who have the right to the land within their political community, that is, all citizens, are entitled to sell.[13] This concept should be interpreted in a very broad sense when considering not only ownership but also the title to alienate an asset, two positions that do not always coincide.

This can occur when it is women to sell.[14] In two deeds of sale from Hellenistic Sicily, two women sell goods without presenting a *kyrios*.[15] In the first case, Dikaiagora,

10 See now Faraguna 2021, pp. 326–327 and Faguer 2020, part. 163–164.

11 Ferrucci 1998, pp. 90–91; on Is. 6 see now Griffith-Williams 2019. On the distinction *aphanes* and *phanera ousia*, referred to in connection with the goods sold by Euctemon see also Faraguna 1997, pp. 19–21 (with earlier discussion) and Ferrucci 2005, esp. pp. 159–162.

12 See recently Pernin 2014, pp. 401–445; Erdas 2020a, pp. 181–182.

13 Since Hennig 1994, p. 305.

14 It is debated whether, in Gortyn, women were entitled to sell their property without a *kyrios*. I.Cret. IV 72 col. v 44–48 grants the right to the heirs to sell property (*kremata*) to the highest bidder if they do not agree on its division, and to share the resulting profit equally ([α]ἰ [δ]| 45έ κα κρέματα δατιόμενοι|μὲ συνγιγνόσκοντι ἀν|πὶ τὰν δαῖσιν, ὀνε͂ν τὰ κρέμ|ατα· κο͂ς κα πλεῖστον διδ|ο͂ι ἀποδόμενοι τᾶν τιμᾶν |50 δια[λ]ακόντον τὰν ἐπαβο|λὰν ϝέκαστος. δατιο-μέ|νοιδ δὲ κρέματα μαίτυρα|νς παρέμεν δρομέανς ἐλε|υθέρονς τρίινς ἒ πλίανς.). The same provisions also apply when a father gives property to a daughter, as suggested by I.Cret. IV 72 col. vi 1–2 (θυγατρὶ ἒ διδο͂ι, κατὰ τὰ αὐτ|ά vac. – "Si un père dote sa fille, on procédera de même", according to the translation by van Effenterre/Ruzé, Nomima II, no. 49). M. Gagarin argues that, in such cases, the woman manages and disposes of the property personally (see recently Gagarin/Perlman, Laws of Crete, pp. 84–86), though his interpretation has been challenged by Maffi with strong counterarguments (Maffi 2012).

15 Camarina 7; Game 2008, no. 81, 2nd cent. BCE, and Morgantina 6; Game 2008, no. 86, 3rd cent. BCE.

daughter of Antallos, sells a prestigious house but also a well and a mill, urban and extra-urban goods that she owns. In the second, rather fragmentary deed, the widow of Sosias sells land with all that it contains (l. 1 [- - πάντα] ἐνέοντα ἐν τοῖς χώ[ροις]), without the presence of a *kyrios*.[16] This is also remarkable because the widow disposes of both her own property and that inherited from her husband, although it is obviously not possible to establish to which of these the sold land belongs.

The two Sicilian examples confirm what has long been known about the more extensive legal capacity of women outside Athens or its areas of influence, while regarding the documents from Morgantina e Camarina the absence of a *kyrios* may not necessarily indicate a change in the status of women in late Hellenistic Sicily.[17] It is noteworthy, however, that ownership and power to sell reside in these cases in the same female person.

In this connection it may be useful to recall a deed of sale from the Tenos register. In the deed (IG XII 5.872 § 20; Game 2008, no. 45) a woman, whose name is lost, with the consent of her *kyrios*, buys land from another woman, Phanikò daughter of Kleosthenes, who has her brother as *kyrios*. The presence of the guarantors at the end of the deed indicates that it is a definitive sale and not a *prasis epy lysei*, which represents the majority of the deeds in the Tenos register. At the same time, the fact that a woman appears as the purchasing party seems to exclude that this is a negotiation or renegotiation of a dowry, as it may be the case in other deeds from Tenos in which women are present.[18] The deed is also particularly interesting with regard to the guarantor. As noted above, he is in fact the seller's brother, who also acts as her *kyrios*. This is possible by taking into account two facts: 1. the guarantor, or guarantors, are always established by the seller, even if the security

16 The first part of the deed is completely missing and the name of the buyer is not known. The indication of the seller is followed by the price of the goods sold (10 talents?) and there is no space for the name of the *kyrios*. The guarantors follow, probably 10 as in other cases.

17 On Camarina 7 and the fragment edited by Cordano 1997, no. 1, see Souza 2016, pp. 159–160, who considers this fragment part of another contract. We refer to Souza 2016 for an up to date discussion of the female role in real estate contracts in Sicily. On female independence in economic transactions see van Bremen 1996, pp. 205–236. Similarly, in the case of the famous διαθήκη of Epikteta from Thera (IG XII 3.330, late 3rd–early 2nd century BCE), Epikteta is assisted by her daughter's husband in founding a *koinon*. The survival of the *koinon* is ensured by the mortgage income from some land the woman has acquired on her own (ll. 31–33: ὥστε ὀφεiλεσθαι αὐτὰς | ἐπὶ τοῖς ὑπάρχουσί μοι αὐτοκτήτοις χωρίοις τοῖς | ἐμ Μελαιναῖ[ς, κτλ.): this does not mean that in acquiring the land she was not assisted by a *kyrios* (who was probably the same son-in-law), but that the land was purchased with Epikteta's money and without contributions from others.

18 On this subject see the useful table in Game 2008, pp. 108–109. The heading of the Tenos register lists dotal endowments together with sales of land and houses as the subject of the document (IG XII 5.872, l. 1: [κατὰ τάδε πράσεις ἐγέ]νοντο χωρίων [καὶ ο]ἰκιῶν καὶ προικ[ῶν] δόσεις), but there is no trace of dowry deeds in it; rather, some assets that are subject to sale are derived from dowries. See now Faraguna 2021, p. 325 nt. 113.

being given is for the benefit of the person making the purchase; 2. normally in deeds of sale the guarantor and seller hold the same legal position (in the Tenos register guarantors are significantly referred to as πρατῆρες).[19]

Returning to the legal position of women in deeds of sale, a look at a deed of *prasis epi lysei* from Amorgos may be useful (IG XII 7.55, late 4th–early 3rd cent. BCE).[20] Although this is not a definitive sale, it is of interest because of the ownership of a set of lands acquired in different ways by the seller before they were sold on condition of release.[21] The owner of various plots of land is always a man, Nikeratos, but his wife Hegekrate with her own *kyrios* (different from her husband) is also involved in the sale of all the assets.[22] Hegekrate is therefore the selling party together with Nikeratos but does not have title to the property, which belongs to her husband alone.[23] Of course, this may have several explanations that escape us. The meticulous description of the ways in which Nikeratos had acquired the landed properties subject to the sale rule out the derivation of at least one of them from his wife's dotal *apotimema*.[24] Instead, it is possible that the wife contributed her own money to the acquisition of part of the property (those *choria* purchased or obtained by mortgage), and that her name simply does not appear as the purchasing party next to that of her husband.[25]

---

19 On personal security in the sale of land and houses see Erdas 2012 and below.

20 See Erdas 2020b, pp. 168–171; Faraguna 2021, pp. 343–344 nt. 184.

21 The assets are of three types: land, house, and tile roof from the division of the inheritance with the seller's brother Anthines (ll. 6–9); land acquired by Nikeratos himself (ll. 9–11); other land acquired by him through a mortgage (ll. 11–13). See Erdas 2020b, pp. 170–171.

22 M. Finley, who included this document among the security *horoi* from Amorgos despite being aware that it was not a *horos*, was not certain that Hegekrates was Nikeratos' wife (Finley 1952, pp. 265–266 nt. 22). The relationship, however, seems to be confirmed by comparison with a *horos*, also from Amorgos (IG XII 7.58), bearing the mortgage of some land and a house with gardens by Xenokles and his wife Eratokrates, represented by her *kyrios* (on this document see Faraguna 2012, p. 136).

23 IG XII 7.55: θεοί. |ἐπ' ἄρχοντος Φανοκράτους, μηνὸς | Ἀνθεστηριῶνος, ἀπέδοτο Νική|ρατος καὶ Ἡγεκράτη καὶ ὁ κύριο[ς] 5| Τελένικος Κτησιφῶντι Πυθίπ|που τὰ χωρία καὶ τὴν οἰκί[α]ν κ[α]ὶ | τὸγ κέραμον ἅπαντα ἅ ἔχε[ι] διε|λόμενος Νικήρατος πρὸς τὸν | ἀδελφὸν Ἀνθίνην, καὶ τὰ χωρία 10| ἃ ἐπρίατο Νικήρατος παρὰ Ἰσχυρί|ωνος ἅπα[ν]τα, καὶ τὰ χωρία ἃ ἔχει | θέμενος Ν[ικήρ]ατος παρὰ Ἐξακέσ|του ἅπαντα [ἀ]ργυρίου δραχμῶν | πεντακισχιλίων, ἐπὶ λύσει· 15| ὑποτελεῖ δὲ μίσθωμα Νικήρατος | Κτησιφῶντι καθ' ἕκαστον ἐνιαυ|τὸν ἀργυρίου δραχμὰς πεντα||[κ]οσίας ἀτελεῖς.

24 On the possibility that in Amorgos, but also in Athens and Tenos, when a wife gives her consent to the sale of property together with her husband we are dealing with a dotal *apotimema* see Faguer 2020, p. 173.

25 Stavrianopoulou 2006, pp. 99–104 opens to the existence in Amorgos of forms of community of property between spouses.

A note on the properties sold and their description

In addition to the name of the seller and the buyer, deeds or records of land sales always include a brief spatial location of the property. The description of the land is essential for proper identification of the property being sold. The information provided varies from deed to deed, but some elements are fairly recurrent. Sometimes the description of the land and the buildings, tools, equipment included in the land can also be very detailed, revealing a wider and more articulated system of land use than is explicitly evident from the deed itself.

This is particularly evident in one of the deeds of sale from Sicily preserved on lead tablets. In the deed Morgantina 1 (Game 2008, no. 83), attributed to Morgantina for reasons of similarity to other texts and dated to the 3rd century BCE, a plot of land is sold as a vineyard, accompanied by the farmhouse above it and some of the objects and tools for working the vines and making wine.[26] The property is described in some detail, even considering the concise nature of the deeds of sale, and presents several peculiarities, both in respect of the terms used to describe it, and the sale procedure, which is partial for the objects and tools, and entire for the vineyard. It is almost certain that the vineyard was part of a much larger estate parceled out for reasons of inheritance and that was originally active in wine production as it was equipped with all the tools for winemaking. Following the division between heirs, it can be assumed that it lost a large part of its productive capacity, which justifies its being put up for sale.

The type of land (*oikopedon, ampelos,* etc.) is sometimes specified in the deeds. The frequent use of generic terms (e.g. *ge, chorion, eschatia*), however, shows that this is not as essential as, for example, the price of the property or the description of its boundaries. In the event that the seller owns several plots in the same territory, it may be useful to specify who the previous owner of the individual plots was, probably in order to unambiguously identify the property and to provide additional security for the buyer against possible risks of eviction.[27] This is the case in the abovementioned deed from the Tenos register with a sale between two women, in which the land being sold is named after Demarchos, the previous owner.[28] This same text also gives the boundaries, which are formed by a road running around it ([ὡς ὁ]ρίζει ἡ ὁδὸς κύκλωι). The datum of the land boundaries is actually the most useful and is mostly reported in the deeds.[29] Boundaries are provided both

26 See below for further thoughts on this document.

27 Faraguna 2021, p. 329.

28 IG XII 7.872 § 20; Game 2008, no. 45, ll. 46–47.

29 The same considerations can be made for the descriptions of real estate in the security *horoi,* although in that case the quick description of the land was justified by the fact that the *horos* was placed next to the land for which it indicated the existence of bonds on the property.

with respect to landscape elements (a road, as in the case just considered, but also a river, a mountain, etc.) and, more frequently, with respect to neighboring properties.

The relationship with the neighbors' land constitutes to all effects and purposes an identifying feature of the property being sold,[30] but it also has a deeper significance. Neighbors often play the role of witnesses in deeds of sale (see, e.g., the μάρτυρες in the deeds of sale from Chalcidic peninsula[31]), and are therefore called upon as parties who have knowledge of the property being sold and who may have responsibilities with respect to the property itself.[32]

These data can be compared with the existence of Solon's laws on neighbors documented by several fragments (Leão/Rhodes 2015, fragments 60–64). Fragments 60a and b deal in particular with the care that must be taken when drawing boundaries between properties. They reveal a special attention to the definition and subdivision of plots of land that undoubtedly had the function of protecting the property from disputes that might arise between neighbors. These could occur primarily with respect to the boundaries of individual plots, but also, one can assume, in cases where plots were sold to third parties.[33]

Price fluctuations, guarantors, and other factors

Real estate prices are conditioned by several parameters, not all of which we can assess. A first piece of evidence is that value varies depending on the type of property. Agricultural estates usually have a higher average value than houses.[34] This

---

30 In a deed of sale from Amphipolis the house (perhaps with *oikopedon*) being sold has the same neighbors as another property whose name is in lacuna. D. Rousset, BE 278 1996 (additions to I.Amphipolis actes IX; see also Game 2008, no. 9): [ἀγαθῆι τύχηι· θεός· ἐπὶ Π]ολυκράτους ἱερέως, ἐπι[στά|του δὲ τοῦ δεῖνος – –]Σ, μηνὸς Δύστρου ὀγδόῃ φθίνον[τος | ἐπρίατο ὁ δεῖνα] παρὰ Δαμασίλεω τοῦ Εὐδήμου οἰκίαν καὶ [οἰκό|πεδον στατήρων ἑ]κατὸν πεντήκοντα ἑνὸς ἡμιστατήρου [βε|5βαίως καὶ παγίω]ς· γείτον<ε>ς κοινοί εἰσιν οἷς γειτονε[ύει | ὁ δεῖνα, ὁ δεῖνα]ΙẸΥΣ Κρατίνου· βεβαιωταί· Εὔδικος [τοῦ δεῖνος | ὁ δεῖνα τοῦ δεῖνος· μάρτυρ]ε̣ς· Κλέϊππος Ζωΐλου, Παυσανίας [τοῦ δεῖ|νος | – – – – – – – – – – – –].

31 See I.Chalcidique actes III and IV (Game 2008, nos. 30 and 29).

32 As Theophrastus states with reference to the polis of Thourioi, on which see below.

33 See, e.g., fragment 60a ap. Digest X 1.xiii: *Gaius libro quarto ad legem XII Tabularum: sciendum est in actione finium regundorum illud observandum esse, quod ad exemplum quodammodo eius legis scriptum est, quam Athenis Solonem dicitur tulisse*, etc. In their commentary on fragment 60–64 Leão and Rhodes explained the existence of these laws as follows: "in a system where agricultural land is subdivided into small parcels, any change in existing boundaries of land can lead to major disputes between neighbours. For this reason, it becomes very important to provide the exact definition of some basic rules, such as the space to leave between plantations bordering a neighbour's land" (Leão/Rhodes 2015, p. 178).

34 See Étienne 1990, pp. 60–61 for the Tenos register but also Game 2008, p. 154 on Sicilian deeds of sale.

clearly depends on the size of the plot(s), although the measurements of the land are almost never specified within the deeds. Another general fact that can be derived from geographically homogeneous sets of texts is the tendency for house prices to be more uniform than land prices, which are usually more variable.[35] This is probably due to the fact that the dimensions of the buildings were not too dissimilar from each other, while the farm plots could have very different extensions.

In a deed of sale from Piano Casazze in the region of Morgantina (I.dial.Sicile II 112; Game 2008, no. 87, 3rd century BCE) an agricultural plot of land (χῶρον) is sold at the very remarkable price of 150 talents.[36] No indication is given as to the location of the estate and therefore the size of the property cannot be deduced, but one can guess that it must have been conspicuous. As mentioned, prices for houses are lower: in a deed from Castel di Judica, in the region of Katane (I.dial. Sicile II 111; Game 2008, no. 91, 3rd century BCE), an unfinished house (οἰκίαν ἀτελέα) is sold for only 3 silver staters. Since the seller's name is the same as the buyer's patronymic, it is perhaps a sale between relatives. This could be the reason for such a low price, together with the precarious condition of the building.[37]

Beyond this, the problem in understanding price fluctuations within a homogenous geographical context is that many deeds cannot be dated with certainty. Furthermore, the differences in prices between town houses offered for sale in the Chalcidic peninsula[38] and the lower prices of houses in Tenos (and the Cyclades in general) and Sicily may be conditioned by various factors: a) Since rural areas have low house prices and high land prices, the difference between property prices in town and in the countryside is conditioned by the use made of them and the territory in which they are located. b) The socioeconomic conditions of a given territory can certainly influence not only prices but also the need to alienate land partially or permanently in order to obtain funds for survival. This might be the case, for example, in the *poleis* of Amorgos, where between the end of the 4th and 3rd centuries BCE several *horoi* and in one case a deed of sale[39] show a somewhat unstable tendency in the management of private lands. Economic instability can

35 See especially the acts from the Macedonian area (Hatzopoulos in I.Chalcidique actes, 76; see also Hennig 1987).

36 Manganaro 1997, no. 7, with Dubois, BE 1999, no. 642.

37 Given such a low price, L. Dubois in I.dial.Sicile II 110, 183–184 suggested that it was a mortgage loan, but nothing in the text suggests this (μηνὸς Προτιβάλιος, ἐπὶ Πίθωνος ἰαρέος | ἐπρίατο οἰκίαν ἀτελέα Ἄλκιππος Π̣υρρίχου | πὰρ Ὀνάσου Ἀλκίππου· ἄμποχος· Μόθων Κέν[τ]ου | τιμά· τρῖς στα[τ]ήρες ἀργυρίου).

38 Within the Chalcidic peninsula, moreover, house sales deeds record a higher average price value in Olynthus than in other settlements, e.g., Stolos (Cahill 2002, pp. 276–278).

39 See below.

also be seen at state level, in a series of documents attesting to large loans granted to the three *poleis* of the island by non-Amorgian private individuals.[40]

These symptoms of distress may conceal financial crises related to the state of the land (drought, poor harvests, etc.). In these cases private individuals could easily resort to forms of partial alienation of real estate that allow them to obtain liquidity without losing possession,[41] while it is perhaps less useful to resort to outright sales. However, it can by no means be ruled out that the sale of part of one's property can be used as a form of investment to strengthen assets weakened by external situations. Social instability due to political factors can also cause prices to collapse, as Hatzopoulos showed for the sales of houses and land in Kellion following the conquest of the Chalcidic peninsula by Philip II in 349 BCE.[42]

In serialized documentation, the price is also a good indicator of the real nature of the deed. In sales where there is an outright transfer of the property, the price of, e.g., houses, is variable; whereas deeds that always present the same prices for the houses being sold may conceal transactions of a different nature, e.g., a *prasis epi lysei,* or dotal *apotimemata.*[43]

With this multifaceted scenario in mind, we can now turn to the price of the properties offered for sale in relation to the number of guarantors. First of all, however, it is necessary to ask who is liable for the integrity of the property in sales of land and houses, and consequently whether it is necessary to resort to personal security.

Documentary evidence shows several cases in which the seller himself partly or wholly provides security for the sale of his goods. The most striking case is a deed from Stolos, in the Chalcidic peninsula, in which the seller is said to be βεβαιωτὴς αὐτός (I.Chalcidique actes 1, mid-4th century BCE).[44] Seller and guarantor are thus in the same legal position with respect to the sale. This can explain why guarantors are not always recorded in the deeds of sale. When present, they are therefore called upon first and foremost to provide security for the integrity of the property

40 Migeotte, Emprunt, nos. 48–56, 168–198; Erdas 2020b, pp. 180–184.

41 In this respect, the situation in Amorgos cannot be compared to that in Tenos, where the sales register covers credit transactions that serve as pure investment and appear unrelated to a state of necessity. See Faraguna 2019.

42 I.Chalcidique actes, 76–77, with Cahill 2002, p. 278.

43 See Étienne 1990, p. 62 on the Tenos register.

44 I.Chalcidique actes 1; Game 2008, no. 31 (between 356 and 349 BCE): οὐνὴ εὐθέα· ἱερεὺς Ἀντίδοτος | Πολυκλέος· Βιλταλὼ Διονυσιφάνεος | παρὰ Φιλίππου τοῦ Ἀννίκαντος τὴν οἰ|κίην ἐμ πόλει ἐξέης Ἀρχίο τοῦ Ὀπώριος |5 40 dr.· βεβαιωτὴς αὐτός· μάρτυρες Ἐπι|κράτης Ὀπώριος, Πολύστρατος Κρασεος, | Ἀρχέστρατος Ἄδωνος· μεὶς Ἡραιών. Sometimes guarantor and vendor are relatives, as in a deed from Olynthus in which the guarantor is the brother of the seller (Robinson 1934, no. 4; Game 2008, no. 16; see Nevett 2000; Cahill 2002, pp. 294–295); while at Amphipolis a seller is also a guarantor together with other relatives for the sale of a house and an *oikopedon* (I.Amphipolis actes XII; Game 2008, no. 12). See Erdas 2012, esp. pp. 352–354.

being sold. In deeds of sale from the Chalcidic peninsula and Macedonia they are called βεβαιωταί, while in Tenos' deeds of sale they are called πρατῆρες, and in Sicilian lead tablets ἄμποχοι.

Let's start with the mention of guarantors of the sale in IG XII 5.872 § 20 (Game 2008, no. 45) cited above, where one of the three guarantors is the brother of the seller (Phanikò). This is not surprising because relationships between guarantors and sellers in deeds of sale are frequent in Tenos and elsewhere as well. Here the three guarantors must provide security for the integrity of the goods, but at the same time their liability extends to their solvency. In fact, it is specified in the deed that the guarantors must provide security all together and each separately for the sale price. The formula refers to the security as a joint and several liability and recalls other types of clauses common outside Tenos.[45] In addition to this type of security in Tenos' deeds one also finds a pro-rata guarantee, according to which a guarantor provides security for part of the property value (see, e.g., IG XII 5.872 § 23, ll. 55–60, where the *koinon* of Thiasites acts as a legal subject providing security together with ten men[46]).

In all these cases, therefore, the security provided by the guarantor is not limited to protecting the integrity of the assets being sold, but also covers the value of the property. Returning to IG XII 5.872 § 20, it is striking that the property sold by Phanikò has a very low value (120 silver drachmas). Therefore, the question arises as to whether there is a relationship between the price of the properties offered for sale and the number of guarantors presented by the seller. This question can only be answered by considering a series of geographically and chronologically homogeneous deeds. In the records from Sicily, for example, we have a

---

45 This is the meaning of the expressions καὶ μέσωι πάντες καὶ χωρίς ἕκαστος παντὸς τοῦ ἀργυρίου or more simply καὶ μέσωι πάντες καὶ χωρίς ἕκαστος. See Erdas 2012, p. 356. Game 2008, p. 106 assumed that this type of guarantee was used when there was no agreement between the seller and buyer parties. The formula is, however, quite common in reference to personal security outside the real estate sales field and always indicates a joint and several liability.

46 IG XII 5.872 § 23, ll. 55–60; Game 2008, no. 50: [Θρα]συγόρας Χαρεστάδου ἐκ πόλεως παρὰ Σιμίου Ἀρίστιος Ἐσχα[τιώ]του καὶ παρὰ Ἀρίστιος Ἐσχατιώτο[υ, οὗ κύρ]ιος Σῖμος Ἀρίστιο[ς Ἐσχατιώτη]ς, ἐπρίατο τὰς οἰκίας καὶ τὸν κέραμ[ον καὶ τὰ χω]|ρία τὰ ἐν Αἰσίλει πάντα ὅσα [ἦν] Ἀρίστιος, καὶ τὰς ἐσχατιὰς καὶ ὕδατος ἀ[γω]γὰς τὰς οὔ[σ]α[ς] τῶν χωρίων τούτων, οἷς γείτονες Ἀλεξῖνος Καλλίο[υ, Κρ]άτης Ἰσοδή[μου, δραχμ]ῶν ἀργυρίου τετρακισ[χιλίων] | καὶ ἑπτακ[οσί]ων, πρατῆρες Ἀρπαλῖνος Ὀνήτορο[ς] Ἐλει̣[θυαιε]ὺς κα̣[τ]ὰ δια[κο]σίας πεντήκοντα, [Π]ασιτέκτων Συμμάχου Κλ[υμενεὺ]ς κα[τ' ὀκτακοσίας πεντήκοντ]α, Ἱέρων Ἱεροπόλιος Ἐ[λειθυαιεὺς] | κατὰ διακοσίας, Εὐθύτης Ἡρακλείου Ἐλειθυαιεὺς κατὰ διακοσίας, Φιλίσκ[ος] Ι. . κανου(?) Θρυήσιος κατὰ ἑκατὸν εἴκοσιν, Θρασυγόρ[ας Μορυ]χί[ωνο]ς [Δονακεὺ]ς κατὰ πεντακοσί[ας, – – – Μο]|ρυχίων[ος Δ]ονακεὺς κατὰ χιλίας ὀκτακοσίας τριάκον[τα], Ἀρχαγόρα[ς Μο]ρυχίωνος Δονακεὺς κατὰ πεντακο[σί]ας, Δημοκράτ[ης . . . . . .]αίου Θε[στιάδη]ς κατὰ ἑκατόν, Κ[– – – –] |60 Κλυμενεὺς καὶ κοινὸν Θιασιτῶν κατὰ ἑκατὸν πεντήκοντα.

certain variety of prices in relation to the number of guarantors, who in several deeds appear as many as ten, though not everywhere. Thus we see the abovementioned deed from the region of Morgantina (I.dial. Sicile II 112; Game 2008, no. 87, 3rd cent. BCE) in which a single guarantor provides security for a plot of land worth 150 talents; while in a deed from Agyrion one guarantor is recorded for a house with all equipment sold for 5 talents and 305 golden litrai (I.dial.Sicile II 110; Game 2008, no. 90, 3rd cent. BCE); and in the abovementioned deed from Castel di Judica the sale of an unfinished house worth 3 silver staters still requires the presence of one guarantor.

A further look at the Sicilian acts that have come down to us confirms what seems to be inferred from these three deeds, namely that there is no rule and sometimes not even a trend in the number of guarantors involved in a sale of land and houses, even when the number of guarantors presented is higher. In a deed probably from Camarina (Camarina 6; Game 2008, no. 80, 2nd–1st century BCE), half of a *choron* and the equipment that was on the property are sold. The land must have been quite extensive, at least judging by the sale price, which is 250 talents. The sale is guaranteed by ten guarantors. In the already-mentioned deed Morgantina 1 (3rd century BCE), vineyard land with all the equipment is sold for a much lower value of 21 talents and 115 litrai,[47] but the guarantors presented are still ten.[48] The two deeds are not contemporaneous, it must be said; however, a possible increase in the sale price of the land is not sufficient to justify the sharp difference between the value of the two plots of land in the face of an identical number of guarantors presented.

I would like to stop briefly on Morgantina 1 (Game 2008, no. 83) for a few remarks on the nature of the deed.

ἐπ᾽ ἱαραπόλου Ὄρθωνος, Θευδα[ισίου *num.*]· ὠνεῖτα[ι ἀμπέ]|λους καὶ τὰ ἑπόμενα πάντα ταῖς [ἀμ]πέλοις καὶ̣ [τοῦ λα]|νοῦ δύο μέρεα, τῶν δ᾽ ἄλλων τὰ ἥμισσα, τοῦ στα[θ]μ̣ο[ῦ] | παντός, ὅ κ᾽ ἦ̣ [ἐ]μβασίεσσιν, καὶ τῶν ἄλλων ἐντ[ὸς] | τὰ ἥμισσα Λύσων Ἱππία ΠΔΗΤ ΔΔ̣ πὰρ Θέστωνος | Δαμάρχου καὶ <ΠΑΙ> πὰρ Σατύρου Δάμωνος ὀρφοβω|τᾶν ἐόντων, πλὰν τῶν ἱερῶν· ἄμποχοι· Νικίας Κρατί[α], | Ἐμμενίδας Δάμωνος, Θεύδωρος Εὐπολέμου, | Φιλονίδας Ἡρακλείδα Ἱάρων Φιλιάρχου, | Φιλίαρχος Ἀπολλωνίδα, Δείνων Φιντία, | Φίλων Ἐμμενίδα, Πολύξενος Ἐμμεν[ί]δ̣[α], | Π̣υρρίας Καραίκου *vacat*

Orthon being *hierapolos*, on [the day] of Theudaisios; Lyson son of Hippias buys vineyards and all that depends on it, two shares of the press, half of the other objects and the whole building farm, which could be used for the crushing operations, and half of the other objects inside, at the price of 21 talents and 115 litrai, to Theston son of Dam-

47 On price see Manganaro 1997, p. 328.

48 Although this deed dates back to the 3rd century BCE, therefore earlier than the previous one.

archos and to Satyros son of Damon, *orphobotai,* excluding the sacred objects. Guarantors: Nikias son of Kratias, Emmenidas son of Damon, Theudoros son of Eupolemos, Philonidas son of Herakleidas, Hiaron son of Philiarchos, Philiarchos son of Apollonidas, Deinon son of Phintias, Philon son of Emmenidas, Polyxenos son of Emmenidas, Pyrrhias son of Karaikos.

As mentioned above, the deed provides for the alienation of a piece of land that was to be part of a larger property intended for wine production. The verb used is ὠνέομαι, is placed at the beginning of the deed (l. 1 ὠνεῖται) and refers to a definitive sale. It must therefore be ruled out that it is a dotal *apotimema.* In such situations, the sale could be an alternative to the pupil *apotimema,* even if it is still a more hazardous operation. This is shown by the case presented by Iseus (On the Succession of Menecles 2.28–29): here Menecles, the plaintiff's adoptive father, attempts to sell a property *(chorion)* resulting from an inheritance, while the orphan's guardian (the guardian is Menecles' brother) prevents the sale[49] in order to force him to mortgage the property in favor of the orphan.[50]

Two elements in the text from Morgantina provide some insights as to the type of deed. The sale of two-thirds of the grape press and the low selling price have led some scholars to suggest that the deed may be a *prasis epi lysei.* But if we assume that this is the sale of the part of an originally larger estate inherited by one or more orphans, this alone could explain the sale of two-thirds of the press[51] and half of the other tools originally used collectively for winemaking. The partial sale of the press is undoubtedly unusual, but it would also be unusual if the deed concealed a *prasis epi lysei,* of which there is no mention in the text. There is also no evidence in the text to support the idea that two-thirds of the press license to use is sold here.[52]

As for the low sale price, as suggested above it may reflect the devaluation of the property as a consequence of the parceling out of the original estate.

49 In the case of Menecles' succession, in fact, being undivided property, any claim by one of the co-owners would have stopped the sale, as Cobetto Ghiggia 2012, 80 nt. 35 points out.

50 The verbs used to describe the sale (which in the end is not carried out except in part and for a total of 70 mines) are πιπράσκω and ὠνέομαι. On the type of land and in general on the sale of the *chorion* see Ferrucci 1998, pp. 113–115; 186–188.

51 On the interpretation of δύο μέρεα (l. 3) as two-thirds see Dubois in I.dial.Sicile II 123.

52 For the interpretation of this deed as a *prasis epi lysei* see Dubois in I.dial. Sicile II 123; for the sale of the license to use the press see Game 2008, no. 83, 158. As Game rightly points out, the press is an expensive tool used in sharing, but there is nothing in the act to suggest that it is alienated in a different manner from the rest of the assets.

Public institutions, private deeds

We are informed of the presence of city officials in charge of drawing up contracts and in general of the city's intervention in land and house sales again by Theophrastus. According to him, sales: 1) may be announced by the herald; 2) may take place in the presence of a magistrate; 3) may be pre-recorded no less than 60 days before the deed (in Athens).[53] In any case, the presence of magistrates (or alternatively witnesses, as in the example of Thurioi that follows this list[54]) according to Theophrastus has the function of establishing responsibility for the sales. The liability concerns the validity of the sale, i. e., the guarantee by the magistrate or the witnesses that the deed is accomplished, is valid, and that there can no longer be any claims on the object of the sale.[55] Theophrastus does not mention this explicitly, but it is inferred from the very definition of *kyria one* (on which see above) that magistrates are charged with a further and major responsibility, related to the registration of the deed. In general, from the varied picture envisaged by Theophrastus follows that there is frequent recourse to the registration of acts.[56] This is evident in the Tenos sales register (IG XII 5.872), where it now seems clear that stone records were made at the end of the year and not close to the registration of the deed itself by the magistrates.[57] This, in turn, makes explicit the different functions that deeds of sale could assume depending on the medium through which they reached us, as well as the various steps that led to the completion of the sale: stipulation of the deed; registration; publication either of the individual deed for private use or of the set of registrations (as in the case of Tenos, precisely).

We have already said that a sale is concluded when the sale price is paid and the measures in connection with the payment of fees have been fulfilled. From the deeds of sale that have come down to us, the first part of the sale, that which goes up

---

53 Theophrastus, fragment 97 Szegedy-Maszak = 650 Fortenbaugh, 2–10.

54 Theophrastus, fragment 97 Szegedy-Maszak = 650 Fortenbaugh, 11–13: Οἱ δὲ Θουριακοὶ τὰ μὲν τοιαῦτα πάντα ἀφαιροῦσιν οὐδ' ἐν ἀγορᾷ προστάττουσι ὥσπερ τἆλλα, διδόναι δὲ κελεύουσι κοινῇ τῶν γειτόνων τῶν ἐγγυτάτω τρισὶ νόμισμά τι βραχὺ μνήμης ἕνεκα καὶ μαρτυρίας.

55 Partsch 1921, p. 116, referring to the responsibility of the magistrate in the registration of deeds speaks of "knowledge of the legal relationships in relation to the properties." He attributes the function of notary to the magistrate. For a restatement of this interpretation see Faraguna 2021, pp. 330–331. On the presence of magistrates in private land sale deeds and the increase in public intervention over time see also Zelnick-Abramowitz 2015.

56 Thus Faraguna 2000 and 2021, pp. 293–367, to whom we refer for further considerations on the topic addressed in this paragraph, and in particular with respect to Theophrastus' *On Contracts* and the registration and execution of deeds of sale, the presence of cadastral lists, and the magistrates involved in the sale.

57 Faguer 2020, p. 161. On the arrangement of the acts in the stele and its significance he refers to Gauthier 1992 and Faraguna 2019. See now Faraguna 2021, pp. 325–327.

to the payment of the price, clearly emerges, especially when the documents are the personal copy of a public record. But, as has been shown also recently by M. Faraguna, they have several elements that can be traced back to the second part of the deed, that relating to registration, which is the task of the magistrates.

I will in conclusion concentrate on a couple of examples among many others. The first is the reference in the heading of several deeds from Olynthus and Macedonia to a definitive deed (οὐνὴ εὐθεῖα).[58] The statement that the deed is concluded, and therefore can no longer be disputed, implies an intervention by magistrates who have accepted it as valid, probably also through the acquisition of registration fees. For this reason when the label *oune eutheia* is present, it could mean that the real estate is transferred from the seller to the buyer in a final and permanent way and the deed is registered by state officials. The statement that the sale was paid in full (τὴν τιμὴν ἔχει πᾶσαν) found in the set of land purchased by Zopyros son of Gorgias, in the Macedonian city of Mieza (dating ca. 250–225 BCE), could also refer to a similar context.[59]

Public intervention, however, can also be determined by any disputes that occur over land that is sold. This may be again the case with Zopyros' plots of land. These are ten spanned over two years' deeds of sale of contiguous lands, all in favor of Zopyros, totaling more than 32 hectares. The structure of these deeds is similar to that of the sale deeds of the Chalcidic peninsula and Amphipolis,[60] with the name of the buyer, the name of the seller, a summary description of the property and its size, the price paid, the guarantors and witnesses and, finally, the mention of the eponymous *epistates* and the magistrates probably in charge of registering the sales (the ταγωνᾶται[61]). In some of these deeds, witnesses of the judges are mentioned (μάρτυρες δικαστῶν), and there is the abovementioned indication that the price was paid in full.[62]

---

58 On *oune eutheia* as 'achat ferme, direct' see Hatzopoulos in I.Chalcidique actes no. II, 23–27; *contra* Thür 2008 (who distinguishes between *oune eutheia*, 'blocked sale', and *katochos*, 'definitive sale'); Game 2008, pp. 44–45 ('achat immédiat'), Erdas 2012, p. 350 nt. 20; Faraguna 2021, p. 371 nt. 178 and now Harris 2023, who, after a lexical and epigraphical analysis, defines it as 'incontestable sale' (see also Harris 2008).

59 SEG 53.613. Deed C, ll. 19–22: Ζώπυρος Γοργία ἐπρίατο πα[ρὰ] Ε[ὐ]πολέμου τοῦ Στάρτ|20ιος ἐν Δροέσται<ς> ψιλῆς πλέθρα [: – ' :], τὰ ἐχόμενα τῶν | ἀμπέλων τῶν Ἀττίνα καὶ τῆς γῆς ἧς παρὰ Βίωνος ἠγόρα|σε Ζώπυρος, τὸ πλέθρον δραχμῶν ⁝ ο' ⁝· τὴ[ν τιμ]ὴν ἔχει πᾶσαν. If the seller has received a deposit, such a clause may indicate that the payment is complete and the deed has been registered (for a discussion of the transfer of property when a deposit has been paid see Theophr. fr. 97 Szegedy-Maszak = 650 Fortenbaugh, 47–55).

60 For which it is therefore possible to think, by analogy with the Zopyros dossier, of a registration made before the magistrate, perhaps aimed at collecting registration fees (Faraguna 2021, pp. 435–436).

61 Helly/Mari 2018, p. 352; Faraguna 2021, p. 345.

62 The phrase τὴν τιμὴν ἔχει πᾶσαν appears only once after the name of the guarantor (Deed B, ll. 12–13), while in the other cases it always refers to Zopyros. If this is not a transcription error on the stele (which is possible), in that one case it may indicate an active role of the guarantor in paying for the land.

The presence of witnesses of the judges[63] and the statement that the sale is valid (because the price has been paid in full) could, however, conceal a dispute over the land that arose around their sale, perhaps relating to the integrity of the property purchased. This would have prompted Zopyros to have the previously recorded deeds transcribed in stone.[64] In conclusion, therefore, even in a private copy that records a series of sales, the presence of the state emerges at several levels, both in the magistrates in charge of the registration and in official figures involved in the transactions as a result of disputes over the property sold.

Bibliography

ARNAOUTOGLOU, Ilias (2023) A Prolonged Birth of a Concept: The Unity of Greek Law: Response to S. C. Todd, in: Philipp SCHEIBELREITER (ed.), Symposion 2022. Akten der Gesellschaft für Griechische und Hellenistische Rechtsgeschichte 29, Vienna, 285–292.

VAN BREMEN, Riet (1996) The Limits of Participation. Women and Civic Life in the Greek East in the Hellenistic and Roman Periods, Amsterdam.

BRESSON, Alain (2016) The Making of the Ancient Greek Economy, Princeton.

CAHILL, Nicholas (2002) Household and City Organization at Olynthus, New Haven/London.

COBETTO GHIGGIA, Pietro (2012), Iseo. Orazioni, Alessandria.

CORDANO, Federica (1997) Su due tavolette di Camarina con contratti d'acquisto, in: La parola del passato 52, 355–362.

DUBOIS, Laurent (2008) Inscriptions grecques dialectales de Sicile II, Geneva.

ERDAS, Donatella (2012) Note sulla garanzia personale negli atti di vendita nella Grecia antica, in: Annali della Scuola Normale Superiore di Pisa 4, 345–364.

ERDAS, Donatella (2018) What Laws Applied to Guarantors? Epigraphic Evidence for Legal Procedure Affecting Personal Security in Athens and Beyond, in: Annali della Scuola Normale Superiore di Pisa 10, 333–358.

ERDAS, Donatella (2020a) Funzionari pubblici e chora. Osservazioni sulla gestione delle terre nelle città greche tra età classica ed ellenismo, in: Michele FARAGUNA/Simonetta SEGENNI (ed.), Forme e modalità di gestione amministrativa nel mondo greco e romano: terra, cave e miniere, Milan, 171–188.

ERDAS, Donatella (2020b) Terre e proprietà nelle Cicladi. Il caso di Amorgos, in: Alessandra INGLESE (ed.), Epigrammata V. Dinamiche politiche e istituzionali nell'epigrafia delle Cicladi, Tivoli, 163–184.

ÉTIENNE, Roland (1990) Ténos II. Ténos et les Cyclades du milieu du IVe siècle av. J.-C. au milieu du IIIe siècle ap. J.-C., Paris.

FAGUER, Julien (2020) Ventes immobilières et sûretés réelles à Ténos et Paros, in: Bulletin de Correspondance Hellénique 144, 155–207.

FARAGUNA, Michele (1997) Registrazioni catastali nel mondo greco: il caso di Atene, in: Athenaeum 85, 7–33.

---

63 These are possibly the *basilikoi dikastai* mentioned in another Macedonian inscription from Tyrissa (SEG 47.999, 3rd cent. BCE). See ZELNICK-ABRAMOWITZ 2015, p. 51 and nt. 43.

64 Zelnick-Abramowitz suggests that the register may have been published because Zopyros' assets had been confiscated by the city-state and had to be resold or auctioned (ZELNICK-ABRAMOWITZ 2015, pp. 49–52).

FARAGUNA, Michele (2012) Diritto, economia, società: riflessioni su eranos tra età omerica e mondo ellenistico, in: Bernard LEGRAS (ed.), Transferts culturels et droits dans le monde grec et hellénistique, Paris, 129–154.

FARAGUNA, Michele (2019) Loans in an Island Society: The Astynomoi-inscription from Tenos, in: Sophie DEMARE-LAFONT (ed.), Debt in Ancient Mediterranean Societies. A Documentary Approach, Genèeva, 215–234.

FARAGUNA, Michele/BOFFO, Laura (2021) Le poleis e i loro archivi. Studi su pratiche documentarie, istituzioni e società nell'antichità greca, Trieste.

FARAGUNA, Michele (2023) Territorio della polis e statuti giuridici e amministrativi della terra: terminologia, concetti, problemi, in: Denis ROUSSET/Pascale DERRON (eds.), Les concepts de la géographie grecque. Entretiens sur l'antiquité classique, Vandoeuvres, 213–265.

FERRUCCI, Stefano (1998) L'Atene di Iseo. L'organizzazione del privato nella prima metà del IV sec. a.C., Pisa.

FERRUCCI, Stefano (2005) La ricchezza nascosta. Osservazioni su aphanes e phanera ousia, in: Mediterraneo Antico 8, 145–170.

FINLEY, Moses I. (1952) Studies in Land and Credit in Ancient Athens, 500–200 B. C. The Horos-Inscriptions, New Brunswick/N. J.

FORTENBAUGH, William Wall et al. (1992) Theophrastos of Eresus. Sources for his Life, Writings, Thought and Influence, II, Leiden/New York/Cologne.

GAGARIN, Michael/PERLMAN, Paula Jean (2016) The Laws of Ancient Crete c.650–400 BCE, Oxford.

GAME, Jean (2008) Actes de vente dans le monde grec: témoignages épigraphiques des ventes immobilières, Lyon.

GAUTHIER, Philippe (1992) L'archonte éponyme à Ténos, in: Revue des Études Grecque 105, 111–120.

GERNET, Louis (1951) Le Droit de la vente et la notion du contrat en Grece d'apres M. Pringsheim, in: Revue historique de droit français et étranger 29, 560–584.

GRIFFITH-WILLIAMS, Brenda (2019) Isaios 6: A Case of Procedural Abuse (and scholarly misunderstandings), in: Christopher CAREY/Ifigeneia GIANNADAKI/Brenda GRIFFITH-WILLIAMS (eds.), Use and Abuse of Law in the Athenian Courts, Leiden/Boston, 95–109.

HARRIS, Edward Monroe (1998) When a Sale is not a Sale? The Riddle of Athenian Terminology for Real Security Revisited, in: Classical Quarterly 38, 351–381 [Harris, E. M. (2006) Democracy and the Rule of Law in Classical Athens. Essays on Law, Society, and Politics, Cambridge, 163–206].

HARRIS, Edward Monroe (2008) Response to Gerhard Thür, in: Edward Monroe HARRIS/Gerhard THÜR (eds.), Symposion 2007. Akten der Gesellschaft für Griechische und Hellenistische Rechtsgeschichte 20, Vienna, 189–202.

HARRIS, Edward Monroe (2016) The Legal Foundations of Economic Growth in Ancient Greece. The Role of Property Records, in: Edward Monroe HARRIS/David Martin LEWIS/Mark WOOLMER (eds.), The Ancient Greek Economy. Markets, Households and City-States, Cambridge, 116–146.

HARRIS, Edward Monroe (2023) The Language of Sale in Documents about Property from Northern Greece, in: Zeitschrift für Papyrologie und Epigraphik 225, 93–102.

HARRIS, Edward Monroe (2024) Unity and diversity in ancient Greek law, in: Classica et Medievalia Supplementum 1, 129–157.

HATZOPOULOS, Miltiades B. (1988) Actes de vente de la Chalcidique centrale, Athens.

HELLY, Bruno/MARI, Manuela (2018) Tagoi, tagai e *tagonatai in Macedonia, in: Francesco CAMIA/Lavino DEL MONACO/Michela NOCITA (eds.), Munus Laetitiae. Studi miscellanei offerti a Maria Letizia Lazzarini, Rome, 261–282.

Hennig, Dieter (1987) Kaufverträge über Häuser und Ländereien aus der Chalkidike und Amphipolis, in: Chiron 17, 143–170.
Hennig, Dieter (1994) Immobilienerwerb durch Nichtbürger in der klassischen und hellenistischen Polis, in: Chiron 24, 305–344.
Leão, Delfim M./Rhodes, Peter John (2015) The Laws of Solon. A New Edition with Introduction, Translation and Commentary, London/New York.
Mackil, Emily (2018) Property Security and its Limits in Classical Greece, in: Mirko Canevaro/Andrew Erskine/Benjamin Gray (eds.), Ancient Greek History and Contemporary Social Science, Edinburgh, 315–343.
Maffi, Alberto (2012) Ancora sulla condizione giuridica della donna nel Codice di Gortina, in: Dike 15, 93–123.
Manganaro, Giacomo (1997) Nuove tavolette di piombo iscritte siceliote, in: La parola del passato 52, 306–335.
Migeotte, Léopold (1984) L'emprunt public dans les cités grecques, Québec.
Partsch, Joseph (1909) Griechisches Bürgschaftsrecht, I. Das Recht des altgriechischen Gemeindstaat, Leipzig/Berlin.
Partsch, Joseph (1921) Die griechische Publizität der Grundstücksverträge im Ptolemäerrechte, in: Festschrift für Otto Lenel zum fünfzigjährigen Doctorjubiläum am 16. Dezember 1921, Leipzig, 77–203.
Pernin, Isabelle (2014) Les baux ruraux en Grèce ancienne. Corpus épigraphique et étude, Lyon.
Pringsheim, Fritz (1950) The Greek Law of Sale, Weimar.
Souza, Randall (2016) Hellenistic Sicilian Real Estate Contracts Inscribed on Lead Tablets: New Readings and Implications for the Economic Independence of Women, in: Zeitschrift für Papyrologie und Epigraphik 197, 149–166.
Stavrianopoulou, Eftychia (2006) "Gruppenbild mit Dame": Untersuchungen zur rechtlichen und sozialen Stellung der Frau auf den Kykladen im Hellenismus und in der römischen Kaiserzeit, Stuttgart.
Szegedy-Maszak, Andrew (1981) The 'Nomoi' of Theophrastus, New York.
Thür, Gerhardt (2007) Die Einheit des "Griechischen Rechts". Gedanken zum Prozessrecht in den griechischen Poleis, in: Etica & Politica 9, 25–54.
Thür, Gerhardt (2008) Ownership and Security in Macedonian Sale Documents, in: Edward Monroe Harris/Gerhardt Thür (eds.), Symposion 2007. Akten der Gesellschaft für Griechische und Hellenistische Rechtsgeschichte 20, Vienna, 173–187.
Todd, Steven C. (2023) The Discovery of the Gortyn Code and Nineteenth-Century Debates over the Unity of Greek Law, in: Philipp Scheibelreiter (ed.), Symposion 2022. Akten der Gesellschaft für Griechische und Hellenistische Rechtsgeschichte 29, Wien, 263–284.
Youni, Maria (1996) À propos de quatre inscriptions olynthiennes: quelques remarques sur la 'sûreté réelle' au 4ème s. av. J.-C., in: Tekmeria 2, 135–153.
Zelnick-Abramowitz, Rachel (2015) Public Registers of Land Sales in Ancient Greece, in: Éva Jakab (ed.), Sale and Community Documents from the Ancient World. Individuals' Autonomy and State Interference in the Ancient World. Proceedings of a Colloquium supported by the University of Szeged. Budapest 5–8.10.2012, Trieste, 41–65.

Alain Bresson (University of Chicago)

Ancient Greek monetary laws and regulations*

Our best information on ancient Greek monetary laws and regulations until the Roman unification of the Mediterranean by Augustus consists of a number of literary sources, inscriptions, and papyri, but these represent only a minuscule fraction of the ancient body of laws and regulations concerning money.[1] Beyond texts, we have another source of information, the coin evidence, which does not provide the laws and regulations themselves, but reveals their consequences. In this respect, we are in the position of the prisoners in the cave, who can only perceive the shadows of the laws. These shadows present us with a formidable challenge. Fortunately, we have a few "puppets" – our current textual documentation of ancient monetary laws and regulations – which are of great importance in making sense of the "shadows dancing on the wall of our cave" – the effects of the whole body of ancient legislation that we perceive through our numismatic evidence.

Leaving aside the specific question of credit-money, it is commonly said that, starting at the end of the Archaic period, money in the ancient world took the form of coinage. This view requires some qualifications.[2] But for the sake of analysis, let us take it as the starting point of the inquiry. In this respect, the main finding of recent numismatic research is that coins were largely minted to fund war. This was first demonstrated for the Hellenistic monarchies.[3] Then the same conclusion was drawn for many civic mints. For the Classical and Hellenistic periods, a long series of civic mints is currently considered to have been merely proxies for Achaemenid satraps or Hellenistic kings, who used them to strike coins to pay their soldiers.[4] It may seem tempting to generalize the model and apply it to earlier periods, returning to the model proposed by Robert Cook in 1958, who suggested that the reason for the initial development of coinage was the need to pay soldiers.[5] It has even been argued that, beyond minting, the circulation of coins was also mainly linked to military milieux and to the immediate expenses of soldiers.[6]

---

* I wish to extend my gratitude to Jane Johnson for her invaluable help in the preparation of this study.

1 For Roman monetary legislation, Rüfner 2016, for the eastern, Greek-speaking provinces Katsari 2011, and Bresson 2017 for the cities of Roman Asia Minor.

2 See below, § 1.

3 de Callataÿ 1997 and 2000.

4 de Callataÿ 2021 and 2022.

5 Cook 1958.

6 de Callataÿ 2019.

The question of how coinage and monetization developed in the ancient world is notoriously complex. While war was undeniably a major factor in minting decisions, it was not the only one, and, above all, the phenomenon of coinage as a whole cannot be reduced to it.[7] Once minted, coins had "a life of their own," and the reasons for their circulation could vary greatly. Moreover, if war was the alpha and omega of both coin minting and circulation in the ancient world, how is it that we have a series of laws and regulations for cities, federal states *(koina)*, kingdoms, and principalities organizing the usage and circulation of coinage?

We face here a fundamental characteristic of the ancient Greek money supply, which to some extent remained valid in the Roman Imperial period: the disjunction between the reasons for minting and the characteristics of circulation.[8] We are used to thinking of money in terms of the public good, circulated by states to satisfy the general needs of their populations and their economic actors. This notion only partially applies in the ancient world, since coinage was first conceived as a tool to serve the immediate needs of the state. But this does not mean that, whatever the reasons for minting coinage, states did not also consider it to be a public good that they had to carefully manage, if only because they collected their taxes in coined money – all of them in the case of the cities, or part of them in the case of the kingdoms, the rest being levied in kind.[9] This explains the bodies of laws and regulations they established.

Money, currency, and the law

The link between law, *nomos,* and money, *nomisma,* was explained by Aristotle himself in the *Nicomachean Ethics.* In Book V, analyzing the conditions of reciprocity within the framework of the community, he explains

> In reality, this measure is need *(chreia)*, which holds everything together; for if people needed nothing, or needed things to different extents, there would be either no exchange or not the same exchange. And currency has become a sort of pledge of need, by convention; in fact it has its name *(nomisma)* because it is not by nature, but

---

7 Bresson 2001 with 2020 for the context of the development of the first coinages in Archaic Lydia and the Greek cities of western Asia Minor.

8 Bresson 2005, p. 50.

9 von Reden 2007, pp. 58–83, for Ptolemaic Egypt, and more broadly 2010, pp. 18–47; see also Bresson 2018, pp. 132–133.

by the current law *(nomos)*, and it is within our power to alter it and to make it useless. (trans. Irwin)[10]

If we accept Aristotle's view, the notion of *nomisma,* money understood as currency, is in essence linked to the rule of law. These lines have recently been commented on by various scholars, such as Sitta von Reden and Stefan Eich.[11] The word *nomisma* derives from *nomizein,* a verb that means, among other things, "to be in common use," or "to enact" (for a legislator). *Nomisma* may have a broad sense of "custom" or "institution," and it may also have a more specific sense of "currency," more precisely of "coinage," and also of (non-monetary) "legal measure." The various meanings coexisted, and this is how, for example, Aristophanes could play on the meanings of "institution" and "money" for *nomisma* in the *Clouds.*[12]

As for the monetary meaning, the sense of "currency" allows us to understand the situation of the states that did not have a coinage of their own. This was famously the case with the Spartans. In the *Lives* of Lykourgos and Lysandros, Plutarch, whose sources date back to the 4th and 3rd centuries, states that the Spartans did not use a precious metal coinage, but only iron spits, the metal of which had been made unusable by being quenched in vinegar when red hot. He explicitly defined this iron money as "iron currency" *(nomisma).*[13] Polybius also referred to their "iron currency as one of the characteristics of the backwardness of the Spartans."[14] The same definition found its way into Pollux's *Lexicon:* "The Lacedaemonians used an iron currency *(nomisma).*"[15] Plutarch also asserts that it was common to people of the past "to use for some iron currencies and for others bronze ones."[16] The iron spits at the Argive Heraion might help us to figure out what these iron or bronze spits looked like, although their interpretation remains controversial.[17]

In the case of Sparta, the word *nomisma* does not apply to a coinage struck in a metal that was gold, silver, or bronze, like the tin coins struck by Dionysius of

---

10 Aristotle, Nicomachean Ethics 5.5.11. 1133a: δεῖ ἄρα ἑνί τινι πάντα μετρεῖσθαι, ὥσπερ ἐλέχθη πρότερον. τοῦτο δ᾽ ἐστὶ τῇ μὲν ἀληθείᾳ ἡ χρεία, ἣ πάντα συνέχει: εἰ γὰρ μηθὲν δέοιντο ἢ μὴ ὁμοίως, ἢ οὐκ ἔσται ἀλλαγὴ ἢ οὐχ ἡ αὐτή: οἷον δ᾽ ὑπάλλαγμα τῆς χρείας τὸ νόμισμα γέγονε κατὰ συνθήκην: καὶ διὰ τοῦτο τοὔνομα ἔχει νόμισμα, ὅτι οὐ φύσει ἀλλὰ νόμῳ ἐστί, καὶ ἐφ᾽ ἡμῖν μεταβαλεῖν καὶ ποιῆσαι ἄχρηστον.

11 von Reden 2003, p. 189, n. 22; Eich 2022, pp. 25–27.

12 Aristophanes, The Clouds 247–248. See also later the case of the philosopher Diogenes the Cynic, Diogenes Laertios 6.20–21, 56, 71, with Eich 2022, p. 28. See also Demosthenes, Orations 24.213 and the play upon *nomisma* as instituted law and currency.

13 Plutarch, Lykourgos 19.1: σιδηροῦν νόμισμα.

14 Polybios 6.49.8: τὸ νόμισμα τὸ σιδηροῦν.

15 Pollux 9.77: σιδηρῷ δὲ νομίσματι καὶ Λακεδαιμόνιοι χρῶνται.

16 Plutarch, Lysandros 17.4: ὀβελίσκοις χρωμένων νομίσμασι σιδηροῖς, ἐνίων δὲ χαλκοῖς.

17 The monetary nature of these iron spits is denied by Kroll 2001, but accepted by Strøm 2009, p. 87.

Syracuse, referred to in Ps-Aristotle's *Economics,* the iron coins used as a temporary expedient by the Clazomenians, mentioned in the same work, or the iron coins of Byzantium, referred to by Strepsiades in the *Clouds.*[18] In all these cases we are dealing with coins, and in the first two the use of the verb "to strike" (*ekopse* or *ekopsan*) indicates a crucial difference, as it refers directly to coined money. In Herodotus' famous reference to the role of the Lydians in the introduction of a gold and silver coinage, "they were the first people we know of who struck and made use of a currency of gold and silver," the key word is "struck" *(kopsamenoi).*[19] It was the striking process that produced the specific form of *nomisma* that would become known as coinage. But *nomisma* in the monetary sense could exist separately from coinage, as proved by the Spartans' iron money.

These observations invite us to go one step further. It is clear that the Greeks of the Classical and later periods created their own image of those they called their first legislators (*nomothetai),* and specifically of their role in monetary matters. Pheidon of Argos is said to have introduced coinage in Greece, and Theseus of Athens to have struck the first Athenian coinage. The texts are indicative of how the Greeks thought of their past, but not of the actual history of the development of coinage.[20]

The case of Solon, however, is more complex.[21] According to Androtion and the Aristotelian *Constitution of the Athenians,* Solon modified both the Athenian system of weights and measures and that of the silver drachm, which was reduced from 1/70 of a mina (6.2 g) to 1/100 (4.3 g).[22] He also established a system of equivalences between a quantity of grain, a *medimnos,* a sheep, and a silver drachm.[23] The authenticity of this legislation has been the subject of heated debate.

The author of the *Constitution of the Athenians* mentions in this passage that "the ancient coin-type was the didrachm."[24] Therefore there is no doubt that he believed that Solon's reform was about coinage. Indeed, the main denomination of Athenian coinage before the Owl (the first Wappenmünzen and the Gorgoneia series) was the didrachm.[25] Clearly, a reliable memory of the monetary situation two centuries before the writing of the *Constitution* had been preserved. But this seems to condemn the authenticity of the reforms attributed to Solon. In fact, coinage was not introduced

---

18 [Aristotle], Economics 2.2.20c 1349a: νόμισμα ἔκοψε καττιτέρου; 2.2.16 1348b: νόμισμα ἔκοψαν σιδηροῦν; Aristophanes, The Clouds 248: σιδαρέοισιν, ὥσπερ ἐν Βυζαντίῳ.

19 Herodotus 1.94.3: κοψάμενοι πρῶτοι δὲ ἀνθρώπων τῶν ἡμεῖς ἴδμεν νόμισμα χρυσοῦ καὶ ἀργύρου κοψάμενοι ἐχρήσαντο.

20 Picard 2001 and 2015; Bresson 2012.

21 van Alfen/Ober 2018, pp. 489–491.

22 Androtion FGrH 324 F 34 (Plutarch, Solon 15.3–4; fragment 64/1a Leão/Rhodes); [Aristotle], Constitution of the Athenians 10.1–2 (fr. 64/1a Leão/Rhodes).

23 Plutarch, Solon 23.3 (fragment 77 Ruschenbusch; fragment 80.2 Leão/Rhodes).

24 [Aristotle], Constitution of the Athenians 10.2: ἦν δ᾽ ὁ ἀρχαῖος χαρακτὴρ δίδραχμον.

25 Kroll 1981.

in Athens before Peisistratus, more or less fifty years after Solon's reform, and there is no doubt that Solon's alleged reform could not have concerned coined money.

Does this mean that Solon's reform of the value of the drachm is just one of the many late forgeries that, for the sake of convenience, have been associated with the famous lawgiver? While everyone agrees that Solon could not have reformed the Athenian coin standard, it has been proposed that he may have reformed the weight of a raw silver drachm, which would have been used before the introduction of coinage. The point of contention is thus the question of the use of raw silver as money in pre-Solonian and Solonian Athens. Its existence is denied by Gil Davis, whose main argument is based on the total absence of Hacksilber hoards in mainland Greece in this period: this region would have transitioned directly from a barley standard to a coined silver one.[26] It is accepted by John Kroll, who underscores the references to gold and silver in Solon's laws and other texts of the period, leaving open the possibility of a Solonian reform of a raw-silver drachm.[27]

The absence, for now, of Hacksilber hoards similar to those that have been found in the Eastern Mediterranean may well reflect the scarcity of silver in mainland Greece, but not its total absence. The silver drachm may have been commonly used as a unit of account, and only rarely as a means of payment, especially to balance accounts. In societies of the Eastern Mediterranean and Mesopotamia, the shekel was a monetary unit in silver centuries before becoming a coin. It is therefore reasonable to assume that Solon reformed the raw-silver drachm, which was later misunderstood as a reform of silver coinage.

We can retain the concept of legislation on the use of raw and weighed silver as money, even if the unit, the drachm, as in pre-Peisistratid Athens, was a specific weight of silver and not yet an object sanctioned by the city, like the Spartan iron *obeliskos* or the coin modeled on it that appeared in Asia Minor in the 7th century. This also shows that the analysis of ancient Greek monetary laws cannot be limited to coinage: they encompassed a broader spectrum of monetary realities, including the use of raw monetary metals.

The decision-makers

At the beginning of Book 2 of Ps-Aristotle's *Economics,* the author specifies the conditions of good administration of the four types of *oikonomiai.* He describes those "of the king, of a satrap, of a city, and of an individual."[28] As for the administration of the king, he in turn defines four types of management: "about coined money,

26 Davis 2012.
27 Kroll 2008.
28 [Aristotle], Economics 2.1.1.1345b: βασιλική, σατραπική, πολιτική, ἰδιωτική.

about input, about output, about expenses."[29] He then defines the nature of the management of coinage: "as for currency, of what kind and when it must be made dear or cheap."[30] Finally, when he explains what expenses *(analōmata)* consist of, he adds: "and whether one must disburse coined money for expenses or goods in exchange of coined money."[31]

All of this assumes that decisions were made by kings or their deputies. Ps-Aristotle does not provide the same information for the satraps and the cities, but implicitly his comments must have also applied to these two forms of administration. Coins were minted by kings, satraps, and cities. In the late Archaic and Classical periods, the coin type, such as the Achaemenid Persian gold darics and silver siglos (the king depicted as a warrior with bow and arrow), could suffice to identify the mint.[32] The coin types of many Greek cities, such as Aigina, with the turtle on the obverse, and Athens, with the head of Athena on the obverse of its coins from c. 514 BCE, could also suffice to identify them.[33] In parallel, starting at the end of the Archaic period, it became increasingly common for cities, minor kings, and dynasts to have a legend clearly identifying the mint, especially as coin types could sometimes be shared with other mints in the same region.

As stated by T. Martin, the minting of a coinage was not per se a necessary demonstration of sovereignty in the abstract sense in which it is understood by modern states.[34] Many smaller Greek cities never had a coinage, and those that did could stop minting for long periods because they lacked adequate sources of metal or found it more convenient to use a foreign coinage. Nonetheless, it should also be noted that a state could impose the use of its coins on its new citizens, as when Smyrna absorbed the settlement of Magnesia by Sipylos c. 245–243 BCE. The treaty regulating the absorption stipulates: "The currency of the city will also be legal tender in Magnesia."[35] When Rhodes absorbed adjacent territories in Caria or the neighboring islands, either incorporating them into its own civic territory or transforming them into subject cities, it made sure that no local mint could operate and that only Rhodian coinage was legal tender in the various parts of its territory.[36]

---

29 Ibid. περὶ νόμισμα, περὶ τὰ ἐξαγώγιμα, περὶ τὰ εἰσαγώγιμα, περὶ τὰ ἀναλώματα.

30 Ibid. τὸ νόμισμα λέγω ποῖον καὶ πότε τίμιον ἢ εὔωνον ποιητέον. The words τίμιον ἢ εὔωνον are commonly regarded as an inauthentic addition. It is here suggested that they might refer to the relative value of the gold and silver coinages, given that the ratio of value between the two metals was constantly changing. This explanation would fit with the "of what kind," that is, gold or silver, of the first part of the sentence.

31 Ibid. καὶ πότερον δοτέον νόμισμα εἰς τὰς δαπάνας ἢ ἀντὶ νομίσματι ὤνια.

32 Alram 2012.

33 Sheedy 2012; van Alfen 2012.

34 Martin 1986.

35 I.Smyrna II 573 + II 2, 376, l. 55: δεχέσθωσαν δὲ καὶ ἐμ Μαγνησίαι τὸ νόμισμα τὸ τῆς πόλεως [ἔνν]ομον.

36 On the coinage of Rhodes, Ashton 2001.

The decision to mint and add a legend identifying the issuing authority was based on practical reasons. Many coinages were used directly to pay soldiers, so it was in the best interest of the minting authority to stress who had minted them. This explains, for example, the frequency with which Thracian kings and minor rulers added a legend with their names to their coins, since Thrace was a major supplier of soldiers and mercenaries from the Archaic to the Hellenistic period.[37]

Remarkably, some of these kings or rulers even added an explicit reference to the nature of the currency or the mark it bore. This is the case with the coins of Getas, a king of the southwestern Thracian tribe of the Edones, who reigned c. 480–460 BCE. Most of his coins simply mentioned that he was the "king of the Edones" *(basileus Edōneōn)*. But a rare series bears the legend "Currency *(nomisma)* of Getas king of the Edones."[38] This is more than one generation before Herodotus, the first author in our literary sources to use the word *nomisma* to refer to coined money.[39] The silver didrachms of the Odrysian king Seuthes – Seuthes I (424–410/5) or perhaps Seuthes II (410/5–390/85) – bore on its obverse either the legend "Money *(argyrion)* of Seuthes" or "Coinage *(komma)* of Seuthes."[40] Much later, Kotys III, a king of southeastern Thrace between c. 31 and 23/2 BCE, struck tetradrachms of the Thasian type with the legend "Coin-type *(charaktēr)* of Kotys."[41]

If for a king, dynast, or satrap the decision-making process is clear, for the city it was the authorities in charge who made the decisions mentioned above. In fact, just like those of the kings and satraps, the cities' decisions were made to serve their own interests, but these interests were of a different nature. This explains why we have a series of civic laws and decrees relating to monetary matters. Undoubtedly they were discussed in the council and at the assembly, just like any other law or decree, before being voted on by the citizens, according to the legal procedure proper to each city. Proposed by the local benefactor Menas, the decree of the city of Sestos in the Thracian Chersonese at the end of the 2nd century BCE specifies:[42] "When the people decided to use a coinage of its own ..."[43]

In some rare cases, we have the echoes of the debate that could take place in the assembly on monetary matters. An early case is the debate in Sparta immediately after the fall of Athens in 404, when the possibility of accepting foreign gold and

37 Paunov 2015.

38 Ex Egger Collection (A. Tkalec AG, 27 October 2011), lot 25: νό[μ]ισμα Ἐδōνέōν βασιλέōς Γίτα. On the military usage of Thracian kings, Rufin Solas 2018.

39 Herodotus 1.94, 3.56, 4.166.

40 Peykov 2011 1# B0090 (https://en.numista.com/catalogue/pieces234192.html; also: BnF Luynes 1827): Σεύθα ἀργύριον. Peykov 2011 1# B0100 (https://en.numista.com/catalogue/pieces236712.html): Σεύθα κόμμα.

41 Prokopov 2006, no. 1860: Κότυος χαρακτήρ; de Callataÿ 2012 for the date and context.

42 See Robert 1973.

43 I.Sestos 1, ll. 43–44: τοῦ τε δήμου προελομέ|ν̣ου νομίσματι χαλκίνῳ χρῆσθαι ἰδίωι.

silver money in the city was discussed.[44] The ephors deliberated on the question and it was decided that the Spartans would keep their old iron spits. As the friends of Lysander opposed the measure, it was decided that gold and silver coinage would be held and used only by the city, not by individuals. Olivier Picard was right to suspect that, even if the point is not made by Plutarch, the friends of Lysander probably suggested that Sparta introduce a coinage of its own.[45]

A second case is that of Syracuse. The history of Greek cities also saw the rise of authoritarian rulers. At some point the tyrant Dionysius of Syracuse (in power between 406 and 367) found himself in dire straits: "As he was short of silver, he struck a tin coinage, and having summoned an assembly he ardently spoke in favor of it. The citizens perforce voted that everyone would accept as silver, not as tin, whatever he got."[46]

As in other matters referred to in the *Economics,* we see that Dionysius needed to obtain a vote of the citizens in order for his new coinage to be accepted.[47] In this case, the vote was forced by the tyrant. We can imagine that the situation was no different in the many cases in which a city minted for a satrap or a king, such as when Sinope minted a coinage for Datames.[48] But even in this case there was certainly a discussion and a vote to pass the law or decree.

Quite at the other end of the chronological spectrum, in the Roman Imperial period, the decision to mint a local bronze coin was still in the hands of the local authorities, council, and assembly.[49] Often it was a local benefactor who underwrote the cost of minting, but he first had to obtain the approval of the local authorities. This is reflected in the legends of some series, which could bear the formula (with a name in the genitive), so-and-so "made a request for a decree," and (seemingly) "made the proposal for a decree and dedicated."[50] Even in this period of elite government, the civic community was still officially in charge of coin minting.

---

44 Plutarch, Lysandros 17.2–4.

45 Picard 2015.

46 [Aristotle], Economics 2.2.20c 1349a: οὐκ εὐπορῶν δὲ ἀργυρίου νόμισμα ἔκοψε καττιτέρου, καὶ συναγαγὼν ἐκκλησίαν πολλὰ τοῦ κεκομμένου νομίσματος ὑπερεῖπεν· οἱ δὲ ἐψηφίσαντο καὶ μὴ βουλόμενοι ἕκαστος ὃ ἂν εἴλετο ἔχειν ὡς ἀργυροῦν ἀλλὰ μὴ καττιτέρινον.

47 Lewis 2021.

48 For the case of Datames, see [Aristotle], Economics 1350b or 2.2.24a and Polyainos, Strategemata 7.21.1, with de Callataÿ 2021, pp. 53–54, and 2022, pp. 52–53.

49 Weiss 2005.

50 "Made a request for a decree" αἰτησαμένου, Ancyra, RPC online I 3111–3112 (under Nero); Eukarpia III 2588 (Hadrian); Alia III 2614 and 2615 (Trajan). "Made the proposal for a decree" ψηφισαμένου, Stratonikeia IV 25110–25111, temp. (Marcus Aurelius). "Made the proposal for a decree and dedicated": ψηφισάμενος ἀνέθηκεν, Mylasa II 11971–198 (Titus). On these formulas, see Weiss 1992, 2000 and 2005, p. 62, and for Mylasa, specifically Delrieux 2010.

Coinage, society, and the law

Thus, unless there was a higher authority, such as a local tyrant, king, or satrap who could impose his own decisions, the decision whether or not to have coined money was in the hands of the civic authorities. But some cities deliberately refused to have their own coinage as a matter of principle. This was the case in Sparta before the 3rd century, in the alleged tradition of its legislator Lykourgos. At least for a while, this city even officially denied its own population the use of foreign coins. By law, only the state could hold and use coins.[51] This is confirmed by our archaeological sources.[52] Sparta had no coinage of its own, and very few foreign coins have been found on its territory. The reasons alleged by our ancient sources for their refusal to introduce coinage are the uselessness of a precious metal in a city that was accustomed to its "ancestral" *(patrion)* money, and the determination to prevent greed and private enrichment.[53] In fact, the real motive may have been the desire of the elite not to be challenged by members of the lower classes who would have benefited from the opportunities of an open and monetized market. The traditional form of *nomisma* fitted well with the traditional form of Sparta's social structure. Yet our ancient tradition also stresses that the Spartans were eager to get rich and accumulated precious metal in their homes.[54] The result was exactly the opposite of what the conservative leaders of the city advocated: the absence of a civic currency triggered private enrichment and inequality, which caused the collapse of the city.[55]

In the *Laws,* Plato advocated a model of the conservative city, in part inspired by Sparta and Crete.[56] This model was also based on the desire to limit the role of the market. Like the Cretan cities, it accepted the use of coined money (some of them began to mint in the 5th century), but it proposed a system of dual currency inspired by Sparta:[57]

> There follows also a law which forbids any private person to possess any gold or silver, only coin *(nomisma)* for purposes of such daily exchange as it is almost necessary for craftsmen to make use of, and all who need such things in paying wages to hirelings, whether slaves or immigrants. For these reasons we say that our people should possess currency *(nomisma)* which is legal tender among themselves, but valueless elsewhere. As regards the universal Hellenic currency *(koinon Hellenikon nomisma)*, – for the sake of expeditions and foreign visits, as well as of embassies or any other missions necessary

---

51 See above, with n. 44.
52 Bresson 2022, pp. 82–84.
53 Plutarch, Lysandros 17.2–4, with Christien 2002, pp. 178–179.
54 Plato, Alkibiades 1.123a.
55 Bresson 2022.
56 Bresson 2019a.
57 Plato, Laws 5.742a-c, tr. Loeb (modified). On the Cretan coinage, see below n. 117.

> for the State, if there be need to send someone abroad, – for such objects as these it is necessary that the State should always possess Hellenic currency. If a private citizen ever finds himself obliged to go abroad, he may do so, after first getting leave from the magistrates; and should he come home with any surplus of foreign currency, he shall deposit it with the State, and take for it an equivalent in home currency; but should anyone be found out keeping it for himself, the currency shall be confiscated, and the man who is privy to it and fails to inform, together with the man who has imported it, shall be liable to cursing and reproach and, in addition, to a fine not less than the amount of the foreign currency.[58]

The paradox is that, albeit in a completely different social framework, a dual currency system of the kind advocated by Plato was adopted by the Ptolemaic kingdom in the Hellenistic period. The kingdom minted a high-quality gold and silver coinage, used for war and foreign trade, and a massive bronze coinage, used in the Egyptian countryside. Peasants lived in a world of bronze coinage, but by law they had to exchange at an unfavorable rate their low-value coins for silver coins to pay their taxes.[59]

Many states in the Greek world followed a different path from that of Sparta and adopted coined money. Coined money was a facilitator of transactions and, as such, was at the core of city life in a huge wave that started with the increasingly widespread introduction of silver coinage in the second half of the 6th century.[60] By establishing a link between rich and poor, as well as between city and countryside, the use of coinage unified cities.[61] It also facilitated the development of civic life, especially in democratic regimes, because it allowed the many small payments to jurors, magistrates, and assembly attendees, on which democratic life was based, to be made conveniently.[62] The best example of this model, and the one that is the perfect antithesis of Sparta, is of course Athens, with its deep monetization based on its exceptionally abundant coinage.

But the decision to mint coins was also a matter of opportunity. Minting a precious metal coinage – commonly silver in the Greek world – required a reserve of precious met al. For a city like late Archaic and Classical Athens, with its enormously productive Laurion mines, this was not a problem.[63] And for late Archaic and Classical Aegina, which played a major role in international trade, it was easy to amass silver reserves. But many cities simply could not accumulate enough sil-

---

58 Plato, Laws 5.742a-c., tr. Loeb.
59 Burkhalter/Picard 2005; von Reden 2007, pp. 111–117; Bresson 2017, pp. 286–298.
60 Kim 2005, with map of active mints c. 480 BCE on p. 10.
61 Martin 1996.
62 Trevett 2001.
63 Flament 2007, pp. 241–253; Bresson 2019b.

ver to be able to mint. This is why most of them never minted silver, or only did so on rare occasions and in small quantities.

Only the largest and richest cities struck precious metal, and typically only for short periods. Even first-rank rulers or cities could find themselves in situations where they were unable to strike a precious metal coinage. We have already seen the tin coins struck by Dionysius of Syracuse, the iron coins of Byzantium, and the iron coins used as a temporary expedient by the Clazomenians.[64] Similarly, in the last phase of the Peloponnesian War, Athens, for want of silver, had to strike an emergency gold coinage in very small quantities, and a poor quality bronze coinage, as mentioned by Aristophanes in the *Frogs* of 405 BCE. It was still remembered by all when he wrote *Assemblywomen* in 392 BCE.[65] Over time, in the late Classical and Hellenistic periods, ever fewer cities were able to mint silver coins, although federal states, most famously the Achaian and Lycian Leagues, managed to have a significant common coinage.

The case of bronze is different. Bronze coinage used as small change was first introduced in Sicily around 450, and the system was quickly imitated all over the Greek world. Minting a bronze coinage did not require large stocks of silver. The innovation opened up the possibility for small cities to have a coinage of their own, if only a bronze one, for daily exchange in the agora and for small payments. Many, although again not all, jumped at this chance and introduced a bronze coinage.[66] The already-mentioned decree of Sestos gives two reasons for the decision to mint a bronze coinage: "so that the type *(charaktēr)* of the city be legal tender and that the people might get the profit linked to this source of revenue."[67] Thus, the two reasons are local pride and profit – the profit from minting, because the value of the coinage would be higher than the cost of minting it, and probably also because of the profit the city would make from the exchange between local and foreign coins.[68]

Most cities, including those with bronze coinage, also had to make some foreign currency legal tender in their own territory. This was Plato's *Hellenikon nomisma*, which in the Classical period was the coinage of Athens, and in the Hellenistic period the gold coinage of Philip and Alexander and the silver coinage of Alexander. For example, three early Hellenistic public loan contracts from Arkesine, on the

64 See above n. 18.
65 Aristophanes, Frogs 718–726 and Assemblywomen 815–822.
66 Brousseau 2013 and Psoma 2013.
67 I.Sestos 1, ll. 43–4§: χάριν τοῦ νομειτεύεσθαι μὲν τὸν τῆς π[ό|λ]εως χαρακτῆρα, τὸ δὲ λυσιτελὲς τὸ περιγεινόμενον ἐκ τῆς τοιαύτης προσόδου̣ | λαμβάνειν τὸν δῆμον.
68 Pace Martin 1986, pp. 238–241, and 1996, pp. 262–264; there is no reason to doubt the pride motivation of the Sestians: see Ellis-Evans 2017, p. 45.

island of Amorgos, show that in the cities of the Cyclades, international coinage on the Attic standard (coins from Athens or coinage in the name of Alexander or Demetrios) was the legally accepted *(dokimon)* means of payment for large amounts.[69]

Minting a coinage

One of the most fascinating discoveries of numismatic research in the last decade has been that of the alloy of electrum, the mixture of gold and silver that, probably starting between 650 and 625 BCE, was used to strike coins in western Asia Minor. The consensus had been that the choice of electrum was linked to the fact that it could be found in the sand of the river Pactolus, the river of Sardis. Thus it would have been struck purely for convenience. It has even been proposed that the introduction of coinage in the form of electrum coins was linked to the need to provide a state guarantee for a metal whose composition was constantly fluctuating.[70]

However, physical analysis has revealed a completely different landscape. We now know that the gold/silver ratio in electrum was precisely defined in each series, and differed from one series to the next:

Table 1: Gold-silver ratio in some early electrum series[71]

Type	% Gold	% Silver	% Copper
Smooth type	55	43	1.5
Striated type	60	39.5	0.5
Facing feline	53	44	2
Phanes type	45.5	51	2.5
Royal Lydian type	55	43	1.5

We can therefore be certain that the alloy was artificial and specially prepared for each series. A lead tablet discovered in the foundations of the late 7th century temple of Artemis at Ephesus is of special interest in the matter.[72] It mentions an operation of "working" together *(ergazesthai)* gold and silver (B l.8). If mixed together to prepare an electrum alloy, the proportions of gold and silver mentioned in the tablet

69 Migeotte, Emprunt 49, ll. 20–21; 50, ll. 20–23; 51, l. 11.
70 Wallace 1987. For an approach that emphasizes the role of local elites and a reconceptualization of the state in the phase of coinage emergence, see van Alfen 2020.
71 Ratios from Blet-Lemarquand and Duyrat 2020 and Gitler et al. 2020 for the Phanes series. The two batches of analyses have provided results that only marginally differ.
72 Kroll 2020.

would be 57 % gold and 43 % silver. This would fit perfectly with what we observe in the alloy of the coins. We cannot be certain that the mixture was intended for minting coins (it could have been for other purposes, such as the fabrication of an adornment for the goddess). But there seems to be no doubt that this tablet was used for the preparation of an electrum alloy.[73]

While most states abandoned electrum in the second half of the 6th century BCE, and the Greek cities that had a coinage switched massively to silver, the two neighboring cities of Phokaia and Mytilene kept an electrum coinage until the second half of the 4th century.[74] Each maintained its own types and mint. But since the standard of the coins was the same, they decided to organize a common system of minting, apparently with one city minting in turn after the other. The characteristics of the alloy of their coins were modified several times.[75] The need to regulate the proportions of gold and silver in electrum coins has been known for a long time, from the treaty between the two cities, which seems to date to the end of the 5th century BCE.[76] They organized a common court and harsh penalties to ensure that those in charge of preparing the alloy for the gold (in Greek, *chrysos,* but electrum is involved) did not reduce the proportion of precious metals: "If someone is caught wittingly alloying a weaker gold, he is to be sentenced to death."[77]

We can thus observe the care that states took in the minting of their coinages. In the case of cities, the quality of the metal, whether gold, silver, or electrum, was carefully defined and checked. This does not mean that the metal was always of the best quality: if a state lacked funds, the purity of the metal could be deliberately lowered by adding copper and lead, a practice referred to by Demosthenes in his speech *Against Timocrates.*[78] This is confirmed by numismatic research. In other words, there could be "good states," which produced good quality silver coins, and "bad states," which produced poor quality ones.[79]

A newly published law of Athens, the law of Epikrates of 354/3 BCE, allows us to go into detail about the management of the mint in this city. First edited by Molly Richardson, the text has been commented by Edward Harris and a new edition has

---

73 Bresson 2020.
74 Bodenstedt 1981.
75 See Gitler et al. 2020.
76 IG XII 2.1; Heisserer 1984; Engelmann 1985 (SEG 33.665); Mackil/van Alfen 2006, pp. 210–219; Bresson 2009.
77 Ll. 13–15: αἰ δέ κε καταγ[ρέ]θηι τὸ χρύσιον κέρ|ναν ὑδαρέστερ̣ο[ν] θέλων θανάτωι ζαμι|ώσθω.
78 Demosthenes, Orations 24.214.
79 For a comparison between the Rhodian mint (high fineness silver) and various Cretan ones (low fineness silver), see Barrandon/Bresson 1997.

been provided by Angelos Chaniotis and Robert Pitt.[80] The stone is badly worn, and it is not possible to read the whole text. However, several key aspects are clear enough. The beginning of the text (ll. 4–6) defines the objectives of the law: the point was to make sure that there was enough money for the rituals to Hephaistos and Athena Hephaistia, "and as much money as possible for the general budget *(dioikēsis)* from the mint *(argyrokopion)*.[81] The silver mint was thus considered a source of income to be used for the cults of Hephaistos and Athena Hephaistia and for the general financial resources of the city, in direct parallel with the decree of Sestos.[82] The motivation clause of the law thus reinforces the view that the minting of a coinage, despite its cost, could be a source of profit for the minting state.

For Harris (implicitly restoring *episēmon*, l. 8), the law regulated the exchange of coins and the purification of the silver from the ore coming from the mine. Matthaiou and Pitt read and restore line 8 differently *([t]o a[r]gyrion to asēmon)*; for them, the law concerned the production of coins from the silver bullion coming from the mine and brought forward by private individuals. In any case, the law (ll. 14–15) also refers explicitly to receiving coins *(episēmon argyrion)*, obviously by the mint, in exchange for Attic currency.[83] Thus, we can be certain that Athenian laws regulated both the production of Attic coins from reminted coins and from bullion. The law of Epikrates defined a specific location in the agora for the main operation at stake (l. 8: *hopou kai*) and possibly referred to a specific location for the exchange of the *episēmon argyrion* (ll. 14–15). Interestingly, the almost contemporaneous law of Olbia defined a specific location for the exchange of gold and silver coins, "the stone in the *ekklēsiastērion*", implicitly distinct from that for the exchange of bullion.[84] The purpose of these specifications was obviously to facilitate control.

The Athenian state made a profit by providing fresh coins to those who brought their coins for reminting (foreign coins, including coins of the Athenian type that were not accepted as legal tender, and possibly also old Attic ones) or silver bullion from the mine. In addition, everyone benefited from an increase in the circulation of fresh coins. This helps us to understand why, from the Archaic to the Hellenistic periods, cities could mint coins on behalf of various kings, satraps, or other minor rulers.[85] In doing so, they were offered, free of charge so to speak, the opportunity

---

80 Richardson 2021, with the new supplements and comments of Harris 2022, Matthaiou and Pitt 2024; see also Kroll 2024. Edward Harris and Selene Psoma are preparing a new edition of the law with full commentary.

81 These lines have been restored and explained by Harris 2022, 69–71.

82 See also below, § 5, for the possible connection between the law of Epikrates and the decree of Dyme against counterfeiters.

83 See Kroll 2024, 45.

84 IOSPE I^2 24, ll. 9–10. On the law, see also below § 5.

85 See above, § 1.

to make a profit and to have their own monetary type widely circulated—the two reasons given by the Sestos decree for the circulation of a coinage. They could also create a closed currency system if they wished.[86] This certainly explains why cities gladly accepted the more or less assertive suggestions of these rulers.

Some of the other clauses of the law of Epikrates that we can make sense of despite the mutilation of the stone refer to various aspects of the coin production, such as the supervision of the slaves working at the mint, the weighing operations, and the actual processing of the met al. The law thus refers to a process (l. 7 *katergazētai* from the verb *katergazesthai*), which in this context refers to the various operations linked to coin minting.[87] Furthermore, the city will have to see to it that there is no delay in the production of the coins (ll. 16–20): the *epistatai,* that is, the officials supervising the mint, will have to force the public slaves *(tous dēmosious)* working at the mint to do their work, so that the individuals *(hoi idiōtai)* will receive as soon as possible the coined money *(episēmon argyrion)* to which they are entitled.

An excellent parallel to the Athenian law is provided by a Ptolemaic papyrus dated to 258 BCE.[88] It is a letter to the *dioikētēs* Apollonios from a person who oversaw the minting of gold in Alexandria. His task was to process (*katergazesthai,* ll. 6 and 15–16) the foreign or old Ptolemaic gold coins in order to exchange them for new Ptolemaic coins. But, by order of his superior, he could only accept a limited quantity of them. Foreign importers, merchants, wholesale buyers, and all the people who brought their coins to the mint complained about the situation. Business suffered and everyone was unhappy (ll. 9–34). The man complains that he is compelled (*anagkazometha,* l. 19) not to receive the coins adequately. As a result, the king's revenue was significantly damaged (ll. 35–37) and his coinage was not "fine and new" (ll. 43–45), as it should be.

The Athenian law *(nomos)* and the reference to a Ptolemaic edict (*prostagma,* l. 14) are direct parallels. They aim to increase the income from the mint (Athens: law l. 6; Ptolemaic Egypt: letter ll. 35–37) by improving and speeding up the minting process. The parallel even extends to the detail of the vocabulary, with references to process, *katergazesthai* (law l. 7/letter ll. 6, 15–16), to compel, *epanagkazein* (law l. 17–18), and *anagkazein* (letter l. 19). Both the city of Athens and the Ptolemaic kingdom should have coins in large quantities and of good quality (law l. 7 *hōs pleiston kai kalliston* / letter 42–45 *chrysion hoti pleiston eisagētai kai to nomisma tou basileōs kalon kai kainon ēi dia pantos*). Interestingly, bottlenecks like those in Athens and Alexandria also occurred at the Zecca, the mint of Venice,

86 See below, § 6.
87 For the meaning of *katergazesthai* in the context of a mint workshop, see Bresson 2015, 127–128 and 131.
88 P.Cair.Zen. 1 59021, with Bresson 2015.

in the 14th and 15th centuries. Merchants complained about the delays in getting their ducats from the mint, and the Venetian state also had to legislate repeatedly to alleviate the situation.[89]

Circulating a coinage

An Eretrian law of c. 525 BCE required that payments to the city be made in "money *(chrēmata)* that is legal tender and of good quality."[90] The question of what is meant here by *chrēmata* is debated, and some have argued that it could just as easily refer to uncoined metal, or even to any kind of commodity used as a means of payment. The reference to "ten staters," a stater being a weight unit but also commonly a coin, makes it almost certain that precious metal coinage is meant here.[91] Eretria was also one of the first cities of mainland Greece to mint a silver coinage.[92] In a regulation from Olympia of c. 525–500 BCE, the payment of a fine in drachms, l. 7, and afterwards, l. 8, the interdiction to pay "with other money *(alotria chrēmata)*" – that is, someone else's or perhaps non-local money – are mentioned in the same context.[93] Elis, the city that controlled Olympia, began to mint its coinage in the late 6th century.[94] Finally, *chrēmata* commonly means money in coined form in the Classical period. Therefore, there is no reason to doubt that coins are referred to both at Eretria and Olympia. The interesting point is that the city of Eretria demanded payment in silver coins, which illustrates the role of coinage in the management of the city's income.

A coinage was therefore either legal tender or not, *dokimon* or *adokimon*. In Athens, also at the end of the 6th century BCE, Hippias recalled all circulating coins *(adokimon epoiēse)* on the pretext of reminting them with a new type.[95] But in fact he put them back into circulation without doing so, probably returning fewer of them to their former owners and thus making a profit on the operation.

---

89 Stahl 2000, 246–255 and Bresson 2015 for the parallel.

90 IG XII 9.1273/4, I ll. 2–3, χρέματα δόκιμα κα[ὶ h]υγιᾶ, with the new restorations and comments of Vanderpool and Wallace 1964; Cairns 1984; Walker 2004, pp. 192–197, and also Ducrey 2004, pp. 78–79 and 145–147, with an excellent photo of the stone. The restoration [h]υγιᾶ (instead of [φ]υγία) proposed by Cairns 1984, pp. 152–153, makes perfect sense in the context, although he was mistaken in assuming that the inscription referred only to weighed silver and not to coined money; the payment of δέκ[α σ]τατε̃ρας, 3 l. 1, did correspond to a payment in coins.

91 Ibid. III l. 1. 1: δέκ[α σ]τατε̃ρας.

92 Walker 2004: loc. cit., for the chronology of the introduction of coinage at Eretria, c. 550 BCE, and although he does not accept Cairns's restoration, [h]υγιᾶ, see 204 n. 69.

93 Minon, I.dial éléennes no. 5.

94 Roy, in Hansen/Nilssen 2004, p. 498.

95 [Aristotle], Economics 2.2.4 1347a.

The case of Athens at the end of the 5th/beginning of the 4th century, already mentioned, shows that cities could impose the use of a specific coinage, such as bronze instead of silver, before suddenly returning to silver a few years later, as Aristophanes comically attests in the *Assemblywomen:*[96]

> Second Man: "And do you remember that decree about the copper coinage?"
> First Man: "Ah! that cursed money did me enough harm. I had sold my grapes and had my mouth stuffed with bronze coins; indeed, I was going to the market to buy flour, and was already holding my bag wide open, when the herald started shouting, 'In the future no one shall accept bronze; silver alone is current'".

A law of Gortyn, c. 250–200 BCE, also imposed the use of a bronze coin for small change on its citizens. But the accompanying measures illustrate their reluctance to use it:

> [Gods. The following decision was taken by] the [city] after a vote with three [hundred] men present. One must use of the bronze coinage that the city has established; one must not accept the silver obols. If someone ever accepts them, or refused to accept the official coinage or bought them with an agio, he will pay five silver staters. Information (about such cases) is to be laid before the *neotas* (the body of young men) and from the *neotas* the Seven chosen by lot shall give their verdict on oath in the agora. Whichever party wins a majority of votes shall win, and the Seven shall exact the fine from the losing party, give one half [to the winning party] and the other half to the city.[97]

This reluctance is easy to explain. There was a risk that bronze coins would not be accepted at face value and that an illegal agio would be charged on transactions. In principle, the city prosecuted the transgressors. But in the real world, things could be more complex.

Cities were also responsible for the quality of the coinage that was circulated. Indeed, confidence *(pistis)* in the coinage was a cornerstone of the life of the city. The famous Athenian law of Nikophon of 375/4 BCE detailed the process of controlling the coins circulating in Athens.[98] To make sense of this law, one must take into account the exceptional role of Athens in the monetary landscape of the Classical period. In the 5th century, and again in the fourth, Athenian coinage was produced in large quantities. Consequently, it was a huge success throughout the eastern Mediterranean. It was so successful that it was widely imitated. In turn, these imitations could be brought back to Athens and mixed with genuine Athenian coins.

---

96 Aristophanes, Assemblywomen 815–822, tr. Loeb (modified).
97 Syll.^{3} 525 = I.Cret. IV 162; tr. Austin 2006, no. 123 (modified).
98 Stroud 1974, whose translation is used below.

So much so that from the end of the 5th century onwards, the Athenian market was flooded with imitation coins struck mainly in Asia Minor, the Levant, and Egypt. The quality of these coins was uncertain. Their fineness was lower than that of genuine Attic coins, which generally contained over 98 % silver. The paradox is that the Athenians might have lost confidence in their own coinage.

To remedy this situation, in 375/4 BCE they passed a law to control their coinage. One tester, a *dokimastēs,* was to operate in the city's agora, and another one at Piraeus, for the merchants active there. The procedure was simple: "Athenian [*Attikon*] money shall be accepted [by all sellers of goods] when a) it is found [by the tester] to be silver and b) has the public stamp *(dēmosios charaktēr).*" If the coins proved to be genuinely Attic, they would be full legal tender. But, another situation could arise:

> a) If anyone brings forward [to the tester] foreign silver [coin] having the same stamp as Attic [coin], <if it is good> (*e*[*an kalon*]) [the tester] shall give it back to the man who brought it forward [for review]; b) but if it has a bronze core or lead core or is fraudulent [*kibdēlos*], he shall cut through it immediately and it shall be [confiscated as] sacred property of the Mother of the Gods and he shall deposit it with the Council.

The fourrée coins, which had a core of base metal, usually bronze, and a thin layer of silver to deceive the users, were immediately destroyed. The good non-Attic silver coins bearing the Attic stamp were returned to their owners. This has been the subject of heated debate among specialists. Some argue that the non-Attic coins were returned to their owners to be exchanged for genuine Attic coins.[99] Others believe that these foreign coins were in fact legal tender in Athens.[100] In addition, the law (ll. 16–18) forced traders to accept the Attic coins deemed authentic by the tester. A similar point is made by a 4th century law of Olbia (see below, § 6), which required transactions to be made in the silver and bronze coinage of the city.[101] This was a crucial difference from societies that used raw silver in their transactions, where the means of payment had no official endorsement and remained private and purely transactional.

As for the fourrée coins, they were the product of counterfeiting. In Greece, it seems that the common penalty for counterfeiting was death.[102] We have seen that in the treaty between Mytilene and Phokaia, the death penalty was imposed for failure to comply with the coin-minting specifications.[103] In the speech *Against*

---

99 See Ellithorpe 2019, with previous bibliography.
100 Psoma 2011, with previous bibliography.
101 The point is made by Psoma 2011, p. 34.
102 The same punishment was imposed in Rome, see Grierson 1956, who however insisted on the limits of the enforcement of this law, but see Hendy 1985, pp. 320–328, for whom it was effectively applied.
103 See above, § 4 and n. 77.

Leptines, Demosthenes reminds his audience that in Athens, counterfeiting coins was punishable by death.[104] In *Against Timocrates,* he mentions that Solon had (allegedly) observed that "in all, or nearly all, states there is a law that the penalty for any man who debases the currency is death."[105]

A decree of Dyme, in Achaia, at the end of the third or first half of the 2nd century BCE (before 146), at a time when the city was a member of the Achaian *koinon,* proclaims: "here are those that the city has condemned to death because they stole the divinity and struck bronze coins."[106] A list of six condemned men follows, in three series of sentences. The nature of the crime with which they were charged is still debated. It seems likely, however, that the coins produced were not small change bronze coins but fourrée coins. One of the counterfeiters was a goldsmith, a man accustomed to manipulating metals. Several of them were clearly not citizens. Whether they were private counterfeiters or employees of the mint who made forgeries for their own profit, a situation that can also be observed in the Middle Ages, is also still debated.

Thus far, the question of why these men were also accused of "stealing the divinity" (*hierophōreon* refers properly to a theft from the divinity, a *phōra* being a theft) has never been answered. But the new Athenian law shows that the revenue of the mint was intended to cover the expenses of the cults of Hephaistos and Athena Hephaistia. It seems possible to infer that there must have been a similar system of cult funding at Dyme, which justified the accusation of theft from the divinity. Consequently, the Dyme convicts are most likely to have been employees of the mint, and the fact that one of them was a goldsmith suggests that this mint employed craftsmen specializing in metalwork.

Maintaining a healthy monetary circulation also involved organizing the exchange of foreign coins. The difference in the official type could be enough to make it necessary to exchange them for local coinage, as they were usually of different standards and unequal fineness.[107] But within the same state it was also necessary to exchange coins of different metals, gold for silver, and precious metals for bronze. From the earliest periods, money exchange was thus inevitably an important part of the ancient Greek monetary landscape. States could legislate in a number of ways.[108] They could, for example, allow money changers total freedom, or create a state monopoly to profit from the activity, selling the privilege

104 Demosthenes, Orations 20.167.

105 Demosthenes, Orations 24.212.

106 GEI 031, with full app. crit. and commentary, ll. 4–7: [τούσδε] ἁ πόλις κατέκριν|[ε θανάτ]ου, ὅτι ἱεροφώρεον | [καὶ νό]μισμα ἔκοπτον χάλ|[κεον].

107 For coinages of unequal fineness, see above, § 4 and n. 79.

108 Bresson 2014 and 2017.

of exchanging coins to one banker only, as was the case in Byzantium, according to Ps-Aristotele's *Economics.*[109]

Monetary policies

One should more broadly include in this survey the monetary policies that states could adopt. For example, imperial cities could legislate on coinage not only for their own territory but also for the cities and other states that were part of their empire. Although its interpretation is much debated, this is famously the case of the Attic decree on coinage from the time of the Peloponnesian War. It was inscribed on stone in the cities of the empire, and fragments of it have been found in seven different cities.[110] As a shadowy reminder of her past glory, Athens launched a new, low-key monetary imperialism at the end of the 2nd century with the Delphian Amphictyonic decree on the Athenian tetradrachm.[111]

A common feature of the monetary policies that were adopted by both cities and kingdoms was the creation of a closed currency system.[112] Only coins of the city were allowed to circulate within the boundaries of that state. People arriving with coins of a different type and origin, or with local coins that were no longer legal tender, had to exchange them for local coins, an operation that was all the more profitable if there was a large difference in weight between the monetary standards. For example, the Ptolemaic and later the Attalid kingdoms had a silver tetradrachm of 14.25 g and 12.5 g respectively, well below the international Attic standard of 17.32 g.[113] If the exchange rate was indeed drachma for drachma, the advantage was considerable for the state that imposed the exchange of currencies on an international standard.

A decree from Olbia on the Black Sea, apparently dated to 340–335 BCE, illustrates a possible local currency monopoly.[114] The stone bearing the decree was found in Hieron, at the entrance to the Black Sea – a site where merchants gathered

109 [Aristotle], Economics 2.2.3 1346b.24–26.

110 IG I³ 1453; Osborne/Rhodes, GHI 155. See Maltese 2021 and Psoma 2024, who interpret the text in different ways from a financial perspective.

111 Choix Delphes 182, with commentary Bresson 2006.

112 For the case of Rhodes, Bresson 1993.

113 Ptolemaic kingdom: de Callataÿ 2005; von Reden 2007, pp. 43–47. Attalid kingdom: Meadows 2013 and Bresson 2018.

114 IOSPE I² 24; I.Kalchedon 16; Dubois 1996, no. 14. Based on philological arguments, Dubois dates the text to the 360s; but see Nikolaev 2023a and b for the numismatic and prosopographic arguments for the late date. The document is a decree (see l. 20, reference to it as a ψήφισμα), but by its general character it did not differ from a law (it is defined as such by Arnaoutoglou 1998, no. 41, translation and short commentary).

when sailing to and from the Aegean Sea. The text advertised the conditions for using and exchanging money in the city. Olbia exported large quantities of grain and other raw materials to Aegean Greece, and the decree was a way of inviting traders to come to its port rather than to other exporting cities of the Black Sea. In this period, the city had its own silver and bronze coinage and, just like everywhere else on the Black Sea, used the electrum coins of Cyzicus, cyzicenes, for high value transactions. The decree makes four main points:

1. First, ll. 4–6, "the import and export of any amount of *coined* gold and silver are free."[115] This means that there were no controls or taxes on imported coins. This was of course very attractive to traders, who would not lose money if they imported money into Olbia. This implies, however, that at Olbia there would be taxes on the import and export of raw gold and raw silver. The law then regulates the process of exchange (ll. 6–13).
2. Second, "let all sales and purchases be carried out with the currency of the city, with bronze and silver of the Olbiopolitans." This means that only the coinage of Olbia could be used in the territory of the city. Olbia thus established a closed currency system, which is confirmed by hoard discoveries.
3. Third, "let gold [that is electrum of Cyzicus] be sold and bought at the following price: one [electrum] Cyzicene stater for ten and a half [silver] staters." The decree established a fixed rate between the local Olbiopolitan coinage and the Cyzicene.
4. Fourth, "let all other coined gold and silver be sold and bought by mutual agreement; let no tax be levied on coined gold and silver whether it is bought or sold." The decree provided for complete freedom of exchange between other coins, including the other electrum coins and the gold darics of the Persian Empire, which we know could be used on the Black Sea.

To what extent was Olbia's policy original? We do not have similar decrees or laws for other Black Sea cities, such as Histros, Pantikapeion, and the cities of Colchis. But since only local coins appear in hoards found in the territories of these cities and the surrounding areas, clearly they also established closed currency systems.[116] This does not mean that their monetary regulations were exactly the same as those of Olbia, but their monetary laws were definitely similar.

115 εἶναι παντὸς χρυσίου ἐπισήμο | [κ]αὶ ἀργυρίο ἐπισήμου εἰσσαγωγὴ[ν] | [κα]ὶ ἐξαγωγήν. On the electrum coins of Cyzicus, see Psoma 2020.

116 A full demonstration of the existence of these closed currency systems was provided at the 2017 unpublished conference "Money on the Margins: Coinage, Forms and Strategies of Intercultural Commerce on the Black Sea Shore in the Classical and Hellenistic Eras."

Conclusion

1. From the Archaic to the Hellenistic periods, all states around the Aegean and beyond faced the same challenge. Should they introduce coinage, and if so, in what form? Although the challenge was common, the answers were not necessarily the same. Some rare cities, such as Sparta, refused to have a coinage, which would have challenged the traditional social order. Others, such as the Cretan cities, delayed minting until the first half of the 5th century or later.[117] Most of those who could afford it did indeed introduce a silver coinage, although these attempts were often short-lived. In contrast, starting in the second half of the 5th century, bronze coinages, which were cheaper to mint, were struck more frequently.
2. But everywhere, even in the states that had no coinage, it was necessary to legislate on the question of money, if only to make one or more foreign currencies legal tender. In cities, it was the councils and the assemblies that decided on these policies.
3. Minting a coinage was strictly regulated. The treaty between Mytilene and Phokaia shows a strict control of the gold/silver ratio in electrum. This suggests that already in the Archaic period the gold and silver proportions of the early electrum coins were regulated by the various minting states. The recently published new Athenian law and the letter of 258 BCE concerning the difficulties of the Alexandrian mint show that the state had to ensure that people received the coins they expected from the mint within a short time.
4. The instability of the coin supply and of the financial situation of many states meant that the nature of the coins that were legal tender had to be adapted accordingly, if only by countermarking part or whole of the previously circulating coinage. States were often forced to pass laws or decrees to meet this challenge. Controlling the quality of the coinage and suppressing counterfeiting were also on the agenda. The common penalty for counterfeiting was death.
5. As exemplified by the case of Olbia, policies of closed currency systems were commonly put into place by various states, cities, or kingdoms.

We can therefore conclude that ancient monetary laws and regulations allow us to go beyond war as the only dimension of interpretation of the ancient Greek monetary landscape. Moreover, despite the undeniable differences in these laws, the similarities between states are striking. On the one hand, similar constraints produced similar results. On the other, communication and imitation, as well as a background of permanent competition, certainly also contributed to the homogenization of ancient Greek monetary laws.

---

117 Sheedy 2012, pp. 117–119.

Bibliography

ALRAM, Michael (2012) The Coinage of the Persian Empire, in: William E. METCALF (ed.), The Oxford Handbook of Greek and Roman Coinage, Oxford, 61–87.

ARNAOUTOGLOU, Ilias (1998) Ancient Greek Laws: A Sourcebook, London/New York.

ASHTON, Richard (2001) The Coinage of Rhodes 408–c. 190 BC, in: Andrew MEADOWS/Kirsty SHIPTON (eds.), Money and its Uses in the Ancient Greek World, Oxford, 79–115.

AUSTIN, Michel M. (2006²) The Hellenistic World from Alexander to the Roman Conquest. A Selection of Ancient Sources in Translation, Cambridge.

BARRANDON, Jean-Noël/BRESSON, Alain (1997) Imitations crétoises et monnaies rhodiennes: analyse physique, in: Revue Numismatique 152, 137–156.

BLET-LEMARQUAND, Marise/DUYRAT, Frédérique (2020) Elemental Analysis of the Lydo-Milesian Electrum Coins of the Bibliothèque Nationale de France Using LA-ICP-MS, in: Peter VAN ALFEN/Ute WARTENBERG (eds.), White Gold: Studies in Early Electrum Coinage, New York/Jerusalem, 337–378.

BODENSTEDT, Friedrich (1981) Die Elektronmünzen von Phokaia und Mytilene, Tübingen.

BRESSON, Alain (1993) La circulation monétaire rhodienne jusqu'en 166, in: Dialogues d'histoire ancienne 19, 119–169.

BRESSON, Alain (2001) Monnayage et société dans les mondes antiques, in: Revue Numismatique 157, 51–68.

BRESSON, Alain (2005) Coinage and Money Supply in the Hellenistic World, in: Zofia ARCHIBALD/John Kanyon DAVIES/Vincent GABRIELSEN (eds.), Making, Moving, Managing. The New World of Ancient Economies (323–31 BCE), Oxford, 44–72.

BRESSON, Alain (2006) The Athenian Mint in the 2nd Century BC and the Amphictionic Decree, in: Annali 52, 45–85.

BRESSON, Alain (2009) Electrum Coins, Currency Exchange and Transaction Costs in Archaic and Classical Greece, in: Revue belge de numismatique et de sigillographie 140, 71–80.

BRESSON, Alain (2012) Le marché des philosophes: Platon, Aristote et la monnaie, in: Véronique CHANKOWSKI/Pavlos KARVONIS (eds.), Tout vendre, tout acheter. Structures et équipements des marchés antiques, Bordeaux, 365–384.

BRESSON, Alain (2014) Le change à Délos et la question du kollybos, in: Bulletin de Correspondance Hellénique 138, 515–533.

BRESSON, Alain (2015) The Cost of Getting Money in Early Ptolemaic Egypt: The Case of Pap. Cair.Zen. I 59021 (258 BCE), in: David KEHOE/Dennis M. RATZAN/Uri YIFTACH (eds.), Law and Transaction Costs in the Ancient Economy, Ann Arbor, 118–144.

BRESSON, Alain (2017) Money Exchange and the Economics of Inequality in the Ancient Greek and Roman World, in: Sitta VON REDEN (ed.), 63rd Entretiens sur l'Antiquité classique Economy and Inequality: Resources, Exchange and Power in Classical Antiquity, Geneva, 271–308 (with discussion pp. 309–316).

BRESSON, Alain (2018) Coins and Trade in Hellenistic Asia Minor: The Pamphylian Hub, in: Bernhard WOYTEK (ed.), Infrastructure and Distribution in Ancient Economies, Vienna, 67–143.

BRESSON, Alain (2019a) Der Status der Sklaven in Platons 'Gesetzen', in: Sabine FÖLLINGER/Evelyn KORN (eds.), Von besten und zweitbesten Regeln. Platonische und aktuelle Perspektiven auf individuelles und staatliches Wohlergehen, Wiesbaden, 199–209.

BRESSON, Alain (2019b) The Athenian Money Supply in the Late Archaic and Early Classical Period, in: Journal of Ancient Civilizations 34, 135–153.

BRESSON, Alain (2020) The Choice of Electrum Monometallism: When and Why, in: Peter VAN ALFEN/Ute WARTENBERG (eds.), White Gold: Studies in Early Electrum Coinage, New York/Jerusalem, 477–496.

Bresson, Alain (2022) Closed Economy, Debt and the Spartan Crisis, in: Stephen Hodkinson/Chrysanthi Gallou (eds.), Luxury and Wealth in Sparta and the Peloponnese, Swansea, 77–96.

Brousseau, Louis (2013) La naissance de la monnaie de bronze en Grande Grèce et en Sicile, in: Catherine Grandjean/Aliki Moussaka (eds.), Aux origines de la monnaie iduciaire Traditions métallurgiques et innovations numismatiques: Actes de l'atelier international des 16 et 17 novembre 2012 à Tours, Paris, 81–96.

Burkhalter, Fabienne/Picard, Olivier (2005) Le vocabulaire financier dans les papyrus et l'évolution des monnayages lagides en bronze, in: Fréderique Duyrat/Olivier Picard (eds.), L'exception égyptienne? Production et échanges monétaires en Égypte hellénistique et romaine, Cairo, 53–80.

Cairns, Francis (1984) χρέματα δόκιμα: IG XII,9,1273 and 1274 and the Early Coinage of Eretria, in: Zeitschrift für Papyrologie und Epigraphik 54, 145–155.

de Callataÿ, François (1997) L'histoire des guerres mithridatiques vue par les monnaies, Louvain-la-Neuve.

de Callataÿ, François (2000) Guerres et monnayages à l'époque hellénistique. Essai de mise en perspective suivi d'une étude sur le monnayage de Mithridate VI Eupator, in: Jean Andreau/Pierre Briant/Raymond Descat (eds.), Économie antique. La guerre dans les économies antiques, Saint-Bertrand-de-Comminges, 337–364.

de Callataÿ, François (2005) L'instauration par Ptolémée Ier Sôter d'une économie monétaire fermée, in: Fréderique Duyrat/Olivier Picard (eds.), L'exception égyptienne? Production et échanges monétaires en Égypte hellénistique et romaine, Cairo, 117–134.

de Callataÿ, François (2012) A Tetradrachm with the Legend ΘΡΑΚΩΝ Overstruck on an Athenian Stephanophoros Tetradrachm of ΑΠΕΛΛΙΚΩΝ – ΓΟΡΓΙΑΣ (88/7 BC) and its Consequences for the Thasian type Coinage, in: Evgeni I. Paunov/Snezana Filipova (eds.), ΗΡΑΚΛΕΟΥΣ ΣΩΤΗΡΟΣ ΘΑΣΙΩΝ: Studia in honorem Iliae Prokopov sexagenario ab amicis et discipulis dedicate, Veliko Tarnovo, 307–321.

de Callataÿ, François (2019) Apparition, utilisation et disparition de l'or monnayé au nom d'Alexandre le Grand: une monétisation massive sans croissance économique?, in: Sophia Kremydi/Marie-Christine Marcellesi (eds.), Les alexandres après Alexandre. Histoire d'une monnaie commune, Athens, 207–248.

de Callataÿ, François (2021) Le financement des armées romaines en Méditerranée orientale au moyen de frappes pseudo-civiques locales: aux racines perses du modèle, in: Richard Ashton/Nathan Badoud (eds.), Graecia Capta? Rome et les monnayages du monde égéen (IIe–Ier siècle av. J.-C.), Basel, 35–62.

de Callataÿ, François (2022) Pseudo-Civic not Civic. The Abundant Double Sigloi Struck by Pamphylian and Cilician Cities (ca 460–333 BCE), in: Phoenix 76, 45–69.

Christien, Jacqueline (2002) Iron Money in Sparta: Myth and History, in: Anton Powell/Stephen Hodkinson (eds.), Sparta: Beyond the Mirage, Swansea, 171–190.

Cook, Robert M. (1958) Speculations on the Origins of Coinage, in: Historia. Zeitschrift für Alte Geschichte 7, 257–262.

Davis, Gil (2012) Dating the Drachmas in Solon's Laws, in: Historia. Zeitschrift für Alte Geschichte 61, 127–158.

Delrieux, Fabrice (2010) Les monnaies de Mylasa au nom de Ti. Claudius Melas. Bienfaits, droit de cité romaine et culte impérial dans la Carie du Ier siècle p.C., in: Fabrice Delrieux/François Kayser (eds.), Hommages offerts à François Bertrandy, I: Des déserts d'Afrique au pays des Allobroges, Chambéry, 107–144.

Dubois, Laurent (1996) Inscriptions grecques dialectales d'Olbia du Pont, Geneva.

Ducrey, Pierre et al. (2004) (eds.), Eretria: A Guide to the Ancient City, Gollion.

Eich, Stefan (2022) The Currency of Politics, Princeton.

Ellis-Evans, Aneurin (2017) The Coinage and History of Achaiion in the Troad, in: Revue de Études Anciennes 119, 25–47.

Engelmann, Helmut (1958) Wege griechischer Geldpolitik, in: Zeitschrift für Papyrologie und Epigraphik 60, 165–176.

Ellithorpe, Corey J. (2019) Athenian Mercantilism: A New Approach to the Coinage Decree & the Law of Nicophon, in: Journal of Ancient History and Archaeology 6, 59–75.

Flament, Christophe (2007) Une économie monétarisée: Athènes à l'époque classique (440–338). Contribution à l'étude du phénomène monétaire en Grèce ancienne, Louvain-la-Neuve.

Gitler, Haim/Goren, Yuval/Konuk, Koray/Tal, Oren/van Alfen, Peter/Weisburd, David (2020) XRF Analysis of Several Groups of Electrum Coins, in: Peter van Alfen/Ute Wartenberg (eds.), White Gold: Studies in Early Electrum Coinage, New York/Jerusalem, 379–422.

Grierson, Philip (1956) The Roman Law of Counterfeiting, in: Robert A. G. Carson/Carol H. V. Sutherland (eds.), Essays in Roman Coinage Presented to Harold Mattingly, Oxford, 240–261.

Hansen, Mogens H./Nielsen, Thomas H. (2004) (eds.), An Inventory of Archaic and Classical Poleis, Oxford.

Harris, Edward M. (2022) Notes on the New Law of Epicrates from the Athenian Agora, in: Zeitschrift für Papyrologie und Epigraphik 222, 65–81.

Heisserer, Andrew J. (1984) IG XII, 2, 1. (The Monetary Pact between Mytilene and Phokaia), in: Zeitschrift für Papyrologie und Epigraphik 55, 115–132.

Hendy, Michael F. (1985) Studies in the Byzantine Monetary Economy c.300–1450, Cambridge.

Irwin, Terence/Aristotle (1999) Nicomachean Ethics, Translation and introduction by Terence Irwin, Indianapolis.

Katsari, Constantina (2011) The Roman Monetary System: The Eastern Provinces from the First to the Third Century, Cambridge.

Kim, Henry (2001) Archaic Coinage as Evidence for the Use of Money, in: Andrew Meadows/Kirsty Shipton (eds.), Money and Its Uses in the Ancient Greek World, Oxford, 7–21.

Kroll, John H. (1981) From Wappenmünzen to Gorgoneia to Owls, in: American Numismatic Society Museum Notes 26, 1–32.

Kroll, John H. (1998) Silver in Solon's Laws, in: Richard Ashton/Silvia M. Hurter (eds.), Studies in Greek Numismatics in Memory of Martin Jessop Price, London, 225–232.

Kroll, John H. (2001) Observations on Monetary Instruments in Pre-Coinage Greece, in: Miriam S. Balmuth (ed.), Hacksilber to Coinage. New Insights into the Monetary History of the Near East and Greece, New York, 77–91.

Kroll, John H. (2008) The Monetary Use of Weighed Bullion in Archaic Greece, in: William V. Harris (ed.), The Monetary Systems of the Greeks and Romans, Oxford, 12–37.

Kroll, John H. (2020) The Inscribed Account on Lead from the Ephesian Artemisium, in: Peter van Alfen/Ute Wartenberg (eds.), White Gold: Studies in Early Electrum Coinage, New York/Jerusalem, 49–63.

Kroll, John H. (2024) The Fragmentary Law of Epikrates (354/3 B. C.): Background and Interpretations, in: Angelos Matthaiou (ed.), The Athenian Law of Epikrates (354/3 B. C.). Four Studies, Athens, 39–48.

Leão, Delfim F./Rhodes, Peter J. (2016) The Laws of Solon. A New Edition with Introduction, Translation and Commentary, London.

Lewis, Sian (2021) Classical Tyrants and the Assembly, in: Dialogues d'histoire ancienne Suppl. 21, 57–77.

Mackil, Emily/van Alfen, Peter (2006) Cooperative Coinage, in: Peter van Alfen (ed.), Agoranomia: Studies in Money and Exchange Presented to John H. Kroll, New York, 201–246.

Maltese, Sebastiano P. (2021) Il decreto ateniese sulle misure, i pesi e le monete. Un testo di politica finanziaria, in: Aevum 95, 3–37.

MARTIN, Thomas R. (1986) Sovereignty and Coinage in Classical Greece, Princeton.
MARTIN, Thomas R. (1996) Why Did the Greek "Polis" Originally Need Coins?, in: Historia. Zeitschrift für Alte Geschichte 45, 257–283.
MATTHAIOU, Angelos P./PITT, Robert K. (2024) The Law of Epikrates Revisited, in: Angelos MATTHAIOU s(ed.), The Athenian Law of Epikrates (354/3 B. C.). Four Studies, Athina, 11–32.
MEADOWS, Andrew (2013) The Closed Currency System of the Attalid Kingdom, in: Peter THONEMANN (ed.), Attalid Asia Minor: Money, International Relations, and the State, Oxford, 149–205.
METCALF, William E. (2012) The Oxford Handbook of Greek and Roman Coinage, Oxford.
NIKOLAEV, Mykola I. (2023a) A New Look at the Olbia Monetary Reform of the Second Half of the 4th century BC, in: Stratum 6, 161–172 (in Russian).
NIKOLAEV, Mykola I. (2023b) Canob, Son of Thrasidamantus, Olbiopolit, in: Revista Arheologică (Chişinău) 24, 62–68 (in Russian).
PAUNOV, Evgeni I. (2015) Introduction to the Numismatics of Thrace, ca. 530 BCE–46 CE, in: Julia VALEVA/Emil NANKOV/Denver GRANINGER (eds.), A Companion to Ancient Thrace, Hoboken, 265–292.
PEYKOV, Alexander (2011) Catalogue of the Coins from Thrace. Part I: Tribal and Rulers' Coinages of Thracians, Paeonians, Celts and Scythians (5th c. B. C.–1st c. A. D.), Veliko Tarnovo.
PICARD, Olivier (2001) Les philosophes grecs et la monnaie, in: Revue Numismatique 157, 95–103.
PICARD, Olivier (2015) Monnaies et législateurs, in: Pierre BRULÉ/Jaques OULHEN (eds.), Esclavage, guerre, économie en Grèce ancienne: Hommages à Yvon Garlan, Rennes, 213–225.
PROKOPOV, Ilya (2006) Die Silberprägung der Insel Thasos und die Tetradrachmen des "thasischen Typs" vom 2.–1. Jahrhundert v. Chr, Berlin.
PSOMA, Selene E. (2011) The Law of Nicophon (SEG 26. 72) and Athenian Imitations, in: Revue belge de numismatique et de sigillographie 157, 27–36.
PSOMA, Selene E. (2013) La monnaie de bronze: les débuts d'une institution, in: Catherine GRANDJEAN/Aliki MOUSSAKA (eds.), Aux origines de la monnaie fiduciaire. Traditions métallurgiques et innovations numismatiques, Bordeaux, 57–70.
PSOMA, Selene E. (2020)"Ηδε Κύζικος πλέα στατήρων: How to Explain the Electrum Coinage of Cyzicus, in: Peter VAN ALFEN/Ute WARTENBERG (eds.), White Gold: Studies in Early Electrum Coinage, New York/Jerusalem, 689–701.
PSOMA, Selene E. (2024) Dismembering a Prussian Myth: The Athenian Standards Decree (IG I^3 1453 a-g), in: Tekmeria 18, 231–282.
VON REDEN, Sitta (1995/2003) Exchange in Ancient Greece, London.
VON REDEN, Sitta (2007) Money in Ptolemaic Egypt. From the Macedonian Conquest to the End of the Third Century BC, Cambridge.
VON REDEN, Sitta (2010) Money in Classical Antiquity, Cambridge.
RICHARDSON, M. B. (2021) The Law of Epikrates of 354/3 B. C., in: Hesperia 90(4), 685–746.
ROBERT, Louis (1973) Les monétaires et un décret hellénistique de Sestos, in: Revue Numismatique, 43–53 (=OMS VI, 125–135).
RUFIN SOLAS, Aliénor (2018) "Sovereignty and Coinage". Le cas du royaume odryse (V^e–IVe siècle av. J.-C.), in: Revue Numismatique 175, 5–20.
RÜFNER, Thomas (2016) Money in the Roman Law Texts, in: David FOX/Wolfgang ERNST (eds.), Money in the Western Legal Tradition. Middle Ages to Bretton Woods, New York, 93–109.
RUSCHENBUSCH, Eberhard (1966) Σόλωνος νόμοι. Die Fragmente des Solonischen Gesetzeswerkes, mit einer Text- und Überlieferungsgeschichte, Wiesbaden.
SHEEDY, Kenneth (2012) Aegina, the Cyclades, and Crete, in: William E. METCALF (ed.), The Oxford Handbook of Greek and Roman Coinage, Oxford, 105–127.
STAHL, Alan M. (2000) Zecca. The Mint of Venice in the Middle Ages, Baltimore.

STRØM, Ingrid (2009) The Early Sanctuary of the Argive Heraion and its external Relations (8th – early 6th cent. BC): Conclusions, in: Proceedings of the Danish Institute at Athens 6, 73–159.

STROUD, Ronald S. (1974) An Athenian Law on Silver Coinage, in: Hesperia 43, 145–188.

TREVETT, Jeremy (2001) Coinage and Democracy at Athens, in: Andrew MEADOWS/Kirsty SHIPTON (eds.), Money and Its Uses in the Ancient Greek World, Oxford, 23–34.

VAN ALFEN, Peter (2012) 'The Coinage of Athens' Sixth to First Century B. C., in: William E. METCALF (ed.), The Oxford Handbook of Greek and Roman Coinage, Oxford, 88–104.

VAN ALFEN, Peter/OBER, Josiah (2018) Muddle Wrestling: Grappling for Conceptual Clarity in Archaic Greek Money, in: Mirko CANEVARO/Andrew ERSKINE/Benjamin GRAY (eds.), Ancient Greek History and Contemporary Social Science, Edinburgh, 485–511.

VAN ALFEN, Peter (2020) The Role of 'The State' in Early Electrum Coinage, in: Peter VAN ALFEN/Ute WARTENBERG (eds.), White Gold: Studies in Early Electrum Coinage, New York/Jerusalem, 547–567.

VAN ALFEN, Peter/Ute WARTENBERG (2020) (eds.), White Gold: Studies in Early Electrum Coinage, New York/Jerusalem.

VANDERPOOL, Eugene/WALLACE, W. P. (1964) The Sixth Century Laws from Eretria, in: Hesperia 33, 381–391.

WALLACE, Robert W. (1987) The Origin of Electrum Coinage, in: American Journal of Archaeology 91, 385–397.

WALKER, Keith G. (2004) Archaic Eretria: A Political and Social History from the Earliest Times to 490 BC, London/New York.

WEISS, Peter (1992) Zu Münzprägungen mit den Formeln αἰτησαμένου und εἰσανγείλαντος, in: Studien zum antiken Kleinasien 2, 167–180.

WEISS, Peter (2000) Euergesie oder römische Prägegenehmigung? Αἰτησαμένου Formular auf Städtemünzen der Provinz Asia, Roman Provincial Coinage (RPC) II und persönliche Aufwendungen im Münzwesen, in: Chiron. Mitteilungen der Kommission für Alte Geschichte und Epigraphik des Deutschen Archäologischen Instituts 30, 235–254.

WEISS, Peter (2005) The Cities and their Money, in: Christopher HOWGEGO/Volker HEUCHERT/Andrew BURNETT (eds.), Coinage and Identity in the Roman Provinces, Oxford, 57–68.

Dorothea Rohde (University of Bielefeld)

Exceptions that prove the rule

The local conditionality of debt cancellations

Thinking alternatives: debt cancellations in the old Babylonian period and the Jewish sphere

Debt was an omnipresent phenomenon in agrarian societies. Peasants borrowed tools, draught animals, food, or seed grain from wealthy landowners. Wars, diseases, and crop failures pushed subsistence farmers without resources into dependence on wealthier people, giving services, land, or children for their support.[1] Debt bondage was the ultimate consequence and therefore a danger to society. This constellation – those dependent through debt on the one hand, those powerful through lending on the other – was addressed in different ways. Monarchical systems in the Old Babylonian Period (c. 1880–1595 BCE), for example, recognized this socioeconomic problem of poorer peasants who could no longer feed themselves and were bound to creditors by debt bondage.[2] The definitive instrument was the so-called Edict of Remission (in Akkadian: *mišarum, andurārum,* in Sumerian: *nig.si.sá, ama.ar.gi*), which they proclaimed in the first year of their reign. When a ruler was in power for a longer period, he issued such edicts at irregular intervals.[3] The core of this was the retroactive cancellation of debts and the abolition of debt bondage.[4] The debtor did not have to pay back the debt or the interest and debt slaves were freed. Debt slavery in particular seems to have been seen as a problem, since Article 117 of the Code of Hammurabi also stipulated that debt slaves were to be released after three years.[5]

1 Halstead/Jones 1989.

2 See Bottéro 1961; Kraus 1984; Bergsma 2006, pp. 19–37; Simonetti 2022.

3 Kraus 1958, pp. 203–204; Komoroczy 1982; Finkelstein 1965, p. 243; Liverani 2011, pp. 352–354; Simonetti 2022, p. 285.

4 See, for example, the famous edict BaM 80.318. Finkelstein 1965, pp. 235–243.

5 CH § 117: "If an obligation is outstanding against a man and he sells or gives into debt service his wife, his son, or his daughter, they shall perform service in the house of their buyer or of the one who holds them in debt service for three years; their release shall be secured in the fourth year." Translation by Roth 1995. – Cf. also Dtn 15:12–18, which demands the release of Hebrew slaves after seven years.

The cancellation of debts in order to stabilize the socioeconomic balance of society radiated into the Jewish sphere.[6] In Jerusalem, for example, Nehemiah decreed the cancellation of debts in the mid-5th century.[7] Dt 15:1–3, on the other hand, states that in every seventh year, the *Šemittah* year, there must be a general wiping out of debts, excluding only strangers.[8] Creditors should forgive loans to neighbors and brothers to alleviate poverty.[9] The regular rhythm put debt relief on a predictable footing.[10] The purpose of these cancellations of private debts, demanded by YHWH, as well as those dictated by monarchs in the Old Babylonian period, was thus to economically rehabilitate the debt-ridden populace, reduce dependence on the wealthier classes, and thus preserve social peace.

Such regular debt cancellation was not practiced in the citizen-centered *poleis* of Greece, although the problem was known there too. Thus, Hesiod warns against the dependence of the debtor on the creditor.[11] As is well known, the indebtedness of large sections of the population in Athens led to social tensions and to the total or partial cancellation of debts under Solon.[12] The abolition of enslavement for debt (at least for citizens) was intended to curb the worst excesses of chronic indebtedness among subsistence farmers.[13] Debt reliefs also occurred in Megara, Croton, and Cumae in the Archaic period.[14]

For the later period, despite more sources, debt cancellations were extremely rare. Thus, although indebtedness was chronic,[15] in only a few cases in the Greek

6 See Gross 2000; Bergsma 2006.

7 Nehemiah 5:1–13. Bergsma 2006, pp. 205–207.

8 Bergsma 2006, pp. 125–147.

9 Significantly, Dt 15:1–11 places debt relief in the direct context of poverty, dependency, and exercise of power.

10 Cf. Dt 15:9.

11 Hesiod, Works and Days 349–354; 394–404.

12 [Aristotle], Constitution of the Athenians 6. Androtion (FGrH 324 F 34) speaks only of the cancellation of interest on debt. – Cancellation of all private and public debts: Stanley 1999, p. 210. For the formation of the narrative of Solon's debt cancellation in the 4th century BCE see Cecchet 2018, pp. 128–130.

13 Plutarch, Solon 15; Solon fragment 36. On the assumption that Solon had not abolished debt bondage, see Harris 2002. For the possibility that Solon followed the Middle Eastern model of royal decrees, see Blok 2017. – The Solonian ban on debt slavery seems to have been circumvented in the 4th century BCE. In any case, Menander (Heros 20–36) mentions how two children worked off their father's debts as "almost" slaves. This kind of debt bondage does not seem to have been far from reality. In any case, Isokrates (14.48) hints at the possibility of children serving as dependent laborers because of financial obligations. Such arrangements were probably not enforceable (cf. Aristotle, Nicomachean Ethics 1162b).

14 Megara: Plutarch, Greek Questions 18. See Forsdyke 2005. Croton: Iamblichus, Vita Pythagorika 262. Cumae: Dionysios of Halikarnassos 7.8.1–2. Cf. the catalogue Asheri 1969, pp. 9–117.

15 [Aristotle], Economics 2.18 (agricultural households rely on credit and are chronically over-indebted). See also Hinsch 2023, pp. 47–48.

world were debts apparently understood as a problem that led to legal or political solutions. This suggests that the legal mentality of the Greek world was shaped by a general norm that interpreted cancellation of private debts as a serious interference with property rights. Exceptions to this rule, i.e., the cancellation of private debt, can only be explained as local exceptions to this general norm. In the following, I will therefore first discuss the different types of debt and their social embedding. I will then turn to the legal provisions to concretize the general norm, i.e., the inviolability of property rights. This leads to the need to elaborate the local conditionality of cancellation of private debts as an exception.

Debt as a sociopolitical problem

Typical of Greek society was its vulnerability: war, disease, environmental influences, and seasonal fluctuations forced people without resources to borrow money in temporary emergencies to feed the family, cover short-term business losses, or finance a dowry. But even wealthy individuals ran into liquidity problems when their assets consisted of land and property, and financial demands temporarily depleted their cash reserves.[16] For example, loans were taken out for seed grain, for a dowry, for the proper burial of a family member, to pay a fine, for release from captivity, or for the performance of a liturgy. Loans were also taken to finance maritime trade or to set up a business. People borrowed small amounts from relatives or friends without interest.[17] Small sums for business activities were also provided by so-called *obolostatai*.[18] *Eranoi* got together and granted an interest-free loan that was enforceable in court.[19] Wealthy individuals, bankers, or temples lent larger sums against interest.[20] In addition, one could become indebted to the *polis* or a temple by holding public property, by contracting a debt to the state, or by failing to pay a fine.[21] As a result, debt was practiced across all socioeconomic strata, and loans were therefore present in all economic sectors and social situations.[22]

However, debt was not only an economic matter, but also formed and depended on a social relationship. Thus, Millett emphasized how reciprocity underpinned all forms of lending.[23] Repayment was therefore a matter of honor, when money was lent between friends and relatives. In the case of the so-called *eranoi* loans,

16 Foxhall 2006, p. 259.
17 Millett 1991, pp. 127–159.
18 Millett 1991, pp. 182–186.
19 Millett 1991, pp. 153–159.
20 Millett 1991, pp. 160–217. For bankers as lenders, see Cohen 1990; Shipton 1997.
21 Hunter 2000, pp. 22–25.
22 Millett 1991.
23 Millett 1991, pp. 27–52.

the social relations between the borrower and the lenders who had come together out of a social obligation to support the borrower, were variable. On the one hand, interest was waived, which illustrates the high level of social obligation,[24] on the other hand, the loans were enforceable, which directly threatened the person of the borrower.

For the rural population in particular, loans had an impact on basic social constellations.[25] The recurring indebtedness of small farmers created asymmetrical social relations and, in the worst case, dependency, which threatened personal freedom and civic status. This also affected the rural and urban middle classes, who were indebted to the *polis*,[26] a temple,[27] but above all to wealthy people and bankers, to finance, for example, commercial transactions.[28] If such debts could not be paid, the consequences were bitter: Greek debt law was ruthless, in particular through rapidly rising interest rates, additional interest charges, harsh liens, and heavy penalties.[29] Penalties included double the amount owed, imprisonment, *atimia* or, for metics, sale into slavery.[30]

The fact that debt was often personalized was crucial: One could stand face to face with one's creditor and hold him responsible for one's plight – unlike today with a loan from, say, an online bank. The fear of the consequences of not being able to pay your debts, or the despair of having fallen into a dependency that could never be resolved, had a name and a face. Even if the dualism of the rich and the poor is too simplistic, it does not lack a kernel of truth: there were rich and poor, and the poor were indebted to the rich through loans. In discourse, this could easily become a collective guilt – the rich against the poor or vice versa – and lead to social division, with demands for debt cancellation and land redistribution. Demands for debt cancellations are therefore primarily to be found in the sociopolitical complex of *staseis*, that is, civil strifes.[31]

---

24 Thus Millett 1991, pp. 98–108, emphasizes that (the amount of) interest was measured according to the quality of the social relationship.

25 Foxhall 2006, p. 259.

26 [Aristotle], Constitution of the Athenians 47.3–48.1.

27 [Aristotle], Constitution of the Athenians 47.4. So, for example, the Temple of Nemesis at Rhamnous (IG I³ 248).

28 [Demosthenes], Orations 24.39. See Cohen 1992 on lending as a possibility for profit maximizing activity. It remains unclear whether bankers invested their clients' deposits in lending, as Cohen 1992, p. 22 claims.

29 Eich 2006, p. 590.

30 Double the amount: [Aristotle], Constitution of the Athenians 48.1. Imprisonment: [Aristotle], Constitution of the Athenians 48.1. Andokides 1.92–93. Demosthenes, Orations 24.96–98. *Atimia:* Andokides 1.73–79; Demosthenes Orations 58.21, 49. Hunter 2000: 26–30. Sale into slavery: Demosthenes, Orations 25.57; Harp. s.v. *metoikion.*

31 Cf. Aristotle, Politics 5.7.1310a4–5 (*stasis* as economically motivated). Plato, Constitution 8.551d (the poor vs the rich).

The inviolability of property rights as a general norm

Economic inequality destabilized social and hence political conditions, threatening the cohesion of the *polis.* If external political conditions were also precarious, the indebted population could become a serious threat to the community as a whole. There was a danger that indebted citizens would betray the city to free themselves from the burden of debt. The military strategist Aineias Taktikos therefore advised (14.1):

> As for the mass of the citizens, it is of the utmost importance in the meantime to foster unanimity, winning them over by such means as lessening the burdens on debtors by reducing or completely cancelling interest-payments. At times of extreme danger, even the capital sums owed may be partially or, if necessary, wholly cancelled as well; there is nothing more alarming than to be constantly under the eye of men in debt. Provide the basic amenities of life for the needy, too.[32]

Aineias Taktikos mentions several strategies for strengthening loyalty to the *polis.* For him, it was crucial to reduce or eliminate financial pressure on the individual as a destabilizing factor for the community that reduced military strength. It was therefore necessary to provide for those who lacked the necessities of life. This also included the cancellation of debts *(chreon apokope)*, which refers to several measures in this context: Relief from or waiver of interest, partial or total cancellation of debt, and debt moratoria.[33]

That such encroachments on property rights, as proposed by Aineias Taktikos, were taken seriously is shown by the oaths and assurances attested in many places not to cancel debts and/or redistribute land. The Thracian king, for example,

32 Aineias Taktikos addresses poverty and dependencies as a threat to the loyalty of the individual to the city in several instances, for example in Aineias Taktikos 5.1–2: "(1) Next, do not leave to chance the appointment of gatekeepers: they should be men of sense and alertness, incapable of suppressing suspicion of everything as it is brought in. What is more they ought to be well-to-do individuals with something at stake in the community –children and a wife, I mean – and not men whom poverty, or the pressure of obligations, or desperation of some other kind might leave open to being persuaded to join a revolution if they did not foment one themselves. (2) Leukon the tyrant of Bosporos used to discharge even members of his bodyguard who got into debt as the result of gambling or other excesses." Translations by Whitehead 1990.

33 See also, for example, the case in 147 BCE, when the General of the Achaian League, Critolaus, ordered the suspension of trails and executions for debt (Polybios 11.38.10). Although these measures should only be valid for the duration of the war against Rome, i.e., it was a moratorium, Diodorus (32.26.3–4) called this measures debt cancellation. Cecchet 2018, p. 135.

assured Thasos that he would not tolerate the cancellation of debts by his subjects.[34] The Archon of Athens, on taking office, proclaimed that he would leave property untouched and the heliasts swore that they would not allow any debt cancellation or redistribution of land.[35] Similarly, in Sparta there was a law forbidding the cancellation of debts and the redistribution of land.[36] A Delphic law and an Eleian decree proclaimed the same.[37] Likewise, according to Pseudo-Demosthenes, the members of the Hellenic League undertook not to cancel debts.[38] And the citizens of the Cretan *polis* Itanos swore in the middle of the 3rd century BCE not to abandon the *polis* and its territories, nor to commit subversion and treason. They also swore not to redistribute land, houses, or property and not to cancel debts.[39] In general, the triad of political overthrow, debt cancellation and land redistribution is common in the discourse.[40] Despite this ubiquitous concern about debt cancellation and the omnipresence of debt cancellation in the discourse on *stasis*,[41] there are very few full debt cancellations.[42] This testifies to a specific understanding of the law: despite the obvious sociopolitical drama, debt cancellations were only carried out in the rarest of cases.

Unfortunately, Aineias Taktikos leaves it open who forgives what debts to whom and in what way. We can assume that debt forgiveness did not apply to small loans between friends or relatives; repayment was a matter of course, regardless of what public institutions or the masses demanded or did. Since social relations between *eranoi* were variable, general debt relief also affected *eranoi* loans, at least in part.[43] Undoubtedly, the main objective of debt reliefs were debts owed to the *polis*, temples, wealthy individuals, or bankers. Thus, there were two types of debt cancellation: Firstly, the cancellations of debts to a public institution such as the *polis* or the temple are the most frequently attested cases. The fact that this type of debt

34 The inscription is reedited by Chankowski/Domaradzka 1999. Cf. Loukopoulou 1999.

35 Oath of the archon: [Aristotle], Constitution of the Athenians 56.2. Oath of heliasts: [Demosthenes], Orations 24.149. Canevaro 2013, pp. 173–180 spoke out against authenticity. As already noted by Cecchet 2018, p. 129 even if the oath is not reproduced verbatim, it is unlikely that the content of the oath is entirely fabricated. Asheri 1969, pp. 20–21 assumes that the oath was introduced in the context of the restoration of democracy in 403 BCE. See also Andokides 1.88.

36 Plutarch, Agis 12.1. Cf. Isokrates, Orations 12.259.

37 Delphi: F.Delphes III 1:294. Elis: Minon, I.dial. éléennes 30.

38 [Demosthenes], Orations 17.10.

39 I.Cret. III 4.8. Börm 2019, pp. 234–237.

40 Isokrates, Orations 12.259.

41 Cf. [Demosthenes], Orations 17.15.

42 Eich 2006, p. 584.

43 At times, however, debt forgiveness or moratoria did not apply to *eranoi* loans, as for example in 147 BCE when Critolaus proclaimed the suspension of trials and executions for debt during the war against Rome. The *eranoi* loans were exempt from this (Polybios 38.11.10).

forgiveness is relatively common is not surprising, since it was not legally problematic: if in Sparta the public debt was canceled on the death of a king,[44] this is at least as unproblematic from a legal point of view as if the Hellenistic king publicly proclaimed cancellation of public debts.[45] Similarly, it is legally unproblematic for citizens to decide in the *ekklesia* to cancel debts owed to the public treasury and the temples entrusted to it. If the community of citizens as creditor agrees to the cancellation of a debt, it willingly renounces its property rights.

Similarly, it was legally unproblematic if a wealthy citizen took over the compensation of the debt, thus proving himself to be an euerget. For example, a certain Protogenes of Olbia was honored in the late third or early 2nd century BCE.[46] During his tenure, he not only revised public contracts to avoid default, but also introduced payment deferrals and interest waivers. In doing so, he (probably) paid for the financial losses incurred by the city.[47] Later he proved to be a financial benefactor once again. At the request of the *demos,* he postponed the payment of public debt and canceled the private debts owed to him and his father.[48]

Legally, socially, and politically, the cancellation of debts owed by private individuals but proclaimed by public institutions (king or *polis*) was much more problematic. Here, in addition to the socioeconomic disparity between debtor and creditor and the resulting tensions, as Aineias Taktikos testifies,[49] there was a conflict of individual rights and loss of honor: on the one hand, the cancellation of debts meant the dissolution of economic dependencies, but on the other hand it also meant a serious intervention in the property rights of citizens. Ultimately, debt relief meant expropriation and dishonoring of the creditors, which was not conducive to domestic peace.[50]

The economic, social, and political complexity has meant that only in very few cases has a complete cancellation of private and public debt actually taken place – and that even in *staseis:* While the slogan of debt cancellation was omnipresent,[51]

---

44 Herodotus 6.59.

45 Cf., for example, Perseus of Macedon, who proclaimed the cancellation of public debts as an euergetic act to stabilize and consolidate society during the war against Rome. Polybios 25.3.1–3. Asheri 1969, pp. 62–64; Cecchet 2018, p. 134.

46 Syll.[3] 495. Migeotte, Emprunt no. 44; Cecchet 2018, pp. 133–134 with Müller 2011.

47 This is not mentioned in the inscription, but he would hardly have been honored if the *polis* suffered losses as a result of these measures. Asheri 1969, p. 54; Cecchet 2018, p. 134.

48 It was not uncommon for private individuals to settle or waive the debts of poorer citizens themselves in order to acquire public prestige and create a clientele. Cf. also Timotheus, who paid debts of poorer fellow citizens out of his own pocket and granted interest-free loans (Memnon FGrH 434 F 3.1).

49 Aineias Taktikos 14.1.

50 Cf. Cicero, de officiis 2.78–79. Börm 2019, p. 212.

51 Börm 2019, p. 284.

over-indebtedness regularly a motive for civil strife,[52] and bloody street battles with a high number of casualities occurred, the consequences of canceling private debts and the associated ambiguity in ownership status were apparently avoided. Debt relief was therefore only a marginal phenomenon because of its serious interference with property rights:[53] The cancellation of debts thus characterized the extreme measures that could be taken in a civil war – without actually being carried out. The demands for debt relief and land redistribution provided a threatening backdrop, but they were not the main political demands.[54] This is also supported by the normative civic oaths, which were obviously formulated after the *stasis;* they testify that internal conditions were to be pacified by eliminating demands for debt relief and/or redistribution of land with God's help.

Instead, in the face of foreign threats, less harsh measures were taken, namely debt relief, i. e., partial encroachments on property rights such as moratoria or the waiving of punitive measures against defaulting debtors, as proposed by Aineias Taktikos.[55] This suggests that the intention was a social compromise, providing debtors with relief in order to maintain their loyalty, but not a direct loss of wealth for creditors. Both the social and legal consequences of such relief were therefore limited. The way in which private debt was dealt with in extreme situations, such as civil war or military threats, testifies to the importance of preserving property rights: cancellation of private debt was to be avoided at all costs.

This general norm, the inviolability of property, was inculcated through morally charged narratives. In 4th century Athens, for example, a rumor circulated that in Solonian times "notables" *(gnorimoi)* were using their knowledge of Solon's plan for debt cancellation to make a profit: they took on debt and bought land, only to refuse to repay it shortly after the debt was canceled. The story shows that in classical times, debt cancellation was reinterpreted to discourage this practice.[56] The moral of such anecdotes should be: Unjustifiably, it was not the impoverished citizens who benefited from debt relief, but the credit-burdened elite.[57]

There were also normative texts, such as the philosophical treatises of the 4th century. In Plato's *politeia,* Cephalus defines justice as "telling the truth and paying one's debts."[58] The definition gives the impression that a common opinion is being

52 Eich 2006, p. 584.
53 Eich 2006, p. 602.
54 Eich 2006, p. 602.
55 Polybios 38.11; Aineias Taktikos 14.1.
56 [Aristotle], Constitution of the Athenians 6.2.
57 Plutarch's remark (Agis 6) that Agis IV's debt relief plan was supported by Agesilaus in order to relieve his own credit burden is in the same vein.
58 Plato, Constitution 331c–d: οὗτος ὅρος ἐστὶν δικαιοσύνης, ἀληθῆ τε λέγειν καὶ ἃ ἂν λάβῃ τις ἀποδιδόναι.

reproduced here.[59] Alongside such affirmative narratives, chilling examples also circulated in Greece. Thus, Plato linked debt forgiveness with the aspiration of demagogues to establish a tyranny, i.e., illegitimate autocracy.[60]

Horror stories like that of Argos also had an impact: Shortly after the Battle of Leuctra, a *stasis* occurred in Argos, and accounts of it spread throughout Greece.[61] Based on Ephorus, Diodorus tells us that in 370 Argos became a democracy in which, according to Diodorus, the nobles took over the offices. Demagogues incited the crowds *(plethos)* against them. Those accused of trying to overthrow democracy were arrested and tortured. First 30 were named, executed, and their goods confiscated. Then many more were suspected. In summary proceedings, without investigation and without the possibility of individual defense, the 1200 (or even 1500[62]) richest people in the city were executed. Significantly, the formal procedures were followed, but irregularly.[63] This *neoterismos* was then known in Greece as *skytalismos,* derived from *skytále* (club). To describe the process as an archaic execution method, as Hans-Joachim Gehrke did,[64] does not do it justice: in mock trials, the richest five per cent or so, because they were rich *(megaloploutoi)*, are summarily sentenced to have their heads smashed in with a club. This is not only a logistical challenge but, as Armin Eich so aptly put it, arbitrary class justice, judicial murder.[65] Such tales of arbitrariness and the mass nature of the executions became widely known, evoked great horror and thus influenced the sense of justice and shaped the general rule. The event was so powerful that even the Athenians performed a purification sacrifice,[66] and Isokrates condemned the bloodbath of the most respected and wealthy *(endoxótatoi kai plousiótatoi)* citizens, which was even worse than the other bloodbaths of external enemies.[67] Even Dionysius of Halicarnassus and Plutarch knew about this event.[68] Respect for property rights was thus a general norm that was morally underpinned and whose non-compliance was perhorresed with negative narratives – despite the realization that property inequalities and the chronic indebtedness of citizens threatened social stability.

59 Hinsch 2023, p. 49. – For example, the moral obligation to repay debts is a common theme in the characters of Theophrastus, such as Theophrastus, Characters 9.6; 17.9; 30.3; 30.13; 30.20.
60 Plato, Constitution 565e–566a; 566e. Cf. Plato, Laws 684d-e; 736c.
61 Diodorus Siculus 15.57.3–58.4. Cf. Swoboda 1918; Gehrke 1985, pp. 31–33; Eich 2006, p. 557.
62 Plutarch, Moralia 814b.
63 Swoboda 1918, pp. 98–99.
64 Gehrke 1985, pp. 32–33.
65 Eich 2006, p. 557.
66 Plutarch, Moralia 814b.
67 Isokrates, Orations 5.52.
68 Dionysios of Halikarnassos 7.66.5; Plutarch, Moralia 814b.

This brings us to the question: If debt cancellation was exceptional and deviated from the general norm, under what conditions was private debt canceled? How do these cases relate to the general norm?

Cancellation of private debt: the local conditionality of exceptions to the rule

In the following, I will leave aside those cancellations that are legally unproblematic, i.e., public debts that were canceled by public institutions like kings, tyrants, or *poleis*.[69] I will also leave aside cancellations of private debts such as that of Corcyra in 427 BCE, since here the killing of creditors took place under the cover of the general turmoil of civil war, i.e., in situations where legal norms were temporarily suspended:

> Throughout the seven days [...] the Corcyraeans continued to murder those of their own people whom they considered enemies. The general charge was of conspiring to subvert the democracy, but some were killed out of private hostility, and others by their debtors who had taken loans and owed them money.[70]

If we leave aside the cases in which legal norms did not apply for the time being, and in which the cancellation of a private debt consisted in the killing of the creditor (as in Argos or Corcyra) or in the fear of being killed otherwise,[71] we are really left with only a handful of examples.[72] Of these cases, those in Sparta in the 240s BCE

---

69 See, for example, the symptomatic episode reported by Pompeius Trogus (Justinus, Epitome 21.1.5): Dionysius II, the tyrant of Syracuse, released 3,000 *nexi*, i.e., defaulting debtors, from prison. Obviously, the debt was public, according to Cecchet 2018, p. 133 following Asheri 1969, p. 26. In Hellenism in particular, monarchs acted as benefactors in the Greek world, granting tax reductions or canceling public debts. Significantly, they did not interfere with private ownership by also remitting private debt. Entire cities thus benefited from the *philanthropia* of the Hellenistic rulers. See Asheri 1969, pp. 83–84.

70 Thucydides 3.81.4. Translation by Hammond 2009. Gehrke 1985, pp. 88–93.

71 Cf. Aelianus, Various History 14.24. In Mytilene and Corinth, rich people had forgiven debts to save their lives, for other creditors who did not forgive debts were killed by their debtors. Fuks 1979–80, pp. 56–57; Cecchet 2018, p. 137.

72 Among the few cases in which debt relief was implemented, in addition to the following, are the events at Heraclea Pontica (Justinus, Epitome 16.4.2; 364 BCE) or decisions and measures taken in Alipheira in Arcadia (IPArk 24 = SEG 25.447; c. 273 BCE; cf. Dössel 2003, pp. 225–234; Rubinstein 2013, pp. 142–147; Börm 2019, pp. 209–214). The burning of debt records, which were stored in the archive, was an unconventional method to get rid of debts. We know this also from Dyme (Syll.^{3} 684: Letter of Q. Fabius Maximus, cf. Davies 2003, p. 330; Börm 2019, pp. 219–222).

and in Ephesos in 86 BCE are two relatively well-documented examples of debt cancellations.

The events in Sparta are recorded in detail by Plutarch, whose moralizing account obscures the intentions of the revolutionary kings Agis IV and Kleomenes III.[73] The motives of the two kings will not be discussed here,[74] but rather the reasons brought forward, the process of canceling the debt and, above all, the local circumstances – which are more or less undisputed and can be gleaned from Plutarch's narrative.[75]

Agis ascended the royal throne in 244 BCE. Shortly afterwards, following in the footsteps of the legendary lawgiver Lykourgos, he devised a *rhetra* to restore the supposedly original state of the Spartans. This was to be achieved, inter alia, by canceling debts and redistributing land.[76] Agis managed to get a sympathizing Spartan to be ephor, who presented the *rhetra* to the *gerousia*.[77] But the council of elders was divided, and the ephor brought the *rhetra* directly before the assembly.[78] However, the *gerousia* rejected the proposal,[79] as did the newly elected ephors.[80] So the *rhetra* had failed, at least legally. Not content with this, Agis launched a coup d'état: he deposed the ephors,[81] freed prisoners,[82] and had the debt contracts *(klaria)* burned in the *agora*.[83] The land was not redistributed.[84] The opposing side eventually organized, and Agis was finally sentenced to death in an unlawful summary trial.[85] About 15 years later, in 226, Kleomenes (235–222) again attempted

---

73 Plutarch, Agis; Kleomenes. See on the revolutionary kings and their reforms Fuks 1962; Oliva 1971, pp. 213–268; Shimron 1972, pp. 9–52; Cartledge/Spawforth 2002, pp. 35–53; Shipley 2017; Cecchet 2018, pp. 132–133; Börm 2019, pp. 73–79; Rohde 2024.

74 Cf. Rohde 2024.

75 What follows is only the events that can be gleaned from Plutarch's history. It should be noted, of course, that Plutarch, our main source for the reforms of the two kings, was a philosophically educated writer who was primarily concerned with portraying the characters of outstanding personalities for the moral education of his readership. Accordingly, Plutarch fictionalized his historical narrative to a certain extent, as can be seen most impressively in the biographies of the Spartan reform kings in comparison with the Roman Gracchi brothers. See in particular De Pourcq/Roskam 2016.

76 Plutarch, Agis 8.

77 Plutarch, Agis 8.

78 Plutarch, Agis 9.

79 Plutarch, Agis 11.

80 Plutarch, Agis 12.

81 Plutarch, Agis 12.

82 Plutarch, Agis 12.

83 Plutarch, Agis 13.

84 Plutarch, Agis 13; 16.

85 Plutarch, Agis 19.

to restore the Lykourgan order.[86] He tried to cancel debts (again!), redistribute the land, and revive the *agoge* and the *syssitia*.[87]

Significantly for both processes, at least according to Plutarch's account, an attempt was made to follow the legal process: The proposal was supposed to go through the institutions (*gerousia* and assembly)[88] – a clear sign that Agis was aware of the general norm that debt relief was an encroachment on property and should therefore be avoided. Only when this failed did the kings try to push through their reforms by extra-institutional means, qua royal authority. On both occasions this ended in *staseis*.

Nevertheless, the efforts of Agis and Kleomenes show that they were aware of the legal difficulties of canceling debts and redistributing land. Why did they try it anyway? Firstly, the social conditions were precarious: the gap between rich and poor was wide,[89] the number of citizens was small,[90] the few wealthy people were keeping the poorer ones in debt.[91] Secondly, there was the unconditional will to restore Sparta's dominance in the Peloponnese.[92] Thirdly, it was crucial that the memory of Lycurgus was kept alive in Sparta and could be activated by Agis and Kleomenes for their own purposes.[93] The Lykourgic order, or what was thought to be the Lykourgic order, provided for the equality of citizens, which was to be manifested in the equality of property.[94] So the fact that debt cancellation was to be implemented in Sparta was clearly due to the local constellation and the Lykourgic tradition. However, this also means that neither external pressure nor economic inequality alone are sufficient to make private debt relief appear feasible. The third factor had to be specific local conditions.

This observation, the dependence of debt cancellation on specific local conditions, is also evident in the case of Ephesos, albeit under different auspices. The general cancellation of debts, which is of interest in this context, dates from 86 or

86 Plutarch, Kleomenes7.
87 Plutarch, Kleomenes10–11.
88 Plutarch, Agis 9.
89 Plutarch, Agis 5. Hodkinson 2000, pp. 399–446.
90 Plutarch, Agis 5. On *oliganthropia* see Decety 2018; Doran 2018. On the demographic aspects of the reforms of Agis and Kleomenes see Doran 2018, pp. 80–82.
91 Cf., for example, Plutarch, Agis 6; 7; Kleomenes 10.
92 Plutarch, Agis 1 and Kleomenes 7. For Spartan foreign policy during this period see Giannopoulos 2011, pp. 159–181; Kralli 2017, pp. 147–245; Shipley 2018, pp. 54–73.
93 Plutarch, Agis 6; 9–10; Kleomenes 10; 16; Comp. Agis, Grachhus 2–3; 5.
94 Plutarch, Lykourgos 8. On the inconsistency of the alleged constitution of Lycurgus and the measures of Agis and Kleomenes, especially on the cancellation of debts, which could not be traced back to Lycurgus, see Hodkinson 2000, pp. 43–45; Thommen 2017, pp. 61–62.

85 BCE.[95] The decree consists of two parts: The first part (ll. 1–19) reaffirms the alliance with the Romans, declares war on Mithridates VI Eupator, and emphasizes the consensus of the Ephesian citizenry. The second part (ll. 20–62) reaffirms the need for cohesion[96] and announces various measures aimed at strengthening the military capability on the one hand and stabilizing social conditions on the other, which should apply equally to all citizens.[97]

Citizens who have been removed from the list of citizens for arrears, or who are on the list of *logistai* as debtors to the *polis* or temple, should be exonerated (i.e., their citizenship restored and their debts forgiven).[98] At the same time, it was decided that citizenship should be extended to certain groups of residents (*isoteleis, paroikoi, hieroi,* freedmen, and foreigners) if they contributed to the defense of the city. Public slaves were to become *paroikoi* in this case.[99]

Other provisions included the waiving of fines to the temple or *polis,*[100] the waiving of repayments on loans from the temple treasury,[101] the suspension of public and sacred trials (with a few exceptions),[102] and the continuing payment obligations on public and sacred leases.[103] Although the measures mentioned were varied

95 Syll.[3] 742 = I.Ephesos 8 = ARNAOUTOGLOU 1998, no. 90: "[...] and the people keeping the old favour towards the Romans, the common deliverers, and promptly obeying whatever was ordered; Mithridates, king of Kappadokia, violating the treaty with the Romans and gathering troops, attempted to dominate over lands not belonging to him and conquered our neighbouring *poleis* by deceit and due to the size of its troops and the suddenness of his attack, conquered our city. Our people, guarding from the very beginning the favour to the Romans, awaiting but the occasion to take up arms for the common salvation, decided to declare war against Mithridates for the hegemony of Rome and for the common freedom. All the citizens have unanimously contributed to this struggle. Therefore, it was decided by the people that, since the whole affair is about war, protection, security and salvation of the temple of Artemis, of the polis and its territory, the generals and the secretary of the Council and the presidents shall bring forward immediately a decree and any other action to be taken in these circumstances and the people shall consider them." Translation by ARNAOUTOGLOU 1998.

96 I.Ephesos 8 ll. 24–25: ἀναγκαῖόν ἐστι πάντας ὁμονοήσαντας.

97 I.Ephesos 8 ll. 40–41.

98 I.Ephesos 8 ll. 27–30.

99 I.Ephesos 8 ll. 43–48.

100 I.Ephesos 8 ll. 30–33: The debts of those who owed penalties to the temple or *polis* should be forgiven.

101 I.Ephesos 8 ll. 35–40: Repayment of loans from the temple treasury was to be abolished. Exceptions were loans granted by associations or their agents against mortgages. As a relief, interest was to be waived from the following year until the foreign policy situation had eased.

102 I.Ephesos 8 ll. 41–43: All public and sacred proceedings should be stopped, except for moving boundary stones and disputing inheritance.

103 I.Ephesos 8 ll. 33–35: The lease of temple land or of public revenue should continue to exist and the payment obligations associated with it should remain in place.

and complex, they were ultimately legally unproblematic from the point of view of the community and the individual. They fit neatly into the familiar pattern of debt relief to public and religious institutions.

What is unusual, however, are the provisions for the cancellation of debts to private creditors. Since the protection of property rights was a high legal good and closely linked to social peace, the *polis* could not, of course, cancel private debts on its own, but the creditors had to do it. And that's exactly what they did: They announced in the People's Assembly that they had "happily and deliberately" waived repayment.[104] This was not the case with the commercial lending of the *trapezitai,* whose very existence would have been threatened by debt relief. Therefore, the obligations were to be maintained, with a temporal differentiation: obligations arising from transactions with bankers made in the year of the decision were to be maintained in all parts. In principle, contracts concluded in previous years remained in force, but accommodation for payment was decided: Both, the bankers' and the customers' payment obligations, were to be extended from the coming year to ten years, with corresponding interest.[105]

The decree reflects the extremely difficult situation in which Ephesos found itself between the two opposing forces of Mithridates Eupator VI and Rome. Ephesos was notoriously flexible in its foreign policy. At first, Ephesos sided with Mithridates, willingly opening the gates of the city to him and, at the same time, pulling down the statues of the Romans in the city.[106] Mithridates returned the favor by enlarging the *asylon* of the Artemision.[107] Ephesos was then particularly eager in its opposi-

---

104 I.Ephesos 8 ll. 48–54: "And the creditors who have lent money for maritime loans, loan agreements, deposits, mortgages, remortgages, sales, agreements, contracts and instalments came to the assembly of the people and happily and deliberately and in agreement with the people absolved the debtors from all the debts, and possession shall remain with the people who possess now unless anyone, in Ephesos or abroad [...] has contracted a loan or concluded an agreement." Translation by Arnaoutoglou 1998. – Perhaps the *polis* had in advance promised the creditors that they would compensate for the defaults, as Cecchet 2018, p. 136 suggests. This could be the case, but the inscription does not prove it. The style of the inscription rather suggests that in such a case it would have been declared that the *polis* would take over the private debts.

105 I.Ephesos 8 ll. 54–60: "And regarding bank affairs, those who have deposited money or given or received pledges during the current year, the exaction of the debts shall follow the law. As for deposits or pledges of earlier years, the bankers and the depositors shall arrange the payment from the following year and for the following ten years and the interest shall be in proportion." Translation by Arnaoutoglou 1998.

106 Appian, Mithridatika 21.

107 Strabon 14.1.23 (641C)

tion to Rome; the so-called Ephesian Vespers in 88 BCE left no doubt as to the attitude of Ephesos and did not exactly increase the Romans' confidence in the city.[108]

However, Sulla showed how the Romans treated Mithridates' friends when he stormed Athens in March 86.[109] This gave Ephesos every reason to take a firm stand against Mithridates: not only did it fear the Romans, but Mithridates' reward system had caused social unrest and made him the largest creditor, so there were good reasons to side with the Romans. The first step was the assassination of Zenobius, which sparked a revolt against Mithridates in the cities of Asia Minor.[110] The king responded to the defection of his allies with an offer: all debts would be canceled, metics would become citizens, and slaves would be freed.[111] His promises of debt relief and citizenship were almost imitated by the Ephesians. After the decree, no one in Ephesos had any financial or personal reason to side with Mithridates and betray the city.

---

108 Appian, Mithridatika 22–23: "(22) In the meantime Mithridates built a large number of ships for an attack on Rhodes, and he wrote secretly to all his satraps and magistrates that on the thirtieth day thereafter they should set upon all Romans and Italians in their towns, and upon their wives and children and their domestics of Italian birth, kill them and throw their bodies out unburied, and share their goods with himself. He threatened to punish any who should bury the dead or conceal the living, and offered rewards to informers and to those who should kill persons in hiding, and freedom to slaves for betraying their masters. To debtors for killing moneylenders he offered release from one-half of their obligations. These secret orders Mithridates sent to all the cities at the same time. When the appointed day came calamities of various kinds befell the province of Asia, among which were the following: (23) The Ephesians tore fugitives, who had taken refuge in the temple of Artemis, from the very images of the goddess and slew them. [...] Such was the awful fate that befell the Romans and Italians throughout the province of Asia, men, women, and children, their freedmen and slaves, all who were of Italian blood [...]." Translation by White 1899.

109 See for literary and archaeological findings Parigi 2019. – Ephesos was also severely punished by Sulla: in addition to fines and a Roman garrison, the leaders of Mithridates' supporters were killed. Appian, Mithridatika 61–63; Granius Licinianus 35.82.

110 Appian, Mithridatika 48. From the point of view of the Ephesians, the assassination of Zenobius was a preventive measure. The general of Mithridates had made an example of Chios (Syll.[3] 785, l. 13–15), which Ephesos did not want to follow: Zenobius had ordered the deportation of the population despite the payment of a fine (Appian, Mithridatika 47). This sealed the revolt (Appian, Mithridatika 48). On the murder of Zenobius see also Niebergall 2011, pp. 14–15.

111 Appian, Mithridatika 48: "Mithridates sent an army against the revolters and inflicted terrible punishments on those whom he captured, but as he feared other defections, he gave freedom to the Greek cities, proclaimed the canceling of debts, gave the right of citizenship to all sojourners therein, and freed the slaves. He did this hoping (as indeed it turned out) that the debtors, sojourners, and slaves would consider their new privileges secure only under the rule of Mithridates, and would therefore be well disposed toward him." Translation by White 1899. Cf. Appian, Mithridatika 58; 62. See also Niebergall 2011 for the recipients of Mithridatic propaganda.

The fact that Ephesos declared war on Mithridates at the same time as canceling the debt was in line with Aineias Taktikos' general advice to strengthen the loyalty of the citizens in a foreign policy crisis:[112] The goal was to avoid social conflict over economic issues that could lead to *stasis* or treason. Moreover, from the outset, there was a financial component to Mithridates' war against the Romans that should not be underestimated:[113] Mithridates needed money to keep his war chest afloat and to retain his allies. The Romans were the perfect target: Italians had prospered through trade, administration, or as *publicani.* They were the beneficiaries of Roman imperialism. When, in this situation, Mithridates held out the prospect that half the property of the murdered Italians would belong to him and half to the murderer, and that the debtors who killed their Italian creditors would continue to be relieved of half their debts,[114] economic motives were combined with the experience of foreign rule: men were killed because they were of a certain origin. It was not only the lower classes who benefited from this, but all sections of the population in the cities of Asia Minor.[115] Ephesos had to counteract these emotional and financial incentives to side with Mithridates by taking appropriate measures to stabilize society.

So even if the cancellation of the debt is easily explained by the foreign policy situation, the Ephesians obviously reacted with a unique act; no other *polis* in this situation canceled private and public debts on a comparable scale. Obviously, the advice of Aineias Taktikos has not been followed in similar cases. The arrangements are also much more complex than the cancellation of debts in Sparta, where simply the *klaria* burned. Unlike the Ephesians, the Spartan kings did not seem to value social peace. Accordingly, another factor was necessary for the implementation of debt relief: And that was the positive experience that Ephesos had had in a similar situation, which encouraged the Ephesians to take such an unusual path in this delicate foreign policy situation. For Ephesos had already decided on a debt cancellation that was impressive in its legal constructions.[116]

Around 300 BCE, at the beginning of a war *(koinos polemos)*, the Ephesians decided to suspend the attachment of collateral for the duration of the war.[117] Debtors whose debts fell due during the war were allowed to keep their mortgaged lands during the military conflict. Two years later, with the end of the war, enforcement of securities became acute again. The insolvency of debtors as a result of the war, the fall in the value of their collateral, and the continued demands of their credi-

112 Aineias Taktikos 14.1.
113 See Glew 1977.
114 Appian, Mithridatika 22.
115 Niebergall 2011, p. 5.
116 Syll.[3] 364 = I.Ephesos 4. Cf. Walser 2008; Asheri 1969, pp. 42–47.
117 For dating the inscription and the historical context see Walser 2008, pp. 47–108.

tors had shaken social stability, which is why the *polis* passed the present *nomos.*[118] It was more than skillful: The compromise provided for the recognition of existing laws and contracts, but tried to find legal solutions that were acceptable to creditors and debtors. For example, the land was to be divided between creditors and debtors according to the amount of the loan, the valuation of the land, and the damage caused by the war. The Ephesian reconciliation agreements are very detailed, but it was assumed that disputes would arise. These were not referred to the usual institutions of the *polis,* but to a body of foreign judges *(xenikon dikasterion).* The actual rules, however, were laid down by the *polis.* As well as demonstrating a commitment to the resolution of social problems and the avoidance of conflict, they are also evidence of a highly developed legal practice.

Thus, while the measures around 300 BCE were only a moratorium, Ephesos went a step further in the war against Mithridates, because of the financial incentives offered by the king. It is therefore no coincidence that two debt cancellations from Ephesos are recorded. The success of the moratorium must have had a positive effect on the willingness to resort to legally difficult exceptions in threatening foreign policy situations: Ephesos was able to point to positive experiences with complex legal regulations that were carved in stone and thus reminded the community that compromises in the field of tension between inviolable property rights and the common good were possible, desirable and, above all, successful in strengthening the community against threats from within.

Conclusion

While Babylonian kings forgave private and public debt early in irregular intervals and Deuteronomy called for cancellation of private debts every seventh year, the Greek world did not know regular debt cancellation – not because of strikingly different socioeconomic conditions, but because of different legal perceptions. In the Greek world, cancellation of private debts was perceived as a profound encroachment on property rights. The inviolability of property rights was the general norm, disseminated and practiced through oaths, normative representations by philosophers, warning anecdotes, and cautionary tales of civil war excesses. Violation of this general norm in the form of a *chreon apokope* was understood as an exception and included debt relief, such as moratoria or the waiving of punitive measures against defaulting debtors.

The contrast with the Babylonian and the Jewish spheres shows that in the citizen-centered *poleis,* encroachments on property rights were seen more as a violation

118 Syll.^{3} 364 = I.Ephesos 4.

of norms than as solidarity with the economically disadvantaged. Debt cancellation was therefore not carried out as a planned means of redistribution, out of a sense of economic justice, or because poverty was generally regarded as a problem, but for purely political reasons, whether in the case of Sparta to strengthen the monarchical position or, as in the case of the fall of Ephesos, to stabilize the community in a particular foreign policy constellation. Cancellations of private debts therefore remained the exception and were only used as a last resort.

Their very exceptional nature confirms the general norm, which makes them particularly interesting for studying the tension between legal unity and pluralism. The two case studies presented here show that these exceptions did not contradict the general rule that debt cancellation was a serious infringement of property rights. Each of these exceptions were legitimized in a particular way. This shows that under certain local conditions the hierarchy of norms could shift to the detriment of the general norm; encroachments on property rights were temporary subordinated to other, locally relevant norms.

Thus, the Spartan kings placed the norm of *homoiotes,* the equality of the Spartans, above the norm of the inviolability of property rights, and legitimized this hierarchy of norms with reference to the Lycurgus order. In Ephesos, a different path was taken. Here the cancellation of private debts was decided in the context of the first Mithridatic War. The defense of the *polis* was considered a higher norm than the inviolability of property rights. This hierarchy of norms was legitimized by the reference to *homonoia,* to being of one mind. Significantly, *homonoia* was achieved in two ways: by emphasizing the exceptional nature of the measure, and by the consent of those who had to accept the encroachment on their property rights. In both cases, the debt cancellations were exceptions to the rule.

Both case studies show that the tension between legal unity and pluralism was not so much rooted in different legal norms, but in the diversity of norms from different spheres. Thus, in certain constellations, a social, political, or religious norm could limit the validity of a general legal norm. The exceptional cases did not override the legal rule, but in certain circumstances rated another norm as more important. This shows that legal norms, as claims to regulate human behavior, were integrated into a flexible hierarchy of norms that could be restructured in specific situations and local contexts.

Bibliography

ARNAOUTOGLOU, Ilias (1998) Ancient Greek Laws: A Sourcebook, London/New York.

ASHERI, David (1966) Distribuzioni di terre nella Grecia antica, Turin.

ASHERI, David (1969) Leggi greche sul problema dei debiti, Pisa.

BERGSMA, John Sietze (2006) The Jubilee from Leviticus to Qumran: A History of Interpretation, Leiden.

BLANSHARD, Alastair J. L. (2006) Debt-Bondage, in: Graham SHIPLEY et al. (eds.), The Cambridge Dictionary of Classical Civilization, Cambridge, 259–260.

BLOK, Josine/KRUL, Julia (2017) Debt and its Aftermath. The Near Eastern Background to Solon's Seisachtheia, in: Hesperia 86, 607–643.

BÖRM, Henning (2019) Mordende Mitbürger. Stasis und Bürgerkrieg in griechischen Poleis des Hellenismus, Stuttgart.

BOTTÉRO, Jean (1961) Desordre économique et annulation des dettes en Mesopotamie à l'epoque paleo-babylonienne, in: Journal of the Economic and Social History of the Orient, 113–164.

BRESSON, Alain (2021) Closed Economy, Debt and the Spartan Crisis, in: Stephen HODKINSON/Chrysanthi GALLOU (eds.), Luxury and Wealth in Sparta and the Peloponnese, Swansea, 77–96.

CARTLEDGE, Paul/SPAWFORTH, Anthony (2002²) Hellenistic and Roman Sparta, London.

CECCHET, Lucia (2018) Debt Cancellation in the Classical and Hellenistic Poleis: Between Demagogy and Crisis Management, in: The European Legacy 23, 127–148.

CHANKOWSKI, Véronique/DOMARADZKA, Lidia (1999) Réédition de l'inscription de Pistiros et problèmes d'interprétation, in: Bulletin de Correspondance Hellénique 123, 246–258.

COHEN, Edward E. (1990) Commercial Lending by Athenian Banks: Cliometric Fallacies and Forensic Methodology, in: Classical Philology 85, 177–190.

COHEN, Edward E. (1992) Athenian Economy and Society. A Banking Perspective, Berkeley.

DAVIES, John K. (2003) Greek Archives: From Record to Monument, in: Maria BROSIUS (ed.), Ancient Archives and Archival Traditions, Oxford, 323–343.

DE POURCQ, Marteen/ROSKAM, Geert (2016) Mirroring Virtues in Plutarch's Lives of Agis, Kleomenes and the Gracchi, in: Koen DE TEMMERMAN/Kristoffel DEMOEN (eds.) Writing Biography in Greece and Rome: Narrative Technique and Fictionalization, Cambridge, 163–180.

DORAN, Timothy (2018) Spartan Oliganthropia, Leiden.

DÖSSEL, Astrid (2003) Die Beilegung innerstaatliche Konflikte in den griechischen Poleis vom 5.–3. Jahrhundert v. Chr., Frankfurt am Main.

EICH, Armin (2006) Die politische Ökonomie des antiken Griechenland (6.–3. Jahrhundert v. Chr.), Cologne/Weimar/Vienna.

ERCIYAS, Deniz Burcu (2006) Wealth, Aristocracy and Royal Propaganda under the Hellenistic Kingdom of the Mithridatids in the Central Black Sea Region of Turkey, Leiden.

FINKELSTEIN, Jacob Joel (1965) Some New Misharum Material and Its Implications, Assyriological Studies 16, 243–255.

FORSDYKE, S. (2005) Revelry and Riot in Archaic Megara: Democratic Disorder or Ritual Reversal?, in: The Journal of Hellenic Studies 125, 73–92.

FOXHALL, Lin (2006) Debt, in: Graham SHIPLEY (ed.), The Cambridge Dictionary of Classical Civilization, Cambridge, 259.

FUKS, Alexander (1962) Agis, Cleomenes, and Equality, in: Classical Philology 57, 161–166.

FUKS, Alexander (1974) Patterns and Types of Social-Economic Revolution in Greece the Fourth to the Second Century B. C., in: Ancient Society 5, 51–81.

FUKS, Alexander (1979–1980) The Sharing of Property by the Rich with the Poor in Greek Theory and Practice, in: Scripta Classica Israelica 5, 46–63.

Gehrke, Hans-Joachim (1985) Stasis. Untersuchungen zu den inneren Kriegen in den griechischen Staaten des 5. und 4. Jahrhunderts v. Chr., Munich.

Giannopoulos, Stavros (2011) Griechischer Stadtstaat und hegemoniale Monarchie. Die Politik Spartas gegenüber Makedonien im 4. und 3. Jahrhundert v. Chr., Frankfurt am Main u. a.

Glew, Dennis G. (1977) The Selling of the King: A Note on Mithridate's Eupators Propaganda in 88 B. C., in: Hermes 105, 253–256.

Gross, Walter (2000) Die alttestamentlichen Gesetze zu Brache-, Sabbat-, Erlaß- und Jubeljahr und das Zinsverbot, in: Theologische Quartalschrift 180, 1–15.

Halstead, Paul/Jones, Glynis (1989) Agrarian Ecology in the Greek Islands: Time Stress, Scale and Risk, in: The Journal of Hellenic Studies 109, 41–55.

Hammond, M. (2009) Thucydides. The Peloponnesian War, Oxford/New York.

Harris, Edward M. (2002) Did Solon Abolish Debt-Bondage?, in: Classical Quarterly 52, 415–430.

Herrad, Imogen (2020) When is Revolt not Revolting? Rule-breaking and Revolt in Sparta in Plutarch's Lives, in: Lennart Gilhaus et al. (eds.), Transgression und Devianz in der antiken Welt, Stuttgart, 75–92.

Hinsch, Moritz (2023) Private Debts in Classical Greece. Bonds of Friendship, Curse of Hatred?, In John Weisweiler (ed.), Debt in the Ancient Mediterranean and Near East. Credit, Money, and Social Obligation, Oxford, 46–66.

Hodkinson, Stephen (2000) Property and Wealth in Classical Sparta, London.

Hunter, Virginia (2000) Policing Public Debtors in Classical Athens, in: Phoenix 54, 21–38.

Kefallonitis, Stavroula (2022) Dette et politique, Besançon.

Komoróczy, Géza (1982) Zur Frage der Periodizität der altbabylonischen mišarum-Erlässe, in: M. Damdamaev et al. (eds.), Societies and Languages of the Ancient Near East: Studies in Honour of I. M. Diakonoff, Westminster, 196–205.

Kralli, Ioanna (2017) The Hellenistic Peloponnese. Interstate Relations. A Narrative and Analytic History, from the Fourth Century to 146 BC, Swansea.

Kraus, Fritz R. (1958) Ein Edikt des Königs Ammi-Ṣaduqa von Babylon, Leiden.

Kraus, Fritz R. (1984) Königliche Verfügungen in altbabylonischer Zeit, Leiden.

Liverani, Mario (2011) Vicino Oriente. Storia Economia Società, Rome.

Loukopoulou, Louisa (1999) Sur le statut et l'importance de l'emporion de Pistiros, in: Bulletin de Correspondance Hellénique 123, 359–371.

Müller, C. (2011) Autopsy of a Crisis: Wealth, Protogenes, and the City of Oblia in c. 200 BC, in: Zofia H. Archibald/John Kenyon Davies/Vincent Gabrielsen (eds.), The Economies of Hellenistic Societies. Third to First Century BC, Oxford, 324–344.

Maffi, Alberto (1999) Emprisonnement pour dettes dans le monde grec, in: Cécile Bertrand-Dagenbach et al. (eds.), Carcer. Prison et privation de liberté dans l'antiquité Classique, Paris, 7–18.

McGing, B. C. (1986) The Foreign Policy of Mithridates VI Eupator King of Pontus, Leiden.

Millett, Paul (1991) Lending and Borrowing in Ancient Athens, Cambridge.

Niebergall, Axel (2011) Die lokalen Eliten der griechischen Städte Kleinasiens und Mithridates VI. Eupator zu Beginn des ersten römisch-pontischen Krieges, in: Hermes 139, 1–20.

Niehr, Herbert (1997) The Constitutive Principles for Establishing Justice and Order in Northwest Semitic Societies with Special Reference to Ancient Israel and Judah, in: Zeitschrift für Altorientalische und Biblische Rechtsgeschichte 3, 112–130.

Nieman, Hermann Michael (2014) Zwischen Ökonomie und Theologie: Schuld und Schulden in der Sicht der Hebräischen Bibel, in: Marianne Heimbucher/Alfred Krabbe/Martin Quilisch (eds.), Wie auch wir vergeben unseren Schuldnern ... Geld – Glaube – Zukunft, Leipzig, 105–123.

Oliva, Pavel (1971) Sparta and Her Social Problems, Amsterdam/Prag.

Parigi, Caterina (2019) Atene e il sacco di Silla. Evidenze archeologiche e topografiche fra l'86 e il 27 a.C., Wiesbaden.

Renger, Johannes (2002) Royal Edicts of the Old Babylonian Period, in: The International Scholars Conference on Ancient Near Eastern Economics 3, 139–162.

Ries, Gerhardt (2013) Der Erlass von Schulden im Alten Orient als obrigkeitliche Maßnahme zur Wirtschafts- und Sozialpolitik, in: Kaja Harter-Uibopuu/F. Mitthoff (eds.), Vergeben und Vergessen? Amnestie in der Antike, Vienna, 3–16.

Rohde, Dorothea (2024) Der hellenistische König und seine enttäuschten Peers. Königliche Erwartungen, aristokratische Ansprüche und die Reformen des Agis IV. und Kleomenes III., in: Jan-Markus Kötter et al. (eds.) Zum Umgang mit Enttäuschungen in der Antike, Stuttgart.

Roth, Martha Tobi (1995) Law Collections from Mesopotamia and Asia Minor, Atlanta.

Rubinstein, Lene (2013) Forgive and Forget? Amnesty in the Hellenistic Period, in: Kaja Harter-Uibopuu/Fritz Mitthoff (eds.), Vergeben und Vergessen? Amnestie in der Antike, Vienna, 127–161.

Shimron, Benjamin (1972) Late Sparta. The Spartan Revolution 243–146 B.C., Buffalo.

Shipley, D. Graham J. (2017) Agis IV, Kleomenes III, and Spartan Landscapes, in: *Historia* 66, 281–297.

Shipley, D. Graham J. (2018) The Early Hellenistic Peloponnese: Politics, Economies, and Networks 338–197 BC, Cambridge.

Shipton, Kirsty M. W. (1997) The Private Banks in Fourth-Century BC Athens. A Reappraisal, in: Classical Quarterly 47, 396–422.

Simonetti, Cristina (2022) The Edicts of Debt Remission. A Political Tool of Economic Intervention, in: Marcella Frangipane/Monika Poettinger/Bertram Schefold (eds.), Ancient Economies in Comparative Perspective. Frontiers in Economic History. Material Life, Institutions and Economic Thought, Cham, 283–293.

Stanley, Phillip Vincent (1999) The Economic Reforms of Solon, St. Katherinen.

Swoboda, Heinrich (1918) ΣΚΥΤΑΛΙΣΜΟΣ, in: Hermes 53, 94–101.

Thommen, Lukas (2017) Agis und Kleomenes als Vorläufer der Gracchen, in: Museum Helveticum 74, 54–65.

Walser, Andreas Victor (2008) Bauern und Zinsnehmer. Politik, Recht und Wirtschaft im frühhellenistischen Ephesos, Munich.

White, Horace (1899) Appian. The Foreign Wars, New York.

Weisweiler, John (2023) Debt in the Ancient Mediterranean and Near East. Credit, Money, and Social Obligation, New York.

Whitehead, David (1990) Aineias the Tactician. How to Survive Under Siege, Oxford.

Zurbach, Julien (2017) Les hommes, la terre et la dette en Grèce c. 1400–c. 500 a.C., Bordeaux.

Ruben Post (University of St Andrews)

A unique federal fiscal and legal institution from Early Hellenistic Achaia

At the beginning of the 3rd cent. BCE, the small *poleis* of Achaia in the northwestern Peloponnese were divided. While they had been united under the aegis of a federal state in the 4th cent. BCE, that *koinon* had disappeared by c. 300 BCE.[1] As Polybios explains, however, the Achaian federal impulse re-emerged in 281/0 BCE when "a change of sentiment prevailed, and they began again to join together" (αὖθις ἤρξαντο μετανοήσαντες συμφρονεῖν).[2] He elaborates:

> καὶ πρῶτοι μὲν συνέστησαν Δυμαῖοι, Πατρεῖς, Τριταιεῖς, Φαραιεῖς: διόπερ οὐδὲ στήλην ὑπάρχειν συμβαίνει τῶν πόλεων τούτων περὶ τῆς συμπολιτείας. μετὰ δὲ ταῦτα μάλιστά πως ἔτει πέμπτῳ τὴν φρουρὰν ἐκβαλόντες Αἰγιεῖς μετέσχον τῆς συμπολιτείας.

> The first to take this step were the citizens of Dyme, Patrai, Tritaia, and Pharai. This is why no stele pertaining to the *sympoliteia* of these cities exists. But about five years afterwards, the people of Aigion expelled their garrison and joined the *sympoliteia*.

Apart from this testimony, almost no evidence for the activity of the new Hellenistic Achaian *koinon* exists for the years 281/0 to 275/4 BCE. The singular exception is a stele from the *polis* of Dyme preserving part of a decree regulating a public finance scheme. Although this inscription is challenging to interpret, it provides the only evidence from the ancient Greek world for a public finance scheme involving the credit institution known as the *eranos* loan; it is also the earliest document attesting to the federal legal system of the Hellenistic Achaian *koinon* at a foundational stage in its history. In this chapter, I will re-examine this neglected inscription in the light of some recent research on Achaian history, Greek public finance, and the *eranos* loan, analyzing its legal and economic context at three distinct levels: the private group, the city-state, and the federal state.

---

1 Larsen 1968, pp. 215–216; Beck 1997, pp. 62–66; Mackil 2013, pp. 62–63, 75–76, 89.

2 Polybios 2.41.11–13.

The inscription

The preserved portion of the inscription, now apparently lost,[3] runs to 16 continuous lines, including the end of the document, interrupted primarily by damage on the left side of the stone. Except where I have noted otherwise, I have followed Athanassios Rizakis' version of this text in the following reproduction.[4]

[-]δο[θῆν]αι ἐκ
[- - c. 8 - - τοὺ]ς πολεμάρχους ὑπὸ τῶν ἐγγ[ύ]ων τῶν [ὑ]πὸ τᾶς πόλιος καθεστα-
[μένων ἐξ]<ε>μεν δὲ καὶ τοῖς προστάταις καὶ τοῖς [ἐρ]ανεσταῖς ἐγγράφειν
[- - - - - - -]ς καὶ δαμοσιοφύλακες κα[ὶ] γραμματέ[α] καὶ ταμίαν· οἱ δὲ π[ο-
[λέμαρχοι ε]ἰ[5] μὴ παρδέξονται τὰς ἐκγρα[φ]ὰς παρὰ τῶν προστατᾶν κα[ὶ]
[παρ' τῶν ἐγγύων][6] τῶν ὑπὸ τᾶς πόλιος καθεσταμένων ἢ μὴ παρ' τῶν ἰδιω-
[τᾶν καὶ τῶν ἐρανε]στᾶν ἢ μὴ ἀποδώσοντι ἐν ταῖς ἁμέραις ἐν αἷς γέγρ[α]-
[πται, ζαμιούτω ἁ γε]ρουσία Δ καθ' ἑκάσταν ἁμέραν ἔστε κα ἀποδοῖεν,
[εἰσαγέτω δε τὰν[7] ζα]μίαν ποτὶ τὸ κατὰ τρίμηνον δικαστήριον· οἱ δὲ γέ-
[ροντες εἰ μὴ ζαμιώ]σοντι τοὺς πολεμάρχους, αὐτοὶ ἀποτινόντω
[τὰν ζαμίαν καὶ ἄτιμο]ι ὄντ[ω] καὶ ἐν τοῖς Ἀχαιοῖς καὶ κατὰ πόλιν· εἰ δὲ
[- - - - c.16 - - - -] ἐ<ρ>άνους τοὺς ἐλάσσονες φερόντων ὥστε
[- - - - c.18 - - - - τ]ὸν φόρον, καθὼς ἐξ ἀρχᾶς ἔφερον, ἐξουσία ἔ-
[στω - - - - - - πλή?]θει[8] ἐρανε<σ>τᾶν. τὸ δὲ δόγμα τοῦτο ἀνα-
[γραψάντω - - - c.12 - - - κ]αὶ ἀναθέντω εἰς τὸ ἱερὸν τοῦ Ἀπόλλω-
[νος, ἀντίγραφα δὲ διαποστεῖλα]σθαι τοὺς δαμιοργοὺς ποτὶ τὰν πόλιν
[ἑκάσταν? ὅπως πάντες παρακολουθῶσι]ν ταῦτα.

... be given from ... the *polemarchoi* by the guarantors appointed by the city; and that the *prostatai* and the *eranestai* be able to register the ..., the *damosiophylakes,* the secretary, and the treasurer as debtors. [If the *polemarchoi*] do not receive the debt registers

3 Rizakis, Achaïe III, p. 36.
4 Rizakis, Achaïe III, no. 1, pp. 36–37.
5 I differ from previous editors in suggesting this restoration, which would appear to fit the lacuna as well as the sense of the sentence (Feyel 1943, p. 115). All editors prior to Rizakis' re-edition read the end of l. 4 as ΟΙΑΕΙ[.]-, but a squeeze now in Berlin apparently provides a clear reading of ΟΙΔΕΠ[.]- (Rizakis, Achaïe III, p. 37). Given that the subsequent section explicitly mentions the *gerontes* punishing the *polemarchoi* for not fulfilling a specified duty, a reference to the *polemarchoi* in the nominative appears the most plausible and economical restoration (cf. Rizakis, Achaïe III, p. 39).
6 I have again broken from previous editors with this restoration, which is based on the use of the phrase τῶν ἐγγ[ύ]ων τῶν [ὑ]πὸ τᾶς πόλιος καθεστα[μένων] in ll. 2–3.
7 I have followed Feyel's restoration here (1943, p. 113).
8 I have followed Feyel's restoration here (1943, p. 113).

> from the *prostatai* and [the guarantors] appointed by the city nor from the *idiotai* [and the *erane*]*stai,* or if they do not repay within the number of days within which it has been written to do so, the *gerousia* shall [fine] them 10 talents per day until they repay, and the fine [shall be submitted] to the trimonthly tribunal. [If the] *gerontes* [do not fine] the *polemarchoi,* they themselves shall be liable for [the fine and lose their citizenship], both among the Achaians and in each city. If ... [of?] those making lesser *eranos* contributions so that ... the instalment, as they contributed/paid from the beginning, it shall be possible [for the assembly?] of the *eranestai* [to do X?]. They shall in[scribe] this decree ... and they shall erect it in the sanctuary of Apollo, and the *damiorgoi* shall [send copies?] to [each?] city [so that all might follow] these instructions.

Although fragmentary, it is clear that the surviving sections outline the procedure for the registration of debts (ll. 1–4), the obligations of the *polemarchoi* and *gerontes* in overseeing the scheme and punishments if they fail to fulfill them (ll. 4–11), some aspect of the repayment of the loans (ll. 11–14), and the order for publication of the decree (ll. 14–17). The missing first part of the inscription must have explained in detail the scheme's operation and the obligations of those involved in it.

Before examining this inscription in detail, let us first consider its general nature and date. In l. 11, it is stated that some of the magistrates charged with overseeing this scheme, whom we will discuss below, were to be punished with the loss of both civic and federal citizenship if they failed to carry out their duties. In l. 16, it is then stated that the decree was to be sent ποτὶ τὰν πόλιν, with the following word most plausibly restored as ἑκάσταν, so that the decree was to be sent "to each city." These statements together indicate that this is a copy of a federal decree of the re-founded Achaian *koinon* which was erected in Dyme.[9] It would follow that the "sanctuary of Apollo" (τὸ ἱερὸν τοῦ Ἀπόλλω[νος]) referenced at the end of the inscription was a federal sanctuary,[10] and this is the key to dating this decree.

In the early Classical period, prior to the foundation of the first formal Achaian federal state, Achaian communal activity was focused primarily on shared worship at the prominent sanctuaries of Poseidon Helikonios near Helike and Zeus Homarios (or Hamarios[11]) near Aigion. After an earthquake and tsunami famously destroyed the former sanctuary in 373 BCE, however, the latter sanctuary became the premier pan-Achaian religious site, and eventually the federal sanctuary of the Classical Achaian *koinon.*[12] This site would once again come to serve as the chief federal sanctuary of the re-founded Hellenistic *koinon,* and thus as the primary

9 Feyel 1943, pp. 122–123.
10 Feyel 1943, p. 123.
11 Cf. Mackil 2013 p. 49, n. 131.
12 Aymard 1967, pp. 284–289; Tausend 1992, p. 25; Morgan/Hall 1996, pp. 195–196; 2004, pp. 474–475; Mackil 2013, pp. 48–50, 194–202; Rizakis 2013; Katsonopoulou 2019.

venue for publishing Achaian federal decrees,[13] but only after Aigion, in whose territory the sanctuary of Zeus Homarios was located, joined in 275/4 BCE.[14] The absence in this inscription of any mention of the sanctuary of Zeus Homarios and the inclusion instead of a reference to a sanctuary of Apollo, otherwise unattested as a federal sanctuary, can only be explained if this document dates to the brief period in which the sanctuary of Zeus Homarios was not the Achaian federal sanctuary, between the *koinon*'s re-foundation in 281/0 BCE and Aigion's accession five years later.[15] Nothing else is known about this sanctuary of Apollo, but it must have been located in the territory of one of the four founding *poleis,* Dyme, Patrai, Tritaia, or Pharai.[16]

The public finance scheme

So much for the character and date of this inscription. What can we ascertain about the nature of the scheme outlined in it? This inscription was first published without commentary in 1878 and has been discussed sporadically since.[17] Emil Szanto made the first attempt at reconstructing the scheme outlined in the text, in a lengthy footnote in his study of Greek citizenship.[18] He argued that this was a civic lending scheme, positing that the *prostatai, eranestai,* and *idiotai* collectively comprised the "guarantors appointed by the *polis*" (τῶν ἐγγύων τῶν ὑπὸ τᾶς πόλιος καθεσταμένων), and that this scheme was established by the government of Dyme to obtain funds with which to make a payment to the Achaian federal government. Adolf Wilhelm subsequently commented on minor aspects of the inscription, which he similarly took to be a civic decree, but did not discuss the finance scheme as a whole.[19]

The first thorough analysis of this inscription was published by Michel Feyel in a 1943 article.[20] He posited that this was a federal decree ordering the foundation of a single *eranos* association in each member *polis,*[21] of which the *eranestai* (whom he took to be the same as the *idiotai*), *prostatai, damosiophylakes,* secretary,

13 Polybios 5.93.10; Walbank 1957, p. 624; Rizakis, Achaïe III, pp. 163–165.
14 Polybios 2.41.11–13; Strabon 8.7.3; Aymard 1936, p. 12.
15 Aymard 1967, pp. 277–293; Rizakis, Achaïe III, pp. 39–40
16 Feyel 1943, p. 123; Osanna 1996, p. 42; Rizakis, Achaïe III, pp. 39–40. No epithet for the god is preserved in the inscription, and there does not seem to have been space in the lacuna that follows for one to have been included (Feyel 1943, p. 123, n. 4).
17 Martha 1878, no. 3.96–98.
18 Szanto 1892, pp. 117–118, 2.
19 Wilhelm 1911, pp. 41–42.
20 Feyel 1943.
21 Feyel 1943, p. 123.

treasurer, *polemarchoi, gerontes,* and trimonthly tribunal were all members.[22] He drew this conclusion from two readings which now appear incorrect. First, he read the end of l. 4 as οἱ ἀεὶ [ἔσονται], interpreting this as an indication that all officials mentioned before that phrase in the inscription were to hold their positions within these *eranos* associations permanently.[23] Second, and following from the first point, he did not read ἐγγ[ύ]ων before τῶν [ὑ]πὸ τᾶς πόλιος καθεστα[μένων] in l. 2,[24] arguing that this otherwise unspecified group of "those appointed by the city" had to be opposed to the *eranestai, prostatai, damosiophylakes,* secretary, treasurer, *polemarchoi, gerontes,* and trimonthly tribunal; if any of these groups were officials of the government of Dyme, he reasoned, their affiliation with the *polis* would have been stated explicitly, just as it was for "those appointed by the city." This interpretation was bolstered in Feyel's mind by the federal nature of this decree: none of these could have been civic officials, he posited, as that would have meant that the Achaian *koinon* had required all member *poleis* to possess the same magistrates, which does not conform with our understanding of Achaian federal governance.[25] As we will discuss further below, the dating of this inscription to the earliest years of the Hellenistic *koinon* and an improved reading of the inscription in several places has invalidated Feyel's interpretation of the decree and his reconstruction of the scheme it outlines. Nonetheless, his analysis of some parts remains invaluable.

After Feyel's article, only two sources have discussed this inscription in any detail, to my knowledge. Gustav Lehmann commented briefly on it in a footnote, following Feyel's reconstruction of the institution it outlines as a federal lending scheme, but refraining from discussing how it operated in detail.[26] Finally, Rizakis in 2008 published his new edition of this inscription with a full commentary, notably improving readings in several places thanks to Klaus Hallof's consultation of a squeeze taken from it now held in the Academy of Berlin.[27] Rizakis posited that this is a federal decree outlining the operation of *eranos* loans made by groups of citizens to be repaid in instalments without interest, but remained agnostic on the question of whether those were ad hoc groups or permanent associations.[28] Despite correcting several of Feyel's readings in his new edition of the text, he largely repeated the French scholar's reconstruction of the finance scheme in his commentary, ignoring several of the problems discussed above.

I will present here for the first time a fresh analysis of the scheme working from

22 Feyel 1943, pp. 115–116.

23 Feyel 1943, p. 116.

24 Feyel 1943, pp. 121–122. Interestingly, Feyel considered but rejected this reading, largely because it did not fit with his misreading of ll. 4–5.

25 Feyel 1943, p. 116, n. 2; cf. Aymard 1967, pp. 171–176.

26 Lehmann 1967, p. 326, n. 393.

27 Rizakis, Achaïe III, no. 1, pp. 36–40.

28 Rizakis, Achaïe III, p. 38.

Rizakis' new version of the text. Given this inscription's highly fragmentary nature, a comprehensive understanding of the functioning of the scheme it describes is beyond our grasp, but enough of the decree is preserved to establish that it outlined a mechanism by which groups of individuals were to lend sums of money to officials primarily through *eranoi,* or collective loans, which were then to be repaid in instalments.[29] The word ἔρανος, which can be translated broadly as "common contribution," originally referred in the Archaic period to a communal meal to which all participants contributed a share.[30] Over time, it came to refer to groups, whether formal or informal, temporary or permanent, in which individuals, typically belonging to the same social network, made material contributions for a specified purpose; by the Classical period, the word *eranos* had come to be associated with the practice of numerous individuals pooling their contributions of money to lend out to one person, often (though not necessarily) a family member or friend, which was then to be repaid in instalments.[31] By the early Hellenistic period, the word could refer to a collective loan to be repaid in instalments; an ad hoc group of lenders contributing to such a loan; or a permanent group to which members contributed in some material way.[32]

Three groups of lenders are mentioned in this inscription: *prostatai, eranestai,* and *idiotai.* Comparative material allows us to understand the role of each. Both the *prostatai* and the *eranestai* can securely be identified as members of *eranos* groups, the former contributors, the latter their representatives; as will be discussed further below, those *eranoi* could have been formal, permanent *eranos* associations,[33] in which case the *prostatai* were their elected presidents, or informal, ad hoc lending groups, in which case the *prostatai* would have been individuals temporarily invested by a group of peers with the responsibility for collecting and handling their contributions.[34] Extensive Athenian evidence indicates that the figure equivalent to the *prostates* in Athens, the *plerotes,* handled the organization of contributions to an *eranos* loan, registered it with the authorities, collected repayment, and settled related legal matters on behalf of all creditors.[35] The identity of and role played by the *idiotai* is less clear, but, given that they appear to have comprised a lending group distinct from the *prostatai* and *eranestai,* they can plausibly be identified as individuals who wished to contribute directly to the scheme as individuals, with-

29 Rizakis, Achaïe III, p. 38.
30 LSJ s.v. ἔρανος A.
31 Millett 1991, pp. 153–159; Cohen 1992, pp. 207–215.
32 Baslez 2006, pp. 165–168; Thomsen 2015, pp. 171–173.
33 As first suggested by Feyel, albeit based on faulty readings of the text (1943, pp. 115–116).
34 Vondeling 1961, pp. 107–108, n. 5; Millett 1991, pp. 158–159; cf. Arnaoutoglou 2003, pp. 70–87.
35 Thomsen 2015, pp. 159–161.

out the benefit of belonging to an *eranos* group and having a representative manage their contribution.[36]

Listed alongside the *prostatai, eranestai,* and *idiotai* are the "guarantors appointed by the city" (τῶν ἐγγύων τῶν ὑπὸ τᾶς πόλιος καθεσταμένων), who appear to have been wealthy private citizens designated by the civic government to make creditors whole if the *polis* defaulted on its repayment. An inscription from the Arkadian *polis* of Alipheira dating to 273 BCE or soon thereafter provides a roughly contemporary comparandum. This document, which enumerates several measures imposed by the *polis* to address outstanding issues in the wake of a period of disruption within the community, stipulates that no private citizen was to be allowed to bring suit against another in relation to existing contracts, "except if someone was appointed as a guarantor on behalf of the *polis* by decision of the council" (εἰ μή τις ἰνγεγύευκε ὑπὲρ τὰν πόλιν δόξαν ταῖ [βωλᾶι]).[37] The circumstances in which these individuals may have been appointed as guarantors for the repayment of funds borrowed by the civic government is unclear, but the insistence that they were to remain legally liable for the repayment of debts even when other debtors were relieved of this burden indicates the seriousness with which the *polis* took this quasi-liturgical responsibility.

Beyond these groups of creditors and guarantors, a complex mix of different officials is mentioned in connection with this scheme. The nature of these administrators, who include the *polemarchoi, gerontes* (members of a *gerousia*), *damosiophylakes,* secretary, treasurer, members of a trimonthly tribunal (τρίμηνον δικαστήριον), and *damiorgoi,* has been disputed. I follow Rizakis' interpretation that these are all civic magistrates with the exception of the *damiorgoi,* who must be federal officials (as discussed below), rather than officials of *eranos* associations as Feyel asserted,[38] for two reasons.[39] First, apart from the generic positions of secretary and treasurer, none of these offices is attested in the extensive epigraphical material produced by Hellenistic associations.[40] Second, what little evidence we have attesting to the governments of Hellenistic Peloponnesian *poleis* suggests that *damosiophylakes, polemarchoi,* and *gerontes* were all generally civic officials: *damosiophylakes* appear to have managed public archives;[41] *polemarchoi* were tasked with regulating the activity of *polis* governments, especially in matters of finance, to combat illegal activity or corruption;[42] and the *gerousia,* although scarcely attested

36 For difficulties with the identification of this group, see Feyel 1943, pp. 120–121.
37 IPArk, no. 24, ll. 17–18; IPArk, pp. 281–285; Rubinstein 2013, pp. 142–146. I thank Lene Rubinstein for bringing this document to my attention.
38 Feyel 1943, pp. 115–116.
39 Rizakis, Achaïe III, pp. 38–40.
40 Arnaoutoglou 2003, pp. 105–113.
41 Rizakis, Achaïe III, p. 33, n. 86.
42 Schaefer 1956; Rizakis, Achaïe III, p. 33.

outside of Sparta,[43] seems to have been a small board of permanently appointed elder officials invested with the power to scrutinize the activities of civic functionaries.[44] As noted above, Feyel argued that because this was a federal decree, these could not have been civic officials, as that would have meant that the Achaian *koinon* had required all member *poleis* to possess the same magistrates, which is not in keeping with other evidence for Achaian federal governance.[45] His objection can be dismissed, however, if this decree dates to the earliest years of the Hellenistic *koinon,* as other epigraphical evidence suggests that the western Achaian *poleis* that comprised its founding members possessed very similar, if not identical, civic structures in the early Hellenistic period.[46]

The last civic body mentioned is the trimonthly tribunal (τὸ κατὰ τρίμηνον δικαστήριον). Although no other mention of such an organ exists in the preserved Hellenistic Achaian epigraphical record, there is evidence from other parts of the Hellenistic world for the right of those accused of wrongdoing to appeal the penalties imposed on them to similar tribunals that met at regular intervals.[47] This tribunal may have heard a variety of cases involving civic governance: an inscription of c. 350 BCE from Tegea in Arkadia states, for instance, that anyone found to be obstructing or damaging a public construction project was to be summarily fined and then later brought before a tribunal to have the penalty assessed.[48]

Finally, the end of the decree references the board of *damiorgoi,* officials attested at both the civic and federal level within Hellenistic Achaia.[49] They are enjoined to do something, almost certainly send copies of this document, ποτὶ τὰν πόλιν followed by a lacuna. As discussed above, this phrase would make little sense in a civic context, and so these officials must have belonged to the Achaian *koinon,* not the *polis* of Dyme. It would follow that the *damiorgoi,* some of the only federal officials attested already in the Classical *koinon,* a board that would go on to become perhaps the single most important body of administrative functionaries in the Hellenistic *koinon,*[50] were tasked with organizing the implementation of this scheme at the federal level.

With these considerations in mind, it is possible to attempt a reconstruction of this public finance scheme. The Achaian *koinon* would have announced in member

---

43 Rizakis, Achaïe III, pp. 286–287, n. 109.
44 Rhodes/Lewis 1997, pp. 538–539; Gawlinski 2012, p. 158.
45 Feyel 1943, p. 116, n. 2.
46 Rizakis, Achaïe III, pp. 32–34, 137.
47 E.g., I.Beroia 1B, ll. 35–37; Feyel 1943, p. 114; Rubinstein 2012. I thank Lene Rubinstein for sharing her extensive knowledge on this topic with me.
48 IPArk no. 3, ll. 15–21.
49 Veligianni-Terzi 1977; Sizov 2017.
50 Larsen 1968, pp. 217, 221–2, 231–2; Veligianni-Terzi 1977, pp. 104–7; Arnaoutoglou 2009–2010, pp. 190–191.

poleis that it was soliciting contributions from lenders. Civic *polemarchoi* were then charged with collecting loans from creditors, and eventually repaying them. These creditors comprised contributors organized into *eranoi,* whether formal associations or informal groups, represented by *prostatai,* as well as the *idiotai,* individuals who did not belong to *eranoi.* Each civic government in turn appointed wealthy private citizens as guarantors to reassure these creditors that they would be made whole if the *polis* defaulted. The *damosiophylakes,* secretaries, and treasurers of each member *polis* were charged with registering the details of these transactions with both creditors and guarantors and handling the necessary documentation.

If the arrangement functioned as intended, the civic *polemarchoi* would have collected the loans from the creditors and in turn sent the total amounts raised at the *polis* level on to the federal *damiorgoi;* the Achaian *koinon* would then have used this assembled income before repaying the loans in instalments by the specified deadline until all creditors were satisfied. If it did not, however, the members of the *gerousia* were tasked with holding the *polemarchoi* accountable. In case of malfeasance, the *gerontes* might levy a sizeable fine on the *polemarchoi* for failing to fulfill their duties; this would only have been provisional, however, until it was submitted for review by the trimonthly tribunal. As the ultimate overseers of this scheme, the *gerontes* faced severe punishment if they did not fulfill their duties properly, being liable to pay the imposed fine themselves and lose their citizenship at both the civic and federal levels if the tribunal found in favor of the *polemarchoi.*

Unfortunately, the inscription as preserved provides no hint as to the purpose of this federal financing scheme. Szanto, Wilhelm, and Schwahn all commented on different aspects of this operation but refrained from discussing its purpose.[51] Feyel speculated that given the federal nature of this initiative, “l’éranos avait pour objet de procurer à chaque cité un fonds de réserve destiné aux dépenses de guerre, et qu’en temps de paix les éranistes étaient chargés de faire fructifier ce même fonds;”[52] he then cautiously posited a connection with the Achaian general Philopoimen’s reform of the Achaian army in the late 3rd cent. BCE, being unaware of the evidence for the much earlier dating of this inscription.[53] Rizakis in his 2008 epigraphical commentary noted that Feyel’s suggestion “est possible bien qu’elle s’oppose à la date proposée pour ce document, vers les premières années de la seconde ligue,” refraining from further speculation.[54] Lehmann suggested instead a connection with a statement in Polybios that Achaian officials on the eve of the Achaian War in 147/6 BCE “made *eranoi* permanent” (τοὺς δ᾽ ἐράνους ἐπιμόνους

51 Szanto 1892, pp. 117–118, n. 2; Wilhelm 1911, pp. 41–42; Schwahn 1931, p. 101, n. 1.

52 Feyel 1943, p. 123.

53 Feyel 1943, p. 124, n. 3.

54 Rizakis, Achaïe III, p. 38.

ποιεῖν),[55] a phrase whose meaning is unclear but which most likely refers to the imposition of a moratorium on the repayment of *eranos* loans until the war was concluded.[56] Again, given the evidence that this inscription is more than a century older, this suggestion cannot be countenanced either.[57]

Given that this finance scheme was established at a time when the Achaian *koinon* is not known to have been involved in any military operations, I would argue that it was most likely a means by which federal officials raised money to cover extraordinary peacetime expenses. In this respect, this scheme would most closely resemble the *epidosis,* or public subscription, which relied on individuals voluntarily donating to the state for a specific purpose,[58] often large construction projects or the purchase of grain.[59] One possible purpose of the scheme was the aggrandizement of the new federal sanctuary of Apollo, which seems to have been a minor local sanctuary heretofore. Another possibility is that western Achaia faced a food shortage early in the new *koinon*'s history and wished to take collective action to obtain grain supplies for its citizens. The abovementioned slightly later inscription from Alipheira in Arkadia (about 115 km away as the crow flies) mentioning individuals appointed as guarantors on behalf of that *polis* also references the remittance of a sum owed to the *polis* as the result of a legal judgment taken against two men "for grain" (τῷ σίτω);[60] the most plausible context in which the *polis* might have had to take such action was the failure of importers to supply grain as contracted in a time of shortage sometime before the document was inscribed, probably earlier in the 270s BCE.[61] In the late 190s or early 180s BCE, when the *koinon,* which had by then grown to encompass almost the entire Peloponnese, experienced a widespread grain shortage, it is known to have imposed a federal grain export embargo to ensure a stable food supply for its member *poleis;*[62] perhaps the Dyme inscription attests to a different, much earlier form of federal intervention in the grain supply in a time of dearth.

The *eranos* loan and the finance scheme

To understand fully the social and economic context of this unique federal finance scheme, we must now address a crucial question: what was the nature of the *eranoi* on which this lending scheme centered? By the Classical period, the term *eranos*

55 Polybios 38.11.10.
56 Walbank 1979, pp. 704–5; Fuks 1970, p. 80.
57 Lehman 1967, p. 326, n. 393.
58 Migeotte, Souscriptions.
59 Mackil 2015, pp. 476–477.
60 IPArk no. 24, ll. 8–9.
61 IPArk, p. 282.
62 Post 2022.

was normally used to refer to loans made by groups of individuals who pooled contributions and lent the collected sum to a single individual to be repaid in instalments.[63] There were, however, by the later 4th cent. BCE two kinds of *eranos* loan: on the one hand, there was the "friendly" loan, which was collected by the borrower him or herself from an ad hoc group of close social relations; on the other, there was the more "professional" loan collected from varied individuals, many with no relation to one another or the debtor, by a third party who managed the funds. We already find in 4th cent. BCE Athenian forensic speeches referencing the latter kind of *eranos* loan, which was legally regulated and often interest-bearing.[64] In time, the term *eranos* also came to be used, however, to refer to permanent organizations in which members contributed to a central fund for some purpose, which I refer to here as *eranos* associations.[65]

Moses Finley and others who shared his view argued that *eranos* associations only emerged in the mid-3rd cent. BCE,[66] but there is good reason to believe that at least in Athens, and very likely elsewhere as well, they existed by the 320s BCE at the latest.[67] The history of *eranos* loans and *eranos* associations outside of Athens has received relatively little attention, but literary and epigraphical references attest to variations of this institution existing in the Hellenistic Peloponnese, central Greece, the Cyclades, Rhodes, and Egypt.[68] One of the sources that is most helpful in illuminating the possible nature of the *eranoi* referenced in the Dyme inscription is a *horos* inscription from Arkesine on Amorgos, dated to c. 300 BCE.[69] This document states that a piece of property was mortgaged[70]

> ...τῶ[ι] ἐράν[ωι] καὶ Ἀρισταγόραι τῶι ἀρχεράνωι καὶ τῆι γυναικὶ αὐ[τοῦ] Ἐχε[- – -] πρὸς τὴν ἐγγύαν ἣν ἐγ[ράψα]το Ξενοκλῆν τοῦ ἐρά[νου ὃν] συνέλεξεν Ἀρισταγόρα[ς κα]τὰ τὸν νόμον τῶν [ἐρανισ]τῶν.

> ... to the *eranos* and Aristagoras, the *archeranos*, and his wife, Eche[-], as the surety for which he recorded Xenokles in the matter of the *eranos*, which Aristagoras had collected in accordance with the law of the *eranistai*.

63 Millett 1991, pp. 145, 153–159; Cohen 1992, pp. 207–215; Bresson 2015, pp. 278–279; Van Berkel 2019, pp. 164–170.
64 Cohen 1992, pp. 209–215; Thomsen 2015, pp. 159–162, 172.
65 Thomsen 2015, pp. 156–162.
66 Tod 1932, p. 75; Finley 1952, pp. 100–106; Jones 1999, pp. 5–6, 222–223, 307–308.
67 Arnaoutoglou 2003, p. 78; Gabrielsen 2006, p. 179, n. 12; Chandezon 2012, p. 188; Thomsen 2015, pp. 154–156, 162–170.
68 Fuks 1970, pp. 79–81; Baslez 2006, pp. 166; Thomsen 2015, p. 173.
69 IG XII 7.58.
70 IG XII 7.58, ll. 8–15.

As in the Dyme inscription, the contributors to this *eranos* are termed *eranistai* and they are represented by an individual tasked with managing their collective loan, termed an *archeranos,* a term which late Hellenistic papyrological evidence indicates could be used interchangeably with *prostates.*[71] Importantly, this inscription indicates that the actions of the *eranistai* were governed by a law or legal code (νόμον τῶν [ἐρανισ]τῶν). Finley asserted that this should be interpreted as a law of the *polis* of Arkesine governing the operation of *eranos* loans,[72] but Christian Thomsen has argued persuasively based on other epigraphical evidence that this should be interpreted instead as a bylaw (or code of bylaws) of a permanent *eranos* association, providing evidence for such organizations outside of Athens decades before the date of the Dyme inscription.[73] Thus, the *eranestai* referenced in the Dyme inscription could have been lenders organized through "friendly" ad hoc *eranos* loans; more "professional" ad hoc *eranos* loans; formal, permanent *eranos* associations; or some combination of all three.

Finally, a note on the clauses that round out the body of the Dyme decree and appear to relate to the actual handling of funds (ll. 11–14). Although these lines are exceptionally fragmentary, they notably include the only actual use of the word ἔρανος in the preserved portions of the inscription, as well as two instances of the verb φέρω and the noun φορός. In Attic forensic speeches dealing with *eranos* loans, which provide us with the most detailed information on this economic institution, the phrase φέρειν ἔρανον simply refers to the act of entering into an *eranos* arrangement, whether as creditor or debtor, while εἰσφέρειν φορᾶς *vel. sim.* is used to refer to the contribution of sums by creditors or the repayment of instalments by debtors.[74] Thus, we can translate the preserved phrase in l. 12, ἐ<ρ>άνους τοὺς ἐλάσσονες φερόντων, as referring to a category of "those making smaller *eranos* loans," while the preserved portion of l. 13, [τ]ὸν φόρον, καθὼς ἐξ ἀρχᾶς ἔφερον, would seem to refer to some circumstance in which repayment instalments were to continue to be made "just as they had been made from the beginning." These lines would thus appear to distinguish between different classes of lenders, suggesting that a relatively broad swathe of society may have contributed to this scheme and that some provisions may have been made specifically for small-time creditors.[75] The *eranos* loan seems to have been a popular credit mechanism among the lower classes of many *poleis* because it often involved lending at low or no interest and allowed for relatively small individual contributions to be pooled for credit pur-

71 BGU 1133, l. 5; BGU 1134, ll. 2–3; BGU 1135, l. 2; BGU 1136, l. 2.

72 Finley 1952, pp. 101–102.

73 Thomsen 2015, pp. 168–169; cf. Arnaoutoglou 2003, pp. 128–129.

74 Demosthenes, Orations 21.184–185; Hypereides 3.11; Lysandros fragment 38; Millett 1991, pp. 153, 294–295, n. 33; Whitehead 2000, p. 301.

75 Rizakis, Achaïe III, p. 39.

poses;[76] indeed, Polybios accused the Achaian *strategos* Kritolaos in 147/6 BCE of aiming to stir up "the masses" (τοῖς ὄχλοις) of the *koinon* when he "made *eranoi* permanent" (τοὺς δ᾽ ἐράνους ἐπιμόνους ποιεῖν) for the duration of the Achaian War, suggesting their widespread popularity later in the federal state's history.[77]

We can thus most plausibly reconstruct the finance scheme as one in which a mixture of groups within the member *poleis* of the Achaian *koinon,* most likely a mixture of formal *eranos* associations, ad hoc *eranos* lending groups, and some other independent private citizens, lent money to the federal state via their civic governments. These lenders do not seem to have been confined to the upper classes; rather, the scheme appears to anticipate contributions coming from varied socio-economic backgrounds within each *polis.* In the early 270s BCE, the four member *poleis,* Dyme, Patrai, Tritaia, and Pharai, were small and relatively poorly connected to surrounding regions by both land and sea.[78] Unlike most of the other regions of the Peloponnese that would eventually join the *koinon,* Achaia was not known for any economic activities or the production of any distinctive commodities, perhaps with the exception of textiles.[79] While Plutarch's statement, drawn from the memoirs of the 3rd cent. BCE Achaian statesman Aratos, that in the early 3rd cent. BCE most Achaians "lived in small cities, possessed land that was neither fertile nor extensive, and were neighbours to a sea that had no harbours and for the most part washed a rocky shore" (μικροπολῖται γὰρ ἦσαν οἱ πολλοί, καὶ γῆν οὔτε χρηστὴν οὔτε ἄφθονον ἐκέκτηντο, καὶ θαλάττῃ προσῴκουν ἀλιμένῳ, τὰ πολλὰ κατὰ ῥαχίας ἐκφερομένῃ πρὸς τὴν ἤπειρον) is somewhat hyperbolic, it is not far off the mark.[80] This would imply that the Achaian *koinon* had modest resources to draw on in this earliest phase of its history. I would posit that this financial scheme was a means of leveraging a commonplace social institution, the *eranos* loan, to mobilize as much of the private capital of these small, relatively poor communities as possible for federal purposes.

---

76 Rädle 1970; Millett 1991, p. 77.

77 Polybios 38.11.9–11.

78 Freitag 2000, pp. 250–256; Morton 2001, p. 114; Bonnier 2016, pp. 78–81.

79 Scattered evidence suggests that the primary economic activity of Achaia and its mountainous hinterland in northern Arkadia was pastoralism, especially the raising of sheep for wool production (Roy 1999, pp. 321–333). Evidence of this has recently come to light with the discovery of a large, specialized dyeing and textile production facility near Helike that operated between the 4th cent. BCE and mid-2nd cent. BCE (Katsonopoulou 2011).

80 Plutarch, Aratos 9.4; cf. Polybios 2.38.1–3.

Conclusion

The inscription studied in this chapter provides unparalleled insight into the early legal and economic history of the Hellenistic Achaian *koinon*. As noted above, Polybios observed of the four original member *poleis,* whom he terms the "founders of the polity of the Achaians" (ἀρχηγοὺς τοῦ τῶν Ἀχαιῶν συστήματος),[81] that "no stele pertaining to the *sympoliteia* of these cities exists" (οὐδὲ στήλην ὑπάρχειν συμβαίνει τῶν πόλεων τούτων περὶ τῆς συμπολιτείας).[82] The absence of such a document would have been notable to Polybios, steeped as he was in Achaian history and politics; we know from an inscription recording the accession of Epidauros to the *koinon* in 243 BCE that already by that date the formal establishment of the legal rights and obligations of member *poleis* vis-à-vis the *koinon* was a crucial element of the accession process;[83] this practice of formally declaring the rights and responsibilities of member *poleis* upon accession probably began soon after, or perhaps as soon as, the federal state expanded beyond its four original members.[84] In the first years of the newly re-founded federal state, the legal relationship between member *polis* and *koinon* was evidently established instead through ad hoc decrees relating to individual institutions. The Dyme inscription is, to my knowledge, the only securely attested example of such a decree.

From this perspective, I would argue that the number and severity of the legal checks imposed on the functionaries involved in this scheme are telling. The *prostatai* and *eranestai* were granted the right to keep formal registers of all officials responsible for repayment, in the same way that public debtors often had to register formally with the state (ll. 3–4).[85] The *polemarchoi* were to be fined for every day they failed to repay the creditors following a deadline, the amount being indicated by a ligature of the letters *deka* and *tau* (ll. 7–8); while the numerical system employed in early Hellenistic Achaia is not well understood, this symbol is attested in the acrophonic *koine* of the late Classical and Hellenistic period as an abbreviation of δεκά τάλαντα, "ten talents," meaning that these officials were to be fined the sum of 60,000 drachmas *per day* for failing to fulfill their duties[86] – several times more than the aggregate lifetime income of most people.[87] If the *gerontes* failed to hold the *polemarchoi* accountable in this way, they not only had to pay this astro-

81 Polybios 4.60.10.
82 Polybios 2.41.12.
83 I.Epidauros Asklepieion 25, ll. 1–13.
84 Walbank 1957, p. 233.
85 Feyel 1943, p. 118, n. 2; Rizakis, Achaïe III, p. 286, n. 108.
86 Tod 1911/1912, pp. 101, 110. The closest parallel comes from an inscription of Elateia in Phokis recording a debt payment made by the Phokians to Delphi in the late 340s or early 330s BCE (IG IX 1.110).
87 Cf. Loomis 1998.

nomical fine themselves, but they were also liable to lose both civic and federal citizenship (ll. 9–11). Lastly, reference is made towards the end of the inscription to a power being granted (ll. 13–14: ἐξουσία ἔ[στω]), followed by a lacuna and the words [-]θει ἐρανεστᾶν; I have followed Feyel's restoration of [πλή]θει ἐρανεστᾶν here, taking this to refer to an "assembly of *eranestai*."[88] If this is correct, then the *eranos* groups may have had their own distinct capacity to address issues that arose in relation to the repayment of the loan and take action to hold accountable the civic officials in charge of this scheme.

Taken together, these regulatory mechanisms give the impression of a federal government keen to convince its citizens that it was a trustworthy debtor. This is the only attested instance from the ancient Greek world of a public financing scheme involving *eranoi*,[89] suggesting that the Achaian *koinon* was innovative in its adaptation of this common social institution to raise funds at the federal level. But in the absence of a robust federal legal structure, average Achaian citizens may have been hesitant to contribute to this novel initiative, prompting the officials of the *koinon* to impose such carefully stipulated checks and harsh penalties. After all, a supra-civic Achaian state had not existed for at least a generation, perhaps two, by 280 BCE.

In this light, a passage of Demosthenes' *Against Aristogeiton*, a speech composed between 338 and 324 BCE addressing the complex case of the debts an individual known as Aristogeiton owed to the Athenian state, is particularly trenchant. Here, Demosthenes reflects on the nature of the legal system using an apt metaphor:[90]

> τί γὰρ ἂν τοῦτον αὐτὸν οἴεσθε ποιεῖν λυθέντων τῶν νόμων, ὃς ὄντων κυρίων τοιοῦτός ἐστιν; ἐπειδὴ τοίνυν οἱ νόμοι μετὰ τοὺς θεοὺς ὁμολογοῦνται σῴζειν τὴν πόλιν, δεῖ πάντας ὑμᾶς τὸν αὐτὸν τρόπον ὥσπερ ἂν εἰ καθῆσθ' ἐράνου πληρωταί, τὸν μὲν πειθόμενον τούτοις ὡς φέροντα τὴν τῆς σωτηρίας φορὰν πλήρη τῇ πατρίδι τιμᾶν καὶ ἐπαινεῖν, τὸν δ' ἀπειθοῦντα κολάζειν. ἔρανος γάρ ἐστι πολιτικὸς καὶ κοινὸς πάνθ' ὅσα, ταξάντων τῶν νόμων, ἕκαστος ἡμῶν ποιεῖ. ὃν ὁ λείπων, ὦ ἄνδρες Ἀθηναῖοι, πολλὰ καὶ καλὰ καὶ σεμνὰ καὶ μεγάλ' ὑμῶν ἀφαιρεῖται καὶ διαφθείρει τὸ καθ' αὑτόν.

> You see what sort of person the defendant is when the laws are in force; what do you think he would do if the laws were done away with? Since then it is admitted that, next after the gods, the laws preserve the state, it is necessary that all of you sit here as the *plerotai* of an *eranos*. Whoever obeys these [viz. the laws] by paying a contribution to the salvation of the fatherland you should honour and praise; but whoever disobeys them you should punish. For everything done by each of us in accordance with the laws is an

88 Feyel 1943, p. 115; Rizakis, Achaïe III, p. 39.
89 Migeotte's magisterial survey of Greek public finance includes no discussion of public financing schemes involving *eranoi* (2014).
90 Demosthenes, Orations 25.21–22.

> *eranos* of the state and the community. He who leaves it unpaid, men of Athens, deprives you of many good, noble, and great things and destroys them to the best of his abilities.

For the early Hellenistic Achaian government, lacking a formal *sympoliteia* agreement with its founding member *poleis,* decrees such as that preserved in the Dyme inscription were of paramount importance in formally establishing the legal rights and obligations between citizen, *polis,* and *koinon.* We may thus see in this inscription the cautious early steps in the creation of a federal law code that would not only preserve this delicate new state, but enable its many accomplishments over the subsequent 130 or so years of its existence.[91]

Bibliography

ARNAOUTOGLOU, Ilias N. (2003) Θυσίας ένεκα και συνουσίας: Private Religious Associations in Hellenistic Athens, Athens.

ARNAOUTOGLOU, Ilias N. (2009–2010) Dispute Settlement between Poleis-Members of the Achaean League. A New Source, in: Dike 12–13, 181–201.

AYMARD, André (1936) Le role politique du sanctuaire federal achaien, in: Mélanges Franz CUMONT (ed.), Annuaire de l'Institut de Philologie d'Histoire Orientales et Slaves IV, Brussels, 1–26.

AYMARD, André (1967) Les assemblées de la confederation achaienne. Étude critique d'institutions et d'histoire, Rome.

BASLEZ, Marie-Françoise (2006) Entraide et mutualisme dans les associations des cités grecques à l'époque hellénistique, in: Michel MOLIN (ed.), Les regulations sociales dans l'Antiquité, Rennes, 157–68.

BRESSON, Alain (2015) The Making of the Ancient Greek Economy. Institutions, Markets, and Growth in the City-States, translated by S. Rendall, Princeton.

CHANDEZON, Christophe (2012) L'argent et le credit dans le monde d'Artémidore, in: Christophe CHANDEZON/Julien DU BOUCHET (eds.), Études sur Artémidore et l'interprétation des rêves, Nanterre, 171–203.

COHEN, Edward E. (1992) Athenian Economy and Society. A Banking Perspective, Princeton.

FEYEL, Michel (1943) Sur une inscription de Dymé (*GDI,* 1615 = *DGE,* 427), in: Revue des Études Greques 56, 264–65, 112–24.

FINLEY, Moses I. (1952) Studies in Land and Credit in Ancient Athens, 500–200 B.C., New Brunswick.

FUKS, Alexander (1970) The Bellum Achaicum and its Social Aspect, in: The Journal of Hellenic Studies 90, 78–89.

GABRIELSEN, V. (2006) The Rhodian Associations and Economic Activity, in: Zosia H. ARCHIBALD et al. (eds.), Hellenistic Economies, London/New York, 163–84.

GAWLINSKI, Laura (2012) The Sacred Law of Andania, Berlin and Boston.

JONES, Nicholas F. (1999) The Associations of Classical Athens. The Response to Democracy, New York/Oxford.

91 Cf. Polybios 2.37.8–11.

KATSONOPOULOU, Dora (2019) Observations on the History and Topography of Two Major Sanctuaries of Poseidon and Zeus in Aigialeia of Achaea, in: Elena C. PARTIDA/Barbara SCHMIDT-DOUNAS (eds.), Listening to the Stones. Essays on Architecture and Function in Ancient Greek Sanctuaries in Honour of Richard Alan Tomlinson, Oxford, 88–97.

KATSONOPOULOU, Dora (2011) The Hellenistic Dye-Works at Helike, Achaea, Greece, in: Carmen ALFARO et al. (eds.), Textiles y tintes en la ciudad Antigua, Valencia and Naples, 237–242.

LEHMANN, Gustav A. (1967) Untersuchungen zur historischen Glaubwürdigkeit des Polybios, Münster.

LOOMIS, William T. (1998) Wages, Welfare Costs, and Inflation in Classical Athens, Ann Arbor.

MACKIL, Emily M. (2013) Creating a Common Polity. Religion, Economy, and Politics in the Making of the Greek Koinon, Berkeley.

MACKIL, Emily M. (2015) The Greek Polis and Koinon, in: Andrew MONSON/Walther SCHEIDEL (eds.), Fiscal Regimes and the Political Economy of Premodern States, Cambridge, 469–491.

MARTHA, Jules (1878) Inscriptions d'Achaïe, in: Bulletin de Correspondance Hellénique 2, 94–101.

MIGEOTTE, Léopold (2014) Les finances des cités grecques aux périodes Classique et hellénistique, Paris.

MIGEOTTE, Léopold (1992) Les souscriptions publiques dans les cites grecques, Geneva/Québec.

MILLETT, Paul (1991) Lending and Borrowing in Ancient Athens, Cambridge.

MORGAN, Catherine/HALL, Judith (1996) Achaian Poleis and Achaian Colonisation, in: Mogens H. HANSEN (ed.), Introduction to an Inventory of Poleis, Copenhagen, 164–232.

MORGAN, Catherine/HALL, Judith (2004) 'Achaia', in: Mogens H. HANSEN/Thomas H. NIELSEN (eds.), An Inventory of Archaic and Classical Poleis, Oxford, 472–488.

OSANNA, Massimo (1996) Santuari e culti: Santuari e culti del Acaia antica, Naples.

POST, Ruben (2022) Warfare, Weather, and the Politics of Grain Shortage in the Early 2nd c. BC Achaian League, in: Historia: Zeitschrift für Alte Geschichte 71(2), 188–224.

RÄDLE, Herbert (1970) Selbsthilfeorganisationen der Sklaven und Freigelassenen in Delphi, in: Gymnasium 77, 1–5.

VON REDEN, Sitta (2010) Money in Classical Antiquity, Cambridge.

RHODES, Peter John/LEWIS, David M. (1997) The Decrees of the Greek States, Oxford.

RIZAKIS, Athanasios (2013) États fédéraux et sanctuaires. Zeus Homarios et la construction de l'identité achéenne, in: Peter FUNKE/Matthias HAAKE (eds.), Greek Federal States and Their Sanctuaries: Identity and Integration, Stuttgart, 13–48.

ROY, James (1993) The Economies of Arkadia, in: Thomas H. NIELSEN/James ROY (eds.), Defining Ancient Arkadia, Copenhagen, 320–381.

RUBINSTEIN, Lene (2013) Forgive and Forget? Amnesty in the Hellenistic Period, in: Kaja HARTER-UIBOPUU/Fritz MITTHOF (eds.), Vergeben und Vergessen? Amnestie in der Antike, Vienna, 127–61.

RUBINSTEIN, Lene (2012) Individual and Collective Liabilities of Boards of Officials in the Late Classical and Early Hellenistic Period, in: Bernard LEGRAS/Gerhard THÜR (eds.), Symposion 2011. Études d'histoire du droit grec et hellénistique/Vorträge zur griechischen und hellenistischen Rechtsgeschichte, Vienna, 329–354.

SCHAEFER, Hans (1956) 'Polemarchos', in: RE Suppl. VIII, 1097–1134.

SCHWAHN, Walther (1931) Das Bürgerrecht der Sympolitischen Bundesstaaten bei den Griechen, in: Hermes 66(2), 97–118.

SIZOV, Sergey K. (2017) The Damiourgoi in the Cities of the Peloponnese and the Achaian Koinon, in: Dialogues d'Histoire Ancienne 43 (2), 11–32.

SZANTO, Emil (1892) Das griechische Bürgerrecht, Freiburg.

TAUSEND, Klaus (1992) Amphiktyonie und Symmachie. Formen zwischenstaatlicher Beziehungen im archaischen Griechenland, Stuttgart.

THOMSEN, Christian A. (2015) The *Eranistai* of Classical Athens, in: Greek, Roman, and Byzantine Studies 55, 154–75.
TOD, Marcus N. (1932) Sidelights on Greek history: Three Lectures on the Light Thrown by Greek Inscriptions on the Life and Thought of the Ancient World, Oxford.
TOD, Marcus N. (1911/1912) The Greek Numeral Notation, in: Annual of the British School of Athens 18, 98–132.
VAN BERKEL, Tazuko A. (2019) The economics of friendship: conceptions of reciprocity in classical Greece, Leiden/Boston.
VELIGHIANNI-TERZI, Chrissoula (1977) Damiurgen, Heidelberg.
WALBANK, Frank W. (1957) A Historical Commentary on Polybius, [Vol. I], Commentary on Books I–VI, Oxford.
WALBANK, Frank W. (1979) A Historical Commentary on Polybius, [Vol. III], Commentary on Books XIX–XL, Oxford.
WHITEHEAD, David (2000) Hypereides. The Forensic Speeches, Oxford.
WILHELM, Adolf (1911) Neue Beiträge zur griechischen Inschriftenkunde. Erster Teil, Vienna.

Zinon Papakonstantinou (University of Illinois at Chicago)

Greek legal pluralism

The case of sport and festivals

In memoriam Ingomar Weiler

Sometime in the late first or early 2nd century CE, the freedman turned philosopher Epictetus visited Olympia during the quadrennial celebration in honor of Zeus. Tens of thousands did the same and Epictetus, who was reputed in antiquity for his pauper's lifestyle, presented himself as outraged by the overcrowding and the overall unsanitary and discomforting conditions that visitors had to endure for the sake of the remarkable spectacle.[1] The picture conveyed by Epictetus was business as usual for the Olympic games, and there are indications that such ebullient enthusiasm for agonistic festivals in the face of adversity had spread all over the Greek-speaking world. In fact, Epictetus wrote this possibly eye-witness account of conditions at the Olympic festival during a period of agonistic renaissance under Roman rule.[2] This was a time of swift and stark multiplication of Greek-style festivals and games that were established on top of an already existing network of festivals and games. This bewildering network of contests entailed regulation at all levels, regarding the terms of competition and prize giving for athletes, the behavior of spectators that could irritate even a stoic like Epictetus, as well as norms germane to logistics and the organization of games (e.g., calendar, financing, and many others). By focusing on select examples of regulations for Greek sport and festivals, in this chapter I explore the advantages and disadvantages of a legal pluralist approach to Greek law. Such an approach, it is argued, can shift the epistemological stalemate detectable in some corners of traditional scholarship in Greek law, and provide invaluable insights on legal orders, normative agency, as well as multiple other parameters of the regulatory systems of Greek communities.

1 Epictetus 1.6.26–27.
2 Robert 1984.

Legal pluralism

With some notable exceptions,[3] legal pluralism as a strand of legal theory remains largely unexplored in the work of most commentators of law in premodern societies. For that reason, a brief overview of legal pluralism as the epistemological paradigm that informs the subsequent discussion of normativity in ancient Greek athletics is in order. Legal pluralism emerged in an attempt to document and comprehend legal manifestations (often described as native or customary law) in the context of colonial encounters and occupation in the modern era. This classic legal pluralism assumed a strict separation and hierarchy between western/colonizer law and the legal norms of the colonized. Eventually this strand of analysis spread to an examination of normative elements in the life of what were perceived as exotic or peripheral groupings within western societies. Since the 1970s and especially the 1980s, there have been systematic attempts to articulate a more sophisticated paradigm of legal pluralism that perceives normative orders as accruing from semi-autonomous social fields.[4] These fields are presented as interacting and influencing one another in the process of forming and instantiating legalities and social control. Even though proponents of this so-called 'New Legal Pluralism' advocate a perception of these processes that is nonhierarchical and often noninstitutional, similar to the initial manifestation this version of legal pluralism retains a strong undercurrent of state legal centrism. Another criticism leveled at New Legal Pluralism is the disempowerment, and at times the outright elision, of the legal subject. All social actors are potentially legal actors but in the so-called 'Social-Scientific Legal Pluralism' (a strand that includes both the 'Classic' and the 'New' Legal Pluralism) social actors are usually assumed as compliant components of a normative field, corresponding to a wider constituency which collectively pursues goals. In addition to the underlying current of state legal centrism, this presentation of homogeneous legal orders comprising consistently behaving actors to a certain extent renders 'Social-Scientific Legal Pluralism' an essentialist understanding of legal complexity. A reaction to such perceived drawbacks is the attempt to decenter legal subjects and perceive them as 'law inventing' as opposed to merely 'law abiding'.[5] This 'Critical Legal Pluralism' attempts to emphasize the wealth of meanings and symbolic systems that emerge in legal situations as well as the legal subjectivity and agency of the individual actor as they meander through the multiple normative communities that constitute their lives. 'Critical Legal Pluralism' sees no criteria or boundaries for legal rules in the

3 E.g., The 'Legal Unity and Pluralism' project at the Käte Hamburger Kolleg, University of Münster.

4 Moore 1973; Griffiths 1986. See the overviews in Merry 1988; Teubner 1992; Melissaris 2004.

5 Teubner 1992; Kleinhans/Macdonald 1997; Webber 2006.

context of normative heterogeneity, internormativity, and normative interdiscursivity carried out by constructed social actors.

This very brief and, by necessity inchoate, précis of developments in the field of legal pluralism brings into focus the almost complete lack of engagement with this strand of legal theory in the field of ancient law, especially Greek law. Indeed, many legal philosophers, anthropologists, and other scholars working in the tradition of legal pluralism have emphatically asserted that all human societies, including premodern societies, are legally plural.[6] Ancient Greek law, in contrast, has been dominated for decades by a strict monist and centralist perception of legality. In Greek law scholarship, law is almost always state law, that is statutory law endorsed by one or more institutional entities associated with the state. Once created, law is essentially perceived as a rational normative regime with stringent boundaries that can only be permeated, thus effecting a change in the law, through renewed state action. The only methodological concession are some attempts to pluralize legal forms within the frame of 'official'/state law in a way that, once again, affirms the primacy of such state-endorsed statutory legislation.[7] Not much space is therefore conceded to normative pronouncements and interactions with the law that do not exclusively originate with the official normative order in the guise of the state. As an example of this approach, one can point to the tentative manner in which non-state normative pronouncements, to the extent that they are even studied, are examined in Greek law scholarship.[8]

Contrary to such rigid approaches, in this chapter I argue that constructively engaging with the concepts provided by legal pluralism can substantially enrich debates on Greek law. It must be acknowledged, however, that engaging with legal pluralism is not devoid of challenges. How to define legal pluralism and understand

---

6 MERRY 1988, p. 879; MACDONALD 1998, pp. 74–75; DAVIES 2010, p. 807; see also GRIFFITHS 1986, for discussion of older scholarship. The main difference between premodern and modern societies is that the latter have established more elaborate disciplinary technologies, especially in connection with the enforcement of State statutory law and dominant ideologies. See FITZPATRICK 1983, esp. p. 50, with references to the work of M. Foucault and other theorists.

7 CANEVARO 2017, in connection with the concept of the Rule of Law in ancient Greece. Canevaro relies partly on the work of L. Fuller, one of the early positivist legal pluralists, (cf. FULLER 1969; WINSTON 1983); and B. Tamanaha who has been critical of the dominant strands of legal pluralism, see von BENDA-BECKMANN 2002; and DAVIES 2006, esp. pp. 578–579. For the pitfalls of the concept of the Rule of Law in ancient Greece see PAPAKONSTANTINOU 2008, pp. 8–9 and 63.

8 One can point to how laws governing various aspect of ritual are denied legal standing on the grounds that they are not state endorsed. See, e.g., an explicit, but not atypical, articulation of this fallacious principle in connection with laws on festivals, athletics, and other activities germane to Greek ritual in HARRIS 2015, p. 3 (with further references to scholarship in the same vein): "First, a law must be enacted and enforced by a political authority, that is, the state."

the interaction between its constituent actors, norms, and social fields has been an intractable problem. One of the most common criticisms against legal pluralism is that it can easily slide into a discourse of panjuridism, namely the tendency to see norms and processes of legal nature even when they do not exist. How far can one go in claiming that the innumerable rules that one encounters in any society have normative power? Are all norms and customs obligatory or are they merely widely adopted practices? Thinking of ancient Greece and at the microlevel, what would be the normative standing of the internal rules of the operation of a single, frequently called in scholarship 'private', association that are accepted as binding by its members,[9] or the rules enacted and enforced by sanctuaries? And what of the relationship of the normative order of an association or sanctuary vis-à-vis other associations, groupings, entities, institutions, states, and their rules?[10]

In an influential article, S. E. Merry suggested that a possible way out of this epistemological predicament is to move beyond essentialist definitions of law and into a historical understanding of legal practices that takes into account the legal pluralism that emerges through the dialectic between normative systems. The same scholar also urges an approach to laws as modes of thought inscribed in institutions and social sites.[11] In this context, it is crucial to acknowledge the plurality of state law, but equally importantly to underscore that there are other forms of social regulation emanating from entities that are only loosely associated, if at all, with the state, that draw on the symbols of legality.[12] Other theorists expand this perspective to think not only in terms of collectivities and orders, but also from the perspective of social actors in a legally plural milieu. To pick up the example presented in the preceding paragraph, in ancient Greece private associations and sanctuaries were two such milieux that frequently acted as sites of jurigenesis. To the extent that can be documented and analyzed, these and other entities amounted to semi-autonomous normative fields: there was clearly some interdependence with state law, but they also had significant freedom to, in certain contexts, promulgate

9 I am referring here to associations of various orientations and membership (professional, ceremonial, etc.) called *thiasoi, eranoi, synodoi, koina, orgeōnes,* to name some common denominations. The emphasis on the 'private' nature of these associations in much of modern scholarship implicitly contrasts them to 'state' entities, but the juxtaposition is largely misleading.

10 Greek associations and the rules governing their organization and operations are fairly, though patchily, documented and several aspects of these associations have received a considerable amount of scholarly attention as of late. See, e. g., Gabrielsen/Paganini 2021, with discussion of recent and older scholarship. The complexity and specificity of association norms contrasts sharply with the scholarly reluctance to acknowledge these entities and their regulations as law-generating fields commensurable to the state, as well as to recognize them as interdependent actors, alongside the state and other entities, in a wider nomic landscape, hence exposing the limitations of the currently dominant approach in Greek law.

11 Merry 1988, p. 889.

12 Merry 1988, p. 874.

and implement their own regulations.[13] Social actors belonged to or substantially interacted, in a simultaneous manner, with one or more of these entities as well as the state. Therefore, social actors had to constantly juggle with and negotiate both non-state as well as state-endorsed norms. In situations in which actors were invited to partake in the operations of a semi-autonomous normative field – e.g., in the course of the activities of a sanctuary, including festivals, games, and other manifestations of religious ritual – said actors could be susceptible to normative procedures of more than a single field. Thus, during a local-caliber and usually privately sponsored contest held in accordance with the terms of an endowment, participants were susceptible to the rules of the ceremony and games as specified by the endowment, as well as to the norms of the community/state in which these activities were held. The multiplicity of sets of binding norms pertaining to particular groupings or activities, each grounded in their own distinctive traditions and cultural vernaculars, suggests that Greeks, from the Archaic to the Imperial period, considered such norms as better responses to conditions in semi-autonomous normative fields. To stick with the example of festivals and games, in diverse political and institutional setups (independent *poleis;* leagues; multicultural empires) Greeks found it more advantageous to regulate agonistic festivals and games with regulations germane to each festival than through comprehensive diktats applicable to all manifestations of this flagship cultural practice. In each instance, then, decentered (vis-à-vis the state) social actors contributed to inventing norms for a particular practice/social field and subsequently negotiated the application, enforcement, and at times resistance to these norms.

In the remainder of this chapter, I intend to explore select aspects of the regulatory framework of Greek sport and festivals as a means to illustrate facets of legal pluralism in the ancient Greek world. I will begin by focusing on regulatory codes for games before turning to endowments providing for athletic practices and, finally, to technical rules for athletic events.[14] State institutional configurations shifted considerably from the Archaic to the Imperial periods, and there is evidence

13 For the notion of the semi-autonomous field see originally Moore 1973; Griffiths 1986. The concept has been extensively elaborated since then in legal philosophy and anthropology, see Davies 2010 (esp. pp. 813–814). For the purposes of the present discussion, normative fields and orders are perceived as malleable aggregates of rules with binding power generated by actors operating in diverse social settings.

14 A legal pluralist approach can extend, among others, to an analysis of the regulatory frameworks of *gymnasia,* including the role and responsibilities of gymnasiarchs; and the normative frameworks governing the *ephebeia*. Aspects of both themes have been examined, but not from a pluralist perspective, primarily through the lens of the better-known gymnasiarchy law of Beroia (SEG 43.381, early 2nd century BCE) and the ephebarchic law of Amphipolis (SEG 65.420, originally of the 2nd century BCE, then reinscribed during the late 1st century BCE).

for legal diffusion and plurality throughout this long chronological span. For the purposes of the ensuing discussion, I will concentrate mostly on the better documented post-Classical world. The aim is to contribute to a thematically focused, processual, and historically situated analysis of legal pluralism that is amenable to the dialectic between normative fields, the plasticity of norms, and the negotiation of legal diversity by social actors in specific micro- and macro-settings.

Regulations of Greek agonistic festivals

a. 'Iso'-designated stephanitic games

Sanctuaries and the multitude of activities hosted therein is an ideal starting point for exploring legal heterarchy in the Greek world. Even though Greek sanctuaries were, in principle, partly controlled or sponsored by state institutions or other entities, sanctuary officials had a considerable degree of independence in issuing regulations regarding cultic matters, finances, festival activities (including religious ceremonies, performances, contests), as well as visitor behavior. Normative pronouncements issued by states and other entities concerning sanctuaries were supplemented by sets of regulations that originated with the sanctuaries themselves and operated concurrently to state statutory enactments. Collectively, the totality of such normative enactments should be viewed as manifestations of multiple normative discourses. Moreover, the wealth of documentation germane to laws issued by and germane to sanctuaries strongly points to a conviction on the part of sanctuary authorities and society at large that norms that developed over time in the context of a particular field of practice were better adapted to that field of practice than externally imposed norms.

Greek sanctuaries traditionally hosted and regulated most aspects of agonistic festivals. Participants in Greek ritual, including agonistic festivals, could hardly fail to notice that, while engaging in cultic acts or competing in games, they were subjected to prescriptions and proscriptions enunciated and enforced by multiple entities and magistrates, only some of whom were formally affiliated with the state. During an agonistic festival athletes and visitors, like Epictetus in the Olympics, were expected to adapt their behavior – or sport strategy, if we think of athletes, and act in accordance with the sanctuary/festival regulations they attended. In a world of hundreds of such agonistic festivals, navigating such regulatory heterogeneity, informed by local knowledge and local action, must have been no easy task.[15] This was also the case regarding competitive sport, one of the most popu-

15 For local knowledge see Beck 2020, esp. pp. 26–29.

lar features of many Greek festivals. Even though common ground did exist, as a rule norms governing competitive sport differed, sometimes substantially, from city to city and from sanctuary to sanctuary. That applies both to the substance of the norms, as well as to the individuals or groups entrusted with their enactment and enforcement. This pluralism of rules and enacting authorities can sometimes be observed even in the most unexpected corners of athletic competition, where one would normally anticipate regulatory homogeneity and consistency across the agonistic landscape.

In the Greek world recurring games were regulated by a set of rules that were enacted by a civic entity, at times in conjunction with the administrative apparatus of a sanctuary. Starting in the Hellenistic period monarchs and later Roman emperors could interfere with the regulatory framework of festivals. In both local and interstate agonistic festivals (and that includes the so-called Big Four, namely the Olympic, Pythian, Isthmian, and Nemean games) the principal enacting authorities and their designated officials were also in charge of the implementation and oversight of the regulatory framework of the games. These legally binding norms were enforced by sanctuary or civic authorities through their appointed representatives, including umpires and other games overseers in major interstate sanctuary games and appointed civic officials, such as the *agonothetai*, in most civic games.[16]

One should not assume the existence of a comprehensive code of regulations for every set of games known from Greek antiquity, although fragments of or references to such codes did exist. Thucydides referred to the "Olympic law" (5.49.1 Ὀλυμπιακός νόμος) and during his visit to Olympia Pausanias claimed to have seen the "disposition of the games" (5.20.2, ἡ διάθεσίς ἐστιν ἡ τοῦ ἀγῶνος). In Pausanias' case the *diathesis* of the games was probably an inscribed set of regulations governing most, but not all, aspects of the Olympic games. In the same passage he also refers to the disc of Iphitus in which the proclamation of the truce *(ekecheiria)*, another practice with legal implications, was written. There were also regulations on technical aspects of the competition, a point to which I will return in the last section of this chapter. Aspects of these regulations, whether integrated in the *diathesis* or promulgated as stand-alone enactments, were often revised and supplemented.[17]

The regulations of the Olympic and other major interstate games were well known to athletes and spectators due to the popularity of the festivals that hosted them. That does not entail that the regulations of these games, to the extent that they are known, were models for regulating and administering games in Greek communities throughout the Eastern Mediterranean. This is the case even for games that were designated as equal to one of the major contests, and hence were

16 For an overview of aspects of the regulatory framework of interstate games not discussed in the present chapter see Weiler 2014; Papakonstantinou 2021; Murray 2021.

17 E.g., SEG 51.523, 3rd century CE.

proclaimed to be 'isolympios', 'isopythios' etc., after one of the major games. Such 'iso'-designated games were not meant to be identical or even "like" the original in terms of their program and other arrangements, as it is sometimes assumed in scholarship.[18] An 'iso' designation engendered identical legal consequences with regard to rewards to victorious athletes and, in rare cases, signified correspondence in the determination of age classes.[19] At times festivals, primarily during the Hellenistic period, that comprised both athletic and thymelic contests would designate the former as 'iso' to one of the major contests with gymnic and equestrian events, but designate the thymelic contests as 'isopythian' after the Pythian games, the oldest and most prestigious of interstate festivals with thymelic events. This state of affairs is well illustrated by a decree of Chios regarding the Soteria in Delphi: the Chians accepted the contest as isopythian for the musical events and isonemean for the gymnic and hippic ones "concerning the age classes and rewards".[20] The clause concerning corresponding age classes between the Soteria and a major contest (in this case the Nemean Games) is rather exceptional if not unique, and unless such correspondence is explicitly mentioned in decrees or other documents granting 'iso' status one should assume only the grant of identical secondary prizes by cities to victors.[21] In the case of the Nikephoria games in Pergamon after 182 BCE the athletic and equestrian contests were proclaimed as isolympian, while the musical

18 E.g., Siewert 1992, p. 113; van Bremen 2007, p. 345, n. 4; Di Nanni Durante 2007–2008, p. 8.

19 Concerning rewards, the process is made explicit in a decree of Gonnoi by which the Thessalian city accepts the isopythian status of the Leukophryeneia: δίδοσθαι δὲ καὶ τοῖς νικήσασιν Γοννέων τοὺς ἀγῶνας τού[τ]ο<υς> ὅσον καὶ τοῖς τὰ Πύθια νικῶσιν δίδοται (Rigsby, Asylia, no. 83 ll. 20–22). For other examples regarding the Leukophryeneia see Rigsby, Asylia, no. 91 ll. 14–15, decree of Sicyon; no. 94, 22–24, Corcyra; no. 95 ll. 29–31, Illyrian Apollonia; no. 96 ll. 30–32, Epidamnos; no. 97 ll. 22–24, Chalkis; no. 100 ll. 36–38, Paros; no. 102 ll. 36–39, Klazomenai; no. 105 ll. 27–30, Knidos; no. 111 ll. 78–80, Antioch in Persis; no. 112 ll. 32–25, unknown city; no. 131 ll. 22–23, an Attalid city. I.Ephesos 1415 ll. 10–15, early Hellenistic (late 4th/early 3rd century BCE) refers to a statute regarding *timai* for Ephesian victors of the Nemean games.

20 F.Delphes III 3.215 ll. 9–11: ἀποδεξώμεθα τὸν ἀγῶνα τὸμ μὲν μουσικὸν ἰσ[οπύθιον, τὸν δε γυ] | μνικὸν καὶ ἱππικὸν ἰσονέμεον ταῖς τε ἡλικίαις καὶ ταῖς τιμαῖς. See also ll. 15–16 and 24–25. The same decree, ll. 17–18, also refers to a Chian statute concerning rewards for victors in Pythian and Nemean games. This decree is dated c. 248–246 BCE. For 'iso'-designated games, especially during the Hellenistic period, see Vial 2003; Parker 2004; Slater 2012, pp. 168–169, with references to past scholarship For a broader assessment of Hellenistic agonistic festivals and other aspects of athletics see Chaniotis 1995; Langefeld 2009; Mann/Remijsen/Scharff 2016; Scharff 2024.

21 Klee 1918, pp. 50–51. Organizers of the overwhelming majority of most 'iso'-designated festivals faced no restrictions in the choice of age classes deployed in their games. For this point see also Crowther 1989, p. 101 and the discussion of the Sebastan games in the following section.

competitions were deemed worthy of isopythian status.[22] Hence Greek cities who formally recognized these arrangements effectively agreed to reward their athletes or horse owners who were victorious at the Soteria in Delphi and the Nikephoria of Pergamon with secondary rewards and benefits (monetary or otherwise) equivalent to victors at the Nemean games (Soteria) or the Olympic games (Nikephoria).[23] Victors in musical events at both festivals were given secondary rewards by their cities identical to rewards granted to victors at the Pythian games. That was the extent of the similarities between the Soteria, the Nikephoria, and the more famous contests – or, to put it differently, the organizers of the Soteria, the Nikephoria, and all other contests bearing an 'iso'-designation were given the freedom to introduce changes or new features to their games, compared to older and more established contests, as they saw fit as long as these changes did not pertain to secondary rewards.[24]

The race between cities to elevate the standing of their civic festivals in the eyes of the Greek world and attach an 'iso' designation to their games at times resulted in normative novelties. In 281/1 BCE the league of the Islanders honored the request to recognize the newly established Ptolemaia games, an *agon gymnikos, mousikos,* and *hippikos* held in Alexandreia, as isolympian, the first of its kind.[25] In the same decree the league acknowledged that victors at the Ptolemaia from the constituent states were to receive honors according to the laws of each of these states regarding Olympic victories.[26] The problem was that the Olympic games did not comprise any musical events in their program, hence the island states with musical victors at the Ptolemaia had to devise a legal solution to the requirement to honor as Olympic victors musical performers who could never compete at the Olympic games. It is not known how exactly the constituent *poleis* of the league of the Islanders dealt with this legal conundrum. In the late 5th century BCE the Great Panathenaia, a festival that awarded monetary or other valuable prizes to victors in gymnic, eques-

22 Syll.³ 629 (= F.Delphes III 3.240) and 630 (= F.Delphes III 3.261). It is sometimes assumed that the Nikephoria also corresponded to these major games in age classes, Syll³ 630 28, but this is not certain. See F.Delphes III 3.261, with comments on page 234.

23 Here I make a distinction between primary rewards, granted by the organizers of a contest to victors at the site of competition, and secondary rewards that were sometimes granted to these same victors by their home cities.

24 The type of secondary rewards that a victor in a sacred contest of the Hellenistic period would expect is intimated in the decree of Tralles concerning the recognition of the isopythian standing of the Leukophryeneia games in Magnesia on the Meander. It specifies that citizens of Tralles who were victorious in Magnesia would expect to receive prizes, allowances, and other honors equivalent to all isopythian contests, ἆθλά τε καὶ σιτηρέσια καὶ τἆλλα τίμια, Rigsby, Asylia, no. 129 ll. 19–20, reign of Attalus II.

25 Syll.³ 390; see Remijsen 2011, p. 104.

26 Syll.³ 390 ll. 39–42.

trian, and musical events, granted primary prizes of the highest market value to victors in musical events.[27] But concerning secondary awards, in principle civic authorities during the Hellenistic and Imperial periods did not seem to distinguish between events when assigning honors to athletic, hippic, or thymelic victors.[28] Hence member states of the *koinon* of the Islanders probably shrugged off the lack of musical events at the Olympic games and rewarded their musical victors at the Ptolemaia in the same fashion as athletic and hippic victors.

One of the best-documented illustrations of such normative plasticity in connection with the establishment of 'iso'-designated contests are the Leukophryeneia games in honor of Artemis, held in Magnesia on the Meander. Following the decision to upgrade the Leukophryeneia, a *gymnikos, hippikos,* and *mousikos* contest, to isopythian status the host city sent out in 208 BCE representatives to formally lodge the request, and received numerous positive responses.[29] Due to the extensive documentation available for the process of elevating the standing of the Leukophryeneia, one can perceive with more clarity some of the legal complexities and maneuvering, exercised by all entities and actors, that went into the implementation of this change. As in the case of the Soteria, the Ptolemaia, and all other 'iso' games, in the case of the Leukophryeneia as well the legal consequences of the recognition of isopythian status were formally promulgated and integrated into the existing legal narratives of all relevant entities. Thus a decree of 208/7 BCE by the Aitolian League through which the *koinon* acknowledged the isopythian designation of the Leukophryeneia in Magnesia on the Meander underscores the legal validity of the decision by ordering the relevant officials to integrate the gist of the

27 IG II² 2311, and more recently SEG 53.192. For the date of this inscription see Papakonstantinou 2024. In the Imperial period thymelic performers at the Sebasta, one of the top-tier games, were awarded high-value primary cash prizes of up to 4,000 drachmas (I.Olympia 56 ll. 53–60). Also during the Imperial period, in the Demostheneia in Oinoanda (SEG 38.1462, 125/6 CE) the monetary prizes granted to victors in thymelic events were considerably higher than the prizes for victors in gymnic events. In contrast, in several games in Aphrodisias during the 2nd/3rd centuries CE (I.Aphrodisias Perphormers, no. 52) victors in gymnic events were on average awarded prizes of higher monetary value than victors in thymelic and artistic events.

28 One should not assume that this was a universal practice. For instance, a fragmentary decree (IG I³ 131, issued probably in the 430s or 420s BCE) concerning the right of *sitesis* in the Athenian *prytaneion* distinguishes between equestrian and other victors in Panhellenic games (ll. 11–18), and it is possible, although in my view not very likely, that it indicates that the secondary rewards (but not the *sitesis* itself) granted to these groups differed somehow. On the *prytaneion* decree see most recently Mann 2023; Tentori Montalto/Cardinali/Pizzoli 2023, pp. 24–26.

29 This was the second attempt by Magnesia to secure the elevated status of their flagship festival, following a failed campaign towards the same objective in 221 BCE. See Rigsby, Asylia, 179–185; Slater/Summa 2006.

decree into the league's legal code.[30] As another decree regarding the Leukophryeneia demonstrates, such legislation often appended a list of all crown games that were recognized by a city and which thus created legal obligations regarding secondary rewards.[31] It is worth noting at this point that the upgraded status of the Leukophryeneia was formally acknowledged not only by kings, cities, and *koina*, but also by the non-state entity of the *synodos* of Dionysiac artists. Their decree refers to their internal set of laws (νόμου) in connection with the award of a crown to the *demos* of Magnesia.[32]

Most entities that were recipients of the Magnesian delegates accepted the terms of the request tout court, including the isopythian status of the Leukophryeneia contest. But some cities chose to depart from some aspects of the formal appeal. As already noted, a request to attach an 'iso' designation to a contest triggered legal implications for honors on the part of the home city of a victorious athlete or performer, but this obligation of reciprocal honors was often extended to the *theoroi* who announced forthcoming iterations of the games to the Greek world. In the case of the Leukophryeneia, and as far as the *theoroi* were concerned, that practically meant that Greek cities who had accepted the contest as *isopythios* were expected to treat the Magnesian envoys in a manner similar to the envoys announcing the forthcoming Pythian games. However, both Corinth and its colony Syracuse, even though they consented to the isopythian status of the Leukophryeneia and hence rewarded their victors in Magnesia with honors identical to Pythian victors, nevertheless decided to honor the Magnesian *theoroi* of the isopythian Leukophryeneia with the honors awarded to those proclaiming the Isthmian games, controlled by Corinth.[33] Moreover, Argos unilaterally decided to honor the *theoroi* of the isopythian Leukophryeneia with honors equivalent to the *theoroi* of the Nemean games held in Argos.[34]

The quest of the Magnesians to legally bind other Greek cities in recognizing their contest as *isopythios* was at times negotiated by the recipients of the request and elicited multiple responses in a way that highlights the plasticity of normative engagement in the Greek world. Some entities accommodated the request of Magnesia by revising their local regulatory frameworks and by appending the Leukophryeneia into the roster of locally accepted 'iso' games. Other recipients of the Magnesian appeal provided a positive response, but legally adjusted the terms of the request to accommodate local exigencies and preferences, for instance in connection with the treatment of Magnesian *theoroi*. Each entity that accepted the

30 Rigsby, Asylia, no. 78.12. καταχωρίξαι ἐν τοὺς νόμους. Cf. Rigsby, Asylia, no. 84 ll. 33–34, Phocian League; no. 85 ll. 35–36, Same, Kephallenia; no. 89 ll. 43–44, Achaian League; no. 94 ll. 34–35, Corcyra; no. 95 ll. 38–40, Apollonia.

31 Rigsby, Asylia, no. 88 ll. 47–50, Megalopolis.

32 Rigsby, Asylia, no. 103 ll. 29–30.

33 Rigsby, Asylia, no. 92 ll. 8–14 (Corinth) and no. 120 ll. 29–40 (Syracuse).

34 Rigsby, Asylia, no. 90 ll. 17–19.

standing of a festival organized by another entity could introduce an extra node in the network of internomic arrangements governing the operation of the festival, by altering some of the terms originally set forth by the host entity. This was multi-sited law that was open and contingent.[35]

b. The Sebastan Isolympia games

One of the best documented 'iso'-designated contests are the Sebastan games held in Naples. Established by Augustus and held since 2 CE, the Sebasta was an *isolympios agon* most likely since its foundation. Organized under the auspices of Roman imperial patronage, often with personal involvement of the emperor himself, the Sebasta Isolympia was fast-tracked since its inception to the exclusive club of prominent games, possibly even joining the circuit of top contests *(periodos)* during the Imperial period.[36] Administrative and regulatory facets of the Sebasta bear traces of this background, especially in comparison to other 'iso'-designated contests, discussed in preceding sections, of the early and middle Hellenistic period. A fragmentary inscription (I.Olympia 56) of the 2nd century CE set up in the sanctuary of Zeus in Olympia provides insights for the regulation of the Sebastan games. The Sebastan games *nomos* displayed in Olympia was in all probability an abridged version of the regulatory framework of these games. Other testimonia, most importantly victor lists of the Sebastan games during the 70s, 80s, and 90s CE, suggest an even more diverse line up of competitions as well as a more complex administrative and normative framework than what the Olympia inscription ostensibly referred to.[37]

---

35 Interestingly, it was partially due to this diffused and diverse normativity that the practice of establishing and seeking the recognition of 'iso' games went largely out of fashion (without completely disappearing, as shown by the case of the Sebasta discussed in the subsequent section) during the late Hellenistic period: the setup left too many gaps and grey areas, for instance it provided a disincentive to athletes and performers to compete at games whose 'iso' standing was not recognized by their native cities. See a preliminary discussion in Slater 2012, pp. 176–177. To be sure, what succeeded this setup in the Imperial period, namely a motley of newly established games, and the frequently uncertain prospect of secondary rewards offered by the victors' home cities, also left a lot to be desired from a legal point of view. One can point to the role of the synods for athletes and artists, and the intervention of Roman authorities in these matters, during the Imperial era. But this is a discussion for another occasion.

36 The composition of the Imperial *periodos* is disputed. For recent attempts to interpret the evidence, including an overview of past theses, see Gouw 2009, pp. 137–153; Strasser 2016.

37 For the victor lists of the Sebasta from the Flavian era see Miranda De Martino 2014, 2017, 2018. The divergences in events and age classes in the 1st century CE victor lists vis-à-vis the 2nd century CE *nomos* discovered in Olympia strongly suggest sweeping changes in the program of the Sebasta, enshrined in legislative enactments. But the exact process whereby such changes were implemented cannot be reconstructed on the basis of the present evidence. For the Sebastan games in general see Caldelli 1998, pp. 28–37; Di Nanni Durante 2007–2008; Miranda De Martino 2022, all with references to past scholarship.

Moreover, the reference in the inscription in Olympia (l. 22) to another *nomos* pertaining to the *apographe* of athletes wishing to compete at the Sabasta clearly points to other statutory enactments that were germane to the operation of the games. Overall, and despite its fragmentary nature and the obvious fact that the Sebasta was not a typical festival with games, several provisions in its extant *nomos* (I.Olympia 56) address basic organizational aspects of athletic contests frequently encountered throughout the Greek-speaking world. It can therefore shed further light on the normative arrangements and operation of 'iso' games, and the degree of overlap or departure from regulatory frameworks of other Greek-style games of the Imperial era, regardless of whether they bore the 'iso' designation or not. For these reasons, the Sebastan games *nomos* deserves a fresh look in the context of any discussion related to the mushrooming of Greek-style games and their concomitant regulatory frameworks in the late Hellenistic and Imperial eras. The objective is to be attentive not merely to the pluralization of the legal, but also the way norms were organized in and around practices.

The *nomos* of the Sebasta comprises a provision that elaborates the procedure, paralleled in numerous other Greek games, of dedicating unwon wreaths when a contest was declared sacred, namely when a tie occurred or when an event was not contested per lack of competitors (ll. 16–18). Other clauses echoing common practices in Greek athletics includes the requirement of registration *(apographe)* of the name, city, and event of athletes with the local officials (in the case of the Sebasta, the *agonothetai*) (ll. 18–20).[38] By the same token, several aspects of the program and organization of the Sebastan games diverged widely from the Olympic games. For instance, the Olympic games lacked musical or other artistic competitions but the isolympian Sebastan games comprised an extensive line up of thymelic events in music, acting, poetry, and oratory.[39] That was not unheard of – I have already pointed out the case of the Ptolemaia in Alexandria, another isolympian contest with thymelic games. Similar to the point made in connection with the Ptolemaia, Greek cities most likely awarded their victors in thymelic events at the Sebasta the secondary rewards granted to Olympic victors in gymnic and equestrian events.

Moreover, and in addition to the usual for top-tier games line up of equestrian events, the Sebastan games sported a more extensive program of athletic events than the Olympic games, comprising a *lampas* (torch race) and an *apobates* race in addition to traditional running and field events. The Olympic and Sebastan games also widely diverged regarding the age classes or other groups eligible to compete in athletic events. In Olympia only two age groups were eligible to compete, boys and men. In Naples, by contrast, in addition to boys and men, the *ageneioi* age class is also attested (IG Napoli I 62), as well as other competition classes: the *sebaste*

38 For the *apographe* in Greek games see Robert 1978, pp. 283–284.

39 Summary in Miranda De Martino 2014, pp. 1185–1188.

krisis (possibly a subdivision of the boys age class), the *klaudiane krisis* (similarly, possibly another subdivision of the boys age class), *paides politikoi* (citizen boys), *parthenoi politikai* (citizen girls), *paides syngkletikoi* (boys of senatorial order), *parthenoi syngkletikai* (girls of senatorial order), *bouleutōn thygateres* (daughters of the local *boule* members), and finally *parthenoi* (young girls from any part of the Greek-speaking world).[40] Admittedly there are still many unknowns in all of this, including whether all of these events and age/civic/gender classes were part of the inaugural Sebasta in 2 CE, or whether some were introduced in later iterations of the contest. Most of the distinct classes of contestants are in fact attested for the 70s, 80s, and 90s CE in the most recently discovered, but still partially published, victor lists of the Sebastan games.[41] But Greek agonistic festivals were dynamic organisms, and it must be considered certain that, similar to many other documented festivals, changes in the program, regulation, and other organizational aspects of the festival were introduced over time.

Comparable to the other 'iso'-designated games surveyed in the preceding section, the better documented regulatory framework of the isolympian Sebasta, as intimated in the fragmentary *nomos* from Olympia and the agonistic program of the festival, was symptomatic of wider trends in Greek sport but also an articulation of local exigencies and legal vernaculars. One can especially underscore the numerous, and distinct from the Olympic or any other contemporary contest known thus far, age and civic classes competing at the Sebasta, including the competitions for male and female youths hailing from the Neapolitan civic elite (senatorial order, *boule*).[42] These competition classes are in fact unique in their specificity which integrates age and social background components that smack of local interests and practices. Far from being slavish and accurate copies of the regulations, program, and other logistical arrangements of the alleged original, the Sebasta and other 'iso'-designated games betoken both internormativity and normative heterogeneity, and they assume active legal agency on behalf of local organizers who molded the regulation, program, and rewards of their games.

---

40 For evidence and preliminary discussion, especially for the competition classes attested in the 1st century CE victor lists of the Sebasta, see Miranda De Martino 2014, 2017, and 2018. The *Sebaste krisis* and *Klaudiane krisis* were documented before the discovery of the 1st century CE victor lists, and were discussed by Robert 1939, pp. 239–244, along with other evidence for *kriseis* in Greek games of the Imperial period. For *kriseis* see also Frisch 1988.

41 See note 37.

42 Restricted eligibility contests, usually open to citizens of specific communities or leagues, are known from other parts of Greece during the Hellenistic and Imperial periods. For examples see Papakonstantinou 2019, chapters 3 and 4. Young unmarried girls had the opportunity to compete in some of the top-tier Greek games during the Imperial period. See Lee 1988; Mantas 1995; Golden 1998, pp. 123–140. These discussions should be supplemented by the newly discovered victor lists of the Sebasta.

c. Reception and athletes' agency

The 2nd century CE regulation of the Sebastan games also allows indirect glimpses on the normative agency of athletes and performers. In an example of regulatory overlap, both the Olympic and the Sebastan games required registration and a 30-day residency and training before competition for all eligible athletes and performers.[43] The organizing authorities of the Olympic and Sebastan games had some procedures in place for the enforcement of this rule as well as the adjudication of infringements regarding registration, training, and other matters. As far as the Sebastan games are concerned, the organizing authorities admitted only illness, robbery, or shipwreck as valid excuses for late registration (I.Olympia 56 ll. 24–25).[44] Writing also in the 2nd century CE, Pausanias relates the story of the Alexandrian boxer Apollonius Rhantes at the Olympic games of 93 CE (Pausanias 5.21.12–14). Apollonius showed up in Elis late for registration but was excused on the grounds of his claim that he was delayed in the Cyclades by contrary winds. Eventually one of his opponents demonstrated that Apollonius was late because he was competing in games in Ionia. Such detailed provisions on timely registration and the prosecution of violators are symptomatic of the overcrowded, overlapping, and at times simply chaotic Greek agonistic calendar of the Imperial period – a state of affairs that none other than Hadrian himself attempted to redress in 133/4 CE (SEG 56.1359).

In such a context athletes emerge as not merely law-abiding, but at times as law-resisting subjects in their attempts to navigate and at times circumvent the strict registration requirements or other expectations of normative character imposed by civic and festival authorities. Two documents, one of the second half of the 2nd century CE and one from the very beginning of the third record the unwillingness of many athletes to compete at the Athenian Panhellenia, a contest established by Hadrian and celebrated for the first time in 137 CE.[45] A few decades after their establishment, the Panhellenia had failed to attract a steady stream, to the extent desired by the organizers, of high-quality competitors. Given the imperial pedigree of the contest, Athenians complained to the emperor, most likely Marcus Aurelius, who issued a binding ruling stripping all athletes who failed to register for the Panhellenia, or did so without a valid excuse, of their *syntakseis* (pensions awarded by

43 But the organizers of the Sebasta awarded a per diem *opsonion* for every day that the athletes were in mandatory residence for practice in Naples, which was also a departure from the Olympics in Elis.

44 See the discussion in Merkelbach 1974, with suggested restorations for the Sebasta regulation, and Maróti 1998.

45 Cassius Dio 69.16.1–2. Follet 1976, pp. 343–345. For the date of the first Panhellenia see Wörrle 1992, pp. 337–349, adjusted by Petzl/Schwertheim 2006, pp. 83–84, and Slater 2008, p. 614.

the athletes' home cities) won in all sacred eiselastic games in Athens.[46] This ruling deprived, in other words, the offending athletes of any *syntakseis* won not only through the Panhellenia, but also at the Athenian Hadrianeia, the Olympieia, and the Great Panathenaia.[47] The emperor further specified that athletes who had never won a victory, and therefore the right to a pension, from the games in Athens, and had failed to provide an adequate excuse for missing the Panhellenia, were banned indefinitely from the games held in that city (ll. 7–9). The same document implies that the Athenian authorities could impose further restrictions and penalties on such athletes at their discretion (ll. 10–11). Finally, Marcus Aurelius declared his intention to report the decision to the athletes' *synodos,* a fairly powerful body of collective normative agency for athletes that issued its own internal regulations and often negotiated on behalf of athletes for favorable conditions and privileges.[48]

Such ostensibly stringent measures did not do much to deter top-tier athletes who continued to abstain, in sufficient numbers, from the Athenian Panhellenia. In 201 CE and in response to an Athenian embassy that complained that athletes continued to scorn the Panhellenia and passed up Athens at the time when the games were taking place, Septimus Severus and Caracalla renewed the measures against offending athletes introduced by Marcus Aurelius some decades earlier.[49] Athletes reluctant to compete at the Panhellenia most likely opted to compete at other sacred games held at the same time in Asia Minor.[50] One plausible explanation for this preference is that collectively the games in Asia Minor offered more valuable prizes that compensated for the loss these athletes incurred from forfeiting the potential *syntakseis* of the Athenian games. Moreover, the fact that the Athenian Panhellenia were held in Hadrian's calendar right before the Olympic games, the ultimate agonistic destination of athletes, and thus would have required an extra trip and stopover for the athletes traveling over from Asia Minor, might have contributed to the decision of many to skip this particular Athenian festival.[51] It all came down, therefore, to timing and enrichment opportunities. Even in a minutely structured and strictly regulated network of sacred games, athletes were ultimately capable of pursuing their preferred competition schedule in the face of civic mandates and imperial diktats.

---

46 Oliver 1989, no. 188, 1–9 with emendations and commentary by Strasser 2010: 595.

47 For the sacred eiselastic games of Athens during the 2nd century CE see Spawforth 1989, 194; for testimonia, see Follet 1976, chapter 8.

48 For evidence regarding the negotiations of the athletes' synod with Roman authorities in attempting to augment athletic privileges see Slater 2015. Any discussion of athletes' secondary rewards during the late Imperial period, including all legal implications of this practice, must now be supplemented by the evidence provided through the revised edition of the papyri from Hermoupolis, Drew-Bear et al. 2020.

49 Oliver 1989, no. 245.

50 For a similar interpretation see Slater 2008, p. 615; Strasser 2010, p. 617.

51 SEG 56.1359, 73–74.

d. Endowments and local-caliber games

Operating in the shadow of the prestigious *periodos* contests of the Imperial era was a vast network of games. Among them, the stephanitic and sacred games offered the highest cachet and considerable material rewards (though not necessarily both at the same time) to successful athletes. These games, some of which are mentioned in the letters of Hadrian of 133/4 CE regulating aspects of the competitive calendar and other matters, regularly attracted the best athletes and performers. Even less celebrated was the pastiche of hundreds of local *themides* and other local-caliber games that attracted mainly athletes from the host city or geographically proximate communities. The overwhelming majority of athletes attested in connection with these games competed only occasionally and for a short span of time, mostly as boys and teenagers, and never achieved (or even attempted to achieve) the heights of athletic glory claimed by the victors of the top-tier sacred games.

Yet even though this multitude of games lacked the éclat of sacred and eiselastic games, in many ways these *themides* and other local contests, along with the activities and games held in local *gymnasia* in connection with the *ephebeia* and the training of local groups of men defined by age, were the true breeding grounds of Greek athletics. In their regulatory frameworks too, such local-caliber games were laboratories of normative innovation, negotiation, and at times exceptionalism. The program and overall normative orientation of individual, post-Classical contests in this extensive network of games was symptomatic of dominant strategies of financing and benefaction in Greek cities. Typically, there were regulatory incongruities, on the substantive and procedural level, between festivals with games financed primarily by a civic authority (or, in the Imperial period, by a civically appointed *agonothetes*) and games fully or partially funded by an endowment. In the latter case, the main sponsor, with the blessing of civic authorities, was allowed some leeway to legally establish, in the regulation of the festival, some practices that might have departed from mainstream Greek athletics. But even in these cases, usually civic authorities had most of the oversight, including the capacity to prosecute violators of festival regulations.

This is the case for the Messenian Badesieia, an obscure agonistic festival established in Kardamyle in the mid-late Hellenistic period (2nd–1st century BCE).[52] The contest and related activities were established through a monetary gift of a certain Komas in a community that already held other athletic and thymelic games (II 8–9). The Badesieia was by all accounts a contest of local appeal. It is not known from any other sources besides this inscription, and we do not know of any athletes who competed there. Nevertheless, even the regulation of a contest of this caliber reveals

52 SEG 65.245 and BE 2016, no. 205.

links with the wider statutory framework of the city. The Badesieia consisted of a *gymnikos agon* (I 1–6, with several lines missing on the top part of the stele), held at a stadium, as well as a judgment contest held at the city's *gymnasion* after a procession (I 6–12).[53] In the latter the victor received a shield *(thyreos)* as prize, which he was expected to dedicate, probably at the *gymnasion*,[54] "as it is written" (I 12) – a reference to another enactment, most likely a local *gymnasiarchikos nomos*. Moreover, the decree establishing the Badesieia stipulates that the exact timing of the annual contest will be determined by a new decree or law (I, 14–15). Focusing on such micro-regulatory practices allows one to evaluate the subjectivity of legal agents on the local level, and better appreciate the extent to which regulatory enactments at times departed from widely held customs. In the case of the Badesieia, an example of such decentralized normativity grounded in localized inclinations and traditions concerns prizes: the Badesieia awarded prizes to victors and runners up (I, 1–6), an extremely rare practice in Greek institutionalized *agones*.[55]

The fragmentary regulation of the Badesieia and the attached decree honoring Komas provide some glimpses of the multiple layers of normative engagement around the theme of athletics in a small community of Peloponnese during the Hellenistic period, but there is no indication in the extant text of any possible input of the sponsor Komas in the program, prizes, or any other aspect of the legal framework of the contest. In principle, founding documents for local games by wealthy sponsors usually underscore which features of the games were pushed forth by the benefactor, hence pointing to explicit instances of individual normative agency over regulatory practices that were very much embedded in a particular cultural milieu. An example is provided by the foundation of Kritolaos from Aigiale in Amorgos in memory of his son Aleximachos.[56] The statute prescribes the process of lending out Kritolaos' monetary gift as well as the organization of a public feast and athletic games. Regarding the prizes presented to victors, a cross-reference is given to the local *gymnasiarchikos nomos* (81–83). Most curiously, the law stipulates that no pankration contest was to be held as part of the new contests and that Aleximachos, the deceased youth, would be declared victor of that event on an annual basis (ll. 83–84). The implication of this clause is that Aleximachos was to receive annually the set prize for the pankration contest. While alive Aleximachos was presumably a pankratiast, so this unusual victory arrangement was a concession to the

53 Unless this was a departure from common practice, the contest in the *gymnasion* was not in *euoplia*, as Themos 2015 suggested, since that was a team event and the Badesieia inscription strongly suggests an individual victor. The reading is doubtful on other grounds as well, see BE 2016, no. 205.

54 Cf. the gymnasiarchy law of Beroia, SEG 27.261.B.67–68 and other parallels in Themos 2015, p. 553.

55 See Crowther 1992 for examples.

56 IG XII 7.515, end of 2nd century BCE.

donor and father of the boy Kritolaos, who most likely envisioned and suggested it. Kritolaos, with the consent of the authorities of Aigiale, essentially carved out a novel legal category for a posthumous, annually declared victory without competition that was semantically proximate to what real-life competing athletes would call an *akoniti* (dust-free, meaning no-contest) victory.

Similar micro-regulatory practices that deviated from established customs in civic agonistic festivals are encountered in most endowed games funded by an individual, as well as in endowments for the funding of activities or institutions connected to athletic training. The so-called 'oil endowments' were as popular as the endowments for games in the Greek world. Oil was the most commonly used commodity by athletes in Greek games as well as in *gymnasia* by trainees, some of whom were part-time or full-time athletes. In the words of N. Kennell, "oil was used in every *gymnasium* by every person taking exercise there."[57] The number of those exercising regularly could easily run up to the hundreds for a mid-size city, and even more for a major urban center. Consequently, the cost of supplying oil to a *gymnasion* even in a small city could be considerable, especially in tumultuous or uncertain circumstances. Similar to many other public services in the late Hellenistic and Imperial periods the burden of oil provision to civic *gymnasia* was increasingly assumed by local elites. At times such benefactors provided oil liberally at their own expense for an entire year (or other extensive period), and they were lavishly honored by their cities for their generosity.[58] In such instances, and to drive the point home, in commemorative discourse payment for gymnasial oil from one's personal purse (ἐκ τῶν ἰδίων; ἰδίαι) was redundantly combined with the statement that the commodity, which was indispensable for athletic training and competition, was granted free of charge (δωρεάν).[59] Other benefactors were only able to supply oil to a *gymnasion* for a few weeks and only for some of the age groups regularly training there.[60] Often, although not always, such limited scope donations occurred in the context of a major local festival, and at times benefactors advertised the extraordinary market prices they had to pay to acquire and then donate the precious commodity.[61] Occasionally the cost was so high that some donors boasted in public that they provided free oil to their local training venue

---

57 Kennell 2001, p. 119.

58 E.g., IG XII 9.234 ll. 12–14, and 24–25, Eretria, c. 100 BCE; IG XII 9.236 ll. 17–18, Eretria, c. 100 BCE; I.Priene 41, 100–75 BCE; I.Lindos II 449 ll. 6–7, Lindos, late 1st century CE.

59 E.g., TAM V 2.1204, 1205, and 1208, Apollonis, all in the context of civic *ephebeia*. In such and similar cases, the claim that ephebes went through their training cost-free probably involved more than the provision of oil.

60 E.g., I.Iasos 87, 121, and 248, Imperial period.

61 Papakonstantinou 2019, pp. 161–162 with examples from Stratonikeia in the Imperial period.

for merely a day per year.[62] Yet other local elites, acting as gymnasiarchs, actually sold oil to ephebes and other trainees at the *gymnasion* below market price, and they even boasted about that.[63] In addition to its use by *gymnasion* trainees of diverse age groups (including teams of *paides, epheboi, neoi,* and other groups) cities, and most often in the Imperial period, local private benefactors broadened on the occasion of some festivals the pool of potential recipients for anointing oil to include other local residents who did not normally frequent the *gymnasion,* as well as visiting foreigners.[64] There were, in other words, virtually limitless, legally compliant options for the supply of anointing oil to *gymnasion* trainees and participants in festivals that were borne out of parochial customs and tastes, and manifested through magistracies, decrees, or legal instruments. Other than the wholesale foundation of new games (as in the case of Kritolaos), the most common legal instrument for the articulation of the normative will of individual donors pertaining to the provision of oil and other material aspects of training and competition was an endowment of special-purpose funds.

Given the occasional scarcity and high premium placed on oil, communities encouraged and welcomed oil endowments, and they were willing to turn a blind eye to some provisions that departed from mainstream practice and legal precedent. In the endowment of Phaenia Aromation from Gytheion in 42 CE, the donor donated funds for the provision of oil in perpetuity to residents of her town as well as to foreigners.[65] The donation was meant to take care of the needs for oil τῷ γυμνασίωι καὶ τῇ πόλει, namely the daily supply of anointing oil for the regular athletic trainees of the *gymnasion* as well as for the dispensation to other members of the community, in the form of anointing oil and its byproducts (mostly unguent), on special civic occasions (ll. 17 and 43). Among the different provisions of the endowment, the granting of the right to slaves to partake of the freely available oil in the *gymnasion* for six days per year during festivals stands out (ll. 38–42). The same clause forestalls any opposition to this concession to the slave population of Gytheion by an archon, a *synedros,* or a gymnasiarch. The implication is that members of the civic elite of Gytheion would most likely object to the idea of slaves having access to the *gymnasion* and its oil, as such practice was against the almost universally followed tradition of precluding slaves as integral participants in Greek training venues and formal competition. Normally slaves would provide their labor in these contexts as auxiliary personnel but would not be allowed to disrobe, as the Hellenistic gymnasiarchy law of Beroia puts it, and train in the *gymnasion* or

62 TAM V 2.828.B, Attaleia; TAM V 2.1197, Apollonis.

63 E.g., SEG 38.675, Styberra, ca. 41–48 CE; SEG 38.679 and 680, Styberra, 74/75 CE.

64 Papakonstantinou 2019, chapter 4, for examples.

65 IG V 1.1208. For legal procedures envisaged in this endowment see Harter-Uibopuu 2004.

compete in Greek games.[66] Phaiania, in other words, along with a few other local benefactors in Greek cities of the Imperial period that allowed slaves to partake for a few days per year, and in a manner commensurate to free citizens, in some activities of the *gymnasion*,[67] went against the regulatory tide and contributed in instantiating a multi-layered normative landscape revolving around the distribution of anointing oil.[68] In that regard it is certainly revealing that, as far as one can ascertain, instances of legally substantive innovation initiated by benefactors – and that includes Kritolaos, Phaenia, and many others – largely relied on civic officials for implementation, enforcement, and redress. In the case of sport-related endowments as well, legal innovation and departure from commonly accepted practices was not tantamount to a large-scale decoupling from civic institutions and their representatives.

Νόμοι ἐναγώνιοι

The contingent and localized nature of much of the regulatory framework governing Greek athletic practices and competition is also suggested by the evidence that points to normative diversity in technical rules for the conduct of particular events, what the Greeks called νόμοι ἐναγώνιοι.[69] These kinds of technical rules were somewhat distinct from the broader genre of the *nomoi* of *agones* which, as the cases discussed in the preceding sections suggest, focused on outlining norms and penalties on administrative and logistical aspects, including requirements for registration, age classes, prizes, and acts of ritual directly related to the contest. A certain degree of standardization of the *nomoi enagonioi* was to be expected, especially in the early stages of the consolidation of a network of institutionalized contests in the late Archaic and early Classical period. At the same time, one expects that the almost

66 Slaves as auxiliary personnel in Greek athletics, see Mann 2014, esp. pp. 280–282. Beroia law, μὴ ἐγδυέσθω, SEG 27.261.B.27–28. For an overview of the role of slaves in Greek athletics see also Golden 2008, chapter 2.

67 Cf. also IG IV 597 and 606, Argos, Imperial period; for more examples see Kennell 2001, p. 122.

68 Harter-Uibopuu 2004 draws attention (e.g. p. 10) to further normative departures in the Phaenia endowment, including in the formal procedures adopted in the indictment of violators of the terms of the endowment.

69 Lucian, Demonax 49. In Philostratos, Images 2.6.3, Philostratos points to an instance of normative diversity in the rules for the pankration as they were implemented in Sparta and the Olympic games, especially the prohibition of biting and gouging. Both were prohibited in Olympia, but Philostratos claims that Spartans allowed biting and gouging in local, i.e., held in Sparta, contests because of the Spartans' constant preparation for war, surely an anachronistic explanation. Nevertheless, it is still noteworthy that a plurality of technical rules between different *agones* and communities is presented by Philostratos as a reality.

complete dominance of social elites in Archaic Greek sport would be reflected on the content, polyvocality (or lack thereof), and dissemination of sport-related rules in Archaic Greece.[70] A *nomos enagonios* of the late 6th century BCE concerning rules for wrestling that was inscribed on a bronze tablet and publicly displayed at the sanctuary of Olympia, was perhaps a manifestation of these processes.[71] Infractions of this set of rules – the one that survives proscribes the breaking of fingers during a wrestling bout – were punished, as the fragmentary text suggests, by flogging and a ban from the Olympic games. It is not an unreasonable assumption that similar pronouncements pertaining to other athletic and equestrian events, comprising technical rules and punishments for their infractions, were on display in the sanctuary in Olympia since the 6th century BCE. Literary tradition attributes the inaugural rules of Greek boxing to Onomastos of Smyrna, first Olympic champion in the event in 688 BCE.[72] No published version of the rules for boxing survives, but the attribution of such rules to Onomastos and the publication of rules for wrestling suggests that during the Archaic period Olympia was perhaps thought of as the epicenter of Greek athletic regulation, especially regarding the *nomoi enegonioi.* Furthermore, the published Olympic rules on wrestling, as well as technical rules about other events that might have been enacted and displayed in Olympia, could have easily served as a convenient reference point for organizing authorities of newly established or overhauled Greek contests of the 6th century BCE. Such a development could have contributed to a partial disembedding of competitive sport from its localized contexts, and the emergence since at least the 6th century BCE of the well-attested – in epinician odes and commemorative victory inscriptions – notion of a distinct, interstate network of institutionalized *agones.*

As the network of institutionalized games gradually expanded in the Classical period and beyond, there are some indications for pluralism and heterogeneity even in the realm of *nomoi enagonioi.* By this assertion, I do not mean to imply that different technical rules were in place in every location or contest; rather, the point advanced here is that a degree of normative diversity might account for some of the seemingly insoluble inconsistencies documented in the evidentiary record of Greek *nomoi enagonioi.* The best example concerns the pentathlon, the only combined event in Greek sport which consisted of five disciplines, namely discus, jump, javelin, footrace (a *stadion* race), and wrestling. The event is documented from the early days of Greek institutionalized sport in the late Archaic period until the late Imperial period, and there were certainly several universal features in the regula-

70 See the remarks by Murray 2021, pp. 100–101.

71 I.Olympia.Suppl. no. 2 ll. 1–4, c. 525–500 BCE. Fragments of another bronze tablet of the same date from Olympia, I.Olympia.Suppl. no. 3, contain references to wrestlers and judges, thus suggesting that it might have been of regulatory character.

72 Pausanias 5.8.7; Iulius Africanus fragment 65 Wallraff, pp. 74–75.

tory framework governing the competition of the pentathlon. The five contested events were always the same; wrestling was contested last; three outright victories in three constituent events were sufficient (and perhaps required) for overall victory in a pentathlon competition. But there are many unknowns and some highly contested points, including what exactly happened when none of the contestants could achieve three victories in the first three or four events.[73] There is an inordinate amount of scholarship on this issue alone. To make things even more complicated the ancient record provides contradictory – or so it seems to us – evidence on the sequence in which the events were contested, and commentators are also divided on this point.[74] Ancient athletes and audiences clearly had no issue figuring all this out, and as a result extant sources do not elaborate these points.

A detailed exposition of all the uncertainties associated with the ancient Greek pentathlon lies beyond the scope of the present discussion. There is, however, some documentation that points to the possibility that in certain cases some of the modalities of the pentathlon, for instance the sequence in which the events were contested as well as the method of determining final placements, were not universally followed in the hundreds of *agones* documented especially in the Hellenistic and Imperial periods. Such local variations, to the extent they existed, were legally enshrined and implemented, presumably with the aid of civic authorities, in a process comparable to any other statutory provision related to festivals and athletics. Moreover, such variations would have added a local flair without substantially altering most of the basic principles (e.g., the high value placed on outright victory versus second or lower placements) governing the operation of the pentathlon. A very fragmentary inscription from Rhodes, discovered in the main *gymnasion,* just a stone's throw away from the stadium where the Great Halieia and other contests of Rhodes took place, points in the same direction.[75] It contains detailed technical regulations for the conduct of the events of the pentathlon. In the first, and still most detailed, discussion of the inscription L. Moretti argued that the regulation from Rhodes, fragmentary and intractable as it may be, strongly suggests

73 Most specialists agree that many athletes were eliminated after the third event. The controversy revolves around the method whereby some athletes were selected to continue to the fourth and, if necessary, the fifth event.

74 Most commentators would agree that the three events unique to the pentathlon (discus, jump, javelin, the so-called pentathlon triad) were contested as a block. The sequence of events was therefore footrace-triad-wrestling or triad-footrace-wrestling, and it is true that there is some ancient evidence that seems to support either of these views. For a discussion of these issues, as well as the contentious and still unresolved issue on how the overall victor was decided see, e.g., Golden 1998, esp. pp. 69–73; Kyle 2015, pp. 117–119; Egan 2007; all with discussion of past scholarship.

75 SEG 15.501, with comments and emendations by Moretti 1956; Bean 1956, p. 368; Brein 1980.

local diversification in the rules governing the pentathlon.[76] The first clause of the extant fragment (ll. 3–4) probably deals with the drawing of lots, frequently used in Greek athletics to arrange pairs of contestants in preliminary rounds of combat sports, qualification heats in running, and possibly other aspects, e. g., the sequence in which athletes competed in certain events, an issue that is clearly of concern in the regulation of Rhodes as subsequent clauses suggest.[77] The next partially, but fairly confidently, reconstructed clause (ll. 5–6) of the same regulation stipulates that athletes will have five attempts at the discus, and the one with the best throw will proceed to try first in the jump.[78] This clause is largely in keeping with other ancient evidence on the pentathlon as well as modern interpretations. First, it is in keeping with the widely held view that the so-called triad, namely the three events unique to the pentathlon, were contested as a block. It is also in keeping with the widespread, although not universally endorsed, scholarly assertion that all contestants competed in all three events of the triad: there is no suggestion, on the basis of the text from Rhodes, that any athlete was eliminated from the jump on the basis of his performance, however poor it might have been, in the discus. The only unique and otherwise unattested feature of the conduct of the pentathlon that this clause contributes is that athletes were allowed five discus throws each.

The remainder of the text of this regulation for the pentathlon is too fragmentary to make coherent sense out of it, but there are still some clues. Lines 7–9 concern the jump, but the meaning is uncertain.[79] Even more baffling are ll. 10–12 which might refer to the footrace or the javelin.[80] Following this, there is an isolated reference to a wrestler, so one can safely conclude that this part of the regulation dealt with the last event of the pentathlon. It seems certain, therefore, that the regulation comprised prescriptions concerning the pentathlon events in the order they were contested. However, it is clear that merely a few lines are dedicated to each event which, in turn, strongly suggests that this set of rules was not a comprehensive code laying out *all* the norms pertaining to the pentathlon. Also of importance is the fact that the text went on for at least a few more lines, and there is also another column of the same text (column A) that comprised references to contests, the *agonothetes,* and the *gymnasion.* These rules, as transmitted by the inscription from Rhodes, must have been applicable to the games held in the city, including the Great Halieia, the flagship agonistic festival of the island that regularly attracted

---

76 Moretti 1956, p. 60. The possibility of changes and local variations in the pentathlon is briefly acknowledged, but not expounded, by Kyle 1990, pp. 299 and 304; Golden 1998, p. 55; and Miller 2004, p. 63.

77 For the possibility, insecure as it may be considering the lacunose state of the stone, that the initial lines deal with drawing lots, see Ebert 1963, p. 19.

78 Moretti 1956: 57 followed by Bean 1956, p. 368.

79 For some reconstructions see the studies in n. 75.

80 Footrace, Bean 1956, p. 368; javelin, Brein 1980, p. 90.

top-tier athletes, including Olympic champions. Such full-time athletes were intimately cognizant of every technical aspect of their event. If the technical rules of the pentathlon were identical throughout the hundreds of games attested in the Greek world, as it is often assumed, then the publication of a copy of these regulations in a location frequented primarily by athletes that constantly traveled and competed in contests year-round would make little sense.[81] The most economical assumption is that this was a Rhodian set of rules for the pentathlon, grounded on local practices and traditions.

I suggest that this text from Rhodes is part of a wider enactment that comprised local norms in connection with a series of sport-related themes, including the conduct of athletic events in games held in Rhodes. These local norms were publicly displayed in the main *gymnasion,* right next to the stadium of the city, for all officials as well as local and visiting athletes to see. These regulations were probably codified in the early Imperial period by officials associated with the major games of the island, such as the *agonothetai* of the Great Halieia. The section dealing with the pentathlon is the best-preserved part. As it stands, there is every chance that this local regulation of the pentathlon as it was conducted in Rhodian games did not radically alter basic features of the pentathlon, e.g., the sequence in which the events were held, or the scoring system, as were known from other Greek *agones,* but introduced a few tweaks of select norms. The otherwise unattested proscription that each athlete will have five attempts at throwing the discus seems to have been a departure from practices in other games in Greece, and thus it is duly expounded in the surviving section of the text. This five-throw rule seems to be at odds with a rather inscrutable passage from Pindar that seems to suggest that pentathletes, at the time Pindar was composing, were allowed a single attempt in the throws and that a foul would automatically disqualify an athlete from the remainder of the competition.[82] If that was indeed a widespread rule for javelin and discus throwing at the time of Pindar, it could have evolved and altered over time (and perhaps not uniformly) as the network of institutionalized contests expanded in the Hel-

---

81 The suggestion by Bean 1956, p. 368 that umpires, and not athletes, were the main audience of the inscription from Rhodes, is not entirely convincing. The display of the document in the main *gymnasion* suggests that this regulation was meant to be read by athletes as well.

82 Pindar, Nemean Odes 7.70–74. The Pindaric passage concerns the javelin, but javelin and discus were technically close and were considered as cognate events also by Pindar, Isthmian Odes 2.35. In Nemean Odes 7.70–74 Pindar suggests that an athlete who stepped over the mark when releasing the javelin was disqualified. This seems to imply a single attempt, since it would have been extremely unlikely that an athlete would have fouled all five attempts, as in the system of Rhodes. This is the interpretation of the passage preferred by many sport specialists, see Gardiner 1907, pp. 268–270; Moretti 1956, p. 59; Harris 1963, p. 28; García Romero 2003, p. 54, n. 27, with an overview of other interpretations of the same passage. Lee 1996 understands the passage as referring to an athlete stepping up to the line for his javelin throw – there is, in other words, no foul.

lenistic and Imperial eras. It is impossible to ascertain, at this point, the antiquity of the Rhodian rules; their promulgation, however, was not necessarily contemporary with the time the inscription under consideration was first displayed in the *gymnasion* of Rhodes.

Local *nomoi enagonioi* rarely survive, but the regulation from Rhodes is not the only extant specimen. A regulation of a contest in Misthia in Lykaonia dated no earlier than the 2nd century CE prescribed that pankratiasts that competed in the games in question were not allowed to wrestle and could only fight standing up, the intention probably being to divest wrestlers from an advantage when competing in the pankration. This rule was certainly at odds with mainstream pankration rules as commonly practiced throughout the Greek world, which apparently prohibited only gouging and biting.[83] If one looks beyond athletic technicalities, such sets of rules, including the fragment from Rhodes containing legally binding regulations of the pentathlon and possibly other events and facets of local *agones,* illuminate a crucial dimension of legal plurality grounded in local cultural forms. To quote D. Menderson, "[p]luralism *is* local knowledge and local action, a recognition of the cultural, communal and individual construction of legality."[84] That this polyphony of substantive norms, procedures, and agents of law, explored throughout this chapter, had reached even the *nomoi enagonioi* is symptomatic of the extent to which micro-regulatory practices, and the diversity they evinced, were embedded in Greek communities during the Hellenistic and Imperial periods.

Conclusion

The preceding selective discussion of regulatory enactments and other documents with legal validity related to the practices of Greek athletics make a strong case for perceiving and assessing law in the ancient Greek world in pluralist terms. Normative pluralism and local diversification, in terms of promulgating authorities as well as substantive and procedural law, are evident in *gymnasion* activities and the administration and content of games, especially during the Hellenistic and Imperial periods. A more thorough analysis reveals the existence of institutional and social configurations (including cities, sanctuaries, and associations) that acted as conduits in the process of negotiating and reshaping norms at the local level. Even individual benefactors could insert their will into the regulatory framework of local games or other facets of sporting practices, thus reinforcing the embeddedness of both law and sport in local cultural forms. All actors, individual and collective, engaged in an internormative dialogue that implemented, negotiated,

83 SEG 6.449, with SEG 39.1418. For rules of the pankration see Poliakoff 1987, pp. 54–57.
84 Manderson 1996, p. 1069 (original emphasis).

and occasionally resisted and altered the contingent components of the polynomic landscape of Greek athletics.

Bibliography

Bean, George (1956) Victory in the Pentathlon, in: American Journal of Archaeology 60, 361–368.

Beck, Hans (2020) Localism and the Ancient Greek City-State, Chicago.

Brein, Friederich (1980) Die Wertung im Pentathlon, in: Fritz Krinzinger et al. (eds.), Forschungen und Funde. Festschrift Bernhard Neutsch, Innsbruck, 89–94.

Canevaro, Mirko (2017) The Rule of Law as the Measure of Political Legitimacy in the Greek City States, in: Hague Journal of the Rule of Law 9, 211–236.

Chaniotis, Angelos (1995) Sich selbst feiern? Städtische Feste des Hellenismus im Spannungsfeld von Religion und Politik, in: Wörrle, Michael/Zanker, Paul, (eds.) Stadtbild und Bürgerbild im Hellenismus, Munich, 147–172.

Crowther, Nigel (1989) The Sebastan Games in Naples (IvOl. 56), in: Zeitschrift für Papyrologie und Epigraphik 79, 100–102.

Crowther, Nigel (1992) Second-Place Finishes and Lower in Greek Athletics (Including the Pentathlon), in: Zeitschrift für Papyrologie und Epigraphik 90, 97–102.

Davies, Margaret (2006) Pluralism and Legal Philosophy, in: Northern Ireland Legal Quarterly 57(4), 577–596.

Davies, Margaret (2010) Legal Pluralism, in: Peter Cane/Herbert M. Kritzer (eds.), The Oxford Handbook of Empirical Legal Research, Oxford, 805–827.

Di Nanni Durante, Diva (2007–2008) I Sebastà di Neapolis, Ludica 13–14, 7–22.

Drew-Bear, Marie Claude François et al. (2020) Les archives du conseil municipal d'Hermoupolis Magna, Berlin.

Ebert, Joachim (1963) Zum Pentathlon der Antike. Untersuchungen über das System der Siegeremittlung und die Ausführung des Halterensprunges, Berlin.

Egan, Rory (2007) How the Pentathlon Was Won: Two Pragmatic Models and the Evidence of Philostratus, in: Phoenix 61, 39–54.

Follet, Simone (1976) Athènes au IIe et au IIIe siècle. Etudes chronologiques et prosopographiques, Paris.

Fitzpatrick, Peter (1983) Marxism and Legal Pluralism, in: Australian Journal of Law and Society 1(2), 45–59.

Frisch, Peter (1988) Die Klassifikation der παῖδες bei den griechischen Agonen, in: Zeitschrift für Papyrologie und Epigraphik 75, 179–185.

Fuller, Lon L. (1969) Human Interaction and the Law, in: American Journal of Jurisprudence 14, 1–36.

Gabrielsen, Vincent/Paganini, Mario C. D. (eds.) (2021) Private Associations in the Ancient Greek World: Regulations and the Creation of Group Identity, Cambridge.

García Romero, Fernando (2003) Ancora sullo sport nei proverbi Greci antichi, in: Nikephoros 16, 47–59.

Gardiner, Norman E. (1907), Throwing the Javelin, in: The Journal of Hellenic Studies 27, 249–273.

Griffiths, John (1986), What Is Legal Pluralism, in: Journal of Legal Pluralism and Unofficial Law 24, 1–56.

Golden, Mark (1998) Sport and Society in Ancient Greece, Cambridge.

Golden, Mark (2008) Greek Sport and Social Status, Austin.

Gouw, Patrick (2009) Griekse atleten in de Romeinse keizertijd (31 v. Chr.–400 n. Chr.), Amsterdam.

Harris, Harold Arthur (1963) Greek Javelin Throwing, in: Greece & Rome 10, 26–36.

Harris, Edward (2015) Toward a Typology of Greek Regulations about Religious Matters: A Legal Approach, in: Kernos 28, 1–28.

Harter-Uibopuu, Kaja (2004) The Trust Fund of Phaenia Aromation (IG V.1 1208) and Imperial Gytheion, in: Studia Humaniora Tartuensia 5.

Kennell, Nigel M. (2001) Most Necessary for the Bodies of Men: Olive Oil and its By-Products in the Later Greek Gymnasium, in: Mark Joyal (ed.), In Altum: Seventy-Five Years of Classical Studies in Newfoundland, St. John's (Newfoundland), 119–133.

Klee, Theophil (1918) Zur Geschichte der gymnischen Agone und griechischen Festen, Leipzig.

Kleinhans, Martha-Marie/Macdonald, Roderick A. (1997) What Is a Critical Legal Pluralism, in: Canadian Journal of Law and Society 12, 25–46.

Kyle, Donald G. (1990) Winning and Watching the Greek Pentathlon, in: Journal of Sport History 17, 291–305.

Kyle, Donald G. (^{2}2015) Sport and Spectacle in the Ancient World, Chichester (UK).

Langenfeld, Hans (2009) Der Hellenismus als Epoche der Sportgeschichte, in: Jens-Frederik Eckholt/Marcus Sigismund/Susanne Sigismund (eds.), Geschehen und Gedächtnis. Die hellenistische Welt und ihre Wirkung. Festschrift für Wolfgang Orth zum 65. Geburtstag, Berlin, 177–199.

Lee, Hugh M. (1976) The TEPMA and the Javelin in Pindar, Nemean vii 70–3, and Greek Athletics, in: The Journal of Hellenic Studies 96, 70–79.

Lee, Hugh M. (1988) SIG^{3} 802: Did Women Compete Against Men in Greek Athletic Festivals?, in: Nikephoros 1, 103–111.

Macdonald, Roderick A. (1998) Metaphors of Multiplicity. Civil Society, Regimes and Legal Pluralism, in: Arizona Journal of International and Comparative Law 15(1), 69–92.

Manderson, Desmond (1996) Beyond the Provincial: Space, Aesthetics, and Modernist Legal Theory, in: Melbourne University Law Review 20(4), 1048–1071.

Mann, Christian (2014) People on the Fringes of Greek Sport, in: Paul Christesen/Donald G. Kyle (eds.), A Companion to Sport and Spectacle in Greek and Roman Antiquity, Chichester/UK, 276–286.

Mann, Christian (2023), The Prytaneion Decree (IG I^{3}131) and sitêsis for Athletes, in: Classical Quarterly 73(1), 26–39.

Mann, Christian/Remijsen, Sofie/Scharff, Sebastian (eds.) (2016) Athletics in the Hellenistic World, Stuttgart.

Mantas, Konstantinos (1995) Women and Athletics in the Roman East, in: Nikephoros 8, 125–144.

Maróti, Egon (1998) Zur Regelung der Sportwettkämpfe der Sebasta in Neapel, in: Acta Ant. Hung. 38, 211–213.

Melissaris, Emmanuel (2004) The More the Merrier: A New Take on Legal Pluralism, in: Social & Legal Studies 13(1), 57–80.

Merkelbach, Reinhold (1974) Zu der Festordnung für die Sebasta in Neapel, in: Zeitschrift für Papyrologie und Epigraphik 15, 192–193.

Miller, Stephen G. (2004) Ancient Greek Athletics, New Haven.

Miranda De Martino, Elena (2014) Les Sebasta de Naples à l'époque de Domitien. Témoignages épigraphiques, in: Comptes rendus de l'Académie des Inscriptiones et Belles lettres 158(3), 1165–1188.

Miranda De Martino, Elena (2017), I Sebasta dell'82 d.C.: restauro delle lastre e aggiornamenti, in: Historiká. Studi di storia greca e romana 7, 253–269.

Miranda De Martino, Elena (2018) I vincitori dei Sebastà nell'anno 86 d.C., in: Francesco Camia et al. (eds.), Munus Laetitiae. Studi miscellanei offerti a Maria Letizia Lazzarini, vol. II., Roma, 267–286.

Miranda De Martino, Elena (2022) Concorsi alla greca nel mondo romano: il ruolo di Neapolis, in: Frederico Rausa (ed.), Essere sempre il migliore. Concorsi e gare nella Napoli antica, Atti del Convegno Internazionale, Napoli, 15–17 maggio 2019, Naples, 13–31.

Moore, Sally Falk (1973) Law and Social Change: The Semi-Autonomous Social Field as an Appropriate Subject of Study, in: Law & Society Review 7, 719–746.

Moretti, Luca (1956) Un regolamento rodio per la gara del pentatlo, in: Rivista di filologia e di istruzione classica 34, 55–60.

Murray, Sarah C. (2021) Rules and Order, in: Paul Christesen/Charles Stocking (eds.), A Cultural History of Sport in Antiquity, London, 95–119.

Oliver, James H. (1989) Greek Constitutions of Early Roman Emperors from Inscriptions and Papyri, Philadelphia.

Papakonstantinou, Zinon (2008) Lawmaking and Adjudication in Archaic Greece, London.

Papakonstantinou, Zinon (2019) Sport and Identity in Ancient Greece, London.

Papakonstantinou, Zinon (2021) Law, Litigation, and Sport in Ancient Greece, in: Alison Futrell/Thomas Scanlon (eds.), Oxford Handbook of Sport and Spectacle in the Ancient World, Oxford, 592–602.

Papakonstantinou, Zinon (2024), Sport Prizes in Archaic and Classical Greece: Funeral Games and the Great Panathenaia, in: Christoph Begass/Christian Mann/Marco Tentori Montalto, Money and Honor in Ancient Athletics, Stuttgart, 91–113.

Parker, R. (2004) New 'Panhellenic' Festivals in Hellenistic Greece, in: Renate Schlesier/Ulrieke Zellmann (eds.), Mobility and Travel in the Mediterranean from Antiquity to the Middle Ages, Münster, 9–22.

Petzl Georg/Schwertheim, Elmar (2006) Hadrian und die dionysischen Künstler: drei in Alexandria Troas neugefundene Briefe des Kaisers an die Künstler-Vereinigung, Bonn.

Poliakoff, Michael B. (1987) Combat Sports in the Ancient World. Competition, Violence and Culture, New Haven.

Remijsen, Sofie (2011) The So-Called "Crown-Games": Terminology and Historical Context of the Ancient Categories for Agones, in: ZPE 177, 97–109.

Robert, Louis (1939) Inscriptions grecques d'Asie Mineure, in: William Moir Calder/Joseph Keil (eds.), Anatolian Studies Presented to William Hepburn Buckler, Manchester, 227–248.

Robert, Louis (1978) Catalogue agonistique des Romaia de Xanthos, in: Revue Archéologique, 277–290.

Robert, Louis (1984) Discours d'ouverture, in: Angeliki G. Kalogeropoulou (ed.), Πρακτικά του Η' Διεθνούς Συνεδρίου Ελληνικής και Λατινικής Επιγραφικής: Αθήνα, 3–9 Οκτωβρίου 1982, [vol. A], Athens, 35–45.

Rigsby, Kent J. (1996) Asylia. Territorial Inviolability in the Hellenistic World, Berkeley.

Roueché, Charlotte (1993) Performers and Partisans at Aphrodisias in the Roman and Late Roman Period. A Study Based on Inscriptions from the Current Excavations at Aphrodisias in Caria, London.

Scharff, Sebastian (2024) Hellenistic Athletes: Agonistic Cultures and Self-Presentation, Cambridge.

Siewert, Peter (1992) The Olympic Rules, in: William Coulson/Helmut Kyrieleis (eds.), Proceedings of an International Symposium on the Olympic Games, 5–9. September 1988, Athens, 113–117.

Slater, William John (2008) Hadrian's Letters to the Athletes and Dionysiac Artists Concerning Arrangements for the 'Circuit' of Games, in: Journal of Roman Archaeology 21, 610–620.

Slater, William John (2012) Stephanitic Orthodoxy?, in: Zeitschrift für Papyrologie und Epigraphik 182, 168–178.

Slater, William John (2015) Victory and Bureaucracy: The Process of Agonistic Rewards, in: Phoenix 69, 147–169.

Slater, William John/Summa, Daniela (2006) Crowns at Magnesia, in: Greek, Roman, and Byzantine Studies 46, 275–299.

Spawforth, Anthony (1989) Agonistic festivals in Roman Greece, in: S. Walker/A. Cameron (eds.), The Greek Renaissance in the Roman Empire: Papers from the Tenth British Museum Classical Colloquium, London, 193–197.

Strasser Jean-Yves (2010) 'Qu'on fouette les concurrents …' À propos des lettres d'Hadrien retrouvées à Alexandrie de Troade, in: Revue des Études Greques 123, 585–622.

Strasser, Jean-Yves (2016) La période et les périodoniques à l'époque impériale, in: Cahiers du Centre Gustave Glotz 27, 53–86.

Tentori Montalto, Marco/Cardinali, Sandy/Pizzoli, Lorenzo (2023) Decreto ateniese relativo alla concessione della sitesis, in: Axon 7, 7–38.

Teubner, Günther (1992), The Two Faces of Janus: Rethinking Legal Pluralism, in: Cardozo Law Review 13(5), 1443–1462.

Themos Athanasios A. (2015) Γίνεσθαι τὸν ἀγῶνα τῶν Βαδησιείων κατ' ἐνιαύτον: Ἐπιγραφὴ καθιερώσεως ἀγώνων ἀπὸ τὸ Ἐξωχώρι Καρδαμύλης, in: Aggelaos Mathaiou/Nikolas Papazarkadas (eds.), Ἄξων: Sudies in Honor of Ronald S. Stroud, Athens, 543–574.

Van Bremen, Riet (2007) The Entire House is Full of Crowns: Hellenistic Agōnes and the Commemoration of Victory in: Simon Hornblower/Catherine Morgan (eds.), Pindar's Poetry, Patrons, and Festivals: From Archaic Greece to the Roman Empire, Oxford, 345–375.

Vial, Christophe (2003) À propos des concours de l'Orient méditerranéen à l'époque hellénistique in: Francaise Prost et al. (ed.) L'Orient méditerranéen, de la mort d'Alexandre le Grand aux campagnes de Pompée. Cités et royaumes à l'époque hellénistique, Rennes, 311–328.

Von Benda-Beckmann, Franz (2002) Who's Afraid of Legal Pluralism, in: Journal of Legal Pluralism and Unofficial Law 47, 37–82.

Webber, Jeremy (2006) Legal Pluralism and Human Agency, in: Osgoode Hall Law Journal 44(1), 167–198.

Weiler, Ingomar (2014), Korruption und Kontrolle in der antiken Agonistik, in: Kaja Harter-Harter-Uibopuu/Thomas Kruse (eds.), Sport und Recht in der Antike, Vienna, 1–30.

Winston, Kenneth (1983) The Principles of Social Order: Selected Essays of Lon L. Fuller, Durham.

Wörrle, Michael (1992) Neue Inschriftenfunde aus Aizanoi I, in: Chiron 22, 337–376.

Laura Gawlinski (Loyola University Chicago)

Personal, local, global

Greek dress in ritual norms

The way one dresses is both informed by personal choices and influenced by cultural contexts, particularly the immediate, local context. Dress mediates between the embodied individual and the communities in which the individual participates, making (public) legal regulations about (personal) dress an appealing opportunity for exploring the topic of this volume. This chapter focuses on a select group of Greek legal texts concerning religious practices that often featured regulations of dress, the so-called sacred laws, or ritual norms.[1] This topic sits at the intersection of questions about unity and local idiosyncrasy for law, for religion, and for dress, and it contributes to the discourse around legal materiality.[2]

Dress and the law

The term dress is used here inclusively following the work of sociologists Mary Ellen Roach-Higgins and Joanne Eicher, who define it as "an assemblage of modifications of the body and/or supplements to the body."[3] This definition includes not just clothing, but also adornment elements like jewelry, permanent physical changes like tattooing, temporary physical changes like hairstyling, and applications like perfumes. Dress studies had traditionally focused on the role of dress as visual communication, but more recently has taken a sensory turn, and considers how the body itself interacts with dress, its feelings, sounds and structures, as well as changes made during wearing.

The elements that make up dress are potentially fruitful for approaching local practice. Textiles, for example, in both their materials and in their production processes, have a strong relationship to regional culture. In *Localism and the Ancient Greek City State,* Hans Beck highlights a modern Canadian example, the additional finger knitted into mittens in Newfoundland for help with hunting and fishing.[4] Likewise, through techniques, materials, and patterns, traditional embroidery

1 For discussion of these terms and the collections of these texts, see below.
2 Bonnet 2023 offers a useful overview of local Greek religion.
3 Roach-Higgins/Eicher 1992, pp. 1. For an overview of Greek dress, see Lee 2015.
4 Beck 2020, pp. 27–28; see also 75–120 on dress.

reveals its place of origin.[5] This level of specificity is more difficult to access for ancient Greece because of the poor preservation of physical remains and the lack of detail provided by the written sources. But with increased efforts toward collecting and analyzing that fragmentary evidence, that picture is beginning to change. For example, textile scholars have now been able to use details like the direction in which wool was spun and the types of weaves to conclude that the differences between Italic and Greek cultural traditions continued to persist despite significant interactions between the two in the Iron Age.[6]

References to Greek dress within the inscribed ritual norms have been used in the growing field of ancient textile studies to trace materials, color, technologies, or use in social settings, such as for creating a religious experience.[7] But what has received less attention is how exactly these source texts are a part of legal history. Why transform notions about who should wear what and when into a legal issue? Why write these particular customs down and engrave them into stone? The fact that a culture treats dress as a legal matter cannot be assumed as "natural." There does not seem to be much precedence for this subject within earlier legal traditions, at least not in what is now preserved. From the Near Eastern legal texts, there remains one extant fragment from Middle Assyrian law (ca. 1076 BCE, from Assur) that mentions dress, primarily veiling practices in the context of regulations about women. The passages are of note because of their uniqueness and the opportunity to consider what does or does not resonate with the later Greek codes:[8]

> Wives of man, or [widows] or any Assyrian women who go out into the main thoroughfare [shall not have] their heads [bare]. Daughters of a man [...with] either a ...-cloth or garments or [...] shall be veiled ..., [...] their heads [... (gap of ca. 6 lines) ...] When they go about [...] in the main thoroughfare during the daytime, they shall be veiled. A concubine who goes about in the main thoroughfare with her mistress is to be veiled. A married *qadiltu*-woman is to be veiled (when she goes about) in the main thoroughfare, but an unmarried one is to leave her head bare in the main thoroughfare, she shall not veil herself. A prostitute shall not to be veiled, her head shall be bare. Whoever sees a veiled prostitute shall seize her, secure witnesses, and bring her to the palace entrance. They shall not take away her jewelry, but he who has seized her takes her clothing; they shall strike her 50 blows with rods; they shall pour hot pitch over her head. And if a man should see a veiled prostitute and release her, and does not bring her to the palace entrance, they shall strike that man 50 blows with rods; the one who informs against

5 E.g., Vogelsang-Eastwood 2016.

6 Gleba 2017.

7 E.g., Brøns 2017a, pp. 325–352; Karatas 2020. The studies tend to focus on the ritual norms in sanctuaries contexts.

8 Translation Roth 1997, pp. 153–154 (A 40), 167–169 (A41).

> him shall take his clothing [*further punishments follow*]. Slave women shall not be veiled, and he who should see a veiled slave woman shall seize her and take her to the palace entrance [*text continues*]. (A 40)
>
> If a man intends to veil his concubine, he shall assemble five or six of his comrades, and he shall veil her in their presence, he shall declare "She is my *aššutu*-wife"; she is his *aššutu*-wife. (A 41)

The focus here is on women in public – as is clear from the reference to the thoroughfare – and the visual marking of social roles and age – as seen in references to wives, daughters, concubines, and sex workers. There are punishments for infractions that include confiscation of garments; even a man who does not report is punished through confiscation of his own dress possessions. Additionally, a description of a veiling ceremony shows dress in action, an investiture ceremony by which a woman could be recognized as having changed legal status. Dress makes intangible identities visible.

The earliest extant inscribed Greek law that legislates dress dates to the end of the 6th, a fragmentary text on bronze from Arkadia (provenience unknown) concerning activities in a sanctuary of Demeter Thesmophoros (IPArk 20):[9]

> [If a wom]an wears a colorfully decorated robe,
> it is to be consecrated to Demeter Thesmophoros.
> If she does not dedicate it, being ill-disposed toward the rite,
> let her perish miserably, and whoever is then *damiourgos,*
> is to pay thirty drachmas. And if he does not pay,
> he is to be guilty of impiety. This (the law? the impiety?) will be valid for ten years. Let this (inscription?) be sacred.[10]

The content shares surprising similarities with the Assyrian law, from its (likely)

---

9 It is likely that there were earlier regulations and more of them. Of special note are the early laws of Solon preserved in Plutarch that limited the number of garments put on the corpse at a funeral (Plutarch, Solon 21) or worn by a woman in public (Plutarch, Solon 21.4). These must be an important part of the story of the history of the practice of regulating Greek dress, especially since these are among the only ones that can be interpreted as sumptuary. For the purposes of this paper, I focus on the inscribed evidence.

10 [Εἰ γυ]νὰ ϝέσετοι ζτεραῖον λõπος, | [ἱερὸ]ν ἒναι τᾶι Δάματρι τᾶι Θεσμοφόροι· | [εἰ δὲ] μὲ ὐνιερόσει, δυσμενὲς ἔασα ἐπὲ ϝέργο | [κακο]ς ζ' ἐξόλοιτυ, κὰ ὅζις τότε δαμιοϝοργε | [ἀφάε]σται δαρχμὰς τριάκοντα· εἰ δὲ μὲ ἀφάετοι, | [ὀφλὲν] τὰν ἀσέβειαν· ἔχε ὅδε κῦρος δέκο ϝέτεα· ἒνα[ι] | [δ' ἱερὸν] τόδε. Translation adapted from Mills 1984 with updates from IPArk 20. See Karatas 2020, pp. 464–466, for the history of the interpretations of the ζτεραῖον λõπος. Grand-Clément 2017, pp. 54–56, examines this text in the context of other Demeter regulations.

focus on women, punishment clauses, and even a male official being liable if punishment is not carried out. These resonances do not imply influence, but rather reflect similar social concerns played out through dress. A notable difference is the religious context of the Greek law, though a civic official (the *damiourgos*) is responsible for ensuring compliance, as Greek sanctuary activity was a public concern.

In fact, what unites the references to dress in the Greek legal inscriptions is their religious flavor, whether it be their festival, sanctuary, or funerary context, or a reference to a religious official or cult practice. These inscriptions have therefore been collected within the various corpora that have come to be referred to as *leges sacrae*, "sacred laws," or, more recently, "ritual norms."[11] These collections are idiosyncratic in many ways, fitting the specific goals of their scholarly compilers. As a result, they are all comprised of texts that represent a mix of legal forms. Scholars generally agree that some texts should be identified as laws or decrees because they feature political issuing bodies, general applicability, and even punishment clauses. At the other end of the scale are shorter, simpler notices, such as "Enter pure into the sanctuary, in a white garment" (I.Priene 205).[12] The latter – which Robert Parker calls "black-tie rules" and Edward Harris refers to as "signs" – are of questionable formal legal status, as some argue that the authority is implied, while others view them as no different from a posting on a modern church that warns a tourist to cover their legs before entering.[13] References to dress are not confined to any one legal category within the ritual norms. Attention to these categories and their defining features can bring out important distinctions about how dress works in different contexts; whether purity, deity preference, or social control is the prevailing issue can be derived from the presence of punishment clauses and the source of authority, features associated with formalized law.

Robert Parker has recently taken up the question of religious (rather than legal) unity across the corpus of ritual norms.[14] Noting the broad geographic and temporal spectrum represented, he cautions against finding a single explanation behind the variety in the inscriptions since specific examples could be chronological or the

---

11 For the shifting terminology and decisions informing compilation, see Carbon/Pirenne-Delforge 2012. On the ancient conception of *hieroi nomoi*, see most recently Gagarin 2022. Carbon/Pirenne-Delforge 2019, p. 104, clarify that a ritual norm is not the same as a "sacred law": "We proposed instead to collect a subset of these inscriptions, the ones which could be seen to qualify as prescriptive and, accordingly, normative about sacrifice and purification." For this reason, I have chosen to talk about *corpora* rather than a single *corpus* here, but for clarity will use the term "ritual norms" through the remainder of this chapter.

12 Translation CGRN 121. See Table 1 below.

13 Parker 2004, pp. 62–65; Harris 2015, pp. 58–60. See further the response prompted by a new purity law from Thyateira (Lydia), which unusually contains an explicit penalty: Parker 2018a, pp. 181–183.

14 Parker 2018b.

result of epigraphic habit. Ultimately, he finds that there are few regional differences and that, in fact, at least in the rules "governing sacrifice and purity" there *is* unity, and, as he puts it, "perhaps something we can call Greek religion."[15]

Leaving aside these complications about the scholarly problems with the shape of the corpus of these texts, let us now turn to the texts themselves. The inscriptions that include rules about dress involve both sanctuary and funerary contexts. I excluded the obviously Roman cases, and I focused on *dress*, excluding references to other textiles, or to clothing offerings.[16] The resulting 29 inscriptions cover a fairly wide geographical and chronological range, with the greatest number in the Hellenistic period. These provide a foundation for investigating questions related to unity and idiosyncrasy in legal dress.

Table 1: Greek ritual norms with rules for dress

CGRN #	Reference #	Date (BCE)	Location
	IPArk 20	late 6th cent.	Arkadia
35*[17]	IG XII 5.593	ca. 425–400	Iulis, Keos
82*	CID I 9	ca. 400–350	Delphi
90	IG XII 1.677	ca. 350–300	Ialysos, Rhodes
213*	SEG 2.710	late 4th–early 3rd cent.	Pednelissos, Pisidia
108*	CIG 3562	3rd cent.	Gambreion, Aeolis
101	IG XII 4.359	ca. 300–275	Isthmos, Kos
127	Rizakis, Achaïe III, no. 6	ca. 300–200	Dyme, Achaia
137	SEG 59.1406	ca. 281	Aigai, Aeolis
124	I.Pergamon 40	ca. 250–200	Pergamon
126	IG V 2.514	end of 3rd cent.	Lykosoura, Arkadia
177	I.Priene B-M 146, 147, 148	ca. 200 BCE	Priene

15 Parker 2018b, p. 80. See also Carbon/Pirenne-Delforge 2019, pp. 109–114 on what is "Greek" about the Greek ritual norms. They take an expansive definition as those texts written in Greek, which allows inclusion of rituals that may have had non-Greek origins or contact.

16 The cut-off point for the latest text is difficult since the line between "Hellenistic" and "Roman" is often blurred. Unless a text made its Roman context clear through Roman names or deities, I chose to include it. Some texts are ambiguous in that they address objects that cannot be carried into a sanctuary, and whether the expectation was that the object would be offered or worn is unclear; I chose to include the ambiguous cases.

17 Texts addressing funerary contexts are marked with *.

CGRN #	Reference #	Date (BCE)	Location
	SEG 36.1221	late 3rd–early 2nd cent.	Xanthos
	SEG 6.775	2nd cent.	Tlos, Lydia
	SEG 26.1334	2nd cent.	Skepsis, Troad
121	I.Priene B-M 205	200–130	Priene
176	I.Priene B-M 144	2nd cent. (ca. 130?)	Priene
181	IG XII Suppl. 126	2nd–early 1st cent.	Eresos, Lesbos
200	I.Magnesia 100a	ca. 150	Magnesia on the Meander
190	IG Cyrenaica 100200	ca. 150–100	Cyrene
221	IG XII 4.320	ca. 125–100	Kos
123	I.Tomis 1	ca. 100	Tomis, Skythia
163	IG XII 4.330	1st cent.	Kos
167	IG XII 4.328	1st cent.	Kos
	I.Délos 2529	116/115	Delos
222	IG V 1.1390	91 (or 23 CE)	Andania/Messene
	I.Kios 19	1st cent.	Kios, Bithynia
173	IG XI 4.1300	2nd or 1st cent.	Delos
	IG II^3 4.376	61/60	Marathon

Looking specifically at the references to dress in the ritual norms – at least the ones from sanctuary contexts – they do seem to offer a picture of unity as suggested by Parker. The differences found across them are often explained as reflecting distinctions in cult rather than in culture. In their content, there are a number of similarities crossing place and time. For example, color coding is consistent: purple is limited in order to ensure that the individuals or small groups wearing it stand out (e.g., CGRN 124, 163, 167, and 222), while white is the most common color required for anyone entering a sanctuary (e.g., CGRN 121, 222), and grey or dark clothes are appropriate for funerals (CGRN 82, 108, 213).[18] The treatment of gender is also shared: when a gender is made explicit (most often it is not), it is always women who are the target of restrictions (e.g., IPArk 20; CGRN 126 and 127). How-

18 On purple worn in sanctuaries, see Brøns 2017b, pp. 113–116; on the universality of white in Greek sanctuary contexts, see Brøns 2022, pp. 241–242. Georgoudi 2022 focuses on purple, gold, and white as they relate to the dress of religious officials. Grand-Clément 2016 examines color in sanctuaries more broadly than dress, including aspects like the animals brought in for sacrifice. For funerary dress, Mills 1984.

ever, closer scrutiny of these texts will show that there is more to uncover about the relationships between these universal subjects and their local enactments. Three significant topics rise from this exploration: the regional concentration of priest sales, the effects of gendered costume, and the contextualization of dress within the spaces where it was worn.

Dress and priest sales: a local phenomenon

The regional concentration of *diagraphai* – the documents concerning the selling and purchasing of priesthoods – is well established. In his exploration of unity across the ritual norms, these are the only texts that Robert Parker identifies as definitively regional, as the practice is localized in the Eastern Aegean (coastal Asia Minor and the nearby islands).[19] In form, they are not laws per se, and perhaps not technically ritual norms either.[20] But they are legalistic texts – contracts or the recording of a completed contract – that attest to the legal framework for cult management. They are also an important source for references to dress worn by priests (the *hiereus*). Of the 25 non-funerary texts in the group of dress regulations, seven are *diagraphai,* nearly a third. Thus, this region specializes in this category of contracts, and these contracts are also arguably overrepresented in our collection of information about the dress of priests: we should consider why these two facts are related.

Table 2: Priest contracts with dress items

Contract	Location	Deity	Dress
CGRN 163 ll. 4–14 (1st cent.)	Kos	Nike	purple chiton, gold ring, olive wreath; dress in white rest of the time (κιτῶνα π[ορ]**φύρεον** καὶ δακτυλίος χρυσέος καὶ στέφ[ανο]ν θάλλινον; [λ]ευχιμονίτω δὲ διὰ βίου)
CGRN 167 ll. 15–18 (1st cent.)	Kos	Zeus Alseios	purple chiton, olive wreath with a gold attachment (κιτῶνα **πορ-φύρεον**, στέφανον θάλινον ἔχοντα ἄφαμμα χρύσεον)

19 Parker 2018b, p. 76.

20 Parker 2018b, p. 80: the sales themselves do not constitute a ritual norm. Harris 2015, p. 75: not a law.

CGRN 221 ll. 20–24 (ca. 125–100)	Kos	Herakles Kallinikos	thoroughly white chiton, white poplar wreath, brooch, gold ring (κιθῶνα διάλευκον, ἐστε[φ]α̣νώσθω δὲ καὶ στεφάνωι λευκίνωι, ἅφαμμα καὶ χρυσέος δακτυλίος)
CGRN 176 ll. 13–24 (2nd cent. [ca. 130?])	Priene	Dionysos Phleos	whatever robe he wants, wreath of golden ivy/gold wreath (στολὴν ἔχειν ἣν ἂμ βούληται καὶ στέφανον κισσοῦ χρυσοῦν; στολὴν ἣν ἂμ βούληται καὶ στέφανον χρυσοῦν; στολὴν ἔχων ἣν ἂν θέληι καὶ στέφανον χρυσοῦν)
CGRN 177 A ll. 10–14 (ca. 200)	Priene	Poseidon Helikonios	gold wreath, gold headband ([στέφανον ἔχο]ντι χρύσεον; [στροφίσκ]ον φορεῖν χρύ̣[σεον])
SEG 26.1334 ll. 7–12 (2nd cent.)	Skepsis	Dionysos Bambuleios	ivy wreath, gold wreath, purple chiton, shoes appropriate for the outfit ([στε]φαν[ού]σθω κισσοῦ στεφάνῳ̣; στέφανομ φορεῖν χρυσοῦν καὶ χιτῶνας **ἁλουργ[ο]ύς** κα[ὶ ὑ]πόδεσιν ἀκόλουθον τῇ ἐσθῆτι)
CGRN 123 ll. 7–15 (ca. 100)	Tomis	Samothracian gods	wreath (στεφανωθήσετ̣[αι δὲ παρὰ] τ̣ῶν μυστῶν; ὑπάρχειν̣ δὲ αὐτῷ τὸν στέφανον εἰς τὸ κατ' [ἀΐδι]ον)

Of the six Eastern Aegean contracts, three are from Kos, two from Priene, and another from Skepsis in the Troad, and five different deities are represented in them (Table 2). From these admittedly limited sources, it appears that specifying the dress of the incoming priest cuts across both cults and cities, suggesting it is local in terms of both religious practice and in legal structure. In addition to these is an inscription from Tomis on the coast of the Black Sea, a contract for the priesthood of the Samothracian gods, probably organized by a private association. The mother city of Tomis is notably Miletus, a city of Asia Minor from which we get a number of other priest sales.[21] This ostensible outlier is the exception that proves the rule if the practice appears there because of its relationship to its roots in the region of *diagraphai*. Additionally, its use for the Samothracian gods connects it to a broader Mediterranean network of the mystery cult, which spread through ini-

21 Only one preserved *diagraphe* from Miletus includes a reference to dress, CGRN 249 (= I.Milet 1). I have excluded it from consideration in this chapter because of its Roman context (presence of Roman names and dated ca. 15–100 CE), but one could argue for continuity from earlier Greek practices.

tiates and *theoroi*.[22] These two connections provide a way of thinking in practical terms about how the local becomes regional, or beyond.

No priest's outfit is identical to another's, but instead draws on elements of dress that signal prestige and authority more generally, elements that would be readable to any Greek who met with any kind of authority figure. Wreaths, gold, purple, and, occasionally, the privilege to choose one's own garment, are some commonalities that appear more than once. But the placement and form of the gold varies: sometimes a ring (CGRN 163 and 221), other times a wreath (CGRN 176 and 177; SEG 26.1334). The shape of the wreaths also differs, perhaps based on the cult, as ivy is used for both priests of Dionysus (CGRN 176, SEG 26.1334). Three priests wear chitons of a color typically translated as "purple" (CGRN 163 and 167; SEG 26.1334), but the term used for the chiton on Kos is πορφύρεον, while the Skepsis priest wears ones that are ἁλουργ[ο]ύς. In a study of *halourgos* by Cecilie Brøns and Kerstin Droß-Krüpe, the authors conclude that in its use in epigraphic sources, that term emphasizes its etymological roots in the mollusk-based dye that produces the color.[23] There are not enough examples to draw definitive conclusions, but we should at least entertain the possibility that there was a significant semantic difference behind the choice of the descriptors used by the two cities, possibly based in local technologies or economies.

How do these outfits relate to the legalistic, mutual obligations between *polis* and purchaser that were involved in acquiring these priesthoods? As an alternative to inheritance or selection by allotment, the ability to become a priest through payment develops later and has been tied to an increase in wealth and a desire to use that wealth to access honors; it is a new avenue for new people to gain clout in the cities that used it.[24] Receiving the right to special dress is just one of the perquisites owed for doing one's civic duty, but the choice to regulate the specifics of these visual markers of authority in writing may suggest that there was some perceived necessity for this display. One reason may be found in the fact that leaving the care of cult practice to the whim of euergetism may have brought out some anxiety. Eftychia Stavrianopoulou argues that,

> The reputation of each individual cult and, additionally, of the religious life of the community was dependent upon the 'correct' filling of the priest's office, i.e., upon the uncontested authority [of the cult specialist] ... for the time period determined by the contract. Since the ritual authority of those who had purchased their priestly offices was

22 Blakely/Mundy 2022, esp. pp. 115–116 on Tomis. See also Cole 1984, pp. 69–75.

23 Brøns/Dross-Krüpe 2018. Georgoudi 2022, p. 84, discusses the term's use in this contract in light of the literary vocabulary.

24 Horster 2013, pp. 192–193; Kató 2013.

> more ambivalent than that of those who had gained it by inheritance, the *polis* had to strengthen the authority of the priest ... and to ensure that the term of office went by without complications.[25]

The attention to a priest's appearance may be such a method of strengthening authority. If a priesthood changed yearly, or the men attaining these positions were in some way unexpected, then recognizable dress could help to both signal and ensure their status. The contracts indicate that the dress items were to be worn at the particular spaces and times related to the deity: the costume is not permanent but tied specifically to their particular sphere of authority. The gold and purple would of course make the purchaser look important, but in these contexts, they would specifically make him recognizable as the priest. The community would thus be more inclined to accept his right to this role.

Other ritual norms link dress to new foundations. Related to the *diagraphai* is CGRN 124, which preserves a letter, likely originating with an Attalid king, that includes specifications for establishing a new priesthood at Pergamon and the contract for that priesthood, including perquisites, requirements, and dress. The priest would be chosen by lot and wear a white *chlamys* and an olive wreath with a small purple *(phoinikios)* ribbon (ll. 1–4).[26] The letter describes the term of office in a shorthand that emphasizes dress: the time when he wears the wreath (ὃν ἂ̣ν χρόνον ἔχηι τὸν στέφανον, ll. 16–17). Still another text establishes a new cult at Aigai for Seleucid kings (CGRN 137): the appointment of the new annual priesthood includes information about the incumbent's dress, a laurel wreath, headband, and clothes as bright as possible (ll. 39–40).[27] Innovation in ritual requires aspects that will already be recognizable, and directly after the clothing description, the new priest is told to sacrifice just like the other priests within the city (ll. 40–44).

The special dress influenced the community through visual communication, and it would also affect the man becoming the priest. It is through the physical transformations of getting and then being dressed that helps make the man the priest, especially since Greek religion did not have seminaries or training to encourage an internal transformation or bestow legitimacy. The ability of dress to influence psychological processes – how we think – is referred to by psychologists as "enclothed cognition," which identifies the connection that is made between the

25 Stavrianopoulou 2009, p. 225.

26 [ὁ δ' ἀε]ὶ̣ λ̣αχὼν φορείτω | [χ]λαμύδα λευκὴν καὶ σ̣τ̣[έ]|φανον ἐλάας μετὰ ταινι|δίου φοινικιοῦ. Canevo 2023, pp. 83–90, reexamines the form and topographical context of the inscription to associate the priesthood with Zeus.

27 ὃς στέ̣φανό̣ν τ̣ε̣ φορ̣ή̣σει δάφνης κ̣|αὶ στρόφιον κ̣α̣ὶ̣ ἐσθῆτα ὡς λαμπροτάτην καὶ μ̣|[ε]τὰ̣ τῶ̣ν τιμούχω̣ν ἐμ πάσα̣ις τα̣ῖ̣ς θυσίαις συν|[θύσε]τ̣αι κ̣α̣ὶ̣ ἐ̣ν̣ τ̣α̣ῖ̣ς̣ ἐ̣κ̣κ̣λησίαις κατάρξετ|[αι] ἐπὶ τοῦ βωμοῦ τῶν Σωτήρων καθάπερ καὶ τοῖς ἄ[λ]λοις θεοῖς

"symbolic meaning associated with an article of clothing and the physical experience of wearing it."[28] Tests reveal how someone performs certain tasks in certain clothing, revealing, for example, that people wearing a nurse's tunic show an increase in empathy, or that children dressing as positive children's characters persist longer with their task.[29] In the case of the men taking on a new contract to become a priest in the Eastern Aegean, putting on items that symbolize authority psychologically makes them the priest. Even for a priest enjoined to wear "whatever he wants," (CGRN 176) the process of consciously choosing the garments and then undergoing a physical transformation by putting on those garments prepares him for his position. It is possible that this experience was widely ritualized, and thus heightened, through public investiture.[30] Tomis provides a specific example of such ritualization in a contract for the priest of the Samothracian gods: the text does not specify a garment, but it does state that the one selected will receive a wreath from the initiates in a wreathing ceremony on the day on which he takes up the priesthood (CGRN 123, ll. 7–10).[31] An unusual example of a life-long priesthood, the contract additionally states that he will wear this wreath for all time (ll. 13–15). This would be a lasting symbol of his role, but the day on which he first received that wreath would be special one. Dress participates in the creation of identity; it does not simply reflect and communicate it. In sum, these priest contracts provide an example of a regional law, local rather than global. By showing how and to what end that law is expressed on the individual body, the use and purpose for laws about dress can be extrapolated more broadly.

Regulating gender expression

A second significant feature is the gendered nature of the dress regulations. The contracts for priesthoods featuring dress perquisites concern adult male religious officials only, but elsewhere in the ritual norms, when gender can be determined, the group being regulated is almost always female (women and girls). Three of the texts addressing women are from the Peloponnese and can be associated with Demeter or Demeter-like cults (see Table 3): a law from Arkadia concerning Demeter Thesmophoros, the oldest of the preserved texts (IPArk 20); a Hellenistic law concerning the sanctuary of Despoina at Lykosoura in Arkadia (CGRN 126); and

28 Adam/Galinsky 2019, p. 157.

29 Adam/Galinsky 2019, pp. 158–159 list recent studies.

30 Chaniotis 2005.

31 στεφανωθήσετ̣[αι δὲ | παρὰ] τ̣ῶν μυστῶν φιλοτιμίας ἕνε|[κε]ν̣ τῆς εἰς ἑαυτούς, ἐν ᾗ̣ ἱερᾶται ἡ̣μέ|ρα̣

a Hellenistic warning sign from Dyme in Achaia (CGRN 127).[32] This clustering within the Peloponnese and the consistency of the deity could be interpreted as showing that the attention to women is regional and/or related to cult. Modesty fits with the character and expectations of the goddess, so restriction of gold, purple, and make-up is not surprising. And as Adeline Grand-Clément has argued for the Arkadian Thesmophoros, if these texts relate to festivals or rituals for women, there would be no reason to address men.[33]

But these interpretations are complicated by details in other ritual norms. At first glance, the characteristics of the Andanian mysteries, a festival in Messenia which included Demeter, appears to support the local and/or cultic explanation for these gendered dress regulations (CGRN 222). In fact, the *diagramma* (as the law calls itself) even uses the same unusual, possibly dialectical form of the word for clothing found in the Lykosoura regulations, εἱματισμός (l. 15; cf. CRGN 126, line 5), and there is an overlap among many of the banned objects (e.g., gold, shoes, and plaited hair). However, there is an important difference in that in addition to rules about dress addressed to women and girls, there are also gender-neutral and male injunctions.[34] The gender-neutral dress codes focus on the initiation and those participating as initiates. At the initiation, all the first-time initiates wear the same headgear, a tiara *(stlengida)*, switched to a wreath to mark their change, while both the sacred men and sacred women (*hierai* and *hieroi*) wear the same white cap (ll. 13–15). The rule that initiates must be barefoot and wear white is then addressed to all members of that ritual category with no distinction by gender or age (ll. 15–16). Dress specifically for men appears later in the document: the group

---

32 The Lykosoura text as preserved does not include an explicit reference to women, and morphology is ambiguous as to gender for the dress regulations; the main reason for assuming a female audience is the types of objects and hairstyles. The reference to breast-feeding (κύενσαν, l. 12) must be to women, but the masculine article used for those sacrificing (τὸς δὲ θύοντας, l. 13) must at least include males.

33 Grand-Clément 2017, p. 56.

34 The relevant portions of the text discussed are ll. 13–23: ᵛστεφάνων·ᵛ στεφάνους δὲ ἐχόντω οἱ μὲν ἱεροὶ καὶ αἱ ἱεραὶ πῖλον λευκόν, | τῶν δὲ τελουμένων οἱ πρωτομύσται στλεγγίδα· ὅταν δὲ οἱ ἱεροὶ παραγγεῖλωντι, τὰμ μὲν στλεγγίδα ἀποθέσθωσαν, | στεφανούσθωσαν δὲ πάντες δάφναι. ᵛεἱματισμοῦ·ᵛ οἱ τελούμενοι τὰ μυστήρια ἀνυπόδετοι ἔστωσαν καὶ ἐχόντω τὸν | εἱματισμὸν λευκόν, αἱ δὲ γυναῖκες μὴ διαφανῆ μηδὲ τὰ σαμεῖα ἐν τοῖς εἱματίοις πλατύτερα ἡμιδακτυλίου, καὶ αἱ | μὲν ἰδιώτιες ἐχόντω χιτῶνα λίνεον καὶ εἱμάτιον μὴ πλείονος ἄξια δραχμᾶν ἑκατόν, αἱ δὲ παῖδες καλάσηριν ἢ σιν|δονίταν καὶ εἱμάτιον μὴ πλείονος ἄξια μνᾶς, αἱ δὲ δοῦλαι καλάσηριν ἢ σινδονίταν καὶ εἱμάτιον μὴ πλείονος ἄξια δρα|χμᾶν πεντήκοντα· αἱ δὲ ἱεραί, αἱ μὲν γυναῖκες καλάσηριν ἢ ὑπόδυμα μὴ ἔχον σκιὰς καὶ εἱμάτιον μὴ πλέονος ἄξια δύο | μνᾶν, αἱ δὲ [παῖδε]ς καλάσηριν καὶ εἱμάτιον μὴ πλείονος ἄξια δραχμᾶν ἑκατόν· ἐν δὲ τᾶι πομπᾶι αἱ μὲν ἱεραὶ γυναῖκες ὑποδύ|ταν καὶ εἱμάτιον γυναικεῖον οὖλον, σαμεῖα ἔχον μὴ πλατύτερα ἡμιδακτυλίου, αἱ δὲ παῖδες καλάσηριν καὶ εἱμάτιον μὴ δια|φανές.

of officials called the Ten *(Deka)* will wear a purple headband *(strophion)* during the festival (ll. 177–179).[35] This group is newly established by this law, so just as in the contracts discussed above, these male officials are given visible markers of their new authority through their dress.

By far the bulk of the dress regulations concern female participants. They affect the women among the initiates, whose garment choices are restricted beyond the command to wear white given to all. They also affect the *hierai,* the women chosen for special administrative duties, as well as women without any special ritual role. The distinctions in dress are used to mark the women by role, age, and status (adult women vs. girls; free vs. enslaved women). It becomes clear that even at a festival that is not exclusive to female persons, they are still the group to whom most of the regulations are addressed. Similar mixed-gender settings are involved in the law on funerals from Gambreion (CGRN 108). In this inscription, the dress of mourners is prescribed, defining the women separately from the men and the children: the women must wear grey, clean clothes, while the men and children can choose to wear white if they prefer (ll. 5–9).[36] Again, women are called out specifically for increased construction of their appearance beyond the common dress code for participants.

Table 3: Dress-related punishments and gender

Regulation	Type	Location	Punishments	Gender
CGRN 82 ca. 400–350	law about funerals (ὁ τεθμὸς πὲρ τῶν ἐντοφήιων, ll. 19–20)	Delphi	50 drachma fine (ll. 26–27)	
CGRN 90 ca. 350–300	law (νόμος, l. 19)	Ialysos, Rhodes	purify shrine and sacrifice; impiety if not done (ll. 27–30)	

35 φορούντω δὲ οἱ | δέκα ἐν τοῖς μυστηρί|οις στρόφιον πορφύριον

36 τὰς πενθούσας ἔχειν φαιὰν ἐσθῆ|τα μὴ κατερρυπωμένην· χρῆσθαι | δὲ καὶ τοὺς ἄνδρας καὶ τοὺς παῖδας | τοὺς πενθοῦντας ἐσθῆτι φαιᾶι, | ἐὰμ μὴ βούλωνται λευκῆι

Regulation	Type	Location	Punishments	Gender
IPArk 20 6th cent.		Arkadia	consecrate the offending garment; death (or curse) if consecration refused with additional fine for *damiourgos;* impiety for *damiourgos* if fine not paid (ll. 2–6)	women (restored, [γυ]νά, l. 1)
CGRN 108 3rd cent.	law [funerary] (νόμος, l. 4)	Gambreion, Aeolis	women banned from sacrificing for 10 years, impiety (ll. 25–27)	women (Γαμβρειώταις, l. 4; γυναῖκας, l. 15; αὐταῖς, l. 25); men (ἄνδρας, l. 7); male? children (τοὺς παῖδας, l. 7)
CGRN 126 end of 3rd cent.		Lykosoura, Arkadia	dedicate the offending objects (ll. 7–9)	women (implied by feminine adornments; pregnancy and breastfeeding, ll. 11–13)
CGRN 127 ca. 300–200		Dyme, Achaia	purify shrine, impiety (ll. 8–11)	women (γυν[αῖ]κες, ll. 2–3; παρσεβέουσα, l. 11)
CGRN 222 91 (or 23 CE)	law or decree (διάγραμμα, l. 5, etc.)	Andania/Messene	offending clothing removed by the *gynaikonomos* and consecrated (ll. 25–26)	women (γυναῖκες, l. 16, etc.); girls (αἱ παῖδες, ll. 17, 20, 21)

At least part of the purpose behind the legal regulation of the dress of women must be control. In fact, these issues were taken seriously enough that the regulation of dress by gender can be linked to the inclusion of punishment clauses (Table 3): seven ritual norms preserve a punishment related to dress infractions, five of which (the majority) also contain references to gendered dress. At Dyme, a woman who has disrespected the rules must purify the sanctuary. In several cases – Lykosoura, Andania, and the Arkadian sanctuary of Demeter Thesmophoros – the offending objects must be handed over and consecrated. In addition, for Demeter Thesmophoros, further stipulations are provided for what happens if the dedication is not made: there is a fine, and if the responsible official (the *damiourgos*) does not follow up on the fine, he becomes liable himself. Both the Gambreion funerary law (ll. 17–18) and the *diagramma* on the Andanian mysteries (ll. 26, 27, 32) also call upon an official titled the *gynaikonomos,* the supervisor of women, whose title indicates a concern for the order of women in the Greek world. Of the ritual norms, there is a substantial overlap between the texts that reference women's dress and those that can be categorized more definitely as proper laws through their issuing bodies and explicit punishments.

Attention to women's appearance in Greek legal regulations is common. The early laws recorded in later literary sources also highlight gender, such as the Solonian limits on the number of garments a woman could wear in public (Plutarch, Solon 21.4), and a Locrian law that equated certain dress objects with sex work (Diodorus Siculus 12.21).[37] Women's dress seems to be a widespread concern that can be universalized even further in light of the Assyrian code presented above. The need to regulate women through their appearance thus can be viewed as a unifying aspect of Greek law, but it is also worth considering how these laws worked at local, community level. A concentration on the details of women's appearance has been recognized as a component of their role as cultural bearers, or cultural markers, primarily discussed in the context of immigration or in subnational cultural opposition, when one community's customs come into conflict with another's. Bronwyn Winter explains that such scholarship has explored "the deployment of women as symbols through their appearance and behavior" as well as their responsibility to transmit nationalist ideals, serving "as participants (willing or not), defenders, and advocates, educators through maternal transmission of values to daughters and sons ..."[38] This can be a useful lens for understanding this form of social control within the ancient Greek *polis,* particularly because of the equation of women with the household; the reason this visual role falls to women has been tied to the home as the traditional sphere of women. As legal scholar Martha Minow explains in the context of certain modern immigrant communities:

---

37 See Mills 1984, pp. 264–265; on Solon's restrictive legislation on Athenian women and their wide and long-lasting influence, Tsakiropoulou-Summers 2019.

38 Winter 2016, p. 1.

> If women stay at home or in some other sense are expected to preserve the distinction between home and work, between private and public, their bodies mark the distinction by the clothing and markings they use, even by their very location. They may continue to dress according to their home tradition even if they do join the workforce or shop in public places.[39]

The distinction between public and private – the *polis* and the *oikos* – offers an opportunity for ancient Greek women to bear similar cultural responsibilities. The public nature of Greek ritual, both festivals and funerals, means that women are on view, as well as also gathering with and viewing one another. This is apparent in the Andanian Mysteries, which played a powerful role in the creation and reinforcement of local history for the formerly enslaved Messenian people. Particularly at the public portions of the festival, the women and girls chosen to participate as *hierai* were on display as a representation of cultural resilience. Their garments were almost certainly not literally "traditional," as the rules are thought to have been a product of their own time, but by prescribing a costume, the appearance of tradition was made manifest.

Even when the idea of cultural conflict with an "other" is not clearly present, ancient Greek ritual activities in which women's appearance is regulated can also be viewed through this lens. In the unusual situation of a gender-restricted festival like the Thesmophoria, the attention to women's appearance is heightened. Adeline Grand-Clément has pointed out that one effect on the women at the types of festivals covered in the three regulations of Peloponnesian Demeter sanctuaries (IPArk 20, CGRN 126, and CGRN 127) is that by restricting more ostentatious modifications of appearance like purple clothing and make-up, everyone no matter their background would look the same, and women would feel a more equal part of their community.[40] Grand-Clément's goal is to uncover the sensorial ritual experience of the individual through such restrictions, but they must have also served as a way to transmit values to one another. The values being upheld would be universally Greek – modesty, fidelity to spouse, piety – but their local enactments are used to community benefit.

Legal space

Examination of the spatial contexts in which the dress of the ritual norms was worn is essential for understanding local idiosyncrasies and lived realities. Even when the regulations of two separate cities share general similarities, the specific

39 Minow 2000, pp. 126–127.
40 Grand-Clément 2017, p. 59.

ways in which those regulations are experienced by individuals and communities in their particular environments make them functionally different and irreplicable. In a review of the history of interpretations of so-called "extra-urban" sanctuaries, Christina Williamson emphasizes that sacred space is fundamentally local: although it may be possible to tie a certain god to certain types of landscapes, or recognize some commonalities among the reasons for the siting of sanctuaries, each case must be accounted for in terms of its local pantheon and politics.[41] Jurisdiction is one important aspect of the relationship between space and the law, as it certainly matters that these dress rules were not in force all the time and everywhere, but only in particular sanctuaries and cemeteries. But legal space also recognizes the interconnectedness among law, geography, temporality, and embodiment.

Among the elements of ritual, the procession (πομπή) is particularly tied to considerations of space. The details of festival processions – route, timing, objects escorted, participants included, etc. – were recognized and appreciated by their audience. Socrates in the opening of the *Republic* explains that he had walked to the Piraeus to see (θεάσασθαι) the new festival for Bendis and remarks on the difference between the procession performed by the locals (ή τῶν ἐπιχωρίων πομπή) and the one by the Thracians (Plato, Politeia 327a). The Hellenistic period brought increased attention to the "staging elements" of public ritual: dress is just one among a number of visual and sensory elements that are itemized in the ritual norms, from hiring professional musicians, to ensuring the aesthetic suitability of sacrificial animals, to selecting and lining up participants.[42] The spectacle created by the prescription of distinctions in dress enabled viewers to read the religious, political, and social identities of the participants, but dress must also be examined from the point of view of the wearers as it activates the senses of touch, smell, and hearing in addition to sight. The phenomenology of processions involves the kinetic encounter of the landscape with its natural and manufactured monuments, and this is experienced by dressed bodies. As Williamson summarizes: "Each kind of space, and the symbols, boundaries, and stories that it harbors, will come with its own kinds of experience and prescribed ways of moving through it, reinforced by pathways, monuments and inscriptions – experiences that were clearly entangled."[43] Dress plays an important role in the creation of ritual memory through this processional choreography.

---

41 Williamson 2021, pp. 18–25.

42 Chaniotis 1995. Williamson 2021, pp. 60–61 on spectacle as memory inducing. Stavrianopoulou 2015 provides a useful overview to the visual and kinesthetic aspects of processions.

43 Williamson 2021, p. 34. See further pp. 53–65 on spatial and ritual memory, with discussion of cognitive processes.

Legal materiality also factored into the spatial experience. First, the texts collected as ritual norms are significantly *inscribed* texts: written onto permanent materials that have survived in the archaeological record, they were physical objects intended for lasting, public presentation.[44] We rarely know the precise details of the display contexts of the dress regulations, but most, if not all, would have been visible to the ritual community.[45] In an inscription about the sanctuary of Alektrona at Ialysos on Rhodes, instructions for publishing what items were forbidden precede the text of the law listing those items (CGRN 90, ll. 5–18). It specifies the number of inscriptions (three), their material (local Lartian marble), and their placement for maximum visibility (at the entrance, above a dining structure, and along a road).[46] A copy (ἀντίγραφος) of the regulations for the Andanian mysteries (CGRN 222, ll. 113 and 114) was made for access within the city of Messene, but the extant inscription, carved into local limestone, was set up at the sanctuary of the Karneian grove where the festival was held.[47] At Pergamon, a royal letter about establishing a new priesthood (CGRN 124) was inscribed on a white marble post, which would have had a different visual effect in terms of its material (white and imported) and its direct incorporation into an architectural setting.[48] The display of inscribed ritual norms was not just informational; even someone who could not read the writing could recognize their semantic values through form, location, and material. Their legal authority could further be supported by a second material aspect, the display of confiscated dress objects. Three of the ritual norms with punishments related to dress (Table 3) warn that illegal objects will become property of the gods.[49] It is likely that the objects would be accessible to sanctuary visitors and thus serve as a visible lesson in dress code and a tangible reminder of the laws and their consequences. This material enforcement would work iteratively in concert with the inscriptions themselves over repeated visits.

44 The bibliography on the materiality of inscriptions, their readership, and their use in collective memory is overwhelming. See Low 2020, pp. 235–239 (includes legal inscriptions) and Day 2019 (inscriptions in sanctuary contexts).

45 The lone bronze inscription in this group, IPArk 20, preserves part of a hole that suggests it could have been nailed up for display.

46 ἐπιμεληθήμειν | τοὺς ἱεροταμίας, ὅπως στᾶλαι | ἐργασθέωντι τρεῖς λίθου λαρτ[ί]|ου καὶ ἀναγραφῆι ἐς τὰς στάλα|ς τό τε ψάφισμα τόδε καὶ ἃ οὐχ ὅ|σιόν ἐντι ἐκ τῶν νόμων ἐσφέ|ρειν οὐδὲ ἐσοδοιπορεῖν ἐς τὸ τέ|μενος, καὶ τὰ ἐπιτίμια τῶ[ι] πράσ|σοντι παρὰ τὸν νόμον· θ̣έμειν δὲ |τὰς στάλας μίαμ μὲν ἐπὶ τᾶς ἐσό|δου τᾶς ἐκ πόλιος ποτιπορευομέ|νοις, μίαν δὲ ὑπὲρ τὸ ἱστιατόριον, | ἄλλαν δὲ ἐπὶ τᾶς καταβάσιος τᾶ[ς] | ἐξ Ἀχαΐας πόλιος. “Lartian stone” (ll. 7–8) is a grey marble found near the ancient Rhodian cities of Lartos and Lindos; see Papavassiliou et al. 2020.

47 Gawlinski 2012, pp. 35 and 60.

48 On the general findspot and possible sacred precincts, see Caneva 2023, pp. 83–84.

49 [ἱερὸ]ν ἔναι, IPArk 20, l. 2; ἀναθέτω ἐν τὸ ἱερόν, CGRN 126, l. 9; and ἔστω ἱερὰ, CGRN 222, l. 26.

Three inscribed ritual norms of the Hellenistic period make explicit reference to jurisdictional spaces and processions, thereby emphasizing both the physical contexts and the performative movement between contexts.[50] The contract for the priest of Dionysus Phleos at Priene (CGRN 176) is organized by both place and time. His dress is always a robe of his choice accompanied by a gold wreath (Table 2), but the description of his outfit is repeated (with minor syntactical variation) as the contract specifies the appropriate places, events, and times that control this perquisite. During the Katagogia festival, the priest leads the procession in his outfit (ll. 21–24), and although we do not know the details of the processional route, the legal construction of the elements of this specific event are clear. He also sits in the front row of the theater in this costume (ll. 13–19), a regulation both spatial (the theater) and temporal (theatrical events with sacrifices). Additionally, during the two months of Lenaion and Anthesterion, months of important festivals of the god he represents, he is to be costumed (ll. 19–21), a regulation defined solely by time, rather than place. Through the visibility of the priest, the local calendar is embodied. A similar chronotopic construction of dress is found in another contract (CGRN 163). The priest of Nike on Kos is told to wear his purple chiton, gold ring, and olive wreath in procession (Table 2), with the precise timing of the event indicated as the 20th of the month Petageitnyos (l. 4–10). This same outfit (τὰν δὲ αὐτὰν ἐσθῆτα, l. 10) is also to be worn within the space of the sanctuary, as well as during other sacrifices (l. 10–12). For this priest, the visual contrast with other contexts is made explicit: he is to wear white the rest of the time ([λ]ευχιμονίτω δὲ διὰ βίου, l. 12).

A fair amount about the route of the procession referenced in the *diagramma* of the mysteries of Andania (CGRN 222) can be reconstructed, which offers an opportunity to examine dress regulations more concretely within their geographical setting.[51] In the section of the text on clothing, the female officials called the *hierai* (sacred women) are prescribed garments based on type and price, differing based on age, but this dress changes for the procession:

> Of the sacred women, the adults must wear a *kalasiris* or *hupoduma* without decorations and a himation worth in total no more than two minas, and the girls a *kalasiris* and himation worth in total no more than 100 drachmas. In the procession the sacred women must wear a *hupodutas* and a wool woman's himation with borders no more than half a finger wide, and the girls must wear a *kalasiris* and a himation that is not transparent. (ll. 19–22)[52]

---

50 In another priest contract, CGRN 167 from Kos, the description of the arrangement of the procession does not mention whether the priest must wear his contractual garments then, but it does include a tangential detail that the processing ephebes and boys wear armor (37–38).

51 Gawlinski 2012, pp. 49–58.

52 For the text, see note 33 above.

The differences emphasize the fact that special dressing is a sensorial act that prepares the body for religious ritual. The regulations require that the women put on garments specifically for the procession, the beginning of the festival, garments that they would have to modify afterwards for other activities. In addition, the description of the garments here are among the most specific of any of the ritual norms. The costume creates bonding through uniformity and results in a procession that would look and feel different from any other procession anywhere else, and even from previous Andanian processions before these rules were codified. Finally, these women would have worn this costume to lead the procession along a route from the *polis* of Messene, through the upper Messenian plain, to the sanctuary of the Karneian grove. The end point was at the foot of Andania, a site (by then likely in ruins) that was considered by the Messenians to be their ancestral home before their conquest by the Spartans. Not long after the defeat of the Spartans by the Thebans at the battle of Leuktra (371 BCE), the city of Messene had been founded at Mt. Ithome to serve as a new capital for the region. The Messenians were challenged to create a history from their fragmented past, and one of the ways this was accomplished was through shared religious experience. A participant in the procession traversed a dynamic landscape charged with communal memories, senses heightened through shared dress, embodying their resilience. This became the lived experience of the law.

Conclusion

The Greek legal texts regulating dress are complicated and fragmentary. Although they cannot provide firm conclusions about the specific patterns, fabrics, or adornments of a local community's traditional dress, they can allow us to read between the lines to find how local enactments of universal concepts could vary, how a region that adopted legal sales of religious authority also chose to use dress to underline that authority, how a community's female members visibly took on the values of the group, or how special dress ignited communal memories as an individual processed through the landscape. These personal, local, and global layers help us to imagine the lived experience of the law as written. Rituals norms about dress indicate that there are concepts that were near-universal in the ancient world, such as the association of the color purple with powerful people, or that male officials should be granted the right to hold women accountable for their dress choices. But it is also clear that within these normative structures exists the possibility for regional variations and hyper-local meaning making. Greek law reflects, encodes, and perpetuates these meanings.

Bibliography

ADAM, Hajo/GALINSKY, Adam D. (2019) Reflections on Enclothed Cognition: Commentary on Burns et al., in: Journal of Experimental Social Psychology 83, 157–159.

BECK, Hans (2020) Localism and the Ancient Greek City State, Chicago.

BONNET, Corinne (2023) Epilogue: A Tribute to Potnia of the Labyrinth, in: Hans BECK/Julia KINDT (eds.), The Local Horizon of Ancient Greek Religion, Cambridge, 376–386.

BLAKELY, Sandra/MUNDY, Joanna (2022) Strong Ties and Deep Habits: The Samothracian Diaspora in Network Perspective, in: Anna COLLAR (ed.), Networks and the Spread of Ideas in the Past: Strong Ties, Innovation and Knowledge Exchange, London/New York, 112–160.

BRØNS, Cecilie (2017a) Gods and Garments. Textiles in Greek Sanctuaries in the 7th to the 1st Centuries BC, Oxford/Philadelphia.

BRØNS, Cecilie (2017b) Sacred Colours: Purple Textiles in Greek Sanctuaries in the Second Half of the 1st Millennium BC, in: Hedvig LANDENIUS ENEGREN/Francesco MEO (eds.), Treasures from the Sea. Sea Silk and Shellfish Purple Dye in Antiquity, Oxford/Philadelphia, 109–117.

BRØNS, Cecilie/DROSS-KRÜPE, Kerstin (2018) The Colour Purple? Reconsidering the Greek Word *halourgos* (ἁλουργός) and its Relation to Ancient Textiles, in: Textile History 4, 22–43.

BRØNS, Cecilie (2022) What to Wear? Dress-codes in: Ancient Greek Sanctuaries, in: Raija MATTILA/Sebastian FINK/Sanae ITO (eds.), Evidence Combined. Western and Eastern Sources in Dialogue, Vienna, 231–260.

CANEVA, Stefano G. (2023) Shaping the Elite of Attalid Pergamon: A Reappraisal of the Epigraphic Dossiers Concerning Priesthoods, in: Electrum 30, 75–101.

CARBON, Jan-Mathieu/PIRENNE-DELFORGE, Vinciane (2012) Beyond Greek "Sacred Laws", in: Kernos 25, 163–182.

CARBON, Jan-Mathieu/PIRENNE-DELFORGE, Vincianne (2019) Two Notes on the Collection of Greek Ritual Norms. Looking Back, Looking Forward, in: Axon 3(2), 103–116.

CHANIOTIS, Angelos (1995) Sich selbst feiern? Städtische Feste des Hellenismus im Spannungsfeld von Religion und Politik, in: Michael WÖRRLE/Paul ZANKER (eds.), Stadtbild und Bürgerbild in Hellenismus, Munich, 147–172.

CHANIOTIS, Angelos (2005) Griechische Rituale der Statusänderung und ihre Dynamik, in: Marion STEINICKE/Stefan WEINFURTER (eds.), Investitur- und Krönungsrituale: Herrschaftseinsetzungen im kulturellen Vergleich, Cologne, 43–61.

COLE, Susan G. (1984) Theoi Megaloi: The Cult of the Great Gods at Samothrace, Leiden.

DAY, Joseph (2019) The 'Spatial Dynamics' of Archaic and Classical Greek Epigram: Conversations among Locations, Monuments, Texts, and Viewer-Readers, in: Andrej PETROVIC/Ivana PETROVIC/Edmund THOMAS (eds.), The Materiality of Text. Placement, Perception, and Presence of Inscribed Texts in Classical Antiquity, Leiden, 73–104.

GAGARIN, Michael (2022) Sacred Laws *(Hieroi Nomoi)* and Legal Categories in Hellenistic Crete, in: Delfim LEÃO et al. (eds.), Our Beloved Polites: Studies Presented to P. J. Rhodes, Oxford, 183–190.

GAWLINSKI, Laura (2012) The Sacred Law of Andania: A New Text with Commentary, Berlin.

GEORGOUDI, Stella (2022) Vêtements et insignes des agents cultuels dans les cités grecques: une esquisse, in: Archimède 9, 79–98.

GLEBA, Margarita (2017) Tracing Textile Cultures of Italy and Greece in the Early First Millennium BC, in: Antiquity 91, 1205–1222.

GRAND-CLÉMENT, Adeline (2016) Couleurs, rituels et normes religieuses en Grèce ancienne, in: Archives de sciences sociales des religions 174, 127–147.

GRAND-CLÉMENT, Adeline (2017) "Il est interdit de …". Rituels et procédures de régulation sensorielle dans le monde grec ancien. Quelques pistes de réflexion, in: Mythos 11, 49–58.

Harris, Edward (2015) Toward a Typology of Greek Regulations About Religious Matters: A Legal Approach, in: Kernos 28, 53–83.

Horster, Marietta (2013) Priene: Civic Priests and Koinon-Priesthoods in the Hellenistic Period, in: Marietta Horster/Anja Klöckner (eds.), Cities and Priests: Cult Personnel in Asia Minor and the Aegean Islands from the Hellenistic to Imperial Period, Berlin, 177–208.

Karatas, Aynur-Michèlle-Sara (2020) Greek Cults and their Dress-codes: The Regulations of Greek Sanctuaries for Clothing, Colour, and Penalties Against Misbehaviour, in: Revue des Études Anciennes 122(2), 445–488.

Kató, Péter (2013) Elite und Priestertümer im hellenistischen Kos, in: Marietta Horster/Anja Klöckner (eds.), Cities and Priests: Cult Personnel in Asia Minor and the Aegean Islands from the Hellenistic to Imperial Period, Berlin, 279–301.

Lee, Mireille M. (2015) Body, Dress, and Identity in Ancient Greece, Cambridge/New York.

Low, Polly (2020) Remembering, Forgetting, and Rewriting the Past: Athenian Inscriptions and Collective Memory, in: Christy Constantakopoulou/Maria Fragoulaki (eds.), Shaping Memory in Ancient Greece: Poetry, Historiography, and Epigraphy, Newcastle, 235–268.

Mills, Harrianne (1984) Greek Clothing Regulations: Sacred and Profane?, in: Zeitschrift für Papyrologie und Epigraphik 55, 255–265.

Minow, Martha (2000) About Women, about Culture: About Them, about Us, in: Daedalus 129(4), 125–145.

Papavassiliou, Eleni et al. (2020) The Usage of Lartian Stone through the Centuries, in: Marina Panagiotaki/Ilias Tomazos/Fotios Papadimitrakopoulos (eds.), Cutting-edge Technologies in Ancient Greece: Materials Science Applied to Trace Ancient Technologies in the Aegean World, Oxford, 165–172.

Parker, Robert (2004) What Are Sacred Laws?, in: Edward M. Harris/Lene Rubinstein (eds.), The Law and the Courts in Ancient Greece, London, 57–70.

Parker, Robert (2018a) The New Purity Law from Thyateira, in: Zeitschrift für Papyrologie und Epigraphik 205, 178–183.

Parker, Robert (2018b) Regionality and Greek Ritual Norms, in: Kernos 31, 73–81.

Roach-Higgins, Mary E./Eicher, Joanne B. (1992) Dress and Identity, in: Clothing and Textiles Research Journal 10(4), 1–8.

Roth, Martha T. ([2]1997) Writings from the Ancient World: Law Collections from Mesopotamia and Asia Minor, Atlanta.

Stavrianopoulou, Eftychia (2009) Norms of Public Behaviour towards Greek Priests: Some Insights from the Leges Sacrae, in: Pierre Brulé (ed.), La norme en matière religieuse en Grèce ancienne. Actes du XIIe colloque international du CIERGA (Rennes, septembre 2007), Liège, 213–229.

Stavrianopoulou, Eftychia (2015) The Archaeology of Processions, in: Rubina Raja/Jörg Rüpke (eds.), A Companion to the Archaeology of Religion in the Ancient World, Malden/Mass., 349–361.

Tsakiropoulou-Summers, Tatiana (2019) Solon's Legislation and Women's Incompatibility with State Ideology, in: Tatiana Tsakiropoulou-Summers/Katerina Kitsi-Mitakou (eds.), Women and the Ideology of Political Exclusion. From Classical Antiquity to the Modern Era, London/New York, 33–56.

Vogelsang-Eastwood, Gillian (2016) Encyclopedia of Embroidery from the Arab World, London.

Williamson, Christina (2021) Urban Rituals in Sacred Landscapes in Hellenistic Asia Minor, Leiden.

Winter, Bronwyn (2016) Women as Cultural Markers/Bearers, in: Renee C. Hoogland et al. (eds.), The Wiley Blackwell Encyclopedia of Gender and Sexuality Studies, Malden/Mass., 1–5.

Lina Girdvainyte (University of Edinburgh)

Roman legal enactments in mainland Greece in the 2nd century BCE

A source of unity in the face of fragmentation?

Introduction

Rome's ongoing conflicts with the Macedonian and the Seleucid kingdoms in the late 3rd and early 2nd centuries BCE set in motion a series of diplomatic exchanges between Rome and the Greek city-states. This included agreements of friendship and alliance, requests for interstate arbitration as well as numerous administrative and legislative interventions, all of which laid the groundwork for Rome's more permanent presence in the region after 146 BCE.[1] In what follows, I examine the nature and the extent of Roman legislative and judical activities in mainland Greece in the early 2nd century BCE. I start with Titus Quinctius Flamininus, the great 'liberator' of the Greeks from King Philip V, whose legislation for Thessaly in the aftermath of the Second Macedonian War was invoked in a local territorial dispute half a century later. I then turn to Lucius Aemilius Paulus, the Roman general whose victory over King Perseus resulted in the abolishment of the kingdom of Macedon, and whose laws for the defeated Macedonians were still in use in the early Imperial period. Finally, I examine the activities of Lucius Mummius whose reorganization of the constitutions of the Achaian city-states after the short-lived Achaian War included some regulations of both public and private nature.

In addition to literary sources a handful of surviving inscriptions provide a rare glimpse into the reception and the use of Roman legal enactments by the Greeks. As such, these epigraphic sources provide some of the earliest and the least ambiguous attestations of Roman regulations and judicial decisions entering the realm of locally applicable law, decades before the establishment of Roman administrative framework in the region. Combining both types of evidence, I demonstrate how Roman legal intervention in mainland Greece considerably predated the region's provincial organization and was styled as part of Rome's liberationist agenda. At the same time, I highlight the ways in which some Greek city-states and individuals utilized regulations emanating from Roman authorities to further their own

1 Rome's hegemony over the Greek world in the late Hellenistic period is a well-treated topic: see, for instance, Gruen 1984; Kallet-Marx 1995a; Eckstein 2008; Burton 2011; and Ferrary 2017.

aims – territorial, political, or otherwise. I argue that this contributed to the emergence of a new legal landscape in the region, one which saw more unity in local administration of justice, particularly in the field of interstate affairs, in the face of increased fragmentation.

"[A]ccording to the laws of the Thessalians, which they use to the present day; laws which Titus Quinctius (Flamininus), consul ... had given them"

In the immediate aftermath of the Second Macedonian War (196 BCE), the Roman general Titus Quinctius Flamininus made an appearance at the Isthmian games in Corinth, where he proclaimed all Greeks who had previously been subject to Philip V free, without garrison or tribute, and in full enjoyment of their ancestral laws.[2] Flamininus' declaration, which largely echoed the earlier pronouncements of Antigonos Doson and Philip V, is one of the earliest examples of Roman appropriation of the Greek slogan of freedom and, as such, has long been recognized as a pivotal moment in Rome's relations with the Greek city-states.[3] By severing their ties with Macedon and pledging loyalty to Rome, the Greeks could enjoy their freedom and autonomy, and henceforth be treated as Rome's friends and allies.[4] The perceived connection between legal autonomy – that is, a city-state's ability to make use of its existing laws and enact new ones – and good relations with Rome is well-illustrated by the case of Pharos on the Illyrian coast. Following the city's destruction by Roman forces in 219 BCE, the renewal of friendship and alliance (συμμαχία καὶ φιλία) between the two was presented as Rome granting Pharos its city, all territorial possessions, ancestral laws, and other privileges.[5] Rather than purely a matter of rhetoric, diplomatic ties between Rome and the Greek city-states at this time paved the way for Rome to gradually establish itself as the authority who could guarantee or withdraw the Greeks' autonomy.[6]

---

2 Polybios 18.46.5, cf. Livy 33.32–34; 34.48–51; Plutarch, Flamininus 10.1–6.

3 See, e.g., Ferrary 1988, pp. 83–88. On Rome's adoption of the Greek freedom discourse, see Dmitriev 2011.

4 Ferrary 1990, pp. 220–221.

5 SEG 23.489, ll. 3–10. Cf. SEG 25.445 from Stymphalos in Arkadia, mentioning the restoration of "the city, the lands, and the laws" of the Elateians by Manius Acilius Glabrio in c.189 BCE (ll. 12–13). On 'ancestral laws' as a fundamental feature of a Greek city in the Hellenistic period: Cassayre 2010, pp. 36–37; cf. Kantor 2006 on Lycia in the Roman period and Kantor 2016, pp. 47–49 on Aphrodisias after the Antonine Constitution.

6 All treaties concluded between Rome and the Greeks eventually came to contain a confirmation of the latter's territorial rights and legal privileges, including the use of ancestral laws. For the argument of a purely rhetorical function of such treaties, see Eckstein 1999.

Among those declared free and in full enjoyment of their ancestral laws by Flamininus were the Thessalians. And yet, it was also they who became the subjects of Rome's first recorded attempt at constitutional restructuring of the Greeks' federal organization. Livy relates how Flamininus, together with a commission of ten senators from Rome, set out to return Thessaly into some form of order in 194 BCE.[7] According to the author, the action was prompted not only by the continuous meddling of the Macedonian king in Thessalian affairs, but also by the "restless character of the people."[8] Among the regulations introduced by Flamininus was the organization of the Thessalian council and jurors on the basis of property qualification.[9] Similar arrangements were seemingly carried out for Euboia, as well as Perrhaibia and Magnesia, reorganized as territorial leagues at this time.[10] Furthermore, certain changes in Thessalian manumission inscriptions from this point onward suggest that Roman regulations may not have been limited to public matters only: a separate payment to the city, in addition to the payment by the freed slave to their former owner, is henceforth attested throughout Thessaly, resulting in considerable procedural uniformity in manumission practices in the region.[11] Other changes, such as the adoption of a new common calendar to facilitate administration have likewise been connected to Flamininus' reforms.[12] The extent to which these measures were, strictly speaking, imposed on the Thessalians is less clear, as Roman intervention at this time may well have been requested by the pro-Roman leading figures of Thessaly, now freed from Macedonian control.

That Flamininus' arrangements for Thessaly and the wider region dealt, at least in part, with territorial rights can be easily inferred from epigraphic evidence. In a letter addressed to the authorities of Chyretiai, a city in the Thessalian region

7 On the institution of the *decem legati*, see Yarrow 2012.

8 Livy 34.51.4–6.

9 Livy 34.51.6: *a censu maxime et senatum et iudices legit.* A number of detailed arrangements were also issued for individual communities, with some compelled to join the Thessalian, the Achaian and the Aitolian Leagues: e.g., Polybios 18.47.6–10. For the Senate's ratification of Flamininus' arrangements: Livy 34.57. Cf. Cicero, against Verres 2.123: property, age, and occupation qualifications imposed in the seemingly contemporary charter of Agrigentum in Sicily, drawn up by Scipio. For Thessalian federalism in the Hellenistic period, see Bouchon/Helly 2015.

10 On the Euboian *koinon*, see Knoepfler 2015, suggesting that the stimulus for federal organization was provided by Flamininus' declaration of the Euboians' freedom from Macedonian control. Cf. Livy 34.51. On the Magnesian League, see Ferrary 1988, p. 105; Knoepfler 1990, p. 479. Note Livy 35.31–32.1 on Flamininus' visit to Demetrias, the seat of the newly organized Magnesian council, in 192 BCE, with discussion of this episode in Armstrong/Walsh 1986, pp. 44–45, who point out that the Magnesians' hostile attitude was directed not towards Rome or their new constitution but rather at the prospect of being returned back to Macedonian control.

11 Zelnick-Abramovitz 2013.

12 Graninger 2011, pp. 95–97.

of Perrhaibia, Flamininus returned to their rightful owners the lands and houses which had previously been confiscated and added to the public domain of the Roman people (εἰς τὸ δημόσιον τὸ Ῥωμαίων, ll. 9–10).[13] The letter demonstrates the commander's concern with the public perception of himself and, by extension, of Rome (ll. 2–7):

> ἐπεὶ καὶ ἐν τοῖς λοιποῖς πᾶσιν | φανερὰν πεποήκαμεν τήν τε ἰδίαν καὶ τοῦ δήμου τοῦ Ῥωμαίων | προαίρεσιν ἣν ἔχομεν εἰς ὑμᾶς ὁλοσχερῶς, βεβουλήμεθα κα[ὶ] | ἐν τοῖς ἑξῆς ἐπιδεῖξαι κατὰ πᾶν μέρος προεστηκότες | τοῦ ἐνδόξου, ἵνα μηδ' ἐν τούτοις ἔχωσιν ἡμᾶς κατα|λαλεῖν οἱ οὐκ ἀπὸ τοῦ βελτίστου εἰωθότες ἀνα|στρέφεσθαι.

> Since in all other matters too we have made clear our own policy and that of the People of the Romans which we have toward you in general, we have also wished in the future to appear in every part to be champions of what is honourable, in order that in these matters too men may not have (the means) to slander us, men who have not been accustomed in accordance with the best principles to conduct themselves.[14]

Flamininus thus moved to return the confiscated lands "in order that also in these matters you may learn our nobility of character and because in no way at all have we wished to be avaricious, considering goodwill and concern for our reputation to be of supreme importance."[15] This act of generosity on Rome's part was, as pointed out long ago by Robert Sherk, a clever ploy to convince the elites of the former Macedonian dependencies that Rome had their interests at heart.[16] Finally, Flamininus authorized the city to restore the possessions of any future claimants, provided their claims were verified and due investigation was carried out by the city officials in accordance with the commander's written decisions (ll. 13–18):

> ὅσοι μέν|τον μὴ κεκομισμένοι εἰσὶν τῶν ἐπιβαλλόντων αὐτοῖς | ἐὰν ὑμᾶς διδάξωσιν καὶ φαίνωνται εὐγνώμονα λέ|γοντες στοχαζομένων ὑμῶν ἐκ τῶν ὑπ' ἐμοῦ γεγραμ|μένων ἐγκρίσεων, κρίνω δίκαιον εἶναι ἀποκαθίστασ|θαι αὐτοῖς

13 IG IX 2.338 = Sherk, RDGE 33, 197–194 BCE, with Armstrong/Walsh 1986, whence SEG 36.542. Cf. Livy 31.41.5: Chyretiai captured and sacked by the Aitolians in 199/8 BCE.

14 Here and thereafter, translation from Sherk 1984, no. 4.

15 Ll. 11–13: ὅπως καὶ ἐν τούτοις μάθητε τὴν καλοκἀγαθίαν ἡμῶν | καὶ ὅτι τελέως ἐν οὐθενὶ φιλαργυρῆσ[α]ι βεβουλήμεθα | περὶ πλείστου ποιούμενοι χάριτα καὶ φιλοδοξίαν.

16 Sherk, RDGE, 33, p. 213. Compare a letter of Manius Acilius Glabrio to Delphi (Sherk, RDGE, 37) in 190 BCE, an appendix to which provides a lengthy list of the owners of properties which were restored to the city and the sanctuary.

> But all those who have not recovered what belongs to them, if they notify you and if it is the truth they seem to be speaking, and if you conduct your investigation in accordance with my written decisions, I decide it is just (for their property) to be restored to them.

Whether these written decisions of Flamininus only concerned the community of Chyretiai or were part of a broader bulk of procedural arrangements concerning the territory the region, it is clear that they were made available to the city's officials in written form, entered into the city's archives and were henceforth treated as part of the city's body of laws. Flamininus' administrative and judicial activities in Greece took several years and involved traveling from one place to another, holding assize-type hearings and pronouncing judgments.[17] According to Livy, the commander spent the entire winter of 195/4 BCE in Elateia "administering justice."[18] All of these ad hoc decisions, prompted by petitions and complaints of various parties, would have found their way into the local civic and federal archives and could be resorted to in future disputes.

An even more illuminating case concerning Flamininus' arrangements for Thessaly comes from the city of Narthakion. Around 140 BCE, a long-standing territorial dispute between Narthakion and the nearby community of Melitaia was brought before the Roman Senate for arbitration.[19] The two communities had quarreled for some time about a piece of land, with various arbitral awards favoring one side over the other. The disputed territory is first referred to as public land and a deserted area (πε|[ρὶ χώρας] δημοσίας καὶ περὶ χωρίου ἐρήμου, face A, ll. 19–20), but the quarrel appears to have involved control over some sanctuaries as well (περὶ τῆς χώρας καὶ τῶν ἱερῶν, face B, l. 13).

As the initiating party in the present iteration of the dispute, the Melitaians pleaded their case first. Having renewed their "goodwill, friendship and alliance" with Rome, the city's ambassadors claimed that the disputed land had been in their possession at the time they entered into friendship with Rome (face A, ll. 16–22).[20] The Narthakians, they asserted, occupied this land unjustly (ἀδίκως, face A, l. 23), and the Senate should see to it that the land is returned to Melitaia. In support of their case, the city's representatives cited several previous arbitral

---

17 See, e.g., Polybios 18.42.5–8 and 18.47.5–13.

18 Livy 34.48.2: *totum hiemis tempus iure dicundo consumpsit.*

19 IG IX 2.89 = Ager 1996, 156 = Sherk, RDGE, 9.

20 On the instrumentality of interstate friendship between Rome and the Greek city-states in the 2nd century BCE, with particular reference to this document, see Snowdon 2014. The number of Greek embassies to Rome to secure some form of diplomatic relations rose significantly after Flamininus' victory: the dispatch of legates to Greece *ad tenendos sociorum animos* (Livy 35.23.5) on the eve of the war with Antiochos demonstrates multiple active alliances in Greece by 192 BCE.

awards in their favor. The Narthakian ambassadors spoke next and, having likewise renewed their friendship and alliance with Rome, just as the opposing party had done, made an analogous claim that they too were in possession of the disputed land at the time of their entry into friendship with Rome (face B, ll. 11–13). The reason behind such claims by both parties was the well-documented guarantee on Rome's part of the territorial integrity and inviolability of her friends and allies.[21] Therefore, the point of entry into diplomatic relations with Rome could be cited by an allied state as confirmation of its territorial rights, thus acting as the limit of legal memory.

In her discussion of this document, Sheila Ager pointed out what she called "the basic flaw in the Roman procedure": namely, that both parties could have an equally valid claim to the disputed land if they had become friends and allies of Rome at different times.[22] But this is only a problem if one holds, as Ager did, that Rome had a general tendency to award the land in Greek territorial disputes to whichever party held it at the time of their entry into friendship with Rome.[23] However, nothing in the text of the inscription indicates the Senate's insistence on the application of such a criterion. More importantly, neither the Senate nor the disputing parties themselves tried to establish which one of them entered into the Roman friendship first.[24] The main argument of the Narthakian representatives was as follows (face B, ll. 13–19):

> περὶ τῆς χώρας καὶ τῶν ἱερῶν κριτηρίοις [νεν]ικηκ[έ]|ναι κατὰ νόμους τοὺς Θεσσαλῶν, οἷς ν̣[ό]|μοις ἕ̣ως τα̣[ν]ῦν χρῶνται, ο[ὓ]ς νόμους Τίτος Κοΐγκτιος ὕπατος ἀπὸ τῆς τῶν δέκα πρεσ|βευτῶν γνώμης ἔδωκεν καὶ κατὰ δόγμα συγκλήτου

> Concerning the land and the sanctuaries they had been in the courts victorious according to the laws of the Thessalians, laws which they use to the present day, laws which Titus Quinctius (Flamininus), consul, after consultation with the Ten Commissioners had given them, also in accordance with a decree of the Senate.[25]

The courts whose decisions followed Flamininus' laws are not specified. Angelos Chaniotis held that this refers to the verdict of Flamininus himself, while Michael

21 See, e.g., *lex de provinciis praetoriis* of 100 BCE: Crawford, *Roman Statutes* 1.12 (Knidos) IV, ll. 5–30. Cf. Snowdon 2014, pp. 430–431.

22 Ager 1996, pp. 427–429.

23 Ager 1996, pp. 327, cf. 412: "The question of ownership was to be determined by Roman politics rather than the legal-historical background of the land."

24 Snowdon 2014, p. 428.

25 Here and thereafter, translation from Sherk 1984, no. 38.

Snowdon assumed this to be the court of the Thessalian League.[26] Neither of these suggestions is sufficiently supported by the text and there is no particular need for speculation: it is clear that the weight of the Narthakians' argument lay not in the authority of any particular judicial tribunal but rather in the continuous validity of Flamininus' regulations for Thessaly. The Narthakian ambassadors further stated that "it was now the third year since they had been victorious before three tribunals – of Samians, Kolophonians, and Magnesians – and that the decisions had been made in accordance with the laws, (and) that they should all be legally binding, just as for others had been done."[27] This, together with the above reference to multiple rulings in accordance with Flamininus' laws, is one of the earliest attestations of Roman legal enactments applied by local judicial tribunals in solving interstate disputes. Having heard the arguments on both sides and having renewed the friendship and alliance with both cities, the Senate ruled in the following terms (face B, ll. 28–32):

> ὅσα κεκριμένα ἐστὶν κατὰ νόμους | οὓς Τίτος Κοΐγκτιος ὕπατος ἔδωκεν, ταῦτα κα|θὼς κεκριμένα ἐστίν, οὕτω δοκεῖ κύρια εἶναι δεῖν | τοῦτό τε μὴ εὐχερὲς εἶναι ὅσα κατὰ νόμους κε|κριμένα ἐστὶν ἄκυρα ποιεῖν·
>
> That whatever decisions had been made in accordance with laws which Titus Quinctius, consul, had given them, it seemed best that these ought to be legally binding, just as had been decided; (and) that it was not an easy thing for that, which in accordance with the laws had been decided, to be made invalid.

So, instead of investigating the case anew – or rather, as was more common, relegating it to another third-party tribunal – the Senate chose to uphold Narthakians' right to the disputed land on the grounds that the earlier decisions taken in accordance with Flamininus' regulations for Thessaly should be legally binding.

What is crucial here is that the initial reference to Flamininus' laws comes from the winning party's arguments. The ambassadors of Narthakion not only referred to Flamininus' regulations for Thessaly as "the laws of the Thessalians ... which they use to the present day," but also stressed that these laws originated from the commander's consultation with the Ten Commissioners and were confirmed by a decree of the Roman Senate (face B, ll.16–19). In other words, the Narthakians

26 Chaniotis 2004, pp. 193–194, suggesting that the Senate adopted Flamininus' organization of Thessaly as a legal *terminus* in this dispute, cf. Snowdon 2014, p. 422: "decisions by a court of the Thessalian League (whose laws T. Quinctius Flamininus had helped re-establish in 194)."

27 Face B, ll. 19–24: περί τε τούτων τῶν πρ̣αγμά|[τω]ν ἔτει ἀνώτερον τρίτῳ ἐπὶ τριῶν δικασ|[τη]ρίων νενικηκέναι, ἐπὶ Σαμίων, Κολοφ̣ων[ί]|[ων], Μαγνήτων, κεκ[ρι]μένα εἶναι κατὰ νόμου[ς] |ὅπως ταῦτα κύρια ᾖ οὕτω καθὼς καὶ ἄλλοις | γεγονός ἐστιν·

grounded the validity of their claim in Flamininus' regulations for Thessaly laid down some fifty odd years ago. The two quarreling communities had previously been part of Phthiotic Achaia and were only assigned to Thessaly following Flamininus' settlement.[28] It may thus be that the newly drafted "laws of the Thessalians" redefined the territory of these communities at the time of their incorporation into Thessaly, which would explain the insistence on Flamininus' regulations by one party, but not the other. The explicit reference to Flamininus' laws was a deliberate legal strategy of the Narthakians who wanted to highlight the applicability of these enactments to all Thessalian communities, including their opposing party. This very sentiment, first articulated by the representatives of Narthakion, was then reiterated in the Senate's final verdict.

Similarly to the written decisions of Flamininus which had to be used by the authorities of Chyretiai in their investigation of local claims to restoration of property, "the laws of the Thessalians" given to them by Flamininus were readily available to the authorities of the Thessalian communities and could be used to assert territorial claims in local as well as Roman judicial tribunals decades later. The dispute between Narthakion and Melitaia conclusively proves that Flamininus' laws for Thessaly constituted lasting rather than temporary measures. Through recurring disputes of the sort, regulations emanating from Roman authorities were legitimized and passed down as applicable law, largely on the initiative and the agency of the Greeks themselves. Since Flamininus' laws were applicable to all Thessalian communities, including ones newly incorporated into the territorial league, they presented the region with (an impression of) a unifying supra-civic legal framework and a common point of reference in interstate affairs. The existence of and the adherence to these regulations further contributed to the increasing perception of Rome as the highest judicial authority in disputes involving city-states allied with Rome. It is of little surprise, then, that grounding one's claim in the validity of regulations emanating from Roman authorities carried extra weight by the second half of the 2nd century BCE.

"When (Macedonia) fell under the power of the Romans, it was left free ... and it received laws from Paulus Aemilius, which it still uses"

A comparable episode of large-scale Roman legislative intervention in mainland Greece took place in the immediate aftermath of the Third Macedonian War, which resulted in the abolishment of the kingdom of Macedon in 167 BCE. The victorious commander Lucius Aemilius Paulus, aided by a senatorial commission from

28 Polybios 18.47.7; Livy 33.34.7.

Rome, undertook an extensive settlement of the region. This included, among other things, an administrative division of the former kingdom into four independent districts, each with its own capital, annually elected executive officials, and district assemblies.[29] A common Macedonian council was also established, responsible for the overall administration of Macedonian affairs, including the collection and payment of tribute to Rome.[30]

Having summoned the leading men of each city to Amphipolis, Paulus declared the Macedonians free: they were to keep their own cities and lands, to use their own laws, and to elect annual office holders.[31] Similarly to Flamininus' proclamation in 196 BCE, this move was intended to make clear to everyone "that the forces of the Roman People brought not slavery to free peoples, but on the contrary, freedom to the enslaved."[32] The confirmation of the continuous use of their laws *(utentes legibus suis)* also indirectly sanctioned the continuity of some royal regulations which had been incorporated into the civic laws of Macedonian communities. For instance, the ephebarchical law of Amphipolis, inscribed under Augustus, contains regulations dating back to the Antigonid period.[33] Likewise, royal boundary demarcations were still invoked in territorial disputes in the 2nd century CE, with their validity routinely confirmed by imperial judges.[34]

However, similarly to Flamininus' arrangements for Thessaly, the restoration of autonomy and territorial integrity of the Macedonians went hand in hand with

---

29 Livy 45.29; 45.32.2. Derow 2015, p. 76 called this "an attempt on the part of Rome to avoid taking over direct control while establishing a system that would make indirect control as easy as possible." On the Antigonid inspiration of this administrative division: Hatzopoulos 1996, pp. 248–254; Daubner 2014, p. 116.

30 Livy 45.32.2: *quod ad statum Macedoniae pertinebat, senatores, quos synhedros vocant, legendos esse, quorum consilio res publica administraretur,* cf. 45.18.6–8; 45.29–30. A property qualification for accessing council seats as well as other key political offices was likely prescribed as well, in parallel with Flamininus' arrangements for Thessaly. On Paulus' use of the Macedonian council as a representative assembly in carrying out his reforms: Edelmann-Singer 2015, pp. 59–60.

31 Livy 45.29.4: *liberos esse iubere Macedonas, habentis urbes easdem agrosque, utentes legibus suis, annuos creantis magistratus.* Cf. Livy 45.18.1.

32 Livy 45.18.1: *ut omnibus gentibus appareret arma populi Romani non liberis servitutem, sed contra servientibus libertatem adferre.* This freedom was to be assured and lasting "under the protection of the Roman People" *(sub tutela populi Romani)*: Livy 45.18.2.

33 SEG 65.420, 24/3 BCE. Cf. OGIS 483: a law from Pergamon, regulating the maintenance of Pergamene buildings and streets, inscribed in the 2nd cent. CE but still referred to as 'royal law' (βασιλικὸς νόμος) on the inscription. See also Alonso 2013, p. 329 on Ptolemaic regulations retaining their legal force in Roman Egypt.

34 See, e.g., AE 1997, 1345, from Doliche, 101 CE: a Roman judge, appointed by Trajan, confirms a boundary demarcation by King Amyntas III; SEG 39.577 & SEG 59.658, from Bragylos, 2nd century CE: restoration of boundaries by a Roman proconsul, carried out "according to the delimitation made by King Philip."

imposition of a new set of regulations. Livy summarized Paulus' legislative activities as follows:

> *Leges Macedoniae dedit cum tanta cura, ut non hostibus victis, sed sociis bene meritis dare videretur, et quas ne usus quidem longo tempore, qui unus est legum corrector, experiendo argueret.*
>
> Paulus laid down laws for Macedonia with such care as to seem to be giving them not to conquered enemies, but to well-deserving allies – laws which not even experience over a long period of time, the one best amender of legislation, could prove faulty in actual use.[35]

The longevity of Paulus' laws, highlighted by Livy, is further confirmed by the 2nd century CE author Justinus, who remarked that Paulus' laws were still in use in Macedonia, either at the time of Pompeius Trogus, i.e., the 1st century CE, or possibly that of Justinus himself.[36] Some of the leading men of Macedonia, ten of each city, who were ordered to attend Paulus' council at Amphipolis,[37] may have acted in an advisory capacity in drafting these regulations. Jean-Louis Ferrary drew a parallel between this passage in Livy and the decree from Pergamon in honor of Menodoros, whereby this leading citizen is recorded to have been a member of "the council established in accordance with Roman legislation" (ll. 13–14: ἐν τῶι κατὰ τὴν Ῥωμαϊκὴν νομοθεσίαν βουλευ|τηρίωι) at the time of Manius Aquillius' organization of Asia, following Attalos' bequest of his kingdom to Rome.[38]

The extent and nature of Paulus' legislative activities in Macedonia are in some ways easier to reconstruct than those of Flamininus. First and foremost, Paulus' laws must have aimed at regulating the self-governance of the four newly organized Macedonian districts and ensuring the upkeep of their so-called constitutions. That this was not a smooth process can be gleaned from Polybios, who mentions a delegation from Rome to look into the Macedonian affairs shortly after 167 BCE, as the Macedonians, "being unaccustomed to a democratic and council-based form of government, were quarrelling among themselves."[39] About a decade later, Macedonian leaders once again requested Roman intervention in settling their internal

35 Livy 45.32.7, translation adapted from Loeb Classical Library. Cf. Livy 45.31.1.

36 Justinus, Epitome 33.2.7: "When [Macedonia] fell under the power of the Romans, it was left free, magistrates being appointed in every city; and it received laws from Paulus Aemilius, which it still uses." Epigraphic evidence from Macedonia continues to attest the four districts, their presiding officials, as well as the council(s) well into the 3rd century CE.

37 Livy 45.29.1.

38 Ferrary 2017, p. 125 on SEG 50.1211, from Pergamon, after 125 BCE.

39 Polybios 31.2.12–13: συνέβαινε γὰρ τοὺς Μακεδόνας ἀήθεις ὄντας δημοκρατικῆς καὶ συνεδριακῆς πολιτείας στασιάζειν πρὸς αὑτούς.

feuds (στάσεις).[40] Roman regulations for Macedonia in 167 BCE provided its people with a new point of reference in managing their internal affairs, thus directly contributing to the reorientation of Macedonian communities toward Rome as the highest arbitral authority.

Paulus' laws would have also provided for those regulatory domains which only came into existence after the abolishment of the kingdom, such as the exploitation of the formerly royal estates and other sources of revenues which had belonged to the kings. Macedonians were prohibited from leasing out said estates and from exploiting their gold and silver mines – "a source of immense revenue," according to Livy – in an effort to prevent "conspiracies and strife."[41] The extent of the region's military organization was, unsurprisingly, strictly regulated too.[42] This administrative, economic, and military reorganization sought to prevent future unification of Macedonia under a single ruler with control over the region's resources.

One of the most restrictive measures introduced by Roman authorities at this time was the ban on intermarriage and acquisition of landed property between the four Macedonian districts, understood as an attempt to dismember the former kingdom.[43] Livy's expression *commercium agrorum aedificiorumque* would appear to be a direct translation of γῆς καὶ οἰκίας ἔνκτησις – the right to acquire land and real estate within the territory of a Greek city, which was normally restricted to the citizens of that city or a territorial league. Paulus' prohibition of this right might imply that property acquisition had been unrestricted across Macedonia under the kings, which was seen as potentially dangerous by Roman authorities.

The effectiveness of these measures for the period between 167 and 146 BCE may seem dubious at first: it is difficult to imagine how Rome could have policed cases of intermarriage or inter-regional landholding without the presence of a Roman magistrate on the ground. This might have been one sphere of responsibility for the new district councils, consisting of representatives of each city. However, unlike more immediate measures such as demobilization or closure of the precious metal mines, the ban on intermarriage and property acquisition between regions

40 Polybios 35.4.10–12.

41 Livy 45.18.3–5, cf. 45.29.11–14. The complete closure of the precious metal mines cannot have lasted very long: locally extracted metals must have been used to finance military campaigns between Rome and the Thracian tribes in the second half of the 2nd century BCE. The royal estates, which came to form part of the Roman *ager publicus* two decades later (cf. Cicero, de lege agraria 1.5) were perhaps placed under a locally-managed exploitation system, redirecting the revenues toward the sum due to Rome as tribute.

42 Livy 45.18.2–8; 45.29.13; Diodorus Siculus 31.8: prohibition to maintain armed forces, except at frontiers, and the ban on cutting timber for ships.

43 Livy 45.29.10: *Pronuntiavit deinde neque conubium neque commercium agrorum aedificiorumque inter se placere cuiquam extra fines regionis suae esse.* Cf. 45.30.2–8. The ban on the use of imported salt (45.29.12) should also be understood as part of the measures aimed at reducing economic contact between regions.

may have been future-oriented. In other words, it was intended to prevent the emergence of local power structures or clanships created through family alliances, large-scale property holding and, by extension, wide-ranging political influence. The inclusion of this ban in the newly drafted Macedonian laws provided Roman authorities with the possibility to act legally if and when such potentially dangerous power structures arose. So, unless these measures were at some point repealed, Roman officials would have been authorized – in theory, at least – to undo ownership or not recognize the legitimacy of children and inheritances which extended across regional bounds. It is therefore significant that, alongside constitutional, administrative, and economic restructuring, Roman legislative intervention at this time also pertained to private law matters.

Beyond Macedonia proper, numerous decisions over public and private property in the Greek cities were also made by Paulus, comparable to those carried out by Flamininus a few decades earlier. Ilias Arnaoutoglou recently suggested that the epigraphically attested confiscations of land by the commander should be viewed in light of his "(quasi-)legislative initiatives."[44] An inscription from Doliche in Perrhaibia, dating to 167 BCE, records Aemilius Paulus not only confiscating properties in northern Greece but also granting them whomever he pleased.[45] The inscription comprises three documents: a poorly preserved edict, containing a list of individuals' names and properties, and two letters by Paulus addressed to the key office-holders of the city of Gonnoi in Thessaly. The listed properties, consisting of agricultural lands (vineyards, olive groves) and buildings, were presumably confiscated from the supporters of Perseus following the war.[46] Unlike in the case of Chyretiai discussed above, where previously confiscated lands were returned to their rightful owners in an act of demonstrable generosity by Flamininus, Paulus reassigned the lands in Gonnoi to individuals who had supported Rome during the war. As could perhaps be expected, this sort of meddling with private property rights was met with some pushback.

In the first letter addressed to the authorities of Gonnoi, Paulus stated that one of his intended beneficiaries, Demophilos of Doliche, was prevented from taking possession of his new properties in Gonnoi by certain individuals who claimed that Demophilos did not have the authorization of Paulus and the ten senatorial com-

---

44 Arnaoutoglou 2020, p. 291. For Paulus holding judicial hearings in cases involving city-states outside the bounds of Macedonia, see Livy 45.28.6–7; 45.31.1–3. Note also Livy 45.31.15: all charges had to be justified by providing documents from the royal or civic archives.

45 SEG 66.400, with Batziou/Pikoulas 2014–2019 [2020], and Bouchon 2014, whence SEG 64.492.

46 For wide-scale accusations of the king's supporters across Greece and the deportation of all those who had held some office under the king to Italy: Livy 45.31.6–9 & 32.3–7; cf. Pausanias 7.10.11–12 on the deportation of over one thousand Achaians, including the historian Polybios.

missioners.[47] Paulus blamed the city's authorities for not taking action to punish the culprits and exhorted them to comply with his earlier ordinance (πρόσταγμα, l. 16). Moreover, the commander asked the city to refer any similar complaints directly to him, thus assuming personal jurisdiction over any other disputes stemming from his confiscations and reassignments of landed properties (ll. 17–19). Here again, the contrast with Flamininus' conduct in Chyretiai is noteworthy: while Flamininus authorized the city to carry out investigations and restore the lands in accordance with his written decisions, Paulus assumed a more direct role in Gonnoi, which had to do with the city's reluctance to cede the properties of its own citizens to the benefit of outsiders like Demophilos of Doliche.

The second letter confirms continuous opposition to the commander's orders: Paulus accused the city's authorities of being completely ignorant (τελέως ἀγ̣νώμονες, l. 23) due to their lack of concern for the matter, despite his multiple exhortations. He then threatened the authorities with "greater punishment for not attempting to do what is right and for associating with these wretches," referring to the two men who refused to vacate the estates assigned to Demophilos.[48] Finally, Paulus informed the city that he had written to the *strategos* and the councilors of the Perrhaibian League to ensure that Demophilos receives the properties assigned to him (ll. 27–29). Paulus' threats and escalation of the matter to federal authorities must have done the trick, since all three documents were inscribed on a large stele in Doliche, the home city of Demophilos.

Granting landed estates in Gonnoi to a citizen of Doliche undermined not only local property rights but also the more general principle among the Greeks that land ownership within a city's territory was intrinsically linked with possession of local citizenship. Paulus' actions can therefore be seen as contradicting the Roman rhetoric of restoring the lands and the use of ancestral laws to the Greeks.[49] As pointed out by Georgy Kantor, if taken at face value, Roman confirmation of the validity of the Greek cities' laws and the integrity of their territories should have prevented the Romans from intervening in local property relations and legal regimes.[50] This and similar episodes thus provide an important glimpse into the reality of many Greek cities confronted with the new, self-proclaimed protectors of their freedom.

One further point stands out with regards to the understanding of Roman rules by the Greeks. Despite the city's apparent reluctance to comply with Paulus' ordinance,

---

47 SEG 66.400, ll. 9–19. This Demophilos could perhaps be identified with one of the two merchants who guided the Roman army through the region during the war: Livy 44.35.10 records his name as Menophilos.

48 Ll. 25–27: ἔδει μὲν οὖν καὶ μείζονι ἐπιμ̣[ονῆ]ι περιπεπ[οηκέ]|[ν]αι πάντας ὑμᾶς οὐ στοχαζομένους τοῦ καλῶς ἔχ[ειν? *vv*] | [καὶ? ἄ]λ̣λ̣ο̣ις μοχθηροῖ̣[ς] συνεπακολουθοῦντας. For the emotional aspects of Paulus' letter, see Chaniotis 2021, pp. 78–80.

49 On this point, note Kantor 2017, pp. 68–69.

50 Kantor 2017, p. 68.

it is crucial that the two men who were accused of obstructing Demophilos' seizure of properties contested the latter's claim not by reference to some civic law or their own rights, but by asserting that Demophilos did not have the approval of Aemilius Paulus and the ten commissioners (ll. 11–12: ὡς μὴ γεγονότος τούτου μετὰ τῆς ἡμ̣ετέρ̣α[ς] | γνώμης καὶ τῆς τῶν δέκα). Thus, similarly to the Narthakians' resort to Flamininus' laws in their dispute with Melitaia, this document highlights considerable awareness on the part of individual Greeks of the kind of legal arguments which might stand a chance in a controversy stemming from Roman regulations.

"[I]n accordance with the decrees (and judgements) of the Romans and the (local) laws"

To complete this examination of Roman rules for the Greeks in the 2nd century BCE, let us take a look at the activities of Lucius Mummius, the Roman general who carried out the settlement of southern Greece following the short-lived Achaian War in 146 BCE. With a notable exception of Corinth, which was destroyed and its territory confiscated, the defeated Achaians were declared free, thus following in the footsteps of Flamininus and Aemilius Paulus.[51] Once again, despite the declaration of freedom, Lucius Mummius, aided by a senatorial commission from Rome, implemented a series of reforms comparable to those of his predecessors.[52]

First, the Achaian and other territorial leagues were dissolved, with a view to rid Greece of potentially anti-Roman federal structures. Furthermore, in Pausanias' words, Mummius "proceeded to put down democracies and established offices based on property qualification."[53] The constitutional restructuring of the Achaian city-states, which involved reorganization of civic councils and introduction of property qualification to access key civic offices, was overseen by no other than the Greek historian Polybios. According to Pausanias, the former member states of the Achaian League "got permission from the Romans that Polybios should draw up constitutions for them and frame laws."[54] Polybios himself claims to have been tasked with visiting the Achaian cities and examining all arising disputes, until people "grew accustomed to the constitution and laws" (μέχρις οὗ συνήθειαν ἔχωσι τῇ πολιτείᾳ καὶ τοῖς νόμοις). Soon, he says, he made the inhabitants "content with the

---

51 Cassius Dio 21.72.3 (Zonaras 9.31): "he caused the walls of some of the cities to be torn down and declared them all to be free and independent except the Corinthians." Cf. Strabon 8.6.23. For the territory of Corinth as Roman *ager vectigalis:* Cicero, de lege agraria 1.5 & 2.87–90.

52 Polybios 39.5–6; Pausanias 7.16.9–10.

53 Pausanias 7.16.9: ὡς δὲ ἀφίκοντο οἱ σὺν αὐτῷ βουλευσόμενοι, ἐνταῦθα δημοκρατίας μὲν κατέπαυε, καθίστα δὲ ἀπὸ τιμημάτων τὰς ἀρχάς.

54 Pausanias 8.30.9: Ἑλλήνων δὲ ὁπόσαι πόλεις ἐς τὸ Ἀχαϊκὸν συνετέλουν, παρὰ Ῥωμαίων εὕραντο αὗται Πολύβιόν σφισι πολιτείας τε καταστήσασθαι καὶ νόμους θεῖναι.

constitution given to them ... and left no difficulty connected with the laws on any point, private or public, unsettled."[55] Indeed, one of the most conspicuous changes in the epigraphic sources at this time is the appearance of *synedria* as a new type of city council replacing the *boulai* across the Peloponnese.[56] This way, Rome sought to ensure that political power in the region lay firmly in the hands of the propertied classes, seen as more likely to be favorable to Rome.[57] The laws referred to by Polybios and Pausanias must have dealt first and foremost with ensuring the observation and the effectiveness of these new constitutions.

This, however, does not mean that the new type of constitution imposed on the Achaian cities was universally accepted. A key piece of evidence for local opposition to Roman constitutional arrangements comes from the Achaian city of Dyme and dates to only about a year after Mummius' settlement.[58] The inscription records a letter of Quintus Fabius Maximus, the Roman governor of Macedonia, to the authorities of Dyme, and concerns a civil disturbance within the city led by a faction of local politicians. The matter was brought to the attention of Fabius Maximus, as the nearest Roman magistrate operating in the area, by the city's own councilors. They informed the governor that the town hall, together with the archive of public records, had been burnt down, and that the leader of this disturbance was a local law-drafter (*nomographos*, l. 24) Sosos, who "drafted the laws contrary to the type of government granted to the Achaians by the Romans" (ll. 9–10: τοὺς νόμους γράψας ὑπεναντίους τῆι ἀποδοθείσηι τοῖς | [Ἀ]χαιοῖς ὑπὸ Ῥωμαίων πολιτ[εία]ι).[59] Since the accusers provided genuine proof (ll. 16–17: πα]|ρασχομένων τῶν κατηγόρων ἀληθινὰς ἀποδείξεις), Fabius Maximus sentenced the main instigator to death, together with one of the *damiourgoi* who had been involved in setting fire to the town hall and the archives. Sosos' fellow law-drafter, who was equally implicated in the disturbance but who "seemed to have done less wrong," was ordered to appear before the peregrine praetor in Rome.[60]

55 Polybios 39.5.2–3: ὃ δὴ καὶ μετά τινα χρόνον ἐποίησε πρὸς λόγον τοὺς ἀνθρώπους στέρξαι τὴν δεδομένην πολιτείαν καὶ μηδὲν ἀπόρημα μήτε κατ᾽ ἰδίαν μήτε κατὰ κοινὸν ἐκ τῶν νόμων γενέσθαι περὶ μηδενός. On the new 'constitution' of the Achaian cities, see Kallet-Marx 1995a, p. 83.

56 On this change, see Hamon 2005 and Piérart 2013, with examples. Cf. Müller 2005 on a similar change in civic councils in Boiotia after the dissolution of the Boiotian League in 171 BCE, and Knoepfler 1990 on Euboia after 168 BCE.

57 But note Heller 2009, p. 8, rightly stressing that the transformation of civic councils into closed bodies with restricted access, or the so-called "régime des notables" in the Greek world ought to be understood as part of a lengthy development which had started in the Hellenistic period.

58 Syll.[3] 684 = Rizakis, Achaïe III 5, 144/3 BCE, with discussion in Kallet-Marx 1995b.

59 Cf. ll. 18–20: νο|μογραφήσαντα ἐπὶ καταλύσει τῆς ἀποδοθείσης πολιτεί|[α]ς ("drafting laws aiming at the overthrow of the constitution given").

60 Syll.[3] 684, ll. 23–27.

The gravity of the crimes brought before him was perceived by the governor as "laying the foundation of the worst state of affairs and of disorder for all the Greeks" (ll. 11–13). More importantly, Fabius Maximus judged this to be "at odds with the freedom returned in common to all the Greeks and with our policy" (ll. 15–16: [τ]ῆ̣ς ἀποδεδομένης κατὰ [κ]οινὸν τοῖς Ἕλλη[σιν ἐ]|λευθερίας ἀλλότρια καὶ τῆ[ς] ἡμετέ[ρα]ς προαιρέσεως·). The latter phrasing bears striking resemblance to the rhetoric of Flamininus' letter to Chyretiai, discussed above.[61] So, on the one hand, it is clear from the letter that the Achaian cities were left free after Mummius' settlement and were able not only to make use of their existing laws but also introduce new ones – otherwise, the office of local law-drafters would make little sense. However, it is equally clear that any new legislation introduced had to conform to Roman regulations. The inscription thus illustrates rather brilliantly the tension between the nominal freedom of the Greeks and their need to conform to Roman rule in mid-2nd century Achaia. Crucially, the events at Dyme were brought to the attention of Roman authorities entirely by local initiative: pro-Roman city councilors utilized the argument of anti-Roman legislation to ensure their opposition was rooted out. In other words, Roman arrangements for the Achaian cities were deliberately invoked by the Dymean councilors as a means to quell the disturbance and maintain control.[62] Their strategy is therefore comparable to the Narthakians' emphasis on Flamininus' laws in their dispute with Melitaia discussed above.

Aside from overseeing the smooth running of the new civic constitutions, Mummius' laws for the Achaians also had to do with some jurisdictional matters between city-states. A very fragmentary inscription from Nemea, dating to 145 BCE and seemingly concerning a longstanding dispute between Argos and Kleonai over the Nemean games, mentions Lucius Mummius and the ten commissioners in relation to their legislation.[63] While it is impossible to tell whether this dispute was settled by Mummius himself or by some other arbitral authority, it is safe to assume that the regulations laid down by the commander inevitably touched upon interstate affairs, following the dissolution of territorial leagues.[64] Polybios' reference to himself as drafting and perfecting "the laws on the subject of common jurisdiction"

61 Cf. Polybios 39.5.1, on Mummius' settlement as a "good example to the whole of Greece of the policy of Rome" (καλὸν δεῖγμα τῆς Ῥωμαίων προαιρέσεως ἀπολελοιπότες πᾶσι τοῖς Ἕλλησιν).

62 Cf. Kallet-Marx 1995b, pointing out that the destruction of civic archives was likely perceived as a much larger offense locally than the drafting of anti-Roman laws.

63 SEG 23.180, ll. 10–13: [– – – Λεύκιον Μόμμιον ἀνθύ[πατον – – –] | [– – –τῶν δέκα πρεσβευτῶ[ν– – –] | [– – –το]ὺς νόμους γεγονότα[ς– – –]. See also Ager, Arbitrations, no. 152 and, more recently, Miller 2001 II, no. 99/100, whence SEG 51.357.

64 For Mummius' role as arbitrator in interstate disputes at this time, see Tacitus, Annales 4.43.3, cf. I.Olympia 52, ll. 52–55, 63–66.

(περὶ τῆς κοινῆς δικαιοδοσίας νόμους) should perhaps be understood in a similar way, as regulations dealing with 'common' or interstate jurisdiction.[65]

Likewise, Polybios' claim that he "left no difficulty connected with the laws on any point, private or public, unsettled" (39.5.2–3: μήτε κατ' ἰδίαν μήτε κατὰ κοινὸν ἐκ τῶν νόμων) suggests that some Roman regulations for Achaia pertained to private law matters too. This would have had to do, at least in part, with Mummius' prohibition of property acquisition across the civic frontiers, reminiscent of Paulus' regulations for Macedonia two decades earlier.[66] This prohibition is best understood in connection with Rome's decision to dissolve territorial leagues, many of which guaranteed landholding rights across the territory of their member states. Though this measure proved to be temporary,[67] its original aim would have been similar to that of Paulus' too, namely, preventing the rise of powerful individuals whose properties and political currency spanned across multiple communities. All this fragmentation aside, the former member states of the Achaian League now shared a degree of unity not only in terms of their new constitutions and laws but also, as seen in the case of Dyme, in terms of constraints placed upon introduction of new legislation.

So, where does this leave us? By the mid-2nd century BCE, numerous legal enactments emanating from Roman authorities in Greece had entered the realm of locally applicable law. These enactments concerned matters both public and private in nature, and were easily accessible to Greek communities and individuals as well as to local judicial institutions. A pair of decrees passed by the city of Demetrias and the Magnesian League around the middle of the 2nd century BCE celebrate foreign judges from Messene for adjudicating their disputes in accordance with the decrees (δόγματα) and judgments (ἀποκρίσεις) of the Romans as well as the local laws.[68] The relevant lines of the decrees read as follows:

> ll. 21–22: τὰς κρίσεις ἐχθέμενοι δι|καίως καὶ ἀκολούθως τοῖς τε δόγμασιν τοῖς Ῥωμαιών καὶ τοῖς νόμοις
>
> ll. 54–55: κεκρικέναι τάς τε δίκας καὶ εὐθύνας δικαίως καὶ κατὰ τὰ δόγματα | τὰ Ῥωμαίων καὶ κατὰ τοὺς νόμους

65 Polybios 39.5.5. On this, see Fournier 2010, pp. 268–269.

66 Pausanias 7.16.9: οἱ τὰ χρήματα ἔχοντες ἐκωλύοντο ἐν τῇ ὑπερορίᾳ κτᾶσθαι ("those with property were forbidden to acquire possessions beyond the boundaries (of their city)").

67 According to Pausanias (7.16.10), territorial leagues were restored a few years later and the ban on property acquisition was waived.

68 Bardani 2013, no. 7, as yet unpublished, cf. SEG 65.249. For a comparable earlier expression referring to a royal decree alongside local laws, see I.Iasos 82, c. 250–220 BCE, ll. 45–46: κατά τε τὸ διάγραμ|[μα τοῦ] βασιλέως καὶ τοὺς νόμους. For the institution of foreign judges, see Scafuro 2014 and Magnetto 2016.

ll. 69–70: τοῖς δὲ διαδικήσασιν ἔκριναν ἴ|σως καὶ δικαίως κατὰ τὰς Ῥωμαίων ἀποκρίσεις καὶ τοὺς νόμους

Foreign judicial commissions, invited to adjudicate lawsuits of another city, customarily settled those lawsuits in accordance with the laws of the inviting city.[69] This explains why the institution of foreign judges, particularly popular in the Hellenistic period, is sometimes held responsible for increased uniformity in Greek law at this time. The phrasing of the Magnesian decrees clearly suggests that Roman legal enactments, in the form of decrees and judicial verdicts, constituted part of the substantive regulations which could be resorted to in local judicial proceedings. Though honorific decrees for foreign judges hardly ever specify the nature of the disputes that the invited tribunals were asked to resolve, a good portion of cases in Magnesia may have had to do with property or debt litigation. If we accept that, around 194 BCE, Flamininus organized the Magnesian League in a way comparable to the Thessalians, some of these Roman 'decrees' and 'judgments' may refer to just that. Flamininus' letter to Chyretiai once again comes to mind, whereby the commander urged the city to investigate cases of property restitution in accordance with his own "written decisions."

A comparable instance of foreign judges' conformity with Roman regulations comes from Boiotia: an admittedly heavily restored decree, issued by the city of Tanagra in honor of judges from Megara, celebrates their judicial assistance which accorded to the conditions set out in their treaties with the Romans.[70] The lack of direct parallels to the Magnesian decrees makes it difficult to judge whether this was a localized phenomenon or a wider practice. Nonetheless, it is significant that the two sets of applicable rules – the local laws and the Roman decrees and judgments – are presented here as complementary rather than competing. Moreover, this is further proof that Roman legal enactments were readily available for consultation by invited judges. This kind of joint application of local and Roman rules in the internal litigation of Greek cities is therefore indicative of the adaptation of local justice to the changing political and legal circumstances.

---

69 See, e.g., SEG 26.677, 2nd cent. BCE: decree of Peparethos in honor of judges from Larissa, celebrating them for their observance of local, i.e., Peparethian, laws: τὴν τῶν ἡμετέρων νόμων τήρησιν (l. 27).

70 IG VII 20, ll. 16–18: [πλὴν εἴ τινα ἄλλως] | προστέτ[ακται ἡμῖν ἐν ταῖς σ]υν[θήκαις τ]αῖ[ς γενομέναις πρὸς] | Ῥωμαίους. Following Rome's decision to dissolve the Boiotian League, its former member states sought to conclude individual agreements with Rome and increasingly turned to foreign judges as an alternative venue for dispute resolution: Cassayre 2010, pp. 81–89.

Conclusion

Several important points stand out from this discussion. By the mid-2nd century BCE, numerous Roman legal enactments, in the form of decrees, edicts, and judicial verdicts, were circulating in mainland Greece alongside local laws whose continuous validity was repeatedly confirmed by Roman authorities. Roman enactments, which pertained to both public and private matters, were incorporated into the realm of locally applicable law, and were readily available for consultation decades, if not centuries later.

The epigraphic sources discussed above not only demonstrate the relevance and applicability of Roman regulations in a number of local disputes, but also highlight how recourse to Roman rules could be used strategically before local as well as Roman judicial authorities. We see this, most glaringly, in the case of Narthakion's dispute with Melitaia, whereby the Narthakians' appeal to the continuous validity of Flamininus' laws – notably, referred to by them as "the laws of the Thessalians" – guaranteed their victory in the judicial hearing before the Roman Senate. Invoking regulations emanating from Roman authorities could be a useful strategy not only in interstate disputes, but also in power struggles within the same community, as seen in the case of civil strife at Dyme. The very fact that Roman legislation to the Greeks went hand in hand with confirmation of their freedom and autonomy may have incentivized local claims to the validity of Roman regulations.

While this was hardly among Rome's immediate aims, Roman legislative activities in the 2nd century BCE contributed to a degree of unity in local administration of justice. More often than not, Roman regulations were aimed at numerous communities at once – the Thessalians, the Macedonians, or the Achaians – thus providing them with an impression of a unifying legal framework and a common point of reference. Furthermore, the increased fragmentation at this time – due to the administrative division of the Macedonian kingdom or the dissolution of territorial leagues – resulted in a growing network of alliances between Rome and individual city-states. This introduced a measure of control on Rome's part, providing Roman authorities with a license to intervene, and resulted in wide-scale orientation of the Greeks toward Rome as the highest arbitral authority. Likewise, despite the continuity of a myriad of local laws and legal regimes, the imposition of new regional and civic constitutions, alongside restrictions on intermarriage and property holding contributed to a degree of uniformity across different parts of the region.

Put together, the historiographical and documentary evidence discussed above illustrate the emergence of a new legal landscape in mainland Greece, one with a mixture of local and Roman rules at play, and a clear perception of Rome as the highest, if not the only, legal authority and source of justice. This, in turn, calls into question the extent to which the introduction of the governor's court in Macedonia in 146 BCE should be seen as a watershed moment in the legal relations between Rome and the Greek city-states.

Bibliography

AGER, Sheila (1996) Interstate Arbitration in the Greek World, 337–90 B. C., Berkeley.

ALONSO, Jose-Louis (2013) The Status of Peregrine Law in Egypt: 'Customary Law' and Legal Pluralism in the Roman Empire, in: Journal of Juristic Papyrology 43, 351–404.

ARNAOUTOGLOU, Ilias (2020) An Outline of Legal Norms and Practices in Roman Macedonia (167 BC–AD 212), in: Kimberly CZAJKOWSKI/Benedikt ECKHARDT (eds.), Law in the Roman Provinces, Oxford, 284–312.

ARMSTRONG, David/WALSH, Joseph J. (1986) The Letter of Flamininus to Chyretiae, in: Classical Philology 81, 32–46.

BARDANI, Voula (2013) Τιμὲς Μεσσηνίων δικαστῶν. Ἐπιγραφικὲς συμβολὲς στὴν ἐξέταση τοῦ θεσμοῦ τῶν ξενικῶν δικαστηρίων, Volos.

BATZIOU, Anthi/PIKOULAS, Yannis (2014–2019 [2020]), Πρόσταγμα καὶ ἐπιστολὲς Λευκίου Αἰμιλίου Λευκίου (Παύλου Μακεδονικοῦ), in: Ηόρος 26–31, 281–302.

BOUCHON, Richard (2014) Démophilos de Doliché, Paul-Émile et les conséquences de la troisième guerre de Macédoine à Gonnoi, in: Topoi 19(2), 483–513.

BOUCHON, Richard/HELLY, Bruno (2015) The Thessalian League, in: Hans BECK/Peter FUNKE (eds.), Federalism in Greek Antiquity, Cambridge, 231–249.

BURTON, Paul (2011) Friendship and Empire. Roman Diplomacy and Imperialism in the Middle Republic (353–146 BC), Cambridge.

CASSAYRE, Aude (2010) La justice dans les cités grecques. De la formation des royaumes hellénistiques au legs d'Attale, Rennes.

CHANIOTIS, Angelos (2004) Justifying Territorial Claims in Classical and Hellenistic Greece. The Beginnings of International Law, in: Edward HARRIS/Lene RUBINSTEIN (eds.), The Law and the Courts in Ancient Greece, London, 185–213.

CHANIOTIS, Angelos (2021) Unveiling Emotions III. Arousal, Display, and Performance of Emotions in the Greek World, Stuttgart.

DAUBNER, Frank (2014) Makedonien I bis IV. Verhinderte Mobilität oder Forscherkonstrukt?, in: Eckart OLSHAUSEN/Vera SAUER (eds.), Mobilität in den Kulturen der antiken Mittelmeerwelt, Stuttgart, 113–124.

DEROW, Peter (2015) Rome, Polybius, and the East (ed. by Andrew ERSKINE/Josephine CRAWLEY QUINN), Oxford.

DMITRIEV, Sviatoslav (2011) The Greek Slogan of Freedom and Early Roman Politics in Greece, Oxford.

ECKSTEIN, Arthur (1999) Pharos and the Question of Roman Treaties of Alliance Overseas in the Third Century B. C., in: Classical Philology 94, 395–418.

ECKSTEIN, Arthur (2008) Rome Enters the Greek East: From Anarchy to Hierarchy in the Eastern Mediterranean, 230–170 BC, Oxford.

EDELMANN-SINGER, Babette (2015) Koina und Concilia. Genese, Organisation und sozioökonomische Funktion der Provinziallandtage im römischen Reich, Stuttgart.

FERRARY, Jean-Louis (1988) Philhellénisme et impérialisme: aspects idéologiques de la conquête romaine du monde hellénistique, Rome.

FERRARY, Jean-Louis (1990) Traités et domination romaine dans le monde hellénique, in: Luciano CANFORA/Mario LIVERANI/Carlo ZACCAGNINI (eds.), I trattati nel mondo antico. Forma, ideologia, funzione, Rome, 217–235.

FERRARY, Jean-Louis (2017) Rome et le monde grec: choix d'écrits, Paris.
FOURNIER, Julien (2010) Entre tutelle romaine et autonomie civique: L'administration judiciaire dans les provinces hellénophones de l'Empire romain (129 av. J.-C. – 235 apr. J.-C.), Athens.
GRANINGER, Denver (2011) Cult and Koinon in Hellenistic Thessaly, Leiden.
GRUEN, Erich (1984) The Hellenistic World and the Coming of Rome, Berkeley/Los Angeles.
HAMON, Patrice (2005) Le conseil et la participation des citoyens: les mutations de la basse époque hellénistique, in: Pierre FRÖHLICH/Christel MÜLLER (eds.), Citoyenneté et participation à la basse époque hellénistique. Hautes Etudes du monde gréco-romain, Geneva, 121–144.
HATZOPOULOS, Miltiades (1996) Macedonian Institutions under the Kings: A Historical and Epigraphic Study, Athens.
HELLER, Anna (2009) La cité grecque d'époque impériale: Vers une société d'ordres?, in: Annales. Histoire, Sciences Sociales 64(2), 341–373.
KALLET-MARX, Robert (1995a) Hegemony to Empire. The Development of the Roman Imperium in the East from 148 to 62 BCE, Berkeley.
KALLET-MARX, Robert (1995b) Quintus Fabius Maximus and the Dyme Affair (Syll.3 684)', in: The Classical Quarterly 45(1), 129–153.
KANTOR, Georgy (2006) Ancestral Laws under Roman Rule. The Case of Lykia, in: Vestnik Drevnej Istorii 259(4), 50–77.
KANTOR, Georgy (2017) Property in Land in Roman Provinces, in: Georgy KANTOR/Tom LAMBERT/Hannah SKODA (eds.), Legalism: Property and Ownership, Oxford, 55–74.
KNOEPFLER, Denis (1990) Contribution à l'épigraphie de Chalcis, in: Bulletin de Correspondance Hellénique 114, 473–498.
KNOEPFLER, Denis (2015) The Euboian League – an 'Irregular' *Koinon?*, in: Hans BECK/Peter FUNKE (eds.), Federalism in Greek Antiquity, Cambridge, 158–178.
MAGNETTO, Anna (2016) Interstate Arbitration and Foreign Judges, in: Edward HARRIS/Mirko CANEVARO (eds.), The Oxford Handbook of Ancient Greek Law, Oxford.
MILLER, Stephen G. (2001) Excavations at Nemea II: The Early Hellenistic Stadium, Berkeley.
MÜLLER, Christel (2005) La procédure d'adoption des décrets en Béotie de la fin du IIIe s. av. J.-C. au Ier s. apr. J.-C., in: Pierre FRÖHLICH/Christel MÜLLER (eds.), Citoyenneté et participation á la basse époche hellénistique, Geneva, 95–119.
PIÉRART, Marcel (2013) Une nouvelle proxénie argienne de la basse époque hellénistique et les synèdres d'Argos, in: Askol'd IVANTCHIK (ed.), Monumentum Gregorianum, Moscow, 275–289.
SCAFURO, Adele (2014) Decrees for Foreign Judges: Judging Conventions or Epigraphic Habits?, in: Michael GAGARIN/Adrian LANNI (eds.), Symposium 2013. Vorträge zur griechischen und hellenistischen Rechtsgeschichte (Cambridge MA, 26.-29. August 2013), Vienna, 365–395.
SHERK, Robert K. (1984) Rome and the Greek East to the Death of Augustus, Cambridge.
SNOWDON, Michael (2014) "In the Friendship of the Romans". Melitaia, Narthakion and Greco-Roman Interstate Friendship in the Second Century BCE, in: Historia. Zeitschrift für Alte Geschichte 63(4), 422–444.
YARROW, Liv Mariah (2012) Decem Legati: A Flexible Institution, Rigidly Perceived, in: Christopher SMITH/Liv M. YARROW (eds.), Imperialism, cultural politics, and Polybius, Oxford, 168–183.
ZELNICK-ABRAMOVITZ, Rachel (2013) Taxing Freedom in Thessalian Manumission Inscriptions, Leiden.

Patrick Sänger (University of Münster)

P.Eleph. 1: A document and its origin

Some thoughts on the methodology of Hans Julius Wolff and Joseph Mélèze Modrzejewski*

Introduction

In the seventh year of Alexander, son of Alexander, in the 14th Year of Ptolemy's satrapy, in the month of Dios; marriage contract (συγγραφὴ συνοικισίας) between Herakleides and Demetria; Herakleides (from Temnos)[1] takes (λαμβάνει) Demetria, who is from Kos, to be his lawful wife, a free man a free woman, from her father Leptines, who is from Kos, and her mother Philotis; (Demetria) brings clothing and jewelry worth 1,000 drachmas into the marriage, and Herakleides is to provide Demetria with everything appropriate to a freeborn woman; and we are to live together wherever it seems best to Leptines and Herakleides, by mutual consent; if Demetria should disgrace her husband Herakleides, she is to be deprived of what she had brought into the marriage; but Herakleides shall prove his accusations before three men, who are acknowledged by both of them; Herakleides shall not be permitted to take another wife home and thereby offend Demetria, or to have children with another wife, or to do evil to Demetria under any pretext; if Herakleides should do anything of the kind, and Demetria can prove it before three men, who are acknowledged by both of them, Herakleides shall return to Demetria the dowry to the value of 1,000 drachmas which she brought with her, and shall also pay 1,000 Alexandrian silver drachmas; Demetria and those who assist her in demanding payment shall have the right to demand payment as if judgment had been rendered, both from Herakleides himself and from all his property on land and sea; this contract (συγγραφή) shall have legal force everywhere, whether Herakleides should use it against Demetria, or Demetria and her assistants should use it against Herakleides to claim payment, as if the agreement had been made on the spot; Herakleides and Demetria shall have the right to keep the contracts separately under their own custody and to use them against each other; witnesses (μάρτερες [*sic!*]): Kleon from Gela, Antikrates

---

* I would like to thank Thomas Ford (Münster) for valuable advice and his help with the English style.

1 As we are dealing with a double document (see below), the translation basically refers to the upper copy of the contract. However, the origin of Herakleides is only mentioned in the lower copy, where he is referred to as Temnites in l. 20.

from Temnos, Lysis from Temnos, Dionysios from Temnos, Aristomachos from Cyrene, Aristodikos from Kos.

Accordingly, the contents of P.Eleph. 1, with which we find ourselves at the beginning of Greek papyrology. This papyrus is the oldest securely dated Greek document and takes us back to the year 310 BCE – about 20 years after Alexander the Great had taken Egypt from the Persian Empire. And the death of Alexander was by this time 13 years ago. According to the papyrus' dating formula, at the time the document was drawn up, Alexander's empire was nominally under the regency of his son of the same name, born to Roxane after his death. In addition to the year of the reign of this Alexander IV, the dating formula also refers to the year after the establishment of the satrapy of Ptolemy, a general of Alexander the Great. The founding father of the Ptolemaic dynasty is here not yet a king, but – as a relic of the Persian imperial administration – satrap of the still united Empire of Alexander the Great with ruling power over Egypt.

The present document P.Eleph. 1 has gone down in the history of papyrology as the so-called "marriage contract of Elephantine." The papyrus illustrates how a Greek immigrant couple, the woman from Kos, the man probably from Temnos (a city in the Aeolian part of western Asia Minor), entered into marriage in Elephantine, which is on the southern border of Egypt, before Greek witnesses who were from Gela in Sicily, Cyrene (in modern Libya), Temnos, and Kos. The couple recorded their marriage agreement in a contract. The form of the deed and the use of certain contract clauses make it clear that it was designed not to lose any of its validity or legal force in the event of any future changes of the couple's location. The deed is a 'double document,' meaning that the text is set down in duplicate. Both spouses have access to a copy of the double document and, in addition, the right to convene a council of three men in the event of a dissolution of their marriage, in order to obtain a divorce with a corresponding settlement. This three-man council can be convened anywhere and is therefore, like the document itself, perfectly suited to a life of high mobility or at least takes into account the possibility of a change of location.

The amount of the dowry indicates that the lifeworld from which the marriage contract originates is that of a wealthy circle of people: the amount of money mentioned corresponds to the average income of several years at that time.[2] Why the couple had moved to Elephantine, whether they had already lived in the town for some time and spent the rest of their lives there, remains a mystery. The reason for their immigration may have been trade, but a connection to the military is also conceivable, as Elephantine was the location of a Greek garrison.[3] Regardless of this, the marriage contract of Elephantine is exemplary of dynamic migration pro-

2 Rowlandson 1998, p. 165.
3 Fischer-Bovet 2014, p. 262; Thompson 2021, p. 29.

cesses that can be traced back to the conquests of Alexander the Great and brought people from all possible regions of the Mediterranean – not only immigrants from the Greek mother country, but also Macedonians, Jews, and other ethnic groups in large numbers – to Egypt.[4]

The place of P.Eleph. 1 in Greek legal history and the associated notion of a *koine*

P.Eleph. 1 is the oldest Greek papyrus text that can be dated with certainty. The great importance of the text for Greek legal history is self-explanatory. Firstly, it is the oldest Greek contract from Egypt; secondly, it gives us the oldest testimony of a Greek marriage contract,[5] and – last but not least – it is the oldest Greek testimony that transmits a private agreement, written in the document type of the *syngraphe*, directly, that is, as an original document. Against this background, it is very interesting that leading figures of legal papyrology and ancient legal history such as Hans Julius Wolff and Joseph Mélèze Modrzejewski have not celebrated P.Eleph. 1 more enthusiastically.[6] To understand this attitude it is first necessary to discuss the conceptual model on which it is based – this will guide us to the heart of the problem at stake in this paper.

Wolff argued strongly that in the Hellenistic era something like a juridical *koine* or – as he also called it – a "Hellenistic legal *koine*" developed in the field of Greek private law which built on the linguistic and factual concordance of Greek particular laws and was particularly able to flourish under the regime of the Ptolemies in Egypt, a country of immigrants.[7] It was Mélèze Modrzejewski who has reminded us that the term "legal *koine*" was shaped in the 1930s by Louis Gernet;[8] by analogy with the established *koine* concept in the context of the supraregional Greek language that emerged rather quickly at the beginning of the Hellenistic era, Gernet urged us not to forget the complexity of the processes behind legal unification. Looking at the *koine* of Greek private law, the "*koinè* du droit privé," he also cautioned that we reach our limits in determining or defining the degree of its "unité and pureté."[9] This advice carries some weight, although it has rarely received the attention it deserves. To be sure, Wolff can certainly not be criticized for having

4 On immigration to Hellenistic Egypt and the related aspects, see, e.g., La'da 2002; Fischer-Bovet 2011; Sänger 2022.

5 Mélèze Modrzejewskis 2005, p. 349.

6 In the following, the references to Hans J. Wolff's and Joseph Mélèze Modrzejewski's research positions refer exclusively to their most recent major works for the sake of convenience.

7 Wolff 2002, pp. 35–43.

8 Mélèze Modrzejewski 2014, p. 148, n. 33.

9 Gernet 1938, p. 278.

applied the concept of a juridical *koine* in an unfounded or unreflective manner, since it undeniably fits in with the model of legal pluralism which he took up in categorizing the systems that would become apparent in the field of private law in Hellenistic Egypt; moreover, indeed, one will have to accept a coexistence of Egyptian and Hellenistic legal traditions and therefore refrain from the idea of a mixed law of any kind.[10] Nevertheless, the question remains as to how much one separates the two traditions; and in this context, despite the by no means obscured insight that Egyptian institutions or modes of behavior may have influenced the development of the Hellenistic traditions or may have been integrated into them,[11] one is inclined to understand Wolff's work more as a plea for the isolation of a Greek legal sphere.[12] This is admittedly with the pointed remark that it was precisely this legal sphere to which the government was naturally close and to which implicit priority may therefore have to be given.[13]

If for Wolff one does not yet gain the impression that the thought-construct he drafted in connection with the juridical *koine* is an expression of a certain ideology, one can hardly avoid this impression in the case of Mélèze Modrzejewski. The isolation of the Greek legal sphere or of the juridical *koine* connected with it which he advocates seems to take on even sharper features. To a certain extent, this is a logical consequence of what Mélèze Modrzejewski repeatedly emphasized as symptomatic of the social order in Ptolemaic Egypt, namely the strong separation – ethnically, socially, and culturally – of "Greeks" or *Hellenes,* so immigrants from the Greek cultural sphere and their descendants, and indigenous "Egyptians."[14] It is not necessary to elaborate here on the problematic nature of this postcolonial and now outdated historical picture.[15] What is decisive for us is the fact that the demarcation of the juridical *koine* from other legal traditions, which is noticeable in Wolff

10 Wolff 2002, pp. 4, 27–28, 79–84.

11 Wolff 2002, pp. 71–98.

12 It is telling how Wolff 2002, pp. 3–4 justified his restriction on the Hellenic sector of the papyrological evidence from Egypt: "Ihm [dem griechischen Recht; note from the author] gegenüber wurden die ägyptischen Züge zunehmend als bloßes, wenn auch keineswegs abgestorbenes Traditionsgut ... empfunden. Demgemäß wird ihnen Beachtung zuteil werden, aber nicht um ihrer selbst willen, sondern nur insoweit, als ihnen entstammende Institutionen und Verhaltensweisen die eigene Entwicklung der hellenistischen Traditionen beeinflußten oder in sie eingeschmolzen wurden, oder als es gilt, die Anwendungsbereiche gegeneinander abzugrenzen."

13 Wolff 2002, pp. 3, 38–39, 71–74.

14 Mélèze Modrzejewski 2014, pp. 108–109, 186–188, 192, 197, 221.

15 The post-colonial approach advocated by Mélèze Modrzejewski is increasingly being relativized by current research on various levels – admittedly in clear historiographical dissociation from any simplification that allowed older research to speak of a "mixed society" in the wake of colonial ideas and under the assumption of a decline of Hellenism; see in general, e.g., Moyer 2011, pp. 30–32; Rowlandson 2013, pp. 218–219; Scheuble-Reiter 2012, p. 140; Fischer-Bovet 2014, pp. 247–250.

but still recognizably relativized, is practically accomplished by Mélèze Modrzejewski. For him, a legal system had emerged in Egypt that resembled "un ensemble compose de la loi royale et de deux fonds de *nomoi* [Egyptian and Greek; note from the author], gardant chacun des caractères distincts en function du clivage social et ethnique."[16] In this rigid construct built on alleged sociopolitical realities, there was virtually no room for influence in either direction, at least at the beginning of Hellenism.

If the character and delimitation of the juridical *koine* as an expression of a common Greek private law is an area in which, as we have seen, Mélèze Modrzejewski not only takes up the view of his older colleague but also noticeably narrows it, both scholars agreed on another point, essential for us in what follows: that the earliest Greek deeds we encounter in Egypt are expressions of Greek written tradition; in terms of contracts, this means that they reflect what we would expect to find against the background of Greek contractual practice. Accordingly, Wolff had stated with respect to P.Eleph. 1 that "an dem hellenistischen Charakter dieses Urkundstyps nicht zu zweifeln [ist]."[17] If Wolff considered a Hellenistic origin for a document dating to 310 BCE – which, moreover, is the oldest Greek contract on papyrus so far – one is justified in asking what the direct comparative examples would be. In fact, they do not exist, and Wolff had something different in mind, because he linked P.Eleph. 1 ideationally with the contractual practice cultivated in the Greek mother country. Unsurprisingly, Mélèze Modrzejewski also emphasized the continuity between classical Greece and the Hellenistic world in the field of private law, and programmatically attributed the changes in this field more to political changes in the wake of the Macedonian conquest than to non-Greek influences.[18] In the context of P.Eleph. 1, he resolutely concluded: "Si le droit romain est un droit des jurisconsultes ('Juristenrecht'), le droit hellénistique est un droit des notaires."[19] All in all, it seems – and here the circle closes – that the aforementioned juridical *koine* is supposed to have continued legal developments whose origin is to be sought in the mother country. And this is absolutely necessary from the perspective of both scholars: For how can something be called *koine* (with reference to the Greek common language), which did not have its beginning in Greece – and did not preserve its purely Greek nature from the beginning? In the depiction of Wolff and Mélèze Modrzejewski, P.Eleph. 1 was thus nothing peculiar insofar as it only confirmed the Greek contract practice that had emerged by then: as a consequence of Alexander's conquest, the desert sands of Egypt could reveal what, due to the less favorable finding circumstances and climatic conditions, was lost forever elsewhere.

---

16 Mélèze Modrzejewski 2014, p. 228.
17 Wolff 1978, p. 60.
18 Mélèze Modrzejewski 2014, pp. 28–29.
19 Mélèze Modrzejewski 2014, p. 131.

In the following, it will be examined whether the previously explained model of a juridical *koine* can be applied to P.Eleph. 1. This does not involve questions of private law in the narrower sense. Rather, the focus will be on the practice of drafting deeds. In this area, however, attention will not be paid to legal formulas and their development, but instead to the materiality, the components, and the external design of the deed. In this way, the fundamental question will be addressed as to whether the formation of a Greek deed such as P.Eleph. 1 can be understood by itself, i.e., out of a pure Greek tradition, or whether other factors may possibly have to be taken into account.

Syngraphe, witnesses, and double document

First of all, possible links to a pre-Hellenistic contract practice in Greece will be discussed. With regard to the stylization of the contractual text contained in P.Eleph. 1, Wolff referred to the *syngraphe* quoted by Demosthenes in his speech contra Lakritos, which concerns a loan;[20] the text (or. 35.10–13) reads as follows:

> Written agreement (συγγραφή)
> Androcles of Sphettus and Nausicrates of Carystus lent (ἐδάνεισαν) to Artemon and Apollodorus of Phaselis 3,000 drachmas of silver for a voyage from Athens to Mende or Scione, and from there to Bosporus, and, if they wish, on the left-hand side as far as the Borysthenes, and back to Athens, at 225 a thousand – and if they sail after Arcturus out of the Pontus towards Hierum, at 300 a thousand – on security of 3,000 Mendaean jars of wine, which will be shipped from Mende or Scione in the twenty-oared ship skippered by Hyblesius. They pledge these, not owing any money to anyone else on this security, nor will they obtain any further loan on it. They will convey back to Athens in the same boat all the goods from the Pontus purchased with proceeds from the outward cargo.
>
> If the goods reach Athens safely, the borrowers will pay the accruing money to the lenders in accordance with the agreement within twenty days of their arrival at Athens in full – apart from any jettison which the fellow-voyagers vote to make jointly and any enemy exaction from them, but otherwise in full. They will place the security intact under the control of the lenders until they pay the accruing money in accordance with the agreement.
>
> If they do not pay within the agreed time, the lenders shall be permitted to pledge the pledged goods and to sell them at the prevailing price; and if the proceeds fall short of the amount which ought to accrue to the lenders according to the agreement,

20 Wolff 1978, p. 61.

the lenders, both singly and together, shall be permitted to exact it from Artemon and Apollodorus and from all their property, both on land and at sea, wherever it may be, in the same way as if judgment had been given against them and they had defaulted in payment.

If they do not enter the Pontus, after waiting in the Hellespont for ten days after the Dog-star, they shall unload in any place where Athenians are not liable to seizure of goods, and after sailing back from there to Athens, they shall pay the amount of interest written in the agreement in the previous year. If any ship in which the goods are being conveyed suffers irreparable loss but the pledged goods are saved, the lenders shall share what is preserved. On these matters nothing else is to prevail over the written agreement.

Witnesses (μάρτυρες): Phormion of Piraeus, Cephisodotus of Boeotia, and Heliodorus of Pithus.[21]

The objective stylization of the contract handed down by Demosthenes and the naming of witnesses following the main text may be comparable to P.Eleph. 1. But in what way does this justify placing both contractual texts in a strict line of development? This question becomes more striking if one considers that in Athens – which must be our point of comparison due to the availability of the sources – the written word as a means of evidence in everyday business gains acceptance only from the early 4th century BCE, for which Isocrates in his Trapezitikos (17.20) provides the first attestation and where Demosthenes (i.a. or. 35.14) provides another contemporary source for this development. Before that, the tradition of oral and, as it were, witnessed contracts was predominant in Athens.[22] Even if Athens becomes more "document-minded" from the early 4th century BCE – as Rosalind Thomas[23] has put it – it will have to be noted that the written record of a contract first became significant in the realm of maritime trade,[24] where "stable and visible land ownership" was of little concern.[25] This is the world we enter with the *syngraphe* cited in Demosthenes and taken up by Wolff, but it is not the context of P.Eleph. 1, which, as we know, is based on a marriage. It is true that we encounter a high-income married couple in P.Eleph. 1 – so that socioeconomic comparison with persons who engaged in maritime trade may seem justified – but the practice of drawing up a marriage contract is, we recall, first attested by P.Eleph. 1. This also concerns the fact that, unlike in Athens of the Classical period, where the heads of the families themselves regulated the conclusion of a marriage, in P.Eleph. 1 this becomes a matter

21 MacDowell 2004, pp. 135–137.

22 On the development from oral but witnessed contracts or transactions to written ones, see Pringsheim 1955.

23 Thomas 1989, p. 42.

24 Cohen 2005, p. 257.

25 Thomas 1989, p. 41.

for the couple.[26] Against this background, the very content of P.Eleph. 1 discourages comparison with earlier examples of the use of written contracts in Athens. We lack any evidence for Athens that would justify assuming before the end of the 4th century BCE that written contracts would have been used extensively in everyday legal life apart from in the business world of high society.[27] The linguistic stylization of P.Eleph. 1 (and the mere appearance of witnesses) may therefore be comparable to the *syngraphe* in Demosthenes contra Lakritos, but the practice of documenting a marriage contract in this way need not automatically be linked to an Athenian tradition in the 4th century BCE – a tradition into which, as already noted, the use of the written word in legal transactions only gradually entered before the beginning of Hellenism. Rather, the appearance of a Greek marriage contract could also be linked more strongly with the local traditions of the place where it was found: with Egypt, where, quite differently from Athens, there was already a flourishing contractual system (based on documents) for any kind of business in pre-Hellenistic times, including marriage certificates, which (in Egyptian language) are attested from the 3rd Intermediate Period (ca. 1070–664 BCE) onwards;[28] and where from time immemorial the written word had had a completely different weight than in Greece; and where a writing material such as papyrus was produced which was ideally suited for writing down all kinds of texts, due to its easy availability.

So, if one wanted to establish a continuity between Greece or Athens and P.Eleph. 1, one should not primarily start with Athenian contract practice, but rather limit oneself to noting the emerging custom of writing down contracts at all, and consider Egypt as a place where this development received dynamizing and accelerating impulses due to the prevailing writing and contract culture. When looking for comparable Greek continuities, one should ask oneself quite fundamentally whether Athens in particular represents the right reference point for the search for continuities, given that in the case of P.Eleph. 1 the contracting parties are, as already mentioned, from Kos and from Temnos. However, it is pointless to speculate whether it was more common in these places than in Athens to write down all possible contracts on papyrus or a similar writing medium, because the sources offer us no support in this respect. Therefore, a local contextualization of P.Eleph. 1 in the south of Egypt should be considered before looking to distant Greece.

This approach also seems more promising with regard to another aspect that Wolff wanted to link to Athens: the previously-mentioned naming of witnesses at

---

26 Mélèze Modrzejewski 2005, pp. 348–349.

27 It was only towards the end of the 4th century BCE that written contracts were apparently made without witnesses, which probably indicates an increase in the importance of the document and its validity in legal transactions; see Pringsheim 1955, pp. 290–292; Thomas 1989, p. 41; and below.

28 Just see, e.g., Lippert 2012, pp. 59–60.

the end of the contractual text, which can also be found in the *syngraphe* quoted by Demosthenes.[29] It is now significant that the end of the development that gives the written word in Athens more authority in contract practice seems to be marked by the fact that the involvement of witnesses is no longer necessary to guarantee the validity of a contract – it is sufficient to deposit the document with a trustee. This step is documented by Hypereides contra Athenogenes (e.g. 8–12) and Lykourgos contra Leokrates (23), where the contract executed in writing no longer requires witnesses;[30] with both speeches we are in the 30s or 20s of the 4th century BCE. Strictly speaking, this means that – if we were to follow the Athenian model – the involvement of witnesses at the time when P.Eleph. 1 was issued no longer corresponded to the zeitgeist. An explanatory recourse to the *syngraphe* in Demosthenes therefore does not impose itself from the outset. Regardless of whether or not the naming of witnesses in a contract was perhaps common in other places of Greece at the time when P.Eleph. 1 was written, in Egypt one does not have to undertake an exhausting search to find parallels: the naming of witnesses is common at the end of Demotic and Aramaic treaties, of which we know numerous specimens from Elephantine belonging to the 5th or 4th century BCE (and beyond), including marriage contracts.[31]

As for the number of witnesses, from this too – and again contrary to Wolff[32] – no argument can be made for or against a Greek origin of the attested practice. It can be stated that in the *syngraphe* cited by Demosthenes, as in all the non-Egyptian examples cited by Wolff, all of which date from Parthian or Roman times,[33] three witnesses are named, whereas in the Greek contracts from Egypt, almost (!) without exception, six are named; and six witnesses are accordingly what we find in P.Eleph. 1, the oldest testimony. In the Demotic and Aramaic contracts a plurality of witnesses is also encountered, but the number varies (between 3 and 16[34]) and does not show any affinity for six. The question of what moved the couple in the case of P.Eleph. 1 to resort to six witnesses must remain open for the time being. If there is an underlying Greek tradition, it is one that we cannot trace at present, at least not for the time from which P.Eleph. 1 originates. Wolff's preferred explanation for the number of witnesses, which he calls the "Greek hypothesis,"[35] is thus anything but incontrovertible. This is ultimately also true for his considerations on the origin of the double document – the last point to deal with here.

---

29 See above n. 20.

30 See above n. 27.

31 See the evidence provided in Porten 1996 (based, as far as the Aramaic documents are concerned on Porten 1968; Porten/Yardeni 1989).

32 Wolff 1978, pp. 63–64.

33 Wolff 1978, pp. 60–63.

34 Based on the Aramaic and Demotic contracts contained in Porten 1996.

35 Wolff 1978, p. 64.

P.Eleph. 1 is special because the papyrus, apart from its other peculiarities already mentioned, also provides the oldest and therefore first ever example of a double document. There is thus no indication as to what kind of tradition this means of drafting a contract is drawing on – also with regard to the Demotic and Aramaic documentation. On the basis of parallels from Kurdistan, Mesopotamia, and Palestine,[36] Wolff constructed a reception "im Zusammenhang mit dem Alexanderzug irgendwo im Perserreich," but at the same time stated that the adoption "müsste an einem, freilich noch nicht gefundenen, Ort geschehen sein, wo die Tradition der babylonischen 'Hüllentafel' *(case-tablet)* unter Anpassung an neue Schreibmaterialien fortgelebt hatte."[37] This is a learned approach, but it must remain a daring thesis as long as these parallels are Greek double documents from Parthian and Roman times found on the soil of the former Seleucid Empire. Why did our couple decide on the form of a double document for their contract, a practice thereafter widely attested in Egypt and the rest of the Hellenistic East?

Rather than reflecting on traditions and reception trajectories, we might do better to approach this question on a very practical level, once again involving the local context. Without being able to clarify the phenomenon sufficiently, I would like to propose an approach that focuses on the fact that no document writer is named in P.Eleph. 1. This is different in the Demotic and Aramaic contracts from Elephantine, where this is regularly the case. The point is that in Demotic and Aramaic contracts it is not just any writers who are referred to, but scribes who, in connection with Demotic texts, were part of the staff of the temple of Khnum at Elephantine or, in connection with Aramaic texts, are to be identified with skilled scribes whose craft was apparently hereditary. They offered their services either, as in the case of the temple staff, in Elephantine or, as in the case of the Aramaic scribes, in Elephantine and the neighboring city of Syene located on the eastern bank of the Nile.[38] The naming of such professional scribes, in addition to the involvement of witnesses, lent additional security to the contracts – a security that Greek contracting parties in early Hellenistic Elephantine may not have been able to establish because of the lack of public structures at the beginning of the Greco-Macedonian xenocracy over Egypt that would have permitted recourse to a skilled circle of professional scribes.[39] Another explanation would be that the

36 Wolff 1978, p. 61 with n. 20.
37 Wolff 1978, p. 62.
38 Demotic contracts: Porten 1996, pp. 278, 280; Aramaic contracts: ibid., pp. 74, 82.
39 Accordingly, Yiftach 2008, p. 205 has already stated (with regard to the emergence of public archives towards the end of the 3rd century BCE): "The double document was used by Greeks immediately after the creation of the Hellenistic monarchies, before the administrative system(s) including an organized system of public archives evolved. Since there were no state archives, the best security one might obtain was through the physical features of the document as detailed above."

aspect of a private act – without official involvement – was deliberately emphasized in the drawing up of a double document, a characteristic that was causally inherent in the double document (and also in the character of the *syngraphe* on which the stylization of the contractual text was based). Thus, the form of a double document could be classified either as an attempt to make a virtue out of necessity, or could be explained as a result of a certain mentality, in which it was unimportant for the security of the contract whether a scribe (or the writer of the document) was named as a kind of official reinsurance or not. No matter how one may think of it: In both cases – which may also be thought of as intertwined – something completely new was created with the double document, the innovative potential of which is based on the fact that the security of the deed was established by the double copy of the contract on one sheet (with sealing of the upper copy), the witnesses, and the deposition of one copy each of the entire document with the two contracting parties. This novelty clearly stood out in Elephantine from the way in which contracts were designed in Demotic and Aramaic; and the search for an underlying tradition must largely remain in the dark, since for the moment it cannot go beyond a purely linguistic level, on which the stylization of the contractual text is comparable to a *syngraphe.*[40]

Thus, the double document seems to be a phenomenon of its own, a phenomenon which, according to our present knowledge, first became tangible in Elephantine in early Hellenistic times or which developed there due to the circumstances. Due to the unclear circumstantial evidence, it also seems to be advisable for the time being to regard the double document as a Greek invention, which was perhaps affected by "foreign influences" that cannot be precisely determined.

Conclusion

According to the foregoing, one can easily construct an alternative narrative for P.Eleph. 1 in contrast to Wolff's depiction. We do not have this contract because it is the product of a flourishing and extensive Athenian contract practice that spilled over into Egypt with the onset of Hellenism; furthermore, dealing with witnesses shows that the Athenian or, in general, "the" Greek tradition does not have to be considered the origin for the idea of contract design. Rather, it is the influence of Egyptian writing culture and the use of witnesses in that very contract practice

40 It should be noted in passing that for the deposition of double documents, which are chronologically documented after P.Eleph. 1, usually a *syngraphophylax,* a custodian of documents, was resorted to (Yiftach 2008, p. 203, n. 2), which, as Wolff 1978, p. 61, n. 25 has already noted, can be compared with the custody of a document with a trustee attested in Athens (mentioned among others in Demosthenes, Orations 33.36).

that led a contract like P.Eleph. 1 to be written down and secured with witnesses. In contrast, the double document could be a Greek innovation of its own, possibly linked to the place of its first attestation; the idea of a reception in the context of Alexander's campaign is anything but compelling.

If we now consider that P.Eleph. 1 is supposed to stand at the beginning of a juridical *koine,* then this beginning turns out to be less clear than Wolff and Mélèze Modrzejewski constructed it – at least when it comes to the materiality, the components, and the external design of a deed or a contract. If we want to reflect on continuities and ruptures of Greek contract practice in the context of early Hellenistic papyri, we should detach ourselves from Athens and focus more on the local context, thereby allowing for the possibility of idiosyncrasies. Admittedly, a single and limited case study cannot fundamentally challenge the seminal work of two great legal scholars such as Wolff and Mélèze Modrzejewski, but perhaps it can at least encourage us to break down the concept of a rather rigid juridical *koine* (in the sense of Wolff and Mélèze Modrzejewski) in favor of a dynamic conception of legal pluralism – a legal pluralism that feeds into different practices of drafting deeds, which are part of a unified system insofar as they are cultivated in Egypt, where the language and the way of drafting do not determine the validity of the contract. From this perspective, then, the common character is established not through a specific language and form or the uniformity of the private law in question, but through legal pluralism itself, placing Hellenistic Egypt in the tradition of the Achaemenid Empire – but that is a subject for another paper.

Bibliography

Cohen, Edward E. (2005) Commercial Law, in: Michael Gagarin (ed.), The Cambridge Companion to Ancient Geek Law, Cambridge, 290–302.

Fischer-Bovet, Christelle (2011) Counting the Greeks in Egypt. Immigration in the First Century of Ptolemaic Rule, in: Claire Holleran/April Pudsey (eds.), Demography and the Graeco-Roman World. New Insights and Approaches, Cambridge, 135–154.

Fischer-Bovet, Christelle (2014) Army and Society in Ptolemaic Egypt, Cambridge.

Gernet, Louis (1938) Introduction à l'étude du droit grec ancien, in: Archives d'histoire du droit oriental 2, 261–292.

La'da, Csaba (2002) Foreign Ethnics in Hellenistic Egypt, Leuven/Paris/Dudley (MA).

Lippert, Sandra (2012) Einführung in die altägyptische Rechtsgeschichte, Berlin.

MacDowell, Douglas M. (2004) Demosthenes, Speeches 27–39, Austin.

Mélèze Modrzejewski, Joseph (2005) Greek Law in the Hellenistic Period. Family and Marriage, in: Michael Gagarin (ed.), The Cambridge Companion to Ancient Geek Law, Cambridge, 343–354.

Mélèze Modrzejewski, Joseph (2014) Loi et coutume dans l'Égypte grecque et romaine, Warsaw.

Moyer, Ian S. (2011) Egypt and the Limits of Hellenism, Cambridge.

Porten, Bazalel (1968) Archives from Elephantine. The Life of an Ancient Jewish Military Colony, Berkeley.

PORTEN, Bazalel (1996) (ed.), The Elephantine Papyri in English. Three Millennia of Cross-cultural Continuity and Change, Leiden.
PORTEN, Bazalel/YARDENI, Ada (1989) Textbook of Aramaic Documents from Ancient Egypt. Vol. 2: Contracts, Jerusalem.
PRINGSHEIM, Fritz (1955) The Transition from Witnessed to Written Transactions in Athens, in: Aequitas und Bona Fides. Festgabe zum 70. Geburtstag von August Simonius, Basel, 287–297.
ROWLANDSON, Jane (1998) Women & Society in Greek & Roman Egypt. A Sourcebook, Cambridge.
ROWLANDSON, Jane (2013) Dissing the Egyptians: Legal, Ethnic, and Cultural Identities in Roman Egypt, in: Andrew GARDNER/Edward HERRING/Katheryn LOMAS (eds.), Creating Ethnicities & Identities in the Roman World, London, 213–247.
SÄNGER, Patrick (2022) Immigrant Soldiers and Ptolemaic Policy in Hellenistic Egypt (Late Fourth Century–30 BCE), in: Georg CHRIST/Patrick SÄNGER/Mike CARR (eds.), Military Diasporas. Building of Empire in the Middle East and Europe (550 BCE–1500 CE), London, 51–81.
SCHEUBLE-REITER, Sandra (2012) Die Katökenreiter im ptolemäischen Ägypten, Munich.
THOMAS, Rosalind (1989) Oral Tradition and Written Record in Classical Athens, Cambridge.
THOMPSON, Dorothy J. (2021) Laying the Foundations for Roman Egypt, in: Roger S. BAGNALL (ed.), Roman Egypt. A History, Cambridge, 1–45.
WOLFF, Hans J. (1978) Das Recht der griechischen Papyri Ägyptens in der Zeit der Ptolemaeer und des Prinzipats, Vol. 2: Organisation und Kontrolle des privaten Rechtsverkehrs, Munich.
WOLFF, Hans J. (2002) Das Recht der griechischen Papyri Ägyptens in der Zeit der Ptolemaeer und des Prinzipats, Vol. 1: Bedingungen und Triebkräfte der Rechtsentwicklung, Hans-Albert RUPPRECHT (ed.), Munich.
YIFTACH-FIRANKO, Uri (2008) Who Killed the Double Document in Ptolemaic Egypt?, in: Archiv für Papyrusforschung und verwandte Gebiete 54, 203–218.

Philipp Scheibelreiter (University of Vienna)

Common concepts in Athens and Rome?

A comparative legal perspective on the ὁμολογία*

Unity and diversity: Greece and early Rome

At first glance, it may seem unorthodox to include early Roman law in the question of unity and diversity in Greek law. The idea pursued in this study of comparing Athenian homology (ὁμολογία), which is currently being discussed more intensively again,[1] with an instrument of early Roman contract law, is not new in terms of its approach. It was formulated as early as 1923 by Egon Weiß, albeit only in parenthesis, and has received little attention in literature.[2] 100 years later, his ideas will now be taken up and scrutinized for their resilience.

A fundamental observation to be made beforehand is that early Rome can also be understood as an ancient polis. This consideration is not new either. Wenger coined the term ancient legal history[3] and placed Roman law in the wider context of the ancient Mediterranean region, which also was defined by Selb as a cultural area with common legal traditions.[4] Because of the development that Roman law then underwent, especially from the middle and late Republic onwards, in view of the unique position it acquired within the legal cultures of antiquity during the so-called classical period (1st century BCE to 3rd century CE) and its monumental significance for the history of European private law, the fact that the *ius civile proprium Romanorum*[5] was

---

* This study corresponds to the lecture I gave in March 2023 at the conference to which this volume is dedicated. I would like to thank the organizers of the conference, Prof. Kaja Harter-Uibopuu (Hamburg) and Prof. Hans Beck (Münster), as well as the panelists. During the writing it soon turned out that it would go far beyond the limits of the space given to the authors to analyze all relevant passages on the law of homology and compare them with the ancient Roman material; cf. now Scheibelreiter 2025.

1 See Platschek 2018, p. 36; Barta 2021; Schanbacher 2021.

2 It is mentioned, for example, in Martini 1999, p. 31; Barta 2011, p. 383 n. 2308; cf. below under 7.

3 Wenger 1905; on the reception see also Selb 1993, pp. 47–50; Thür 2006, pp. 3–4; Höbenreich 2006, pp. 18–19.

4 Cf. Selb 1993.

5 In connection with the ancient civil transactions *mancipatio* (Gaius, Institutes 1.119; 2.65) and *in iure cessio* (Gaius, Institutes 2.65), Gaius speaks of these as institutes of the *ius proprium civium Romanorum.*

originally merely the law of a city and its citizens,[6] which was organized in a similar way to a Greek polis,[7] fades into the background. Nonetheless, the three elements of Rome's "mixed constitution" – cited prominently by Cicero[8] – have their counterparts in the institutions of classical Athens: Both polities are based on a popular assembly, each has a "consultative body," the βουλή or *senatus,* and both Athens and Rome have annually changing supreme officials (ἄρχοντες or *consules*) with comparable administrative functions.

These examples amount to at least striking similarities in terms of the internal organization of the two city-states. This should not obscure some serious distinctions – here are a few examples:[9] In Rome officials were elected, whereas in Athens, where – unlike the Roman magistrates – they had to give account of their performance in office,[10] they were drawn by lot. Rome had three (with the *concilium plebis:* four) popular assemblies constituted according to different organizational criteria, whereas there was only one in Athens.[11] The Athenian βουλή was an elected body for a fixed term with a monthly changing composition,[12] whereas membership of the senate was in principle permanent.[13] Finally, the delimitation of the judicial competences of the archons is not as clear as that between *prator urbanus* and *praetor peregrinus.*[14]

On the other hand, major parallels can be identified in procedural law. Both in classical Athens and according to the two older types of procedure in Roman law *(lege agere, agere per formulas),* the procedure is divided into two parts:[15] An initial procedural stage to initiate the trial or establish a court, where the respective trial program is determined with an official (the ἄρχων or *praetor*),[16] is followed by a

6 Cf. Kunkel/Schermaier 2005, p. 17: "Nur der römische Bürger hat Anteil am römischen Recht."

7 In this sense also Wenger in Kohler/Wenger 1914, p. 155.

8 Cicero, de re publica 1.69.

9 As further examples, Hölkeskamp 2023, pp. 65–70 emphasizes the different weighting of individual votes in Rome compared to the more egalitarian principle in Athens or that, unlike in the *comitia,* motions were debated in the ἐκκλησία. After all, unlike the archons, the officials in Rome were not to be regarded as "Mandatare des Volkes," but stood "über dem Volk" as holders of official powers, cf. (Cicero, de legibus 3.2.5–6).

10 Hölkeskamp 2023, p. 73.

11 Hölkeskamp 2023, p. 65.

12 Cf. only Bleicken 1995, pp. 226–234; Hansen 1995, pp. 256–259.

13 Since the *lex Ovinia* (312 BCE) – cf. Elster 2003, pp. 84–89 – the expulsion of a member of the senate was possible, by the censorial *lectio senatus* for moral reasons. In this respect, membership of the senate was not, as previously, to be regarded as lifelong, cf. Mommsen 1887, pp. 418–424; Kunkel/Wittmann 1995, pp. 443–445.

14 Cf. Bleicken 1995, p. 94; Scheibelreiter 2015, p. 86.

15 Cf. only Thür 1977, pp. 155–156; Thür 2000, pp. 33–34.

16 See in general Scheibelreiter 2018; see also Thür 2007.

second stage at the court of judgment (δικαστήριον) or the *iudex/recuperatores.*[17] Parallel structures can also be recognized with regard to the jurisdiction concerning foreigners[18] in Athens (ἄρχων πολέμαρχος)[19] and in Rome *(praetor peregrinus).*[20]

In no way should it be claimed here that Rome was modeled on Athens. However, early Rome can also be understood as a city-state in the Mediterranean region, just like a Greek polis in the *Magna Graecia* or the motherland. Against this background, a much-discussed provision of Attic law, the so-called law of homology, will now be scrutinized and contrasted with a sentence from the law of the Twelve Tables. It will be shown that a sentence of the *lex duodecim tabularum* can contribute to a better understanding of this much more widely documented νόμος.[21] Again it should be emphasized that it is not intended to postulate any mutual influence between the two provisions or even the existence of a Greek legal transplant in the Rome of the early Republic.

The law of homology

The phrase:[22] ὅσα ἂν ἕτερος ἑτέρῳ ὁμολογήσῃ, κύρια εἶναι is still the subject of discussion. The sources speak of a νόμος,[23] which is why a law of homology can also be assumed.[24] Some authors trace this back to Solon.[25] The translation of this sentence is not easy.

The verb ὁμολογεῖν literally means "to speak in the same way"[26] and thus establishes the relationship to a counterpart or his explanation. This ὁμολογεῖν could be

17 Cf. Kaser/Hackl 1996, pp. 192–201; Platschek 2023, p. 380.

18 Cf. Scheibelreiter 2015, pp. 84–87.

19 [Aristotle], Constitution of the Athenians 58.2.

20 Pomponius, Digest 1.2.2.27–28.

21 More often the law of the Twelve Tables is interpreted with the help of Greek law, cf. Kunkel/Schermaier 2005, p. 32; Scheibelreiter 2020, pp. 16–17. Hofmann 1870; Wenger 1953, pp. 366–367; Martini 1999, pp. 26–30 provide an overview of Greek parallels to the law of the Twelve Tables.

22 Hypereides 3.13; cf. Demosthenes, Orations 47.77; Demosthenes, Orations 48.11.54. Phillips 2009, pp. 93–94 or Gagliardi 2014, pp. 178–179 give the whole evidence.

23 Plato, Symposion 196c; Demosthenes, Orations 42.12; Demosthenes, Orations 47.77; Demosthenes, Orations 56.2; Deinarchos 3,4; Hypereides 3.13.

24 In Plato, Symposion 196c; Demosthenes, Orations 56.2 is the plural (νόμοι), which is why Maschke 1965, pp. 165–171; Avilés 2012, pp. 64 and 68–71; Gagliardi 2014, pp. 188–190 and 2015, p. 380 n. 21; Schanbacher 2021, pp. 70–76 assume several laws of homology.

25 Thus Phillips 2009, pp. 106–107; Dimopoulou 2012, p. 232; in contrast Wolff 1957, p. 61; Thür 2013, pp. 6–7; undecided Gagliardi 2014, p. 192. In Ruschenbusch 2014, Leão/Rhodes 2015 and Schmitz 2023, the law of homology is not taken into account.

26 Cf., e.g., von Soden 1971, pp. 10–11; Thür 2013, p. 1; Gagliardi 2014, p. 177; Gagarin 2018, p. 42.

interpreted on the one hand as "recognizing" or "establishing" a fact[27] and on the other hand as "accepting" an offer.[28] In this second sense, ὁμολογεῖν would mean "to agree."[29] Understood in this way, the ὁμολογεῖν as a speech act would establish an obligation, which tempted some authors to compare ὁμολογεῖν with Roman legal categories like the consensual[30] or the verbal contract.[31]

Since some evidence for the Athenian law of homology has a procedural context, the law of homology has a procedural context:[32] A party was not allowed to deviate from assertions about facts or legal relationships that had been made in the first stage of the proceedings (ἀνάκρισις or δίαιτα) in the subsequent proceedings before the judgment court.[33] Rather, according to the law of homology, the speaker had to "say the same thing" (ὁμολογεῖν) as in the first part of the proceedings. The shortcoming of this catchy theory, however, is that it cannot explain the so-called "voluntary homologies," i. e., evidence for the law of homology, which do not show any reference to the ἀνάκρισις,[34] or can only be explained unsatisfactorily.[35]

The adjective κύριος can in turn be translated as "authoritative"[36] to denote a fact that is beyond dispute.[37] Others translate κύριος, in the sense of the result of a contract, as "binding."[38] In the following, the neutral translation variant "lawful" is chosen because it allows for both meanings.

---

27 Wolff 1957, pp. 53–54; Rupprecht 1975, p. 281.
28 Kussmaul 1969, p. 30.
29 Schanbacher 2021, p. 67.
30 Thus Mitteis/Wilcken 1912, p. 73 n.1; Beauchet 1897, pp. 21–22; Lipsius 1915, pp. 684–686; Cohen 2006, pp. 73–84; Phillips 2009, p. 106; Gagliardi 2014, p. 185; but in contrast Todd 1993: 265; Scafuro 1997, pp. 128–129; Jakab 2006; Carawan 2006, p. 342; Thür 2013, pp. 6–7; Schanbacher 2021, p. 71 n. 36.
31 Cf. Weiss 1923, pp. 432–433; Platschek 2018.
32 Thür 1977, pp. 152–158; Jakab 1994, pp. 195–197 and 2006, p. 86; Carawan 2006, p. 350 n. 16; Kästle 2012, pp. 194 n. 158; cf. also the preliminary work of Partsch 1924, p. 273; Wolff 1957, pp. 53–61; von Soden 1971, p. 3.
33 Cf. only Thür 1977, pp. 156–158; Jakab 1994, p. 196; Thür 2007, p. 134.
34 Thür 1977, pp. 156–157 refers to Hypereides 3.13; Demosthenes, Orations 47.77; Demosthenes, Orations 48.11.54; Plato, Symposion 196c.
35 Cf. Avilés 2012, pp. 54–55; Thür 2013, pp. 8–9; Platschek 2013, pp. 59–60; Platschek 2018, p. 36.
36 See also Hässler 1960, pp. 27–28; Thür 2013, p. 8; Platschek 2013, p. 264.
37 For example Wolff 1978, p. 146; Thür 2013, p. 9; Dimopoulou 2014, p. 266.
38 For example Whitehead 2000; Cohen 2006, pp. 73–75; Lanni 2007, p. 226; Harris 2013, p. 366; Gagliardi 2014, p. 198.

The function of the law of homology

In the beginning, the context and function of the law of homology must be examined more closely: What does a speaker who invokes this law intend to achieve for his argument?

The important function of the law (νόμος), namely that of a non-technical piece of evidence (ἄτεχνος) read out during the trial,[39] plays a subordinate role within the evidence.[40] In most of the passages, the authority of the law is cited or referred to in order to defend a certain point of view or to support an argument. In the following, the two references[41] that cite the law of homology in connection with contract law will be examined in more detail.[42]

On the law of homology and Hypereides 3,13[43]

The abovementioned quotation for the law of homology[44] comes from the speech of Hypereides against Athenogenes, its only evidence in connection with a contract of sale.[45] Epicrates wants to buy the slave Midas and his sons in order to set them free. Their owner Athenogenes offers Epicrates the drugstore managed by the three slaves as a package deal. Epicrates, who is in love with one of the slaves and therefore acts hastily and inattentively, agrees to this proposal and makes the purchase.[46] As a result, he also has to take over the debts of the deal, which Athenogenes had presented to him as insignificant: These are the debts to the named creditors Pankalos and Prokles and "if Midas owed anything to anyone else."[47] Epicrates agrees. Shortly afterwards, however, he learns that the debt is significantly higher than he had expected on the basis of Athenogenes' account.[48] Consequently – as is generally

39 Aristotle, Rhetoric 1375a.24.

40 In the law of homology only in Demosthenes, Orations 47.77; cf. also Hypereides 3.13.

41 Hypereides 3.13 and Demosthenes, Orations 52.1.

42 On exegeses of Isokrates, Orations 18.24–25; Deinarchos 3.4 and Demosthenes, Orations 42.12; 47.77; 48.11.54 cf. Scheibelreiter 2025, 41–56.

43 Cf. Blass 1898, pp. 81–90; Worthington/Cooper/Harris 2001, pp. 87–89. The speech dates to between 330 and 324 BCE.

44 See above under 2.

45 Carawan 2006, p. 344; cf. also Gagliardi 2015, p. 387.

46 Cf. also Maffi 2008, pp. 211–214.

47 Hypereides 3.6: εἴ τῳ ἄλλῳ ὀφείλει τι Μίδας.

48 Instead of 40 mines now 5 talents (= 300 mines), cf. also Schanbacher 2021, p. 71.

assumed[49] – he brings an action for pecuniary damage (δίκη βλάβης). Epicrates' argumentation cannot be explained in detail here.[50] Overall, however, the speaker endeavors to portray Athenogenes as an impostor and brings five laws into play to prove this. However, none of these laws directly applies to the facts of the case.[51]

Before doing so, he tries to take away the effect of a possible argumentation by Athenogenes with the law of homology and says:[52]

> ἐρεῖ πρὸς ὑμᾶς αὐτίκα μάλα Ἀθηνογένης ὡς ὁ νόμος λέγει ὅσα ἂν ἕτερος ἑτέρῳ ὁμολογήσῃ, κύρια εἶναι. τά γε δίκαια, ὦ βέλτιστε. τὰ δὲ μὴ τοὐναντίον ἀπαγορεύει, μὴ κύρια εἶναι.

> Yet Athenogenes will soon be telling you that, in law, whatever one man *homologates* another is *lawful*. Yes my friend – fair *homologies*, that is. With unfair ones it is just the opposite: they shall not, the law says, be *lawful*.[53]

Epicrates quotes the law of homology and adds that it does not apply to the present situation: For what one has confirmed to another would only be lawful (κυρία) if it had a just content (δίκαια). As twice in Plato,[54] the word κύρια is also equated here with δίκαια, which was probably not contained in the law.[55] By means of the limiting particle γε, Epicrates restricts the scope of application of the law of homology,[56] which could be understood as a description of a defense in the sense of a Roman *exception*.[57] Considerations according to which Epicrates wishes to annul the contract due to an error caused by Athenogenes[58] overlook the fact that Epicrates nowhere explicitly raises this argument.[59]

---

49 MEYER-LAURIN 1965, p. 17; MEINECKE 1971, p. 348; OSBOURNE 1985, pp. 56–57; WHITEHEAD 2000, p. 268; COOPER in WORTHINGTON/COOPER/HARRIS 2001, p. 96 n. 27; PHILLIPS 2009, p. 91; THÜR 2013, pp. 5 and 6; GAGLIARDI 2014, p. 200; GAGLIARDI 2015, p. 387; GAGARIN 2018, p. 35; in contrast, SCHANBACHER 2021, p. 71 n. 34. MASCHKE 1926, pp. 166–167 or DIMOPOULOU 2014, p. 273 suspect an action regarding fraud; in contrast, MEYER-LAURIN 1965, pp. 15–17; CARAWAN 2006, p. 346; GAGLIARDI 2015, p. 386; SCHEIBELREITER 2019, p. 41 n. 56.

50 On the speech, see WENGER 1903; CARAWAN 2006, pp. 344–351; THÜR 2013; GAGARIN 2018; SCHEIBELREITER 2019, pp. 37–43; SCHANBACHER 2021, pp. 71–74.

51 Cf. on this SCHEIBELREITER 2019, p. 41 n. 53.

52 Hypereides 3.13.

53 Translation: WHITEHEAD 2000, p. 274, with adaptations set in italics.

54 Plato, Symposion 196c; Plato, Kritias 52d-e.

55 Thus PHILLIPS 2009, p. 96 n. 22 and 105; THÜR 2013, p. 7.

56 Cf. also PHILLIPS 2009, p. 92 n. 11.

57 Cf. KÜBLER 1934, pp. 87–88; SCHEIBELREITER 2019, pp. 39–40; similarly CARAWAN 2006, pp. 345–346.

58 So also LIPSIUS 1908: 685; CANTARELLA 1966, pp. 91–92; CARAWAN 2006, p. 345.

59 See also PHILLIPS 2009, pp. 104–105; MEINECKE 1971, p. 349; SCHANBACHER 2021, pp. 72–73.

But what will Athenogenes refer to with the law of homology? The announcement that Athenogenes would immediately quote the law of homology (ἐρεῖ δὲ πρὸς ὑμᾶς αὐτίκα) suggests that Epicrates knew from the first section of the trial[60] that Athenogenes would bring this νόμος as evidence – because only then could he use this evidence before the judges.

It is often assumed that Athenogenes intended to prove the binding nature of the sales contract by recurring to the law of homology. However, this is countered by the fact that the contract of sale is not referred to in the speech as ὁμολογία, but technically as ὠνὴ καὶ πρᾶσις[61] (contract of sale) or, more generally, as συνθῆκαι[62] ([text of the] contract).

Epicrates himself traces the stages of the conclusion of the contract: (1) Athenogenes explains the individual points of the purchase contract. He also mentions the liabilities of the business. Epicrates should assume these, no matter how high they are: οἷα γίγνεται, ταῦτα, ἔφη, σὺ ἀναδέξῃ.[63] (2) Epicrates agrees to assuming the business debts: ὡς γὰρ εἰπόντος αὐτοῦ ταῦτα ἐγὼ προσωμολόγησα.[64] (3) Athenogenes reads out the already prepared text of the treaty:[65] ἦσαν δὲ αὗται συνθῆκαι πρὸς ἐμέ.[66] (4) Athenogenes seals the deed (σημαίνεται)[67] and adds the name of the buyer (προσέγγραψας).[68] (5) Epicrates pays the price of 40 mines: τὰς δὲ τετταράκοντα μνᾶς ἐγὼ καταβαλὼν τὴν ὠνὴν ἐποιησάμην.[69] Since the τὴν ὠνὴν ποιεῖν can indicate the conclusion of the purchase contract,[70] this is concluded at the moment of payment of the purchase price.[71] (6) The payment of the purchase price is recorded in the deed.[72]

---

60 Probably before the *archon polemarchos*, since Athenogenes was a metic (Hypereides 3.33), cf. Whitehead 2000, p. 268.

61 Hypereides 3.5: ἐγὼ δέ σοι ἀποδώσομαι αὐτοὺς ὠνῇ καὶ πράσει; 3.6: ἐὰν δὲ πριάμενος σὺ ὠνῇ καὶ πράσει; 3.7: εἰ δὲ πριάιμην ὠνῇ καὶ πράσει; cf. also 3.21 (where Epicrates refers to himself as πριάμενος) and 3.22 (where we read of the ὠναί); cf. on the term also Pringsheim 1950, pp. 111–114; Szegedy-Maszak 1987, p. 68.

62 Hypereides 3.8.10.11.12.14.18.21.22; cf. also 3.17, where Epicrates refers to Athenogenes as the one who "concludes such a contract": Ἀθηνογένει … συνθεμένῳ τοιαῦτα.

63 Hypereides 3.6; similarly Hypereides 3.10.

64 Hypereides 3.8.

65 Thür 2013, p. 5 reconstructs the wording.

66 Hypereides 3.8.

67 Hypereides 3.8.

68 Hypereides 3.8.

69 Hypereides 3.9.

70 On the ὠνὴν ποιεῖν as "to buy," cf. Plato, Laws 849b.

71 Cf. Pringsheim 1950, p. 192; Meyer-Laurin 1965, p. 16; Meinecke 1971, p. 348 n. 12; Carawan 2006, pp. 344 and 350; Thür 2013, p. 9; Gagliardi 2014, p. 182; Gagliardi 2015, p. 385; Schanbacher 2021, p. 65.

72 Carawan 2006, pp. 349–350; Thür 2013, p. 9.

It is noticeable that Epicrates describes his confirmation of the assumption of debt as προς-ὁμολογεῖν[73] or this contractual provision as ὁμολογία.[74] Epicrates thus declared that he would assume the debt that Athenogenes had included as a provision in the contract of sale. The ὁμολογία, which Athenogenes would demand be honored and the validity of which Epicrates contests, is therefore not the entire contract of sale, but the agreement contained therein[75] on the assumption of the business debts.[76] According to Epicrates, this was not in accordance with the law (δίκαιον[77]), as Athenogenes had concealed the actual amount of the debt from Epicrates, perhaps knowingly.[78] Only if Athenogenes could prove to him that he had informed him of the amount of the debt would he confirm its existence and not have brought a lawsuit:[79] ἐπεὶ ἐὰν δείξῃς προειπὼν ἐμοὶ τοὺς ἐράνους καὶ τὰ χρέα, ἢ γράψας ἐν ταῖς συνθήκαις ὅσους ἐπυθόμην, οὐδὲν ἐγκαλῶ[80] σοι ἀλλ› ὁμολογῶ ὀφείλειν. Epicrates speaks here of the general clause "if Midas still owes something to someone else."[81] Conversely, this means that Epicrates refuses to admit the existence of the debt due to the circumstances surrounding the conclusion of the contract.

Epicrates' aim is to avoid having to pay the debts: οὐ δεῖ με τὰ χρέα διαλύειν.[82] If one assumes with the majority of the literature that the speech is based on a claim for pecuniary damages (δίκη βλάβης),[83] the question arises as to how these debts could be declared as pecuniary damage.[84] Only the purchase price already paid could be understood as real damage. Assuming this, he could sue for the 40 mines (duplicated[85]) from Athenogenes with the δίκη βλάβης, as this advance payment was frustrated. According to Greek legal understanding, this would mean the loss of ownership of the business.[86] However, Epicrates does not want to contest the

73 Hypereides 3.7: ὁμολογήσας αὐτῷ τὰ χρέα ἀναδέξεσθαι; Hypereides 3,8: προσωμολόγησα.
74 Hypereides 3.7: ἐν ὁμολογίᾳ λαβών.
75 The fact that ὁμολογία could be used to designate individual contractual provisions is also shown by the law on the warranty for material defects (Hypereides 3.15) cited by Epicrates in the following, cf. below under 7.
76 Cf. also Wenger 1903, p. 15.
77 Hypereides 3.13.
78 This is what the speaker implies in Hypereides 3.7.12.14.21.
79 Hypereides 3.6. The contract has also just been read out in court (Hypereides 3.14).
80 Only]ω σοι ἂν ὁμολογῶ has survived from the end of the sentence. The gap before σοι ἂν ὁμολογῶ was filled by Kenyon 1907, Hypereides 3.14 *ad locum* with οὔκετ' ἐγκαλ]ῶ. Blass 1894, p. 66 – followed by Burtt 1954, p. 440 and Jensen 1963, p. 76 – had added ἀντιλέγ]ω instead.
81 The contract had just been read out (Hypereides 3.12).
82 Hypereides 3.20; cf. Hypereides 3.21. So also Gagliardi 2014, p. 200; Gagliardi 2015, p. 387.
83 Cf. n. 49 above.
84 So Phillips 2009, p. 91 n. 8; Carawan 2006, p. 346. According to Gagarin 2018, p. 35, the aim of the action is either the cancellation of the contract or of the debt.
85 Demosthenes, Orations 21.43; cf. Scheibelreiter 2020, p. 94 n. 203.
86 Meyer-Laurin 1965, p. 17; Meinecke 1971, p. 348; Thür 2013, p. 6; Gagliardi 2014, p. 199.

contract of sale (which he was very keen to conclude)[87] and reverse it:[88] The subject of the legal dispute is rather the invalidity of the assumption of those debts, the extent of which Athenogenes had concealed from him. Epicrates had homologized this assumption (ὁμολογήσας αὐτῷ τὰ χρέα ἀναδέξεσθαι),[89] and he had to fight this ὁμολογία by trying to cut off his opponent's argument based on the law of homology.

The law of homology and Demosthenes 56 (against Dionysodorus) 2[90]

In the speech against Dionysodoros, who together with Parmeniskos received a maritime loan from the orator Darius (and another creditor named Pamphilos), the law of homology is cited at the very beginning:[91]

> τῷ οὖν ποτὲ πιστεύοντες καὶ τί λαβόντες τὸ βέβαιον προιέμεθα; ὑμῖν, ὦ ἄνδρες δικασταί, καὶ τοῖς νόμοις τοῖς ὑμετέροις, οἳ κελεύουσιν, ὅσα ἄν τις ἑκὼν ἕτερος ἑτέρῳ ὁμολογήσῃ, κύρια εἶναι.

> In what then do we place our trust and what security do we take when we put our money at risk? We have you, gentlemen of the jury, and your laws, which require that whatever *homologies* one man voluntarily makes with another be *lawful*.[92]

With this quote, Darius appeals to the judges to observe "their" laws. The law of homology appears to be a program on which the following speech is based.

With regard to the term ὁμολογία/ὁμολογεῖν[93], which is used several times in the following, the main question is therefore what exactly it refers to in each passage.[94] In any case, the conclusion of a loan itself also requires the transfer of

87 Thus, for example, Maschke 1926, p. 167; Meyer-Laurin 1965, pp. 17–19; Meinecke 1971, p. 347, 348 n. 13 and 349; Harris 2000, p. 52; Lanni 2007, p. 226; Barta 2010, p. 39 with n. 152; Gagliardi 2014, p. 199.

88 Carawan 2006, p. 346; Thür 2013, pp. 6 and 7; Gagliardi 2015, p. 387; cf. also Jakab 2006, p. 88.

89 Hypereides 3.7.

90 Cf. Blass 1893, pp. 582–588; Bers 2003, pp. 92–94; MacDowell 2009, pp. 284–287, who dates the speech to 323/22 BCE.

91 Demosthenes, Orations 56.2.

92 Translation: Bers 2003, p. 95, with adaptations set in italics.

93 Demosthenes, Orations 56.1 (twice), 6, 11, 12, 13.

94 Three times, the confirmation of facts by the defendants in the trial (in Demosthenes, Orations 56.37 and 39: that the ship is still intact; Demosthenes, Orations 56.46: that they have received the loan but have not yet repaid it) is technically referred to as ὁμολογεῖν.

the money.[95] This is also confirmed by the creditors when they state at the outset that they have not only promised to grant a loan (without obligation), but have also paid out the money:[96] ἡμεῖς δ' οὐ φαμεν δώσειν, ἀλλ' εὐθὺς τῷ δανειζομένῳ δίδομεν τὸ ἀργύριον.[97] Consequently, it is not the loan itself that is described as ὁμολογία, but the contractual document that contains the confirmation of the maritime borrower that they have money and owe repayment: This "paper" is typically deposited with the creditors.[98] So when they demand that "Dionysodoros should pay the money he confirms (to have received)" (τῶν δὲ χρημάτων ὅσα μὲν αὐτὸς ὁμολογεῖ ἀποδοῦναι ἡμῖν),[99] this is to be understood in a specific technical sense as a literal reference to the text of the deed. In the course of the speech, the deed is usually referred to as συγγραφὴ δανείου using the technical[100] term,[101] once as συγγραφή, of which the debtors have confirmed (ὁμολογεῖν) that it is lawful.[102] Furthermore, ὁμολογία is used in the sense of "issuing a receipt," which the creditors hold out the prospect of upon repayment of the loan.[103]

In the majority of cases,[104] however, the plaintiff refers to the ὁμολογίαι as the conditions under which the contract was concluded: On the one hand, the lenders had demanded that Dionysodoros and Parmeniskos adhere to a certain route and import the grain purchased with loan funds from Egypt only to Athens;[105] otherwise, double the amount of the loan would be due as a penalty.[106] "Under these conditions" (ἐπὶ ταύταις ταῖς ὁμολογίαις) they lent the money:[107]

---

95 Cf. also Schuster 2005, p. 43.

96 Demosthenes, Orations 56.1.

97 Cf. also Demosthenes, Orations 53.9.

98 Demosthenes, Orations 56.1: τὴν ὁμολογίαν καταλέλοιπε τοῦ ποιήσειν τὰ δίκαια.

99 Demosthenes, Orations 56.16. The statement λαβὼν γὰρ ἀργύριον φανερὸν καὶ ὁμολογούμενον (Demosthenes, Orations 56.1) is perhaps to be understood similarly as: the borrower received cash, for which a receipt was issued.

100 See Schuster 2005, pp. 133–136; Avilés 2012, p. 53.

101 Demosthenes, Orations 56.3, 9, 10, 12 (twice), 15, 16, 20, 27 (three times), 31 (twice), 34, 35, 38 (three times), 48, 50.

102 Demosthenes, Orations 56.16: ταῦτα δ' ἡμῶν λεγόντων, ὦ ἄνδρες δικασταί, καὶ ἀξιούντων Διονυσόδωρον τουτονί, τὴν μὲν συγγραφὴν μὴ κινεῖν μηδ' ἄκυρον ποιεῖν τὴν ὁμολογουμένην καὶ ὑπ' αὐτῶν κυρίαν εἶναι.

103 Demosthenes, Orations 56.15: ἀλλὰ κατὰ μὲν τἀργύριον, ὃ ἂν ἀποδιδῷς, ὁμολογήσομεν ἐνάντιον τοῦ τραπεζίτου ἄκυρον ποιεῖν τὴν συγγραφήν, … – but with regard to the money you return to us, we will confirm in the presence of a banker that the contract document is no longer valid.

104 The attribution of Demosthenes, Orations 56.13 is not clear, where the speaker says that he and his partner would "concede" (ὁμολογοῦσι … σεσιτηγηκέναι) their own grain transport to Rhodes if they agreed to the low interest rates that Dionysodorus proposes to them.

105 Demosthenes, Orations 56.3, 5, 6, 11, 20, 45.

106 Demosthenes, Orations 56.20.

107 Demosthenes, Orations 56.6; thus interest was owed for the outward and return journey and had to be paid on the return to Athens, cf. Schuster 2005, pp. 68–69.

ἀποκριναμένων δ' ἡμῶν, ὦ ἄνδρες δικασταί, ὅτι οὐκ ἂν δανεισαίμεν εἰς ἕτερον ἐμπόριον οὐδὲν ἀλλ' ἢ εἰς Ἀθήνας, οὕτω προσομολογοῦσι πλεύσεσθαι δεῦρο, καὶ ἐπὶ ταύταις ταῖς ὁμολογίαις δανείζονται παρ' ἡμῶν ἐπὶ τῇ νηὶ τρισχιλίας δραχμὰς ἀμφοτερόπλουν, καὶ συγγραφὴν ἐγράψανθ' ὑπὲρ τούτων.

> We answered, gentlemen of the jury, that we would make the loan with the prospect of no market than Athens, and so they agreed that they would sail here. On these terms they borrowed three thousand drachmas [on the security of their ship] for a roundtrip voyage, and they wrote out the contract with these terms.[108]

The borrowers therefore agreed to the conditions (προσομολογοῦσι) under which the loan was to be granted. The loan is to be given/taken if Dionysodoros and Parmeniskos agree to adhere to a certain trade route, namely: Athens – Egypt – Athens.[109] The phrase "on condition that" is typically expressed with ἐφ' ᾧ τε. For example, it is stated several times that the loan was given "on the condition that the ship would return to Athens" (ἐφ' ᾧ τὴν ναῦν καταπλεῖν Ἀθηνάζε).[110] The speaker now also speaks of the loan being given "under these agreements" (ἐπὶ ταύταις ταῖς ὁμολογίαις δανεισάντων τὸ ἀργύριον)[111] or taken out "under/to these agreements" (ἐπὶ ταύταις ταῖς ὁμολογίαις δανείζονταις:[112] ἐπὶ ταύταις ταῖς ὁμολογίαις δανεισάμενοι, ἐφ' ᾧ τε καταπλεῖν Ἀθηνάζε[113]). Synonymously, Darius also speaks of "the harbour that the parties establish" (ὅ τι ἂ συνθῶνται ἐμπόριον).[114]

This means that these ὁμολογίαι describe the conditions for granting the loan, i.e., provisions of the loan agreement, but not the loan agreement itself. And so a distinction is also made between contracts and agreements:[115] The sequence of words τὰς μὲν συγγραφὰς καὶ τὰς ὁμολογίας used by Darius does not necessarily have to be understood as a hendiadyoin.[116]

---

108 Bers 2003, p. 96.

109 Cf. also Meinecke 1971, pp. 352–354.

110 Demosthenes, Orations 56.3; cf. also Demosthenes, Orations 56.5, 20, 49.

111 Demosthenes, Orations 56.11.

112 Demosthenes, Orations 56.6.

113 Demosthenes, Orations 56.42.

114 Demosthenes, Orations 56.10.

115 Demosthenes, Orations 56.48: εἰ μὲν γὰρ ὑμεῖς τὰς μὲν συγγραφὰς καὶ τὰς ὁμολογίας τὰς πρὸς ἀλλήλους γιγνομένας ἰσχυρὰς οἰήσεσθε δεῖν εἶναι καὶ τοῖς παραβαίνουσιν αὐτὰς μηδεμίαν συγγνώμην ἕξετε, ἑτοιμότερον προιήσονται τὰ ἑαυτῶν οἱ ἐπὶ τοῦ δανείζειν ὄντες, ἐκ δὲ τούτων αὐξηθήσεται ὑμὶν τὸ ἐμπόριον.

116 Thus Gagliardi 2014, p. 183. Comparable formulations can be found in Plato, Kritias 52c-d, where Socrates refuses to flee Athens with the argument that the laws admonished him not to act "contrary to the contracts and agreements, according to which you agreed with us to live as citizens" (παρὰ τὰς συνθήκας τε καὶ τὰς ὁμολογίας καθ' ἃς ἡμῖν συνέθου πολιτεύεσθαι); cf. also Plato, Kritias 52d-e.

Dionysodoros and Parmeniskos, however, had not returned to Athens but, in view of the falling prices in Athens, had set up a more lucrative grain trade between Rhodes and Egypt. They thus acted contrary to the agreement (παρὰ τὴν συγγραφήν[117] or καταφρονήσαντες τὴν συγγραφήν[118]).

Another provision that was violated by the defendants concerns interest: Their amount had also been fixed (διομολογησάμενοι τοὺς τόκους τοὺς εἰς ἑκατέρων τῶν ἐμπορίων τούτων),[119] Darius speaks of the τόκοι ὁμολογηθέντες.[120] Since the loan had been taken out for the outward and return journey (δάνειον ἀμφοτερόπλουν),[121] a considerable sum can be assumed. Dionysodoros wants to deviate from this and only offers to pay interest for a shorter distance or period of time, namely the journey to Rhodes.[122]

The provisions agreed in the loan agreement regarding the trade route and interest (ὁμολογίαι[123]) are to be distinguished from the loan agreement itself,[124] but are, as just seen, closely linked.

Therefore, the damage alleged by the plaintiff with the δίκη βλάβης could also only mean the nonpayment of the agreed interest:[125] The nonpayment of interest can also be regarded as damage to the creditor's assets (βλάβη).[126] Then, of course, the citation of the law of homology specifically served to demand compliance with the *pactum* on interest agreed in the course of the loan: The law of homology serves as an argument in favor of the fact that full interest is owed.[127]

---

117 Demosthenes, Orations 56.3.
118 Demosthenes, Orations 56.10.
119 Demosthenes, Orations 56.5.
120 Demosthenes, Orations 56.12.
121 Demosthenes, Orations 56.6.
122 Demosthenes, Orations 56.12.13.
123 See also Wallace 2014, p. 217.
124 Gagliardi 2014, pp. 196–197 argues differently in favor of seeing the consensus (which he identifies as the ὁμολογίαι) of the parties as a constitutive element for the establishment of the contract in the case of Greek loans.
125 Gagliardi 2015, p. 384. Carawan 2006, p. 351 assumes differently that the main allegation in this speech is that the debtors thwarted the creditor's right of access to the ship to be exercised by way of security.
126 Cf. Scheibelreiter 2020, pp. 189–190 with n. 560.
127 In this respect, Gagliardi 2015, p. 384 is correct when he assumes that the plaintiff's δίκη βλάβης is based on a violation of the ὁμολογία by Dionysodoros. However, the ὁμολογία is not the loan agreement, but its interest clause.

ὁμολογία as contract clause?

The two examples have shown that the homologies, the legality of which is argued with the help of the law of homology, do not refer to the contracts themselves, but to individual agreements in connection with obligations to perform established in a different way.[128]

This understanding of ὁμολογία also coincides with Plato's use of the word, who, referring to a version of the law of homology in his *nomoi* in connection with the contract for work,[129] speaks of the ὁμολογῶν not having acted "according to the homologies" (κατὰ τὰς ὁμολογίας). The plural used here by Plato could also be explained very well by the fact that it refers to individual contractual clauses.[130]

A further example from the Corpus Demosthenicum can help to reinforce the interpretation of ὁμολογία as a secondary agreement to which the law of homology refers:

In his defense speech against Kallippos (Demosthenes, Oration 52)[131] Apollodoros, who is litigating with Kallippos over the payment of funds deposited in the bank of his now deceased father Pasion, refers to a statement of claim that had been brought against his father in this matter:[132]

> λαγχάνει αὐτῷ δίκην, οὐ μὰ Δι' οὐχ ὥσπερ νῦν ἀργυρίου, ἀλλὰ βλάβης, ἐγκαλέσας βλάπτειν ἑαυτὸν ἀποδιδόντα Κηφεσιάδῃ τὸ ἀργύριον, ὃ κατέλιπε Λύκων ὁ Ἡρακλεώτης παρ' αὐτῷ, ἄνευ αὐτοῦ ὁμολογήσαντα μὴ ἀποδώσειν.
>
> He initiated a suit – not, by Zeus, for money *(dike argyriou)*, as in the present case, but for damages *(dike blabes)*. He complained that my father had injured him when he gave Cephesiades the money Lykon had deposited with him, after my father had *confirmed* that he would not pay it out without Callippus' consent.[133]

Pasion, so the accusation goes, had harmed the plaintiff (Kallippos) by handing over the money of Lykon from Herakleia deposited in his bank not to Kallippos,

128 This result is confirmed in Demosthenes, Orations 42.12 and Demosthenes, Orations 47.77, where the modification of payment deadlines (established by judgment or by law) is made by means of ὁμολογία.

129 Plato, Laws 920d.

130 For example, Plato speaks of the fulfillment period of a contractor as the χρόνος εἰρημένος or as χρόνος ῥηθείς (Plato, Laws 921a) and χρόνοι ὁμολογηθέντες (Plato, Laws 921c); cf. Martini 1997, p. 52.

131 Cf. Blass 1893, pp. 514–518; Bers 2003, pp. 46–47; MacDowell 2009, pp. 100–102.

132 Demosthenes, Orations 52.14.

133 Translation: Bers 2003, p. 50, with adaptations set in italics.

who as πρόξενος of the Herakleiotes in Athens was making claims, but to Kephesiades:[134] Lykon had, of course, instructed Pasion to do so, according to the books from which the plaintiff Apollodoros also quotes.[135] Accordingly, the payment to Kephesiades was made by the slave Phormion,[136] with whom Kallippos had consulted the books of Pasion.[137]

Three years later, Kallippos, who – unsuccessfully[138] – pursued the recovery of the amount,[139] filed the abovementioned δίκη βλάβης against Pasion. The property damage resulted[140] from the act of – as Kallippos claims, unauthorized – payment of the money (τὸ ἀργύριον ἀποδιδόναι).[141] However, Kallippos in his claim (ἔγκλημα[142]) also invokes a homology (ὁμολογήσαντα) of Pasion, according to which Pasion would involve Kallippos in the payment of the money to Kephesiades or inform him of it.[143] Whether this ὁμολογία really existed or is merely alleged here is speculative, but also irrelevant in the present context. In fact, the ὁμολογία in the ἔγκλημα of Kallippos is merely mentioned as an – albeit essential – additional element of the facts charged against the defendant, an ancillary *pactum* which regulated the modalities of the payment of a deposit debt in more detail.

---

134 Demosthenes, Orations 52.7 and 18; the payment is made by the Phormion employed in Pasion's bank.

135 Demosthenes, Orations 52.6. Lykon and Pasion check Lykon's credit balance, which is to be paid to Kephesiades before Lykon gives the order: (Λύκων) προσέταξε τὸ ἀργύριον ὃ κατέλειπεν ... Κηφισιάδῃ ἀποδοῦναι. On this recently Jakab 2021, pp. 359–360; Kaiser 2023, pp. 203–214.

136 Demosthenes, Orations 52.7.

137 Demosthenes, Orations 52.5–6.

138 Demosthenes, Orations 52.12.

139 Demosthenes, Orations 52.9–11.

140 Demosthenes, Orations 52.14. The damage to property does not result from the violation of the homology itself – so Gagliardi 2014, p. 194 n. 86 – but from the payment to Kephesiades, cf. Wolff 1957, pp. 44–46; Martini 2005, pp. 75–76; Scheibelreiter 2018a, p. 222 n. 84.

141 Cf. Thür 1986, p. 133 n. 19; MacDowell 2009, p. 102; Kaiser 2023, pp. 213–214.

142 Cf. Scheibelreiter 2018a, p. 222.

143 According to a second version, Kallippos had been personally introduced to Pasion by Lykon and the latter had promised to pay the money to him; this, of course, is disputed by Apollodoros (Demosthenes, Orations 52.18). Kaiser 2023, p. 212 equates the ὁμολογία from Demosthenes, Orations 52.6 (Pasion declares Kallippos not to make a payment without him) with that of Demosthenes, Orations 52.20 (Pasion declared to pay the money to Kallippos).

The law of homology and the *uti lingua nuncupassit* sentence

Weiss already noted: "Wenn wir hören, das attische Gesetz habe verfügt: ὅσα ἂν τις ἑκὼν ἕτερος ἑτέρῳ ὁμολογήσῃ, κύρια εἶναι, so ist dies, von der im Worte selbst mitgedachten Zweiseitigkeit des Rechtsausdrucks abgesehen, nichts anderes als der bekannte Satz der Zwölftafeln (VI,1)."[144]

This sentence[145] reads: *Cum nexum facit mancipiumque, uti lingua nuncupassit, ita ius esto.* – If one performs nexum and mancipium, as he has pronounced with his tongue, so it shall be right.[146]

The *mancipatio*[147] as an ancient civil transaction for the transfer of power of disposal over a person or thing is already assumed in the Twelve Tables.[148] With the *uti lingua nuncupassit* sentence, however, the *decemviri* could have further developed the *mancipatio,*[149] perhaps in "positivization" of an established legal practice.[150] Twelve Tables 6.1 speaks of *nuncupationes,* ancillary legal provisions (in classical times: *leges mancipio dictae*[151]), which, declared solemnly and orally,[152] concern certain characteristics of a purchased item, such as the size or condition of a property,[153] but also reservations on the part of the seller (*mancipium dans*[154]). How the *nuncupationes* were integrated into the *mancipatio* ritual as declarations by only one party[155] is

---

144 Weiss 1923, p. 431; cf. also Martini 1999, p. 31 n. 25. Kussmaul 1969, p. 34 and Avilés 2012, pp. 53–54 speak of ὁμολογίαι as *pacta.*

145 Twelve Tables 6.1; cf. Festus, s.v. *nuncupata pecunia,* p. 176, 5–6 [Lindsay]; on the source situation cf. Crawford 1996, pp. 654–656; Albanese 2003, pp. 21–22; Flach 2004, pp. 96–100; Humbert 2018, pp. 241–245.

146 The ablative *lingua* is erroneously rendered in the nominative in Crawford 1966, p. 654 ('as his tongue has pronounced'); on this see Scheibelreiter 2025, 102–103, nt. 447.

147 Cf. fundamentally Kaser 1971, pp. 41–48; Kaser/Knütel/Lohsse 2021, pp. 96–99; Wolf 1998; Pfeifer 2023.

148 The Twelve Tables neither introduced it nor recognized it (for the first time), cf. Simon 1965, p. 148; Wolf 2009, p. 611. On the dating of the *mancipatio* cf. Wolf 1998, pp. 517–521.

149 Manthe 2019, pp. 43–44.

150 Cursi 2014, p. 149; Cursi 2018, p. 343.

151 On the question of whether the *leges dictae* also go back to the *nuncupationes* cf. Finkenauer 2018, pp. 188–190. Behrends 1982, p. 63 and Randazzo 1998, p. 58 understand only the purchaser's assertion of ownership as *nuncupatio.*

152 Cf. Düll 1937, p. 1467.

153 Kaser 1971, p. 47; Albanese 1992, pp. 60–61; Kaser/Knütel/Lohsse 2021, p. 98; Schermaier 2003, p. 391 with n. 19; Babusiaux/Koch 2022, p. 297; Pfeifer 2023, p. 516. Liebs 2004, p. 277 refers Twelve Tables 6.1 only to purchases of land, since in those the acquirer could not inspect the object of sale for defects before *mancipatio.*

154 Finkenauer 2018, p. 184; likewise Biondi 1953, p. 142.

155 Cf. also Wieacker 1988, p. 327.

unclear:[156] According to the most important source,[157] when acquiring ownership of a slave, only the acquirer *(mancipium accipiens)* acts by means of an act of seizure and the assertion of ownership: *hunc ego hominem ex iure Quiritium meum esse aio* ("this slave belongs to me according to Roman civil law"),[158] to which the transferor remains silent.[159]

The sentence Twelve Tables 6.1 created concrete possibilities for a *mancipatio*[160] that corresponded to the interests of the parties and gave legal effect to the seller's declarations: *ita ius esto.*[161]

Law of homology and Twelve Tables 6.1 have a similar structure, apart from the *cum*-sentence which restricts the scope of *nuncupatio* to libral acts:

	[*Cum nexum facit mancipiumque,*]
ὅσα ἄν ἕτερος ἑτέρῳ ὁμολογήσῃ,	*uti lingua nuncupassit,*
κύρια εἶναι.	*ita ius esto.*

The subordinate clause introduced with ὅσα/*uti* is followed by the main clause denoting the legal consequence. This legal consequence is dependent on a speech act (ὁμολογεῖν, *nuncupare*).

Significant differences between the two laws are immediately apparent. They concern (1) the possible two-sidedness of the homology (ἕτερος ἑτέρῳ), (2) the different introduction of the constituent clause, (3) the freedom of form of the ὁμολογία (in contrast to *nuncupatio*). Finally, it is also necessary to clarify (4) whether the legal consequences (κύρια εἶναι/*ita ius esto*) could correspond to each other.

Ad (1): Weiß already considers the possible two-sidedness included in the law of homology to be problematic for a comparison with the one-sided *nuncupatio.* But the ὁμολογῶν also declares himself one-sided: ὅσα ἄν ἕτερος ἑτέρῳ ὁμολογήσῃ describes the declaration of only one party.[162] The law on the warranty for material defects referred to in the third speech of Hyperides,[163] which in the usual addition

156 The *nuncupationes* could have been declared by the transferor before the *mancipatio* ritual – thus Simon 1965, p. 147; Kaser 1971, p. 415 n. 18; Finkenauer 2018, p. 184; Manthe 2019, p. 43 – or inserted by the transferee in his assertion of ownership; cf. for example Albanese 2003, pp. 18–19.

157 Gaius, Institutes 1.119.

158 This formula is also handed down in Gaius, Institutes 1.119 cf. Boethius, ad Cic. top. 5.28.

159 On *nuncupatio* in the context of the *testamentum per aes et libram* (Gaius, Institutes 2.104) cf. only Babusiaux 2021, p. 146; Rüfner 2023, p. 527.

160 Cf. Cardilli 2014, p. 105; Cardilli 2018, p. 404.

161 Düll 1976, p. 81; cf. also Digest 2.14.48 (Gaius 3 on the Twelve Tables), which Fercia 2015, p. 32 and Zahn 2021, pp. 315–316 refer to Twelve Tables 6.1.

162 On the perhaps synonymous use of ἑτερος ἑτέρῳς and πρὸς ἀλλήλων cf. Plato, Symposion 192c.

163 Hypereides 3.15; cf. above under 4.

to the incompletely preserved text as νόμο[ς ἐστὶ περὶ ὧν ὁμολογοῦν]τες ἀλλήλοις συμβάλλουσιν (law which concerns those who declare and contract with each other) says nothing about the necessary reciprocity of homology:[164] Thus, the ὁμολογεῖν corresponds to the unilateral προλέγειν,[165] the notification of a defect in the sold slave by the seller.[166] Apart from that, no reference is made here to the law of homology.[167]

Ad (2): The pronoun ὅσα ("what", actually: "how much") introduces a conditional relative clause that requires the subjunctive aorist + the particle ἄν, which gives the clause a general-abstract sense. The neuter plural ὅσα denotes the wording of "whatever is being declared."[168] In conjunction with the adjective of the main clause (κυρία), this creates a new legal situation.[169] The function of *uti* ("as"), which corresponds to the *ita* of the main clause, is similar. "That which is to be lawful" *(ius esto)* is defined by the *nuncupatio.*

But linguistically, too, there is a prominent parallel for the similar use of the Greek ὅσα and the Latin *uti* with the Athenian *archon*'s *(eponymos)* promise of protection of possession and the *interdictum uti possidetis:*[170] The *uti nunc possidetis – quominus ita possideatis*[171] of the interdict correlates with the ὅσα τις εἶχεν (...) ταῦτα ἔχειν.[172] Here, the ὅσα-phrase corresponds functionally to the Latin *uti*-phrase.

Ad (3): According to the sources, a fundamental difference is that the *nuncupatio* originally had a solemn, perhaps even religious character.[173] It may suffice to note here that the ὁμολογία has no comparable ritual context. A formal element, as is necessary for the conclusion of the Roman *stipulatio* with the question-answer scheme, cannot be identified for the ὁμολογία of classical Athens.[174]

---

164 In contrast, Gagliardi 2015, p. 380 wants to derive a reciprocity of obligation from the plural ὁμολογίαι used in the law of homology.

165 Cf. Plato, Laws 916b and Pringsheim 1950, pp. 473–478; Herrmann 1990, p. 91; Jakab 1997, p. 88; Ruschenbusch 2001, p. 18.

166 Otherwise, he is threatened with ἀναγωγή; on that cf. Jakab 1997, pp. 86–88.

167 Gagliardi 2014, p. 181 suspects this.

168 Cf. also the ὅσα ἄν ἕτερος ἑτέρῳ ἐπικαλῇ in Plato, Laws 761e.

169 In contrast, Gagliardi 2014, p. 178 n. 7 and 198 and Schanbacher 2021, pp. 74–75 wanted to relate the ὅσα to the 'goods' of an exchange transaction. Even if one agrees with the authors mentioned above that justice of exchange is implied here, this does not apply at all to the extension of a term (Demosthenes, Orations 42.12; 47.77); cf. also Avilés 2012, pp. 58–59.

170 For this striking parallel, see Scheibelreiter 2015.

171 *Uti nunc eas aedes, quibus de agitur, nec vi nec clam nec praecario alter ab altero possidetis, quo minus ita possideatis, vim fieri veto;* for the reconstruction see Lenel 1927, pp. 470–473.

172 [Aristotle], Constitution of the Athenians 56.2.

173 Varro, de lingua latina 6.60; Festus, s.v. *nuncupata pecunia,* p. 176,5–6 [Lindsay].

174 Cf. Platschek 2018, pp. 32–39, who compares *stipulatio* and ὁμολογία.

Ad (4): The main clause κύρια εἶναι, which denotes the legal consequence, has a clear parallel in the *ita ius esto*.[175] The meaning of the word sequence[176] is disputed: The translation "that shall be lawful"[177] was understood as a reference to the immediate enforceability, for example, of the *nuncupatio*[178] or, more generally, to the possibility of the party to a libral act to have a legal formative effect.[179]

In this respect, too, there is comparability with the Greek κύρια εἶναι, whose interpretation varies between "authoritative" in the sense of directly enforceable, and "binding the parties." If the evidence is taken into account, which does not speak of κύρια εἶναι as the legal consequence of the law of homology, but of δίκαια εἶναι,[180] then this – understood as an interpretation of κύριος in the sense of δίκαιος[181] – comes even closer to the Latin *ius esto*. All interpretations of *ita ius esto* have in common that the *nuncupationes* create a certain, authorized legal state.[182] And this also applies to κύρια εἶναι.

Conclusion

The excursus on early Roman law has of course also shown the limits of the comparability of the law of homology and the *uti lingua nuncupassit* sentence: The *nuncupatio*, unlike the form-free ὁμολογία, was part of a ritual that followed certain formalisms. The legal consequence that could affect the *mancipio accipiens* if he violated a condition of the *mancipio dans* made by means of *nuncupatio* (for example a *reversio in rem*) also has no documented parallel in Greek law. The comparison

175 Cf. the suspension of legacies in Twelve Tables 5.3: *uti legassit suae rei ita ius esto*. Schanbacher 1995, p. 18 and 2020, pp. 35–38 relates this to the legal consequence ἐξεῖναι of the Solonian testamentary law (Solon fragment 134d [LegDrSol] = fragment 49a [Ruschenbusch] and [Leão/Rhodes]); cf. on this Ruschenbusch 2014, pp. 94–102; Leão/Rhodes 2015, pp. 78–83; Schmitz 2023, pp. 815–822. However, no Greek influence on the law of the Twelve Tables must be assumed, but so Delz 1966: 81; cf. however the legal consequence κύριον εἶναι in Solon fragment 117a (LegDrSol) = 76a (Ruschenbusch) and (Leão/Rhodes), according to which self-imposed statutes of associations are legal, and which Gaius in Digest 47.22.4 (Gaius 4 on the Twelve Tables) uses comparatively for a Twelve Table provision.

176 Cf. also Twelve Tables 12.5 and on this Albanese 1992: 52.

177 Thormann 1969, p. 260; Düll 1976, p. 39; Flach 2004, p. 96.

178 Cf. Kaser 1949, pp. 103–104, 118–121 and 1983, p. 86; Simon 1965, pp. 150–151; Humbert 2018, p. 248.

179 Cursi 2014, p. 154; Cursi 2018, p. 345.

180 Plato, Symposion 196c.

181 As the δίκαιος as the narrower term could be included in the κύριος, this is not absolutely necessary.

182 Cf. Wieacker 1988, p. 269; Cursi 2018, p. 342.

of the two speech acts must be made on a more fundamental level, which can be achieved above all through the formulation of the legal propositions:

Thus, the ὁμολογήσῃ can be contrasted with the *nuncupassit* just as the κύρια εἶναι with the *ita ius esto*. Both speech acts are also to be understood as unilateral declarations which do not establish a legal relationship, but modify a right established in a different way. In the case of *nuncupatio*, this arises from *mancipatio*, whereas ὁμολογία has a further field of activity. In doing so, however, they shape the legal relationship between the parties and also create a new legal situation: they are κύρια or *ius*.

The evidence for the law of homology and the references to it in the Attic court speeches lead to the conclusion that ὁμολογία does not necessarily mean a contract and that its conclusion does not necessarily create an actionable obligation. Rather, as a unilaterally formulated provision, the ὁμολογία is used to organize an already existing or established legal relationship.[183] In none of this evidence does the law of homology serve as proof or argument for the validity and binding nature of the contracts themselves: In the context of contract law, the law of homology is cited to argue in favor of the existence of individual contractual provisions such as interest (Demosthenes, Oration 56) or the assumption of debts (Hypereides 3). This interpretation of the ὁμολογία in the context of the law of homology as a *pactum* between the parties is fundamentally supported by the comparison with *nuncupatio*.

In this sense, despite all the differences between the law of classical Athens and that of early Rome, a comparison can be made on the level of content, which can be interpreted as "analoge Gestaltung in weit auseinander liegenden Ländern"[184] as well as the result of a "notwendigen Parallelbildung bei gleicher kulturell-ökonomischer Grundlage."[185]

Bibliography

ALBANESE, Bernardo (1992) Brevi Studi di diritto romano, in: Annali del Seminario Giuridico dell' Università di Palermo 42, 4–180.

ALBANESE, Bernardo (2003) Brevi studi di diritto romano, in: Annali del Seminario Giuridico dell' Università di Palermo 48, 9–82.

AVILES, Domingo (2012) The Athenian Law(s) on Homologia, in: Mouseion 12, 52–71.

BABUSIAUX, Ulrike (2021²) Wege zur Rechtsgeschichte. Römisches Erbrecht, Köln/Weimar/Wien.

BABUSIAUX, Ulrike/KOCH, Elena (2022) Römische Kautelarpraxis zur Kreditsicherung. Eine Exegese zur sog. Formula Baetica, in: Thorsten KEISER/Peter OESTMANN/Thomas PIERSON (eds.), Wege zur Rechtsgeschichte. Die rechtshistorische Exegese. Quelleninterpretationen in Hausarbeiten und Klausuren, Wien/Köln, 280–305.

BARTA, Heinz (2011) Graeca non leguntur? II/1, Wiesbaden.

183 Similarly, CARAWAN 2006, p. 350.

184 Thus WENGER 1905, p. 30 in connection with Greek and Roman purchase forms.

185 Cf. SELB 1993, p. 50.

Barta, Heinz (2021) Homologie. Das Entstehen des modernen Vertrages im antiken Griechenland, Wien.
Beauchet, Ludovic (1897/1969) Histoire du droit privé de la republique Athénienne 4: Le droit des obligations, Paris/Amsterdam.
Behrends, Okko (1982) La mancipatio nelle XII tavole, in: Iura 33, 46–103.
Bers, Victor (2003) Demosthenes, Speeches 50–59, Austin.
Biondi, Biondo (1953) Contratto e stipulatio. Corso e lezioni, Milano.
Blass, Friederich (1893³/1979) Die attische Beredsamkeit. Dritte Abteilung. Erster Abschnitt: Demosthenes, Leipzig/Hildesheim/New York.
Blass, Friedrich (³1894) Hyperidis orationes sex, Leipzig.
Blass, Friedrich (1898) Die attische Beredsamkeit, 3. Abteilung. Zweiter Abschnitt: Demosthenes' Genossen und Gegner, Leipzig.
Bleicken, Jochen (⁴1994) Die athenische Demokratie, Paderborn.
Burtt, John O. (1954) Minor Attic Orators II, London/Cambridge/Mass.
Cantarella, Eva (1966) In tema di invaliditá del negozio giuridico nel diritto attico, in: Labeo 12, 88–93.
Carawan, Edwin (2006) The Athenian Law of Agreement, in: Greek, Roman, and Byzantine Studies 46, 339–374.
Cardilli, Ricardo (2014) Nexum e damnatio, in: Jan Hallebeek et al. (eds.), Inter cives necnon peregrinos: Essays in honour of Boudewijn Sirks, Göttingen, 93–113.
Cardilli, Ricardo (2018) Il *nexum* e l'oportere nelle XII tavole, in: Maria F. Cursi (ed.), XII Tabulae. Testo e commento I, Napoli, 401–424.
Cohen, Edward (2006) Consensual Contracts at Athens, in: Hans-Albrecht Rupprecht (ed.), Symposion 2003, Wien, 73–84.
Crawford, Michael (1996) Roman Statutes II, London.
Cursi, Maria F. (2014) La mancipatio decemvirale e il nuovo diritto dei plebei, in: Jan Hallebeek et al. (eds.), Inter cives necnon peregrinos. Essays in honour of Boudewijn Sirks, Göttingen, 145–160.
Cursi, Maria F. (2018) La mancipatio e la mancipatio familiae, in: Maria F. Cursi (ed.), XII Tabulae. Testo e commento I, Napoli, 339–380.
Delz, Josef (1966) Der griechische Einfluss auf die Zwölftafelgesetzgebung, in: Museum Helveticum 23, 69–83.
Dimopoulou, Athina (2014) Ἄκυρον ἔστω: Legal Invalidity in Greek Inscriptions, in: Michael Gagarin/Adriaan Lanni (eds.), Symposion 2013, Wien, 249–275.
Düll, Rudolf (1937) Nuncupatio, in: RE 17(2), 1467.
Düll, Rudolf (⁵1976) Das Zwölftafelgesetz, München.
Elster, Marianne (2003) Die Gesetze der mittleren römischen Republik. Text und Kommentar, Darmstadt.
Fercia, Riccardo (2015) Negotia fiduciaria, trust, categoria generale di contratto, in: Studi Urbinati di scienze giuridiche, poltiche ed economoche. Nuova serie A 53, 19–32.
Finkenauer, Thomas (2018) Drittwirkende pacta im klassischen Recht, in: Zeitschrift der Savigny-Stiftung für Rechtsgeschichte. Romanistische Abteilung 135, 178–260.
Flach, Dieter (2004) Das Zwölftafelgesetz, Darmstadt.
Gagarin, Michael (2018) Hyperides's against Athenogenes and the Athenian law of Agreements, in: Paula Perlman (ed.), Greek Law in the 21st Century, Austin, 35–53.
Gagliardi, L. (2014) La legge sulla ὁμολογία e i vizi della volontà nei contratti in diritto ateniese, in: Michael Gagarin/Adriaan Lanni (eds.), Symposion 2013, Wien, 177–214.
Gagliardi, Lorenzo (2015) The Athenian Law on homologia and the Regulation of Duress and Fraud in Contractual Bargaining, in: Revue historique de droit français et étranger 93, 375–391.

Hässler, Manfred (1960) Die Bedeutung der Kyria-Klausel in den Papyrusurkunden, Berlin.
Hansen, Mogens H. (1995) Die Athenische Demokratie im Zeitalter des Demosthenes. Struktur, Prinzipien und Selbstverständnis, Berlin.
Harris, Edward M. (2000) Open Texture in Athenian Law, in: Dike 3, 27–79.
Harris, Edward M. (2013) The Rule of Law in Action in Democratic Athens, Oxford.
Herrmann, Johannes (1990) Kleine Schriften zur Rechtsgeschichte (ed. by Gottfried Schiemann), München.
Höbenreich, Evelyn (2006) Der "Königsgedanke", in: Gerhard Thür (ed.), Gedächtnis des 50. Todesjahres Leopold Wengers, Wien, 17–32.
Hölkeskamp, Karl-Joachim (2023) Theater der Macht. Die Inszenierung der Politik in der römischen Republik, München.
Hofmann, Franz (1870) Über den Einfluß des griechischen Rechts auf die Abfassung des römischen Zwölftafelgesetzes, in: Franz Hofmann (ed.), Beiträge zur Geschichte des griechischen und römischen Rechts, Wien, 1–42.
Humbert, Michel (2018) La loi des XII Tables, Roma.
Jakab, Èva (1994) Bemerkungen zur Vertrauenshaftung im altgriechischen Recht, in: Gerhard Thür (ed.), Symposion 1993, Wien, 191–197.
Jakab, Èva (1997) Praedicare und cavere beim Marktkauf, München.
Jakab, Èva (2006) Antwort auf Edward Cohen, in: Hans-Albrecht Rupprecht (ed.), Symposion 2003, Wien, 83–91.
Jakab, Èva (2021) Parakatatheke und letztwillige Verfügungen. Zum Hintergrund von D. 32,37,5, in: Zeitschrift der Savigny-Stiftung für Rechtsgeschichte. Romanistische Abteilung 138, 338–378.
Jensen, Christian (1963) Hyperides. Orationes, Stuttgart.
Kästle, David J. (2012) Νόμος μεγίστη βοήθεια. Zur Gesetzesargumentation in der attischen Gerichtsrede, in: Zeitschrift der Savigny-Stiftung für Rechtsgeschichte. Romanistische Abteilung 129, 161–205.
Kaiser, Wolfgang (2023) Berechtigende Verträge zugunsten Dritter im griechischen Recht?, in: Zeitschrift der Savigny-Stiftung für Rechtsgeschichte. Romanistische Abteilung 140, 193–228.
Kaser, Max (1949) Das altrömische Ius, Göttingen.
Kaser, Max (^{2}1971) Das römische Privatrecht, München.
Kaser, Max/Hackl, Karl (1996^2) Das römische Zivilprozessrecht, München.
Kaser, Max/Knütel, Rolf/Lohsse, Sebastian (^{22}2021) Römisches Privatrecht, München.
Kenyon, Frederic G. (1907) Hyperidis orationes et fragmenta, Oxford.
Kohler, Josef/Wenger, Leopold (1914) Allgemeine Rechtsgeschichte. Erste Hälfte: Orientalisches Recht und Recht der Griechen und Römer, Leipzig/Berlin.
Kübler, Bernhard (1934) Griechische Einflüsse auf die Entwicklung der römischen Rechtswissenschaft gegen Ende der republicanischen Zeit, in: Atti del congresso internazionale di diritto romano (Bologna e Roma XVII-XXVII Aprile MCMXXXIII). Roma, [Vol. 1], Pavia, 79–98.
Kunkel, Wolfgang/Wittmann, Ronald (1995) Staatsordnung und Staatspraxis der römischen Republik. Zweiter Abschnitt. Die Magistratur, München.
Kunkel, Wolfgang/Schermaier, Martin (^{14}2005) Römische Rechtsgeschichte, Köln/Weimar/Wien.
Kussmaul, Peter (1969) Syntheke, Diss. Basel.
Lanni, Adriaan (2007) Athenian Approaches to legal predictability, in: Eva Cantarella (ed.), Symposion 2005, Wien, 225–235.
Leão, Delfim/Rhodes, Peter J. (2015) The Laws of Solon. A New Edition with Introduction, Translation and Commentary, London/New York.
Lenel, Otto (^{3}1927) Das Edictum perpetuum, Leipzig.
Liebs, Detlef (^{6}2004) Römisches Recht, Göttingen.

Lipsius, Justus H. (1908/1915) Das attische Recht und Rechtsverfahren, [Vol. 2–3], Leipzig.
MacDowell, Douglas M. (2009) Demosthenes the Orator, Oxford.
Maffi, Alberto (2008) Economia e diritto nell' Atene del IV. Secolo, in: Edward M. Harris/Gerhard Thür (eds.), Symposion 2007, Wien, 203–222.
Manthe, Ulrich (⁶2019) Geschichte des römischen Rechts, München.
Martini, Remo (1997) Sul contratto d'opera nell'Atene classica, in: Gerhard Thür/Julie Vélissaropoulos-Karakostas (eds.), Symposion 1995, Köln/Weimar/Wien, 49–55.
Martini, Remo (1999) XII Tavole e diritto Greco, in: Labeo 45, 20–37.
Martini, Remo (2005/2012) Diritti greci, Bologna.
Maschke, Richard (1926) Die Willenslehre im griechischen Recht, Berlin.
Meinecke, Joachim (1971) Gesetzesinterpretation und Gesetzesanwendung im attischen Zivilprozeß, in: Revue internationale des droits de l'antiquité 18, 275–360.
Meyer-Laurin, Harald (1965) Gesetz und Billigkeit im attischen Prozeß, Weimar.
Mitteis, Ludwig/Wilcken, Ulrich (1912) Grundzüge und Chrestomathie der Papyruskunde. Zweiter Band: Juristischer Teil. Erste Hälfte. Grundzüge, Leipzig/Berlin.
Mommsen, Theodor (1887³/2017) Römisches Staatsrecht II/1, Berlin/Darmstadt.
Osbourne, Robin G. (1985) Law in Action in Classical Athens, in: The Journal of Hellenic Studies 105, 50–58.
Partsch, Josef (1924) Juristische Literaturübersicht (1912–1923), in: Ausbildung – Prüfung – Fachpraxis 7, 258–287.
Pfeifer, Guido (2023) Libralakte (mancipatio, nexum, solutio per aes et libram), in: Ulrike Babusiaux et al. (eds.) Handbuch des römischen Privatrechts Band I (§§ 1–57), Tübingen, 514–517.
Phillips, David (2009) Hypereides 3 and the Athenian Law of Contract, in: Transactions of the American Philological Association 139, 89–122.
Platschek, Johannes (2013) Das Edikt de pecunia constituta, München.
Platschek, Johannes (2018) Die Stipulationen in Plautus' Pseudolus, in: Heinz-Günther Nesselrath/Johannes Platschek (eds.), Menschen und Recht, Tübingen, 31–52.
Platschek, Johannes (2023) Formularprozeß. Verhandlung in iure, in: Ulrike Babusiaux et al. (eds.), Handbuch des römischen Privatrechts Band I (§§ 1–57), Tübingen, 372–412.
Pringsheim, Fritz (1950) The Greek Law of Sale, Weimar.
Randazzo, Salvo (1998) Leges mancipii. Contributo allo studio die limiti di rilevanza dell'accordo negli atti formali di alienazione, Milano.
Rüfner, Thomas (2023) Das testamentum per aes et libram und die anderen Formen letztwilliger Verfügungen, in: Ulrike Babusiaux et al. (eds.), Handbuch des römischen Privatrechts Band I (§§ 1–57), Tübingen, 518–553.
Rupprecht, Hans-Albrecht (1975) Review of H. Freiherr v. Soden, Untersuchungen zur Homologie in den griechischen Papyri Ägyptens bis Diokletian (Köln 1973), in: Zeitschrift der Savigny-Stiftung für Rechtsgeschichte 92, 280–284.
Ruschenbusch, Eberhard (2001) Ein altgriechisches Gesetzbuch. Aus dem Kontext von Platons Gesetzen herausgehoben und in das Deutsche übersetzt, München.
Ruschenbusch, Eberhard (²2014) Solon: Das Gesetzeswerk – Fragmente. Übersetzung und Kommentar (ed. by Klaus Bringmann), Stuttgart.
Sánchez Moreno-Ellart, Carlos (2023) Der Verkauf der geraubten Kallirhoe (Char. II 14 2–3). Griechisches Recht und römisches Recht im Roman "Chaireas und Kallirhoe" von Chariton von Aphrodisias, in: Philipp Scheibelreiter (ed.), Symposion 2022, Wien, 343–372.
Scafuro, Adele (1997) The Forensic Stage, Cambridge.
Schanbacher, Dietmar (1995) Ratio legis Falcidiae, Berlin.
Schanbacher, Dietmar (2020) Zum Phänomen der Rechtsrezeption in der Antike, in: Zeitschrift der Savigny-Stiftung für Rechtsgeschichte. Romanistische Abteilung 137, 1–38.

SCHANBACHER, Dietmar (2021) Theophrast zur Vertragsgerechtigkeit beim Kauf, in: Dike 24, 61–83.
SCHEIBELREITER, Philipp (2015) ὅσα τις εἶχεν – ταῦτα ἔχειν: Eine rechtsvergleichende Studie zur Proklamation des Athener *archon (eponymos)*, in: Zeitschrift der Savigny-Stiftung für Rechtsgeschichte 132, 68–95.
SCHEIBELREITER, Philipp (2018) Prozessprogramm und Subsumption in Rom und Athen, in: Lorenzo GAGLIARDI (ed.), Antologia giuridica romanistica ed antiquaria II, Milano, 171–196.
SCHEIBELREITER, Philipp (2018a) Nomos, enklema und factum, in: Gerhard THÜR/Uri YIFTACH/Rachel ZELNICK-ABRAMOVITZ (eds.), Symposion 2017, Wien, 211–250.
SCHEIBELREITER, Philipp (2019) Aristoteles vor dem Prätor. Von der Ethik der Einrede, in: Clemens JABLONER et al. (eds.), Vienna Inauguration Lectures. Antrittsvorlesungen an der Rechtswissenschaftlichen Fakultät der Universität Wien, [Vol. 4], Wien, 31–83.
SCHEIBELREITER, Philipp (2020) Der "ungetreue" Verwahrer. Eine Studie zur Haftungsbegründung im griechischen und frühen römischen Depositenrecht, München.
SCHEIBELREITER, Philipp (2025), Ὁμολογία und nuncupatio – Das attische Homologie-Gesetz in seinem Kontext, in: Zeitschrift der Savigny-Stiftung für Rechtsgeschichte. Romanistische Abteilung 142, 29–139
SCHERMAIER, Martin J. (2003) Bona fides im römischen Vertragsrecht, in: Luigi GAROFALO (ed.), Il ruolo della buona fede oggettiva nell'esperienza giuridica storica e contemporanea. Atti del Convegno internazionale di studi in onore di Alberto Burdese (Padova – Venezia – Treviso, 14–15–16 giugno 2001), [Vol. 3], Padova, 387–416.
SCHMITZ, Winfried (2023) Leges Draconis et Solonis (LegDrSol). Eine neue Edition der Gesetze Drakons und Solons mit Übersetzung und historischer Einordnung I–II, Stuttgart.
SCHUSTER, Stephan (2005) Das Seedarlehen in den Gerichtsreden des Demosthenes, Berlin.
SELB, Walter (1993) Antike Rechte im Mittelmeerraum, Köln/Weimar/Wien.
SIMON, Dieter V. (1965) Begriff und Tatbestand der iniuria im altrömischen Recht, in: Zeitschrift der Savigny-Stiftung für Rechtsgeschichte. Romanistische Abteilung 82, 132–187.
FREIHERR V. SODEN, Heiko (1973) Untersuchungen zur Homologie in den griechischen Papyri Ägyptens bis Diokletian, Köln.
SZEGEDY-MASZAK, Andrew (1987) The Nomoi of Theophrastus, Salem.
THORMANN, Karl Friedrich (^{2}1969) Der doppelte Ursprung der Mancipatio, München.
THÜR, Gerhard (1977) Beweisführung vor den Schwurgerichtshöfen Athens. Die Proklesis zur basanos, Wien.
THÜR, Gerhard (1986) IG V/2,159: Testament oder Orakel?, in: Gunter WESENER et al. (eds.), Festschrift für Arnold Kränzlein. Beiträge zur Antiken Rechtsgeschichte, Graz, 123–135.
THÜR, Gerhard (2000) Das Gerichtswesen Athens im vierten Jahrhundert v. Chr., in: Leonard BURCKHARDT/Jürgen VON UNGERN-STERNBERG (eds.), Große Prozesse im antiken Athen, München, 30–49.
THÜR, Gerhard (2006) Leopold Wenger – ein Leben für die Antike Rechtsgeschichte, in: Gerhard THÜR (ed.), Gedächtnis des 50. Todesjahres Leopold Wengers, Wien, 1–4.
THÜR, Gerhard (2007) Das Prinzip der Fairness im attischen Prozess. Gedanken zu ἔχινος und ἔγκλημα, in: Eva CANTARELLA (ed.), Symposion 2005, Wien, 131–150.
THÜR, Gerhard (2013) The Statute on Homologie in in Hyperides' Speech against Athenogenes, in: Dike 16, 1–10.
TODD, Stephen C. (1993) The Shape of Athenian Law, Oxford.
WALLACE, Robert W. (2015) Did Athens Have Consensual Contracts? A Response to Lorenzo Gagliardi, in: Michael GAGARIN/Adriaan LANNI (eds.), Symposion 2013, Wien, 215–221.
WEISS, Egon (1923) Griechisches Privatrecht auf rechtsvergleichender Grundlage, Leipzig.
WENGER, Leopold (1903) Die Erzählung in der Rede aus Hypereides gegen Athenogenes, in: Jahresbericht des k.k. Staatsgymnasiums in Cilli, Cilli, 1–27.

WENGER, Leopold (1904) Römische und Antike Rechtsgeschichte. Akademische Antrittsvorlesung an der Universität Wien, gehalten am 26. Oktober 1904, Graz.
WENGER, Leopold (1953) Die Quellen des römischen Rechts, Wien.
WHITEHEAD, David (2000) A Commentary on the Forensic Speeches, Oxford.
WIEACKER, Franz (1988) Römische Rechtsgeschichte, München.
WOLF, Joseph G. (1998) Funktion und Struktur der mancipatio, in: Melanges de droit Romain et d' Histoire Ancienne. Hommage à la mémoire de André Magdelain, Paris, 501–524.
WOLF, Joseph G. (2009) In Mancipio esse, in: Martin AVENARIUS/Rudolf MEYER-PRITZEL/Cosima MÖLLER (eds.), Ars Iuris. Festschrift für Okko Behrends zum 70. Geburtstag, Göttingen, 611–620.
WOLFF, Hans J. (1957) Die Grundlagen des griechischen Vertragsrechts, in: Zeitschrift der Savigny-Stiftung für Rechtsgeschichte. Romanistische Abteilung 74, 26–72.
WOLFF, Hans J. (1978) Das Recht der griechischen Papyri Ägyptens in der Zeit der Ptolemäer und des Prinzipats, [Vol. 1–2], München.
WORTHINGTON, Ian/COOPER, Craig/HARRIS, Edward M. (2001) Dinarchus, Hyperides, & Lycurgus, Austin.
ZAHN, Bastian (2021) Si quid universitati debetur. Forderungen und Schulden privater Personenvereinigungen im römischen Recht, Wien/Köln/Göttingen.

Index Inscriptionum